Sandalwood and Carrion

Sandalwood and Carrion

Smell in Indian Religion and Culture

JAMES McHUGH

OXFORD
UNIVERSITY PRESS

OXFORD
UNIVERSITY PRESS

Oxford University Press is a department of the University of Oxford.
It furthers the University's objective of excellence in research,
scholarship, and education by publishing worldwide.

Oxford New York
Auckland Cape Town Dar es Salaam Hong Kong Karachi
Kuala Lumpur Madrid Melbourne Mexico City Nairobi
New Delhi Shanghai Taipei Toronto

With offices in
Argentina Austria Brazil Chile Czech Republic France Greece
Guatemala Hungary Italy Japan Poland Portugal Singapore
South Korea Switzerland Thailand Turkey Ukraine Vietnam

Published in the United States of America by
Oxford University Press
198 Madison Avenue, New York, NY 10016

Library of Congress Cataloging-in-Publication Data
McHugh, James.
Sandalwood and carrion : smell in Indian religion and culture / James McHugh.
p. cm.
Includes bibliographical references (p.).
ISBN 978-0-19-991630-6 (hardcover : alk. paper)—ISBN 978-0-19-991632-0 (pbk. : alk. paper)—
ISBN 978-0-19-991631-3 (ebook) 1. India—Religion. 2. Rites and ceremonies—India.
3. Smell—Religious aspects. 4. Smell. 5. Odors—India. I. Title.
BL2015.R48M34 2013
152.1′660954—dc23 2012003121

1 3 5 7 9 8 6 4 2

Printed in the United States of America
on acid-free paper

To my parents

CONTENTS

PART FIVE SMELL AND RELIGION

PREFACE

This book is about smells, perfumes, and stinks. Of course, smelling requires people (or animals, or, indeed, gods) to do the smelling and also odorous objects such as flowers, corpses, or elephants to smell. Cambridge Massachusetts, where I started work on this book as a dissertation, smells rather dull for the most part: produce is sold chilled and wrapped; feces and urine are whisked away into sealed sewers; the people of Cambridge (generally) deodorize their bodies and wear little if any fragrance; and on Valentine's Day, the roses have no scent.

In premodern South Asia, as in premodern Europe and North America, the situation was quite different. People, rich and poor, lived in a world that was more varied and pungent in terms of smell: cows roamed the streets; incense burned in homes and temples; gardens were planted with fragrant flowers; bodies were adorned with garlands and scented pastes, and corpses burned on smoky pyres. Not only was the environment more odorous, but also educated people appear to have been far more interested in and articulate about smells than we are. A quick reading of almost any literary text in Sanskrit will reveal a large number of elaborate references to perfumes, flowers, and even stinks; it would appear that the ideal love life involved the complex use of aromatics; many religious texts abound in olfactory imagery, and the rituals devised for honoring both gods and people frequently use diverse fragrant substances.

How might one go about studying smells and perfumes for a whole subcontinent over a period of many centuries if not millennia? As a scholar of texts, I have chosen to work on the written sources that survive and, given the enormous variety of sources that deal with smell in one way or another, I have taken an interdisciplinary approach. Hence, I have used a wide range of Sanskrit texts, and I also draw on the work of scholars of religion, history, material culture, anthropology, and art history. This study is also comparative: I compare the Hindu, Buddhist, and Jain religious traditions in respect to matters of smell,[1] and in places I compare South Asian discourses on smell with notable features of Western discourses about the senses.

There are two important issues I should address at the outset. First, there is the question of what I mean by "South Asian religions." Most of the texts I discuss belong to what we would broadly call Hindu, Buddhist, and Jain traditions. I mainly work with sources in Sanskrit and related languages. This narrowed the scope of the book, and I hope scholars of other South Asian languages will be interested in exploring smells and aromatics in the texts they study. I do not work on sources in Persian and Urdu, so, for the most part, I will not talk about Islamic traditions in South Asia, though I will at times allude to changes in olfactory practices and sensibilities found in later periods when Persianate courtly culture was thriving in parts of South Asia.

In recent years, many scholars have productively debated the utility and also the historicity of such terms as "Hinduism" and "Buddhism," and rightly so, because in a post-Orientalist academy it was necessary to scrutinize such categories.[2] Such discussions—an intellectual culture of conceptual de-aggregation—formed the background of much of my graduate school education. Thus, this book is, in some sense, an exploration of the different ways in which the study of smell and aromatics can bring a new, material, and aesthetic perspective to such matters as the nature of diversity within what earlier scholars might have labeled as a single tradition. This particular perspective can also point to sites of similarity—at least olfactory ones—within one internally differentiated "-ism" or between separate "-isms." My method of examining these questions is to look in great detail at cases from specific contexts and compare them with others—in my opinion, such a hands-on method is the only way to approach these larger concerns. For example, in chapter 2, I explicitly tackle these issues, when I build on the sophisticated work of John Clayton on how dialogue between different religious traditions can clarify doctrinal distinctions and articulate sectarian identities. Throughout the remainder of the book, I continue to explore variation and commonalities in South Asian religious texts and practice, reading a large variety of texts in diverse registers (e.g., literary, mercantile, liturgical) that belong to different religious traditions, all seen through the unique lens (to use a jarring visual metaphor) of smell and aromatics. For example, in the later chapters of the book that deal with sandalwood, I argue that at an early stage some Buddhists developed a distinctive and novel use for sandalwood (or at least they composed certain types of texts that *represent* such a novel use). It seems that quite quickly Jains also adopted this particular representation of the use of sandalwood in one of their narratives, and, after some time, this new use for sandalwood was common in many sources. I make no attempt, however, in this book to argue for one single thesis about smell in premodern South Asia. The picture is far more complex, and instead I try to show a variety of ways in which the study of smell and aromatics can elucidate our understanding of South Asian religions.

The second matter I should discuss is the time period I cover. Perhaps "premodern" is the best term for this time period, though throughout the book I have used other terms ("medieval" etc.), whilst not being too attached to any of them, and readers might be advised to pay more attention to the approximate century I am talking about in any particular case.[3] The Sanskrit texts I study in this book date from several centuries before the Common Era to the seventeenth century CE. Admittedly, examining such a vast period is one of the greatest challenges of this study. At the same time, taking such a broad survey has allowed me to observe some major changes and patterns in smells and aromatics in South Asia as represented in Sanskrit sources, which I discuss in detail throughout the book. One might even propose a historical periodization according to aromatic material culture and olfactory aesthetic sensibilities—a history that might show correlations to the extent of trade networks and outside contacts at various times. It is not just a case of Sanskrit texts referring to new materials at a certain period, such as when people began to write in English about a new material like tobacco, because certain items fade in and out of prominence over the centuries, yet remain on the scene for a very long period. To illustrate, there is no mention of musk in the (critical editions of the) Sanskrit epics, not to mention any ambergris, and the latter only appears at a much later period. Most probably, these materials were not known at the times and places where these texts were produced. On the other hand, costus root, which is celebrated in an early text, the *Atharvaveda*, is less esteemed as an aromatic in later periods, though it is still relatively well-known. As a scholar mainly of discourses and practices within South Asia, I must leave it to historians of trade to relate these changes to actual patterns of exchange. But such work might also be of considerable use in dating and locating texts. For example, only as I was in the very final stages of editing this book did I realize the potential use of certain words used to refer to civet in the approximate dating of texts—the hermeneutic circle of looking at these materials becomes ever more productive.[4]

At this point, I should also make a few remarks about terminology and the form of this book. In English, as in Sanskrit, it is possible to differentiate between the things we smell—odors—and the sense we use to smell: "smell." But in English the word "smell" not only refers to the sense, but can also refer to odors; so it is possible to talk of "an odor in the basement" and "a smell in the basement." In chapter 2, on the philosophical accounts of smell and odors, I have been careful to maintain the distinction between "odors" and the sense of "smell" in order to avoid confusion. I have not, however, marked this distinction between "smell" and "odor" throughout the rest of the book, as the term "odor" tends to have somewhat negative and stinky connotations in English, whereas the noun "smell," though not entirely neutral, is a little less loaded. I often use the word "perfume" in a very general sense to mean a fragrance-artifact made from aromatic materials, and in many cases my more general usage of this term encompasses preparations such as pastes, waters, and incenses. At other times, I am more specific, and I single out incenses, rubbing pastes, and so forth. In these instances, I use the word "perfume" to translate the name of preparations called *gandha* in Sanskrit.

In many cases throughout the book, I provided my own translations of Sanskrit texts (unless otherwise noted translations are my own), even when other scholars already produced better translations of the same texts. I did this to maintain consistency in translating certain Sanskrit terms for aromatics, as well as various smell-related words. Thus my, at times, clunky translations are meant above all to bring out the olfactory aspects of these texts. For commonly available Sanskrit works, I did not provide the original texts in the notes, though I provided the Sanskrit text for works that are harder to find and where I do a particularly close reading of a certain passage.

Readers will observe that this book is at times quite heavy on notes. This is deliberate, because I hope these notes, along with the several excursuses on important aromatic substances, will constitute a useful sourcebook on smells and perfumes for scholars of South Asian religions and culture.

This book progresses from abstract, philosophical accounts of smell, via literary accounts, to the material world of perfumes and aromatic raw materials. Thus, I begin by exploring religio-philosophical classifications of the "primary odors" and the differing hierarchies of the senses used by Hindus, Buddhists, and Jains. Then I explore the smellscapes of Sanskrit texts and the role of odors in narratives. The later chapters describe the more concrete arts of perfumery, representations of the trade in exotic aromatics, especially sandalwood, and I conclude by examining why aromatics figured prominently in certain religious rituals. The book is thus organized into five parts: Smells in Theory, Smells in the World, Smells in Practice, Aromatic Materials, and Smell and Religion. Although the chapters build on one another, readers with a particular interest, say perfumery, might wish to go straight to those chapters. Likewise, readers with little background in the study of Sanskrit and South Asian thought could happily skim over the more technical discussions, especially in chapter 2.

In chapter 1, I introduce the study of smell from a general theoretical and methodological perspective. Although South Asian religious discourse and practice abounded in complex smells, until now, scholars have frequently reduced these odors to the simple category of "perfume" and then effectively ignored them. I argue that it is first important to be aware of the assumptions implicit in much Western scholarship on smell, and I discuss these ideas in some detail. I also explore some previous contributions to the study of smell in other disciplines, and, finally, I discuss the career and work of the Indian scholar P. K. Gode who effectively paved the way for such studies as the present one.

The theory of olfaction was relatively similar in Hindu, Buddhist, and Jain philosophies: odor is either good or bad, and consists of particles carried to the nose by the wind. The place of smell in the hierarchies of the senses these traditions commonly used, however, varied greatly. In chapter 2, I explore these commonalities and differences in South Asian sense-theory and, building on the work of John Clayton, I propose that dialogue between religious traditions not only marks difference but also leads to convergence in certain cases.

If the fundamental smells were often thought to be "good smell" or "bad smell," what are typical examples of these as represented in South Asian texts, and how do these odors and odorants relate to other systems of value and to social hierarchies? In chapter 3, I examine a number of sources that describe smells, including typologies of elephants and a text on prognostication through the smell of semen. Using a number of prominent cases, such as the smell of lotus and the smell of earth, I consider the greater religious and cultural implications of some of the most frequently mentioned smells. In introducing many fundamental features of the smell world of Sanskrit texts, the chapter also provides a foundation for much of the material that I discuss in the remainder of the book.

What do smells make people do in South Asian narratives? In chapter 4, through a close reading of two well-known episodes from the epic *Mahābhārata*—one involving a fragrance, and one a stink—I propose that smells in South Asian narratives, as well as in other contexts, very often serve to unite the smeller with an odorous other (e.g., god, person, or flower) who is removed in space. This differs from the notion of smells as invoking memories, so prominent in modern European discourses, whereby smells unite the self with the former self removed in time, though not necessarily in space.

Given the diverse natures of smells, and their powerful affective potencies, it is only natural that people sought to exploit them to please gods, placate kings, and arouse lovers. In chapters 5 and 6, I explore perfumes in early and medieval South Asia. In chapter 5, I examine texts on the art of perfumery, presenting a brief survey of these materials with particular emphasis on sources that treat perfume at some length. Perfume names in medieval South Asia are a rich source of information on the aspirations expressed through aromatic culture: "Moon Juice," "Who Goes There?" "Uproar." I focus in detail on a text called the *Essence of Perfume* (*Gandhasāra*) that presents perfume formulae in a strikingly playful and literary manner.

What were perfumes and incense actually like and what did people do with them? In chapter 6, I explore the theory and practice of perfumes. Premodern South Asian people did not talk of "top notes" and "base notes" but of "allies" and "enemies" in the structure of a perfume. Perfumes ranged from simple pastes of sandalwood and saffron to complex oils containing dozens of ingredients subject to numerous processes. I also analyze a literary episode involving a perfume-addicted, love-sick prince as a case study to confirm and to complicate what we have learned so far about the uses and meanings of smells and perfumes in medieval South Asia.

The most valued components of perfumes were precious and exotic materials: sandalwood, aloeswood, musk, camphor, saffron, and incenses. In chapter 7, I discuss the imaginary worlds where these materials were said to originate: forests filled with worm-eaten woods and remote places where deer roamed with perfume-filled navels. The materials produced in such places were more valuable for these strange origins, and, despite these origins, texts prescribe these materials above all others as offerings to gods and enlightened beings.

Sandalwood is arguably as important a raw material to South Asian religions and civilization as jade is to China or porphyry was to the Roman Empire at certain times. In chapter 8, I provide a comprehensive account of this material. The word "sandalwood" and terms for it in Sanskrit, in fact, refer to a large number of woods valued as much for their cooling properties and colors as for their fragrance. Taking sandalwood as an example, I present several texts on the evaluation and artifice of aromatics and conclude that faking this costly material was clearly both common and very profitable.

Early Buddhist literature contains many references to people who trade and evaluate luxury goods for a living. In chapter 9, I examine one such episode from a Buddhist story that describes the fortunes of a seafaring sandalwood trader. Commercial prowess resulting from past good deeds translates to profit in the form of abundant sandalwood that devotees can use to glorify the body of the Buddha, and this demonstrates the virtue of the mercantile way of life. I also suggest that early Buddhist texts mention, for the first time, large artifacts made of sandalwood, such as statues. Prior to this, texts only mention the use of sandalwood paste. It appears that this novel material—bulk sandalwood—is, for various reasons, the ideal material for "framing" the body of the Buddha. From this point on, sandalwood became an ideal material to frame the bodies of important persons.

Building on the wide-ranging study of smell, perfumes, and aromatics in the previous chapters, in chapter 10, I answer the question of why people offered these materials to the gods. A passage from the *Mahābhārata* provides a clear answer to the question, "Why do we give flowers and incense to the gods?" After a close reading of this text, I briefly examine two later sources. Here, it appears that aromatic practices (and the olfactory sensibilities of the gods) changed over time, from offering a simple incense made of Indian myrrh to using far more complex perfumes made of exotic aromatics. Although adornment is shared between the "sacred" and "profane" worlds, nevertheless, there are important differences between the olfactory tastes and sensory capacities of the gods and of humans, such that we can justifiably talk of religious olfactory aesthetics.

Finally, I should note again that there are many aspects of smells and aromatics I have not been able to consider in this study, especially given the vast extent of Sanskrit textual culture, not to mention texts in Tamil and other South Asian languages. I have not, for example, done a philological study of the several terms for odors and smelling: how does a *parimala* differ in fragrance or meaning from an *āmoda*? Texts that discuss perfumery at length are relatively few in number; yet, even in those cases there is a vast amount of material still to study, and my accounts of these sources are therefore quite preliminary. For example, a text such as the fascinating *Haramekhalā* clearly deserves a more detailed treatment than I gave it in this book. Moreover, formulae for perfumes and incenses in ritual texts, *purāṇas*, *tantras*, and *āgamas*, are also numerous and associated with quite different religious traditions, theologies, and rites, and I have only begun to scrape the surface of that variety. Neither did I examine such questions as how beings called *gandharvas* are connected with smell, nor the nature and history of a mythical mountain called *gandhamādana*. As for smells in literature, again, I only took a very few examples from some better-known texts. In this respect, I want this study to be a primer that will encourage and enable other scholars to incorporate more detailed reflections on smells and aromatics in the materials they study. But on the incompleteness of this book, I should leave the final word to the great scholar P. K. Gode. In describing his sense of being overwhelmed by the smells and perfumes of Sanskrit literature, he noted in his very charming style:

> The rich odour of the references to *Gandhaśāstra* [perfumery] in literary sources attracts me, but I am unable to enjoy it like the bee in the thicket of golden buds of *Ketakī* [fragrant pandanus flowers] blinded by dust and helpless in his efforts to live in it or move about owing to the loss of his wings cut off by the prickles on the buds.[5]

ACKNOWLEDGMENTS

A great number of people helped me complete this book over the years, and it is a pleasure to acknowledge their contributions. This book is developed from my PhD dissertation, which I could never have done without the ongoing wonderful support, academic and personal, of my advisors Lawrence McCrea, Anne Monius, and Parimal G. Patil. Parimal was a strong supporter of this project from the start and was invaluable in shaping my research. Anne taught me to read in ways I had never thought were possible, and Larry has been a real paṇḍit at all times. Dr. Sreeramula Rajeswara Sarma was an outside reader for the dissertation, and he introduced me to an enormous number of fascinating sources and also provided translations of some of the works of Ṭhakkura Pherū for this book. Michael Witzel was also very informative on many occasions. During my time at Harvard, many other people were of great help in all sorts of ways: Ali Asani, Kenneth Boss, Tom Burke, Pramod Chandra, Beatrice Chrystall, Diana Eck, Jane Grey, Janet Gyatso, Lilian Handlin, the late Oscar Handlin, Leonard van der Kuijp, Bob LaPointe, Dan Lusthaus, Kevin McGrath, Jennifer Petrallia, Alex Rehding, Jennifer Roberts, Susan Sills, Oktor Skjaervo, Ron Tesler, and Cynthia Verba. The Harvard Graduate Society provided a very useful dissertation writing award.

I also owe much to the perfume industry both in America and India. Christophe Laudamiel provided me with wonderful comments on this project, but above all he introduced me to the world of contemporary perfumery, and even went as far as to create several fragrances (and one stink) to accompany this project when it was a dissertation, and these are now archived at Harvard. Christopher McMahon of White Lotus Aromatics introduced me to the world of traditional perfumery in contemporary India through his excellent website. Many kind people working in the world of perfumery and incense-making in India have also contributed to this project, in particular Mr. J. N. Kapoor at R. P. Fragrances in Kanauj; the staff of Gulab Singh Johri Mal in Delhi; the helpful directors and employees of Vasu and Cyclebrand Agarbatti in Mysore, as well as of Nesso; and the state sandalwood oil distillery in Mysore. Many years ago, the scholar of occultism and purveyor of aromatics, Ray Sherwin, fired my enthusiasm for this subject with a little black tin of stinky civet in 1980s Leeds.

Before and after my time at Harvard, this book is also the culmination of many years of learning with some wonderful teachers. At Oxford: Jim Benson (who also kindly provided some advice on Pāṇini for this book), Richard Gombrich, and Alexis Sanderson. At Cambridge: John Smith and Jenny Teichman. Also at Cambridge Eivind Kahrs was particularly influential in introducing me to Sanskrit in the first place. Stephanie Jamison has been incredibly helpful and kind in many ways over the years. The University of Southern California has been very supportive of my research in many ways. The Office of the Provost and the Grant Program for Advancing Scholarship in the Humanities and Social Sciences at the University of Southern California provided generous support for travel and research in India in summer 2010. I am also grateful to the useful discussions at the Religion and Material Culture working group supported by the Center for Religion and Civic Culture at the University of Southern California. Many friends and colleagues at the University of Southern California have been very supportive: David Albertson, Lisa Bitel, Janet Hoskins, Peter Mancall, Lori Meeks, Don Miller, Sally Pratt, Megan Reid, Varun Soni, Ann Marie Yasin, Duncan Williams, and Linda Wootton. The Society for the Humanities at Cornell University provided a home for me during a very productive year of writing. People who supported me during my time at Cornell include Mary Ahl, Anne Blackburn, Bronwen Bledsoe, Daniel Boucher, Joshua Clover, Kay Dickinson, Megan Dirks, Durba Ghosh, Daniel Gold, Carter Higgins, Timothy Murray, Quentin Pearson, Celeste Pietruzsa, Eric Tagliacozzo, Shawkat Toorawa, and Robert Travers. Adam Smith discussed my work with me on many occasions and also kindly read the first chapter.

Another large group of people shaped the way I thought about this project, either through my readings of their published work or through conversations over the years: Daud Ali, James Benn, Clare Batty, Shane Butler, Robert Campany (who very kindly read a whole draft of the book), John Cort, Whitney Cox, Paul Dundas, Emma Jane Flatt, Jordan Goodman, Phyllis Granoff, Jane Iwamura, Dinah Jung, Klaus Karttunen, Anya King, Mark McClish, Susanne Mrozik, John Nemec, Patrick Olivelle, Sheldon Pollock, Anne Porter, Karin Preisendanz, Andy Rotman, David Shulman, Alison Simmons, Frederick Smith, Donald Swearer, and Dominik Wujastyk. The two anonymous readers of the manuscript contributed many excellent and useful comments, and I cannot thank them enough for their hard work.

In India, I benefited from the advice of many scholars: Dr. M. A. Jayashree, Dr. Shubhachandra of Mysore University, Dr. Bhatt of the Maharajah Sanskrit College in Mysore, Bhaṭṭāraka Cārukīrti Swami Jī, the Bhaṭṭāraka of Śravanabelagola, as well as Surendra Bothra, and Kamal Chand Sogani in Jaipur. More recently, I am indebted to everyone, especially Dalip Singh, at the Anup Library in Bikaner, as well as to everyone at the Bhandarkar Oriental Research library in Pune where Saroja Bhate was very helpful. Also I thank Dr. K. N. Hota and Dr. J. D. Sathe at the Sanskrit Dictionary Project at the Deccan College in Pune. In Tirupati, I was grateful to discuss my work with Dr. A. V. Ramana Dikshitulu, and my work there was greatly aided by Dr. Mohan Babu and Lakshmi Manchu. I also thank the American Institute of Indian Studies for giving me the opportunity to study Hindi in Jaipur. In Thailand, Phramaha Bhatsakorn Piyobhaso of Mahachulalongkorn University in Bangkok kindly shared his immense knowledge of Pali materials with me on several occasions.

Many friends have shared ideas with me over the years: Erik Braun and Arthur McKeown have been especially patient in helping me shape this project, and Richard Meyer and David Roman have been extremely kind to me. I also want to thank Simona Bramer, Colin Chamberlain, Nawaraj Chaulagain, Kenny Cupers, John Dolio, Holly Gayley, Clare Gillis, Elon Goldstein, David Harvey, Justin Jennings, Mari Jyväsjärvi, Alex Keefe, Paul Kosmin, Mark Lane, Amod Lele, Emma Lloyd, Justin McDaniel, Finnian Moore Gerety, Ryan Overbey, Rajam Raghunathan, Christina Rosenberger, the Sabhani family in Jaipur, Sunil Sharma, Stephanie Spray, Beth Sternheimer, Byron Suber, Elly Truitt, Miriam Underhill, and Cameron Warner. Also, I thank the staff of Silverlake Wine and Intelligentsia Coffee in Los Angeles. Paul Hotham's interest in the project was very encouraging.

I would like to thank Cynthia Read at Oxford University Press for her enthusiastic support of this book. Also at Oxford University Press, I thank Charlotte Steinhardt for all her hard work, as well as Jaimee Biggins and Brian Hughes. I also thank everyone who worked on this book at TNQ Books and Journals, especially Venkat Raghavan, Srinivasa Raghavan.

I should also thank Peter, Cordelia, Clare, and Mat for their support throughout the writing of this book. Last, but far from least, I would like to dedicate this book to my parents who supported me for many years in many ways, and without whom I could never have begun doing what I am doing now.

Sandalwood and Carrion

PART ONE

SMELLS IN THEORY

1

Introduction

> The good historian resembles the ogre of legend. Wherever he smells human flesh, he knows that is where his prey is.
>
> —Marc Bloch, *Apologie pour l'histoire ou métier d'historien*

Why Perfume Is Not Superficial

To begin with, according to a medieval Indian king renowned for his good taste, perfumes are quite literally neither deep nor superficial. In an eleventh-century Sanskrit treatise on literary language, King Bhoja discusses the varieties of ornamentation of poetic language and compares these linguistic ornaments to bodily ornaments.[1] According to Bhoja, when it comes to the human body, some ornaments, such as clothes, garlands, and jewelry, are external, and some, like clean teeth and trimmed nails, are internal. Perfumes (along with incense, bathing materials, kohl, mouth fresheners, and betel-wraps) are said to be "internal-external." This is presumably because they are applied to the actual surface of the body, and because they were thought to affect it internally and physiologically in a variety of ways—as this book will explain. Perfumes as internal-external bodily ornaments are, according to Bhoja, analogous to such ornamental features of literary language as the bitextual, punning passages common in some Sanskrit poetry: literary ornaments that take advantage of both the form (external) and meaning (internal) of the word.[2] As we shall see, not only are perfumes ornaments of an internal-external nature, but also some of the medieval Sanskrit texts that describe how to make perfumes are considerably poetic and ornamental in nature. In some cases, formulae for perfumes can be read on the one hand as a list of ingredients and on the other as lines of poetry. For example, a recipe I examined called for a certain, rather important, aromatic substance derived from marine snails; the phrase used to describe it can also refer to "the shame of a respectable woman." Medieval South Asian perfumes are neither superficial nor simple.

Even if Bhoja had not alluded to the internal-external nature of perfumes—and in any case we might not necessarily think of perfumes as internal-external today—I would still argue that perfumes in South Asian religion and culture are not superficial in the sense of "frivolous." In other words, I argue that even if perfumes *are* literally superficial, that is not a bad thing, and our typical reaction to the term "superficial" perhaps says more about us than about things that happen to lie on the surface. In a recent summary and review of his own work, anthropologist and scholar of material culture Daniel Miller begins with a set of reflections on "Why Clothing Is Not Superficial."[3] Miller wants to move away from a semiotic analysis of clothing as signs and symbols, according to which "clothing was a kind of pseudo language that could tell us about who we are."[4] Reflecting on his own work on style in Trinidad, on the study of the sari he wrote with Banerjee,[5] as well as on other studies on clothing in Madrid and London, he notes that in different ways in different places "clothing plays a considerable and active part in *constituting* the particular experience of the self, in determining what the self is."[6] The way we normally use the word "superficial" reflects our "depth ontology," according to which our *being* is inside us and opposed to our exteriors.[7] This metaphorical way of understanding the inner self might not be the same everywhere. Indeed, Miller suggests that the people he worked with in Trinidad tended to see the real being of a person located on the outside, and they viewed the inner depths with suspicion. According to Miller, clothes are not mere symbols but can constitute the self, and the very notion of "superficiality," as we tend to use the word, reflects a localized self-interpretation that we cannot assume is the same in all places at all times. For some people in early and medieval South Asia—predominantly the elite and the gods as imagined and worshiped in the temple—perfumes and aromatics made you somehow different. Exactly what people claimed perfumes achieved and how perfumes did it is the subject of much of this book. Indeed, what perfumes did for people, and how people understood them to be transformative varied greatly from one context to another. As an example, we might understand the prominent renunciation of perfumes and garlands practiced by Buddhist monks not as a rejection of scented frivolity and superficiality but as an implicit confirmation of the assumed transforming powers of perfume in certain times and places.[8] By contrast, if someone practicing an ascetic lifestyle today avoids perfume, this choice seems insignificant in construction of one's self (despite the best efforts of the perfume advertising industry)—not something important enough to proclaim in public. Currently, when perfume is avoided, it is often because people are allergic to some of their components or wary of the synthetic materials they might contain, not because wearing perfume might result in something socially significant, such as an involuntary seduction.

Not only perfumes but also material things in general were vital to many forms of religious practice in South Asia: from Vedic sacrifices to medieval temples, the fine details of the materiality of religion were of great concern to many scholars who composed texts dealing with the ideal material aspects of religion, as well as with potential impediments to these ideal conditions. In South Asian religions it was (and is) important to have the correct stance with regard to certain types of *things*, whether this meant using the right incense for a certain type of divine being or strenuously avoiding involvement with certain things. In South Asian ascetic traditions, the quest to transcend or to control materiality arguably led to an obsessive attention to the details of material culture, which is clear from such sources as Buddhist *vinaya* texts. As Miller states, regarding this *immaterial* culture of religion: "the greater the emphasis upon immateriality, the more finessed becomes the exploitation of the specificities of the form of materiality by which that immateriality is expressed."[9]

At the very least, then, we should not assume from the outset that perfumes only functioned as external signs to convey meanings or identities located elsewhere, that we might therefore just as easily study by looking at other, perhaps more explicit, sources. Many people in early and medieval South Asia cared a lot about how people, gods, reliquary stūpas, and other things and places smelled, and this is reflected in the texts we have from many periods. In these texts, there is no shortage of lavish descriptions of smells and perfumes, and the elaborate use of aromatics was a major feature of many religious, royal, and erotic practices. A good perfume, scholars explained, should be like a well-run kingdom, with the correct balance of allies (mild materials), neutrals, and enemies (pungent materials). A good perfume should also be harmonious with incenses and garlands, the season, and the humoral character of the person—god or human—wearing it. The skilled use of perfumes delighted the gods, appeased kings, and excited lovers. The mastery of olfactory aesthetics served the most important goals of life. One Buddhist text, describing the sort of conversation that the Buddha does not engage in, lists talk of perfumes and garlands along with talk of kings, thieves, and clothes.[10] The lists of practices in this text are idealized representations of the lived world; nevertheless, if one were to create such a list today, and represent the sort of typical distracting conversations for a Buddha to avoid, one might mention talk of presidents, crimes, clothes (and probably shoes), but not garlands or perfumes. Perfume is simply not a common topic for gossip any more.

The art form of perfumery that developed in temples, monasteries, and courts relied on exotic aromatics, making the elite world of smell an intrinsically and self-consciously global affair. A sophisticated religious discourse on the goals of life emphasized that the pleasures of the senses were a valid end in themselves. Fragrances and stinks were a common model for describing other values, be they aesthetic, ethical, or related to matters of ritual purity and auspiciousness. And in a system where karmic results frequently took the form of aesthetic phenomena—where evil often quite literally stank—such categories are difficult to distinguish or, at least, cannot be treated in isolation. There are many narratives—Hindu, Buddhist, and Jain—in which bad people find themselves with a notably stinking body at some point in their series of rebirths. Hell stinks and, of course, so does death, and the ultimately fetid nature of the human body is lavishly described in Buddhist texts such as the *Bodhicaryāvatāra*. Suffering, impermanence, diseases, poverty, foul food, and all the other things people wished to escape in South Asian religions tend to smell quite bad. The existence of stinking plants is, as we shall see, explained by linking them to a primordial poison. Conversely, good people are often fragrant, and the best material for making a substitute body of the Buddha appears to be sandalwood. Fragrances make people happy, including the gods. As Vidya Dehejia discusses, beauty and adornments are auspicious sights to behold, including in a religious context,[11] and in the case of smells, we find that the term for a "good" smell is often interchangeable with the term for an "auspicious" smell. As we will see in several cases, one's smell indicates one's karmic past and innate nature, and since smells are almost universally classed as fragrances and stinks, personal odor is usually a good litmus test for one's standing in the universe.

Thus, whatever people were trying to achieve—pleasing the gods, exorcising demons, or making love—in the discourses and practices of early and medieval South Asia, smells were an essential part of the process.

Smell, Religion, Material, and Texts

In early and later medieval South Asia, the study of aesthetic phenomena was highly developed in many areas, particularly in the realm of literary and dramatic theory, and also in the realm of the visual arts. Diverse genres of texts also touched on matters of olfactory aesthetic phenomena. Philosophical texts that examine perception discuss the fundamental nature of the act of smelling and of odors. According to many of these texts, odors are fundamentally either fragrant or bad smelling. Smell was understood to be a contact sense, requiring bodily contact with odorous particles released from an odorant, such as jasmine flower, for perception to take place. However, unlike touch and taste, which were universally accepted as contact senses, smell permits perception of objects from a distance, in the way that sight and hearing do. Smelling certain materials, such as corpses, can produce ritual pollution in an orthodox brahmanical context, and, indeed, given the diffusive nature of smell, the stinks of impurity were harder to control and therefore avoid. At the same time, although smell allows one to perceive the odorous qualities of objects from afar, unlike sight and hearing, this is at the spatial whim of the wind, an intermediate element that is vital for smelling to occur, just as light is for vision. Wind, an element so vital to the diffusion of odors, was closely associated with the sense of touch, and thus the wind that carries a perfume also has tactile features. Odors, consisting of particles carried by the tactile wind, are thus decidedly non-aetherial. A diffusing odor actually expands the reach of the particles of an odorant, such as a flower, across space, and thus an expansive fragrance was an apt metaphor for the wide reach of virtue and the spread of fame.

There are other ways people thought that odors reach us. Smells not only travel via the wind but they can also be detected from close and intimate contact, as in an erotic encounter. Smells can also spread from one object to another by diffusion of particles. In early and medieval South Asia, this latter process was noted and called *vāsana*, sometimes translated as "perfuming." In this process, the odor of a flower or other odorant diffuses into an object, for example, a special oil-based matrix in perfumery, or, more simply, from flowers into a cloak.[12] Therefore, the actual sensory quality of the original object can be smelled at another place and, perhaps more important, at another time. Effectively, smells can be *recorded* by *vāsana*. These recorded smells are not representations of smells in the way portraits of lovers are visual representations nor are they repetitions, as in the case of a lover's words repeated by a fateful parrot or mynah bird that overheard a secret confession. These smells are the actual smell quality of the original odorant, the very same odor particles. *Vāsana* is not only exploited in perfumery, but a closely related term has an important application as an explanatory model in some religio-philosophical theories.

The exploitation of the sense of smell required the manipulation of matter. Unlike some arts, the art of perfumery is entirely dependent on special raw materials. The most important of these ingredients were precious, rare, and above all exotic, even to those who lived in the "land of spices." Accounts of contacts with producers of aromatics are an important source of elite representations of marginal and subordinate social groups, who are often said to inhabit remote lands abounding in precious commodities. Although the diffusion of South Asian textual discourses of olfactory aesthetics was limited to parts of Asia, actual aromatic substances from Asia have played an important role in Western traditions of perfumery over a lengthy period. From the writings of Theophrastus to Jacques Guerlain's classic perfume Shalimar, Western olfactory aesthetics has long gained prestige from acknowledgment of the Eastern origins and exotic Oriental aura of key materials, such as spikenard and sandalwood. South Asians, on the other hand, celebrated the Western regions as the fragrant lands of frankincense and coral.

But one might ask how I came to single out the sense of smell and perfumes, over other senses or types of material culture, as a theme to analyze. After years of reading Sanskrit texts, I noticed that across diverse genres there were many references to smells and also to various aromatic substances, such as sandalwood and varieties of jasmine. When I looked these up in one of the major Sanskrit dictionaries, I would often find the translation "a particular perfume" or "a particular fragrant substance." Translators and scholars were forced to reduce what was obviously a very complex and quite prominent feature of these texts to a few simple terms in English, leaving an impoverished understanding. Once I started to think about Sanskrit texts, South Asian religion, and history in terms of smell and aromatics, I realized that I had taken on a large topic because the references were so numerous, and thus this book is merely a preliminary and general survey. But I hope that, serving as a primer and reference book in this area, the book will encourage other scholars to complicate, expand, and even refute this work.

Can thinking about smell and perfumes tell us anything that we might not learn through other more conventional modes of inquiry? Smells and aromatics played and still play an important role in South Asian religions. Even today, religious institutions are filled with particular fragrances. For example, the strong and distinctive perfumes of camphor and sandalwood noticeably pervade parts of the important temple of Veṅkateśvara at Tirumala in South India. If one envisions the principal sacred god worshipped in that temple, Lord Veṅkateśvara, the image that comes to mind is a large, white mark made of camphor—a pungent aromatic—that covers almost half the image's face. This striking camphor forehead mark also highlights the multisensory nature of aromatic materials in South Asian religions. Perfumes were not just smells, but they were also visual, tactile materials. Conversely, objects thought of primarily in visual terms, such as flowers, often had strong smells, tastes, and other sensory qualities.

Perfumery is an especially interesting aspect of South Asian history to study because perfumery is not just a matter of mixing aromatics in a vessel, but it is effectively a network,[13] where texts meet practice, trade, geography, politics, and religion in a literal and material manner. As an artifact, a jar of medieval South Asian perfume was both the focus and product of several discourses, such as theories of perfumery, pharmacology, scriptural injunctions, literary associations, ideas of wealth and statecraft, as well as the sort of olfactory dialogues with other perfumes that the scholar Alain Corbin describes regarding France (discussed later). Perfume and incense were materially constituted from things with remarkable olfactory properties, such as camphor and musk. These were usually only available from specific places, and they had to be transported to the Indian subcontinent from great distances, often with great difficulty. Perfumes—expensive, rare, and aesthetically striking—were a vital part of religious and royal practices, both for the body and for the environment, both in private and in public. Given the nature of my sources—Sanskrit texts—I will focus above all on the connections of perfumes to various discourses. I will also discuss the relations of perfumes to institutions, such as temples and royal courts. However, because of the difficulties of historically locating many of my sources with any precision, these latter observations will be a little more general. And, given my training and sources, I will focus least of all on the actual trade and origins of aromatic materials, though, it is important to remember that odorous *stuff* found in widely scattered parts of Asia and the Arabian peninsula is always a part of the picture, and that the nature and origins of real materials powerfully shaped other aspects—discursive, economic, and institutional—of the world of smell in medieval South Asia. Conversely, over the centuries, many sources of aromatics, such as trees and animals, and the places they were found, like Sumatra and Timor, were shaped by the other parts of the network, that is, by the discourses, institutional uses, and demand for aromatics.

Through global trade, perfumes and spices for a long time played a significant role in the history of South Asia and beyond. Tellingly, India was characterized in medieval European discourses as the land of spices, perfumed by paradise.[14] In terms of the real long-distance trade in the primary aromatic materials of the old world—namely, sandalwood, musk, camphor, aloeswood, saffron, frankincense, and ambergris—the Indian subcontinent was "on the way to everywhere."[15] As the study of the European demand for spices is crucial to a complete understanding of the global spice trade, so this study of attitudes toward the consumption of aromatics in South Asia might likewise shed light on patterns of trade across the Indian Ocean, where cultural habits of consumption traveled along with spices and other commodities.

The Study of the Senses, Material, and Smells

This book is part of a general turn in the academic study of religion and history toward the analysis of the body, the senses, and material culture. In the study of the religions of South Asia, we are fortunate to possess a number of excellent studies of the various sensory modalities. Perhaps the most influential book on visuality in South Asian religion is Diana Eck's *Darśan: Seeing the Divine Image in India*.[16] Also, recent years have seen work by Rotman on visuality in early Indian Buddhism, as well as a study by Dehejia of adornment in Indian art and literature.[17] I might also mention the interesting work by Mrozik that includes a discussion of the aesthetics of the body of the Buddha.[18]

This "embodied turn" in the study of religion has been established for quite some time.[19] While I do not want to attack any straw persons for being shockingly neglectful of certain terribly important topics, nevertheless, for the most part, the academy has not followed its nose, and the study of the sense of smell has lagged behind the study of the other senses, such as visuality and the body. Major exceptions to the tendency to ignore smell in the study of religion are two excellent full-length studies of smell in early Christianity,[20] by Beatrice Caseau and by Susan Ashbrook Harvey.[21] Caseau's work, like this book, is an initial survey of the terrain; yet, she also tries to "keep a balance between this material world of fragrances and its religious and literary expression in a rhetoric of fragrances."[22] I was especially inspired by Susan Harvey's sophisticated work, which places far more emphasis on the nuances in discursive features of an absolutely enormous variety of late antique and early Christian texts.

In addition to enriching our understanding of South Asian religions by emphasizing and analyzing olfactory phenomena, I also try to dissolve a divide sometimes perceived in the study of religions between the textual/theological as opposed to the material/substantial. Sometimes studies of these two aspects of religion and culture are implicitly presented as opposed to each other. In the introduction to a recent edition of the religious studies journal *Numen* on "Religion through the Senses,"[23] the editors of the journal note that "for far too long, religion has been equated with doctrine, especially with those systematized doctrines known as 'theologies,'" and that "scholars have tended to study the normative, textual, versions of the traditions with which they have been concerned, in many cases disregarding the lived, physical, components of those traditions."[24] I agree entirely with these sentiments, as this book demonstrates, but I wish to emphasize that the "embodied turn" in the study of culture and religion noted earlier is not incompatible with the more traditional study of texts and doctrines—far from it. This is a small but important point: to move beyond the *exclusive* study of doctrines and scriptures is not to abandon them totally.

A common idea of smell as primal alternates between disregarding smells as bestial and embracing the positive power of smells as intimate and unconscious, while retaining the same essential paradigm of the nature of smell. Similarly, if we turn away from doctrines and examine only the body, we still propagate the same dichotomy between text and material—a dichotomy that I believe unproductive in examining the South Asian materials in this book, which constitute an elite and intellectual *textual* discourse of the senses, the body, perfumes, and smells. Some of the perfumes we will read about are complex and even, at times, intellectual artifacts. Any proposed divide between theory and practice is questionable for another reason, namely, because for many of the people who had recourse to the Sanskrit texts I discuss, theory was their practice and texts were their tools.

The recent work of historian Daud Ali transformed our understanding of the courtly and luxury material culture of early medieval South Asia.[25] In many respects, this book builds on his work, but I limit myself to the theme of smell and aromatics, and I focus more on the religious aspects of luxury material culture. Phyllis Granoff has produced a number of very fine studies of the material culture of South Asia in its wider religious and intellectual contexts.[26] My thinking has also been greatly informed by the work of Sheldon Pollock and in particular by his interest in the cosmopolitan nature of Sanskritic culture.[27] Where Sanskritic cultures were found, so were certain perfumes and aromatics, together with certain practices involving and certain attitudes toward these materials, as in the case of sandalwood. Yet, as I discuss in chapter 7, the desire for the rare and exotic that we see in many Sanskrit texts often forced writers to acknowledge the existence of, and look beyond, the limits of cosmopolitan Sanskritic culture. They had to imagine the distant and dangerous origins of the most valued aromatic materials so essential for cosmopolitan urban life. Nevertheless, such visions of remote wild places are entirely dependent on the idea of a civilized center.

This book also has many similarities with an important book on ecology and medicine in early India, namely *The Jungle and the Aroma of Meats*, by Francis Zimmermann.[28] Like that book, I explore one theme from a number of perspectives, and I share an interest in the overlapping and combinatorial systems of classification that characterize much premodern scholarship in Sanskrit. In his examination of the theme of meat and landscape, Zimmermann does not limit his studies to texts, and he achieves some interesting results by comparing his written sources with contemporary scientific discourses, such as maps of species distribution. I pursue that sort of comparison here because I believe this kind of work can expand and enrich our understanding of both texts and history, though, translation between premodern and modern sources is a practice that needs to be approached with extreme caution.

Last, but by no means least, the publication of the magisterial *History of Indian Medical Literature* by G. Jan Meulenbeld has utterly transformed any study of South Asia that is concerned at all with medicine, minerals, plants, and so on, as the present study indeed is.[29] In my discussions of the dating and context of many, if not most, sources I am heavily indebted to that work.

Beyond studies of South Asia, I also acknowledge Edward Schafer's book on the exotic material culture of T'ang China.[30] In choosing to include several excursuses on important aromatic materials, I have emulated that fascinating book, which is both a discussion and a reference work. And, more recently, historian Paul Freedman has produced an excellent study of spices in medieval Europe in which he reflects at length on their imagined exotic origins in the East.[31]

Not only has the study of the body risen in prominence in the humanities in recent years but so too has the study of the senses, including smell, and Mark M. Smith recently produced a very useful survey and analysis of these histories of the senses.[32] Although few in number, there exist some very good studies of the sense of smell and of perfumes by scholars of history, literature, and anthropology. Anthropologists Constance Classen and David Howes have led the way in the study of smell in the English-speaking world. Along with sociologist Anthony Synnott, as well as Jim Drobnick, these scholars have been responsible for several edited volumes on the study of the senses and on smell.[33] The social and intellectual history of smell in eighteenth- and nineteenth-century France was described quite brilliantly by the historian Alain Corbin, in what is without a doubt the most original and influential historical study of the sense of smell: *Le miasme et la jonquille: l'odorat et l'imaginaire social, XVIIIe-XIXe siècles* (translated as *The Foul and the Fragrant*).[34] In that book, Corbin describes the development of some major Western intellectual assumptions concerning the sense of smell. I will pause to repeat some of those materials, because such ideas have informed and continue to inform so much recent thinking on smell in Europe and North America.

We might begin by considering the notion that smell is primitive, bestial, and sensual; an animal sense that has been diminished in adopting the human upright posture, and a sense that, if overdeveloped, marks one as a savage. It is worth quoting at length Corbin's account of these important ideas:

> A few fairly simple stereotypes demonstrate the paradoxical nature of the sense of smell. Olfaction as the sense of lust, desire, and impulsiveness is associated with sensuality. Smelling and sniffing are associated with animal behavior. If olfaction were his most important sense, man's linguistic incapacity to describe olfactory sensations would turn him into a creature tied to his environment. Because they are ephemeral, olfactory sensations can never provide a persistent stimulus of thought. Thus the development of the sense of smell seems to be inversely related to the development of intelligence.

> Unlike the senses of hearing and sight, valued on the basis of a perpetually repeated Platonic prejudice, olfaction is also relatively useless in civilized society. According to Count Albrecht von Haller, "The sense of smell was less important to [man], for he was destined to walk upright; he was to discover from a distance what might be his food; social life and language were designed to enlighten him about the properties of the things that appeared to him to be edible." The best proof of this claim is that the sense of smell is more highly developed among savages than among civilized men.[35]

Not only is smell a bestial and savage sense, but it is also an inferior sense and "disqualified" from serious aesthetic inquiry:

> The sense of smell is at the bottom of the hierarchy of the senses, along with the sense of touch. Furthermore, Kant disqualified it aesthetically.[36]

Last, but not least, is the association between smell and memory. This is the positive side of the nature of smell, as described previously: given the primal nature of the sense of smell, a certain special, nonintellectual, *affective* power is attributed to it, especially in terms of the ability of odors to recall memories:

> As the sense of affective behavior and its secrets (in Rousseau's frame of reference, the sense of imagination and of desire), the sense of smell was viewed as capable of shaking man's inner life more profoundly than were the senses of hearing or sight. It seemed to reach the roots of life. In the nineteenth century it was elevated to being the privileged instrument of recollection.[37]

Although Corbin writes of eighteenth- and nineteenth-century discourses of smell, this idea and the others he mentions will no doubt be familiar to any contemporary reader—these are fundamental assumptions about smell that are shared by many educated people, whether or not they ever studied the sense of smell.

In *The Foul and the Fragrant*, not only does Corbin describe the history of ideas concerning smell and the role of smell in literature, but he also relates these discourses to the world of perfumes. Corbin notes how in nineteenth-century France:

> Democrats dreamed of "la Belle République"; Michelet invented "the People"; socialists designed the happiness of mankind; positivists preached the education of the masses. Meanwhile, however, other dialogues were taking place at a more fundamental level; heavy animal scents and fleeting perfumes spoke of repulsion and disgust, sympathy and seduction.

> Despite Lucien Febvre's injunctions, historians have neglected these documents of the senses.[38]

And most important to this book, Corbin shows how the world of perfumery played a part in the social and political history of the time:

> After the Revolution, with its fascination with corpses and scorn for vegetable scents, the return of musk took on symbolic value. Sprinkled with eau de cologne, drenched in vapors from animal perfumes, the imperial couple broke with rose water. The Restoration also expressed itself in terms of smell. In this respect the faubourg St.-Germain evinced the morbid sensitivity of a chlorotic girl. Vegetable impulses reimposed their delicacy; their function was to dampen female impulses and so signal a new system of control.[39]

This cultural history of perfumery, first undertaken by Corbin, has recently been developed by the scholar of French literature Richard Stamelman in his book *Perfume: Joy, Obsession, Scandal, Sin: A Cultural History of Fragrance from 1750 to the Present*.[40] I might add that the works of Corbin and Stamelman on perfumery have strong echoes of the brilliantly original opinions on the history of perfume expressed by the character Des Esseintes in Huysmans' *A rebours*.[41]

A number of scholars have explored aspects of the history of smell and perfumery in South Asia. The assumptions associated with the dominant Western discourses of smell outlined by Corbin for nineteenth-century France inform some earlier work so strongly that it is interesting to consider them briefly here. The most famous early Indological paper to discuss matters pertaining to smell was Edward Washburn Hopkins' paper on "The Sniff Kiss in Ancient India" from 1907.[42] This paper appears to accept the thesis, mentioned previously, that smell is primitive and bestial. Hopkins discusses the history of the kiss in Indian culture, noting that in the early Vedic texts the vocabulary of kissing is absent and instead sniffing is the norm. The paper is, in fact, a thorough and useful survey of the vocabulary for kissing and sniffing-as-kissing, but most interesting, to us, is that Hopkins is very much of the opinion that sniffing—a "savage custom"[43]—is rather primitive compared to civilized kissing. He explains, "We may start with the assumption that there was a primeval barbarism to which kissing was unknown." He observes that the earlier stage of sniffing was recognized as bestial even by the ancient Indians: "The complete parallel with the action of animals is recognized in the literature."[44] But this bestial sniffing develops into proper kissing: "First comes the sniff-kiss . . . Then comes the real kiss."[45]

If we consider the next idea Corbin mentions—that smell is excluded from serious aesthetic inquiry—we should turn to a short article from 1931 by E. J. Thomas on perfume blending (*gandhayukti*).[46] This is, as far as I am aware, the first article that concerns the topic of perfumery in early India per se, and E. J. Thomas argues (admittedly, on thoughtful philological grounds) that the young Buddha was not so much trained in the art of perfumery as in the scholarly art of *bookbinding*.

John Strong, in 1977, wrote a thought-provoking article on the *gandhakuṭī*, or "perfumed chamber," of the Buddha.[47] That article, owing to the analysis of the role of smell in the ideal environment for the Buddha, was the starting point for my reflections on sandalwood and Buddhism in chapters 8 and 9 of this book.[48] David Shulman wrote an insightful article titled "The Scent of Memory in Hindu South India."[49] Shulman explored both Tamil and Sanskrit materials. I agree with Shulman's analysis of smell as connected to separation and longing. The bridging of various forms of social separation by means of diffusive odors is something we shall see often in this book. Shulman also emphasizes the aspects of smell as related to memories. I am less keen on emphasizing that aspect in this study, where my focus is on presenting the Indian understanding of smell (though my lack of attention to Tamil materials is, admittedly, a significant gap in this book). Although smells are found in Sanskrit literature in contexts of remembering and longing for absent lovers, smells are no more prominent than other sensory stimuli when it comes to memory. Smells often occur in Sanskrit love poems as part of complexes of other motifs, such as the springtime sandalwood-scented wind from the south that cools love fevers; or as part of a very common lotus-mouth comparison; and also in erotic nighttime settings where, in the darkness, one has to rely on smells (perfumes) and sounds (jingling anklets) to experience, to locate, or to be reminded of one's lover. When memories are triggered by sensory stimuli, smells are present, but other stimuli are just as common. It is not the case that when smells are present memories are automatically triggered. There is, nevertheless, no reason why scholars should not apply the important smells-evoking-memories theory to South Asian materials. As stated, however, in this book, I primarily explain and discuss indigenous South Asian theories of smell, both explicit and implicit. Finally, in a recent and excellent short article, Minoru Hara presents a survey of the usage of the Sanskrit word *gandha* (odor, perfume), and many of the examples he cites can be used to supplement the materials I discuss in this book.[50] Hara also discusses certain nuances of usage that I have not focused on in this study, which I intend to be less philological and more historical.

In the study of Islam, including the study of Islam in South Asia, there have been several recent studies of smell and perfumery. Anya King produced a seminal study of musk in Islam and is working on the history of Islamic perfumery. Ali Akbar Husain wrote a book entitled *Scent in the Islamic Garden: A Study of Deccani Urdu Literary Sources* in which he also discusses some later perfumery practices, and Emma Jane Flatt is currently working on the socio-cultural construction of smell in Indo-Islamicate courtly cultures. Dinah Jung has recently completed a fascinating ethnography of the complex world of perfumery in Yemen.[51]

At this time, therefore, quite a number of books and studies are available on smell and perfumery in various religious traditions, as well as in diverse areas and historical periods. The serious and comparative study (not to mention teaching) of smell in history, culture, and religion is now far more feasible than it would have been thirty years ago, though many important topics remain relatively unexplored.[52]

I have, however, yet to mention another body of scholarship on perfumery in South Asia produced by South Asian historians. In a recent short survey of cultural history as a historiographic phenomenon,[53] the historian Peter Burke does not mention the achievements of such scholars as Moti Chandra and P. K. Gode in this area, and where Indian historians are noted it is the Subaltern Studies Group that takes pride of place.[54] Arguably, those Indian cultural historians did not produce methods or theories that had an impact on the writing of history as generally as the Subaltern Studies Group; yet, Coomaraswamy, Moti Chandra, and P. K. Gode, nevertheless, took a highly original approach to the history of India that implicitly reveals a theoretical stance through the topics they chose to study. These people were immensely productive scholars, and P. K. Gode, in particular, explored Sanskrit texts in a way that was extremely prescient in its attention to material culture and to later Sanskrit sources.

It would appear there was a blossoming of interest in Indian perfumery in the decade or so preceding independence. Majumdar's article of 1935, in the journal *Indian Culture*, seems to be the earliest detailed review of this subject, providing an extremely useful survey of materials in Sanskrit on cosmetics and perfumes.[55] He lists the principal sources of data—from Pali materials, the *Arthaśāstra*, and other pertinent texts—adds some short translations, then notes the erosion of these Indic traditions, at least among the elite of the day. The rest of society still used traditional cosmetics, the luxuries of the past:

> In modern times the articles of toilet have multiplied rather frightfully, thanks to the inventions and industries initiated by the West. But these luxuries are still beyond the reach of the majority of Indians who are content with their poor old things.[56]

In 1940, Moti Chandra published a lengthy article, "Cosmetics and Coiffure in Ancient India."[57] This article is slightly more detailed than Majumdar's, but it follows a similar chronological account, relying on many of the same primary sources. As the title indicates, Chandra includes an account of coiffure. Both authors collected a vast amount of data, and the articles are exceptionally valuable as catalogues of sources, although, unlike P. K. Gode, they do not supply previously unknown sources. In a similar vein is R. T. Vyas' excellent introduction to his edition of the perfumery texts called the *Gandhasāra* and the *Gandhavāda*. In 1989, the unique manuscript containing two perfumery manuals, found by P. K. Gode, was finally edited and published by Vyas, then the director of the Oriental Institute in Vadodara (Baroda). An eminent scholar of Sanskrit, R. T. Vyas was able to draw on the progress made by Gode, and he added a lengthy introduction to the text, which provided a wealth of data. He also included appendices to the volume containing the most important Sanskrit textual sources on perfumery, such as extracts from the *Bṛhatsaṃhitā* and the *Agnipurāṇa*. But it is to the work of P. K. Gode, which deserves a wider audience, that I now turn.

The Delight of the Mind: P. K. Gode

> In his eyes, the march, for instance, of betel leaf across the plains of Bhārat is an event of no less historical importance then the famous march of Bonaparte across the Alps.[58]

It is not an exaggeration to say that my study of the cultural history of smell in South Asia would not have been possible were it not for the achievements of the remarkable Indian scholar Parshuram Krishna (P. K.) Gode. Gode transformed the range of resources available to scholars of South Asian perfumery when he discovered two texts that are far longer and more complex than any of the previously known sources. He also wrote several papers on the topic and effectively laid the foundations for the present study.

Gode was born in 1891 at Deorukh in Ratnagiri District, Maharashtra.[59] For over forty years, he was the curator of the Bhandarkar Oriental Research Institute in Pune until his death in 1961.[60] Though his full-time job was curator, he, nevertheless, managed to write a staggering number of papers: 474 according to the final edition of his bibliography.[61] Many of these papers concerned matters of the chronology of texts, but he also wrote extensively on matters of the cultural history of India.[62] As S. R. Tikekar states:

> He was concerned with the history of India no doubt; but not the history of this or that royalty; not of this Nawab or that Sultan. It was in fact the real history of India: a part of the history of our vast Sanskrit literature, a history of Indian life in general; a history of her plants, of her fruits and of the things we use in daily life . . . Kings may come and kings may go; but the society and its occupations and pastimes have a permanent interest.[63]

In presenting a history of the more "permanent" aspects of "daily life," Gode's work shares some similarities with French historians, such as Marc Bloch, Lucien Febvre, and later Fernand Braudel of the *Annales* school, who were also preoccupied with writing a new type of history, or a "total history," considered in the long perspective, the *longue durée*. Yet Gode differs in many important respects from such historians. He is rarely motivated by theoretical concerns, and his work consists for the most part of numerous short papers, as opposed to long comprehensive studies.

Although his work consists of meticulous textual documentation with little theoretical analysis, he, nevertheless, did pose innovative questions regarding Sanskrit texts. Not only did he mine Sanskrit texts for a new type of information, but also the range and period of texts he studied was remarkable: he was by no means only interested in the "golden age" of classical Sanskrit philosophy and literature. Gode was a scholar who could write papers such as "Date of the Rājavinoda of Udayarāja, a Hindu Court-poet of Mahamūd Begḍā—Between A.D. 1458 and 1469," as well as a paper on "References to Tobacco in Some Sanskrit Works Between A.D. 1600 and 1900."[64] Gode created a timeless store of valuable data for subsequent generations of cultural historians, who, because of his efforts, are able to write what is considered today a more conventional, and more theoretical, cultural history of India. To reiterate, in the case of this book, it is in large part thanks to the data provided by Gode that I was able to write on the topic of smell in medieval India at all.[65]

How to Study Smells and the "Period Nose"

While Gode and scholars like him provided the data for this book, in terms of method, I drew in part on the historical and textual work of the scholars mentioned, especially Alain Corbin and Susan Ashbrook Harvey. I have also found the work of scholars of material culture very useful. I earlier noted Daniel Miller when discussing the notion of superficiality. The range of Miller's research furnishes a useful model. Miller writes about matters of considerable theoretical complexity with an admirable simplicity and clarity that I aim to emulate. There is, however, one major difference between the present study and those produced by Miller (as well as the work of Baxandall that I discuss later). Where Miller, and to a certain extent Baxandall, have access to the material culture they are studying, I do not.[66] I might have access to sandalwood and musk but not to medieval Indian incenses and the rituals that used them.[67] Instead, I work with texts that often describe or prescribe an ideal material world. Whether this is an ideal temple functioning in the prescribed manner, a bountiful aromatics market, or the perfectly delightful room of the man-about-town described in the *Kāmasūtra*; what I study is material culture as described in texts. But these texts were composed in South Asia for a South Asian audience, and thus they contain implicitly or explicitly an indigenous theory of material culture: how *things* ought to be, and how the world ought to smell. These texts were not composed and received in a bubble but were in part the product of complex dialogues about matter, smells, perfumes, and so on. Unpacking these texts in order to read these various South Asian "thing-theories" for the case of smell and aromatics is my method here, and this requires the analysis of texts in the light of material-culture theory.

One scholar who I believe strikes a balance between the study of texts and the study of material culture, while providing a nuanced account of sensory perception in a particular historical context, is Michael Baxandall. In 1972, Baxandall published a now famous study of Italian renaissance art entitled *Painting and Experience in Fifteenth Century Italy*.[68] In that book, he argued that fifteenth-century patrons and viewers of paintings, given their specific "cognitive style," saw and assessed paintings differently than we do—Baxandall called this way of seeing the "period eye." Baxandall carefully examined several areas, for example, economics and education, to understand this visual conditioning. In this, he resembles Erwin Panofksy, who attempted to show how medieval scholasticism and the complex structures of Gothic architecture were both produced from the same "mental habit."[69] Panofsky usually describes the two practices in parallel, especially by noting structural similarities, and he assumes they therefore influenced each other by "diffusion." In contrast, Baxandall is far more specific in his study of the diverse sources that he claims influenced the "cognitive style" and the "period eye" of fifteenth-century Italy. In this emphasis, he again differs from Panofsky, who when suggesting connections between Gothic architecture and scholasticism not only remains vague on the details, but he is also primarily concerned with the *production* of Gothic architecture. Baxandall not only addresses the production of paintings but also the *reception* of paintings as seen by the "period eye."

One major criticism of Baxandall is that his theories are reminiscent of a Zeitgeist, with all that such theories entail in terms of ignoring social diversity and artistic individuality.[70] Yet, Baxandall seems quite aware of these issues from the outset, and he goes to some lengths to limit whose "period eye" he is describing—merchants, princes, heads of religious houses, and so forth. He notes that even within these groups there would have been considerable variation, and therefore, he explains that his book "will be concerned with more generally accessible styles of discrimination."[71]

Baxandall does not intend his study, "a primer in the social history of pictorial style," to be of use solely to art historians; he asserts at the end of the book:

> Much of the book has been given up to noting bits of social practice or convention that may sharpen our perception of the pictures. It is symmetrical and proper to end the book by reversing the equation—to suggest that the forms and styles of painting may sharpen our perception of the society . . . It would be foolish to overstate the possibilities, but they are real. They arise from the fact that the main materials of social history are very restricted in their medium: they consist in a mass of words and a few—in the case of the Renaissance a very few—numbers.[72]

Baxandall's methodology is particularly attractive to me because he is so meticulous in his reconstruction of the education and training of a certain class of person. He refers not only to the pigments specified in contracts between patron and painter but also to such matters as theories of symbolism of colors of the period, handbooks of commercial arithmetical education, and prominent aesthetic categories used in contemporaneous sources. Moreover, many of the materials we possess in Sanskrit on perfumes and aromatics correspond to those he relies on, making his work a very detailed model to follow. But, like Baxandall's book, one might accuse this study of smell in South Asia of oversimplifying the issues and ignoring much diversity. After all, our sources include a huge geographic area, a vast period of time, and numerous genres of texts. Moreover, unlike Baxandall, I have not limited myself to exploring one type of period nose, but, at various points in the book, I look at olfactory perceptions in different times and contexts, such as in early mercantile Buddhism and in medieval courtly culture. The goal of my method is therefore to emphasize diversity, not to ignore it. In this study, I have tried to present a variety of different discourses, highlighting where possible the diverse contexts (religious or social) in an attempt to produce the most differentiated account of uses of, and responses to, smells and aromatics in South Asia. Nor have I limited myself to the period noses of various humans, but I also explore the imagined olfactory sensibilities of gods and other beings as represented in various sources. Thus, this book contributes to the exploration of diversity within the category of "the elite"—a heterogeneous term that is as important to unravel as "the subaltern."

Like Baxandall's book, my examination of cognitive styles, mental habits, educational practices, and so forth will help us to understand better the meaning of smells in South Asian texts and consequently those texts themselves. But this particular topic—smells, perfumes, even perfume names—should also "sharpen our perceptions of the society." As Baxandall writes, we should not overstate this matter; yet, we should also note that, as in the case of Renaissance Italy, our sources from this time and place are "very restricted in their medium."[73]

Now, we turn from Western intellectual history to examine what some early Indian theorists said about smell and odors. Their ideas are not only interesting in themselves, but they are also quite useful in thinking about the materials in the remainder of this book.

2

Earth, Wind, Foul and Fragrant

The Theory of Smelling and Odors in Early South Asia

> Having thus listened to the discourses of poetry, and pondered their merits and demerits, the king should then, with enthusiasm, have the logicians dispute.
> One wants a discussion between two who are of equal descent, knowledge, and renown.
> The subject of the discussion is song, dance, or indeed music . . .
> Then, amongst the disputers, the king should announce defeat for those who have reached the state where they are defeated, and victory for the others.
> Thus the king should pass the rest of the day with the diversion of *śāstra*,
> And he should have abundant gifts of favor given to the poets and logicians.
>
> —Someśvara, *Mānasollāsa*

The Sport of Argument

King Someśvara III was a twelfth-century South Indian king of the Kalyāṇa Cāḷukya dynasty, who reigned from 1124 to 1138 CE.[1] He composed, or at least put his name to, a substantial encyclopedia of courtly life, the *Mānasollāsa*, or *Delight of the Mind*, in which he presented a number of activities, from fishing to wearing luxurious footwear, as varieties of pleasure for an ideal king. This is not the last we will see of this text, because it contains some important materials on perfumery. Some of the delights of the mind were more intellectual in nature, and, in particular, scholarly disputation was one of the royal entertainments (*vinodas*). After his meal, the ideal king would summon his poets and philosophers, seat them as appropriate, and listen, and no doubt comment, as they displayed their skills. Satisfied by a demonstration of poetic skill, the king would then turn his attention to the delights of logic. To enjoy the "sport" of scholarly disputation, he would have two expert debaters engage in verbal combat; just as he might command a pair of wrestlers to fight for his amusement. According to this account, the king selected the topic, and he adjudicated who won the debate. It seems from this passage, that Someśvara liked most of all to hear debates about songs, dance, and music; subjects apparently close to his heart.

But this book is not about music or logic, it's about smell: stinks, perfumes, and the act of smelling. Nevertheless, in this chapter, many of the materials under scrutiny should be understood as the products of a lively tradition of scholarly disputation. These texts are intrinsically, and often explicitly, dialogical. What the intellectuals chose to talk about, what they chose not to talk about, the unwavering maintenance of difference on some matters, and the silent revision of positions on others are generally the product of a long and complex dialogue that was no doubt conducted both in writing and in person. Both in idealized representations, as just depicted, and probably also in actual practice, such scholarly debates were not entirely isolated from the rest of cultivated life and intellectual activity. The religio-philosophical materials discussed in this chapter arguably both inform and reflect a wide variety of discourses, be they medical, ritual, or legal.

Smell is a type of sensory perception, one of the ways people can know about the world, whatever the real nature of that world might be according to a given philosophical or theological tradition. South Asian systematic accounts of the fundamental nature of the world and of perception therefore tend to contain a description of smelling and odors. These accounts of perception range from those that are brief and simple to others that are more detailed. In reading the accounts of smelling and odors found in South Asian intellectual discourses from the turn of the first millennium CE to the seventeenth century CE, three major topics of interest tend to stand out, and these topics will form the subject of this chapter. First, there is the basic nature of the act of smelling, something that appears to be relatively simple and uncontested, and is not the focus of a great deal of debate. Second, there is the tricky (even today) question of the fundamental nature of odors: how many types of odor are there? The latter question is connected to debates on why some objects made of earth (the element with the special quality of odor in some systems) apparently have no odor. Finally, there is the matter of how smell relates to the other senses: is it better or worse than sight, for example, or just different, and in what way?

What Is the Use of Smell Scholasticism?

Before I present those three topics, it might help to reflect on why one should think about this particular subject at all. Why should someone in the twenty-first century be interested in early South Asian theories of smell? Then there is the further question of why quite a lot of people in South Asia were ever interested in theorizing smell.

For people engaged in academic pursuits in the twenty-first century, the study of South Asian theoretical material concerning smell is a part of the study of the senses in South Asian religious and cultural history more generally. The historical study of South Asian religions—Hindu, Jain, and Buddhist—relies quite heavily on texts. Therefore, an understanding of the theory of smelling, the nature of odors, and the order of the senses as known to traditional South Asian scholars is a prelude to a good reading of texts in many genres. Perhaps Alain Corbin puts it best with regard to the more recent historiography of the senses:

> Before embarking on an enquiry, they [historians] must know the representations of the sensory system and the ways in which it functioned. In short, they must be capable of deciphering all the references and of detecting the logic of the evidence ordered by the dominant scientific convictions of the period under consideration. Clearly, a document subject to belief in the theory of animal spirits cannot be analysed using the same key as a text that refers to the cerebral topography outlined by Brocq. The way in which authors see the localization and configuration of the central seat of sensibility, the circulation of messages by the circuit of nerves, *is essential to an understanding of their writings. It implicitly orders their perception of the hierarchy of the senses.*[2]

In an analogous manner, an exploration of the South Asian foundational theories of smell and of the "hierarchy" (perhaps not always the most appropriate term in South Asia) of the senses will permit a richer reading of a variety of other texts on the senses and related subjects. It is significant that Corbin highlights the importance of the hierarchy of the senses. In South Asia, the order of the senses is a particularly interesting subject of inquiry from a comparative point of view. In European intellectual life, discussion of the senses was for a long time dominated by the classical Greek hierarchy of the senses. In South Asia, three different orders of the senses were commonly used by scholars belonging to three major sectarian groups, who produced numerous texts and who were no doubt in dialogue with one another. Thus, with regard to the role of smell in South Asia, it is not possible to assign this sense a single hierarchical rank in intellectual life, even amongst scholars and the educated elite. Depending on the sectarian context, and also on the emphasis in classification, the place of smell in the order of the senses could change quite radically.

The History of Minor Ideas

Now for the second question: Why were South Asian intellectuals interested in smell? Although the theory of smell was never the central preoccupation for the schools of thought discussed later, the nature of the world and the nature of perception were, and it was as part of this larger field enquiry that the study of smell came to matter. Despite fundamental disagreements on the nature and reality of the world (setting aside the issue of the order of the senses), by the early centuries of the Common Era, the basic model of smell presented by most schools of thought was relatively uniform: certain things (but not all) in the world possess an odor. When these things are perceived by sentient beings, if those beings have a sense of smell, they can perceive the quality of the odor possessed by that object. These odors are carried to the smell organ in the form of particles via the wind. Only the sense of smell can perceive the odors of these things and hence come to know about certain qualities of certain things in the world. The fundamental qualities of odor are often said to be twofold (sometimes threefold): fragrant and not-fragrant (sometimes also neutral).

The act of smelling mattered to scholars producing accounts and analyses of human perception and experience, and the nature of odors was important to scholars trying to produce a comprehensive account of what the world was made of and what it was like. Above all, the study of perception (including smell) is a vital part of epistemology—the study of the nature of knowledge. A comprehensive account of experience, of ways of knowing about things, or of the structure of the world, would therefore be indispensable to scholars trying to understand and possibly change the condition of sentient beings in the world, in many cases for what we might call religious or soteriological reasons.

As noted previously, within these analyses, smell was rarely the central topic of debate but rather part of a well-stocked armory of definitions that scholars had at their disposal. Ideas about smell and many other minor issues were frequently updated, especially when this sort of intellectual endeavor became more systematic and communication was made easier by the increasing use of a common intellectual language: Sanskrit.[3] In that context, the relative unimportance of this topic proves in itself interesting, because it would appear that ideas concerning minor issues developed in a manner quite unlike those concerning more central ones. The history of ideas may well not follow the same course when the idea in question is not of enormous importance to the traditions that are in energetic dialogue. In a series of essays, John Clayton argued that the South Asian tradition of interreligious debate not only firmed up differences between traditions but was also, in part, constitutive of tradition.[4] Examining the quieter corners of philosophical systems might well allow us to build on this theory: maybe debate did not always firm up differences and maybe not all differences were the sorts of things that could be debated. I return to these questions at the end of the chapter, after a close examination of the materials on smell. But for now, bear in mind that large parts of several philosophical and religious texts from South Asia, such as the Buddhist *Abhidharmakośa*, were concerned with a vast number of such points. A detailed history of one minor idea may shed light on the broader history of a large part of these texts. After all, these numerous smaller questions—the "complete picture" as it were—clearly mattered to South Asian scholars, and thus they should matter to us.

As I noted in the introduction, it is the practice of much contemporary scholarship to challenge essentialist descriptions of religious traditions, for example, to talk of "Buddhisms" as opposed to "Buddhism." If we look at the order in which the senses tend to be listed, however, we see a consistent use of a certain order within one tradition, such as Buddhism, which is different from the order consistently used within another tradition, such as Jainism. In a climate where internal difference and diversity are emphasized, we should remember that there are nevertheless many things, large and small, that do appear to unite certain religions. The sources examined in this chapter tend to use three orders of the senses, and these correspond to what we usually today call Hindu, Jain, and Buddhist schools of thought. Indeed these three separate orders of the senses seem to be very old indeed.[5] They are found quite regularly, though not universally, in our sources from very early times onward, and it is on the basis of these sectarian divisions that I have, as far as possible, organized the chapter. In addition to this somewhat rough sectarian structure, I then present the texts chronologically (as far as possible, given the usual difficulties in dating very old South Asian texts) because I consider the historical development of ideas concerning odors.

Sources

There is no early or medieval South Asian theoretical treatise devoted to the subject of smelling and odorants. Instead, I had to collect passages from a variety of works in order to produce a relatively rounded and complex picture of how this sense and its objects were theorized over the centuries.[6] The sources I have used to produce this account vary, from earlier and less systematic materials, such as an account of the nature of odor in the *Mahābhārata*, to somewhat later and highly systematic texts, such as commentaries on the aphoristic *sūtra* texts foundational to some schools of thought. Large doctrinal compendia such as the Buddhist *Abhidharmakośa* constitute another type of source. Although I refer to a wide range of materials in this chapter, I have been obliged to present them selectively since the total number of texts that, in some shape or form, treat smell is enormous.[7]

I also note that some of the earlier and less systematic sources might in some scholarly contexts be considered to be rather "proto": for example, "proto-Sāṃkhya."[8] This observation is indeed relevant to my discussion of the chronological development of some ideas concerning smell. Yet, the fact that these materials are early and unsystematic and were superseded by other texts in the realm of systematic philosophical thought does not by any means imply that they vanished from intellectual discourse. In some areas of intellectual life, these earlier, and often far less technical, materials might have been partners in dialogue. For example, a much later systematic philosopher, Vijñānabhikṣu, writing possibly in the late sixteenth century,[9] referred to this sort of "proto" material in providing his own particular account of Sāṃkhya.[10] Thus, in later periods, these old ideas evidently remained in circulation.

The Act of Smelling

How did people understand the basic physical act of smelling? It appears that the nature of smelling was relatively uncontested, and in its basic outline is more or less what nonspecialists think today in Europe and America. Moreover, the theoretical and technical understanding of the act of smelling is entirely consistent with (and possibly even at times reflects) less technical accounts of the act of smelling found in a variety of other genres—literary, legal, and so on—that will play a role in later chapters.

In outline, smelling was understood as follows. The sense of smell is located in the nose. Objects in the world that possess odor give off tiny particles that are moved by the wind to the sense of smell in the nose, and then the odor is experienced. This means that smell is a sense that, like touch, requires actual physical contact with matter. However, unlike the sense of touch, the sense of smell involves indirect contact, with tiny particles, and this is mediated by the wind. For this reason, one synonym for "wind" is "odor carrier" (*gandhavaha/-vāha*). When I smell a piece of rotten meat, tiny odorous particles of the meat leave the meat and are carried by the wind to my nose where they touch my organ of smelling. This account has several implications:

- Smell has the strange, almost paradoxical, nature of being both a remote sense and a contact sense.
- Smelling depends on a third factor, the wind, in order to occur.
- If you smell something, you have effectively touched part of it, and this might have repercussions in a context where ritual impurity can be transferred by physical contact.

Perhaps the clearest account of this process is that found in a text called the *Nyāyamañjarī* (*A Cluster of Flowers of the Nyāya Tree*) of the ninth-century poet and philosopher Kashmirian Jayanta Bhaṭṭa.[11]

> The sense of smell, for its part, is only effective when contacted, because of binding to the odor which has as its substrate that mass of atoms,[12] which spreads from such things as a jasmine vine agitated by the wind. And the shrinkage and so on of the substance by virtue of the efflux of atoms is not to be conjectured—because of the superabundance of atoms. For this very reason people hand down the tradition of penance in the case of smelling a ritually impure substance, in order to remove the fault/sin arising from contact with that substance by means of the odor.[13]

This is quite a dense and technical passage. First, Jayanta Bhaṭṭa notes that the sense of smell (*ghrāṇa*) only works when contacted (when it has *prāpyakāritā*). This is because the sense of smell binds to the odor (*gandha*) whose substrate is a mass of atoms that has spread from something odorous, such as a jasmine vine which has been agitated by the all-important wind. But, as Jayanta observes, the fact that there is an efflux of atoms (*paramāṇu*) does *not* make the odorous substance shrink—this is because the atoms are so enormously abundant in the odorous substance. This comment is presumably addressed to the possible objection that this theory is flawed because odorous substances do not shrink on losing their atoms. Moving on from these philosophical issues, Jayanta relates the theory he espouses to religious law. His theory explains why it is taught (in texts on *dharma*) that people need to do a religious penance (*prāyaścittam*) in the event that they smell ritually impure substances (*aśucidravyaghrāṇe*). By this final move he achieves two things. First, he provides a clear theoretical explanation for why penances exist for smelling ritually impure substances. Second, the tradition of such penances, which only really make sense in the light of his account of the sense of smell, suggests that a theory of smell very much like the one he espouses is also implicit in revered religious texts on *dharma*.

This latter point is particularly interesting in the study of smell more broadly in South Asian religions. In the *Law Code of Manu*, the *Mānava Dharmaśāstra*, an important and early South Asian treatise on *dharma*, there is some clarification of what is implied by the prohibition of smelling certain substances:

> Making a Brahmin cry, smelling liquor or substances that should not be smelt (*ghrātir aghreyamadyayoḥ*), cheating, and sexual intercourse with a man—tradition calls these sins that cause exclusion from caste.[14]

The precise category of sin involved here is called "causing exclusion from caste" (*jātibhraṃśakaram*). As Olivelle notes, the exact implications of the terminology for this type of sin is not entirely clear; although, it is a less serious category of sin than the most serious category. Here, it is helpful to note the manner in which these lesser sins evidently correspond to the greatest sins of the most serious category (*mahānti pātakāni*).[15] Those most serious sins are "killing a Brahmin, drinking liquor, stealing, and having sex with an elder's wife."[16] The sins listed previously that cause exclusion from caste are all somewhat modified versions of the same sorts of activities: Instead of "killing a Brahmin," the sin is "making a Brahmin cry"; instead of "drinking liquor," there is "smelling liquor"; instead of "stealing," there is "cheating"; and instead of "having sex with an elder's wife," there is "sexual intercourse with a man." Therefore, smelling liquor or impure substances, though it involves contact with impure substances, is not considered quite as bad: smelling is similar to eating but not quite as direct or intense in terms of contact and ingestion, just as cheating is a somewhat less direct form of theft than actually physically stealing something.

But what exactly are Brahmins forbidden to smell here? The text says smelling liquor/intoxicants or substances that should not be smelt (*ghrātir aghreyamadyayoḥ*). The term for liquor/intoxicants used here (*madya*) appears to be a broad term covering a variety of substances,[17] and the *Law Code of Manu* does not contain any clarification as to what is meant by "substances that should not be smelt." To find out how some scholars might have understood this term, we turn to commentators on this verse, in particular to a celebrated commentary on the *Mānava Dharmaśāstra*, the *Manubhāṣya* of Medhātithi, probably dating from the ninth century CE.[18]

Medhātithi explains this part of the verse as follows, in the form of a reply to someone who denies there are things that should not be smelled:

> "What, however, is a substance that should not be smelt? For there is nowhere a prohibition on smelling, like there is a prohibition on eating. And it is not possible to understand that what is not to be eaten is not to be smelt: it is the case that ghee and so forth acquired for a sacrificial offering should not be eaten, but it is not the case that it should not be smelt."
>
> We say: on account of their stinking bad-smell garlic, onions, human excrement, and so forth disturb[19] the sense of smell: that is what should be understood. And because of the association with liquor, those very things that are not to be eaten are to be understood [as included here too.] Not [however] stinking[20] timber.[21]

The hypothetical opponent suggests that there is not a prohibition on smelling a thing, apparently trying to do away with this restriction. This opponent argues that, although it is forbidden to eat certain things, such as ghee and other materials used in a Vedic sacrifice, it is not forbidden to smell these things. The logic appears to be that smelling some of the sacrificial materials in a Vedic fire sacrifice would be unavoidable, even though these materials are not to be eaten. Medhātithi responds to this on two levels. First, he notes that "things that should not be smelt" implies things that disturb the sense of smell, such as garlic, onions, and human excrement. Second, he deals with the reference to liquor and says that things forbidden to eat are included in this category. His refutation implies that substances, like alcohol, that are *intrinsically* forbidden, unlike ghee, to eat and/or drink (at least for certain members of society) are not to be smelled.

Medhātithi's enumeration of materials that are not to be smelled is not surprising –they are especially odorous materials forbidden in the Brahmin diet. What is striking, is the suggestion that there were actual (or imaginable) opponents to the idea that smelling could be a sin. Presumably, for these opponents, given the diffusive nature of many smells, including those of things forbidden to eat, this sin would appear impossible to avoid at certain times: taste does not diffuse, but smell does, and if smelling certain things is a sin, then this might make life quite difficult, especially in the context of a fire sacrifice. No doubt, it is for this reason that some commentators qualify this sinful act of smelling with the word "intentionally" (*kāmataḥ*) here.[22]

The second aspect of the act of smelling that I highlight is the strange nature of smell, in that the objects of smell (for example a jasmine flower) may be far away from the perceiver. In this respect, smell is like sight: I can both see and smell a white, fragrant jasmine flower from a distance. But, the movement of the odorous particles of the jasmine flower is entirely at the whim of the wind.[23] Smell is, therefore, not as reliable a way of perceiving distant objects as sight; although, coupled with the tactile nature of wind, it is possible to know in what direction a certain odorant lies. Yet, as smell depends on wind, sight depends on light, and at night, in the dark, smell may be the best option for finding your way around. (A dark night also presents opportunities for a variety of secret activities, which can give scent-trails furtive and erotic connotations.)

Taking advantage of the limitations and possibilities implied by the theoretical (and possibly everyday) understanding of smell, some Sanskrit poets seem to have delighted in creating clever perception-conceits. Perhaps the most famous of these occurs in the literary play *Ratnāvalī*, by the seventh-century King Harṣa; a text that like most literary Sanskrit (*kāvya*) abounds in olfactory references.[24] In one passage, the character of the king charmingly sniffs his way around the royal pleasure garden in the dark on his way to a secret tryst:

> This is surely the border of *campakas*; this is that beautiful *sinduvāra*, and this is the dense hedge of *bakula* trees; this is the row of *pāṭalas*.
> The path in this place, though concealed by double-darkness, becomes clear by means of the signs of the trees recognized by constantly sniffing the varied perfume.[25]

Smell has replaced sight as the sense that leads a person through space, mainly because it is dark. Moreover, the fact that this is the only way to navigate the garden suggests how dark it is. The "landmarks" the king uses to navigate are perfumes indicating the location of various fragrant flowers. It is almost as if the darkness has reduced the King's abilities to those of a bee moving through the fragrant flowers in search of sweet nectar: a very common image in Sanskrit poetry. Smell is fulfilling the function of vision here, something it can do on rare occasions. This is very much smell out-of-place, providing cognitive information to navigate, which is ideally left to the sense of sight. It is this transformation of the sense of smell to a substitute for vision—the king is guided not by visible forms but by clouds of fragrance (a highly incongruous yet beautiful use of smell)—that makes this passage so memorable. Of course, its incongruity only reinforces the normal cognitive role of vision, and the delightful, fragrant, and erotic aspects of the passage reinforce the common role of smell as an attractant.

Finally, the notion of the wind as a carrier of odors plays a prominent part in many of the texts I describe elsewhere in this book, so I will dwell no further on this matter here.

The Classification of Odors

Anyone who has ever tried will be aware that producing a finite enumeration or classification of smells is a difficult task.[26] Though motivated by a variety of philosophical and theological agendas, a number of South Asian scholars from the last few centuries BCE until the mid-first millennium CE consciously tried to produce such a classification as part of various larger attempts to describe the fundamental nature of the world and of experience. I will first examine the history of these attempts to classify odors, as produced by thinkers with broadly Hindu, Jain, and Buddhist sectarian affiliation. Noting the manner in which different sectarian accounts became increasingly similar over the centuries, I will then reflect on the possible reasons for this change.

Hindu

I begin by examining odors as presented in schools of thought that are today generally described as Hindu. It would appear that the earliest Hindu source on the classification of odors is a passage from the *Mahābhārata*. Though odors are mentioned in many contexts in numerous early texts, I am not aware of any explicit treatment of the classification of odor prior to the following passage.[27]

I will discuss this passage from the *Mahābhārata* in the same section as some passages from texts produced by a school of thought frequently referred to as Nyāya-Vaiśeṣika because of the close association of two philosophical schools: the logically and epistemologically oriented Nyāya school and the more ontologically oriented Vaiśeṣika school. Both the passages in the *Mahābhārata*, and the Nyāya-Vaiśeṣika texts display some notable features of what Frauwallner calls the "nature-philosophical" school of Indian philosophy.[28] This school, he claims, is characterized by an interest in the nature of the external world, as well as a doctrine of individual souls. He places both Jainism and Vaiśeṣika in this category, as well as the following dialogue in the *Mahābhārata* between Bhṛgu and Bharadvāja. Indeed, the latter passage does share several concerns with Jainism, and it appears to be in conversation with schools of thought that have concerns that we might identify as typically Jain. For example, the passage refers to a soul-like entity called a *jīva* and discusses the senses of plants.[29] On this topic, the passage from the *Mahābhārata* contains an argument that plants are said to have all five senses, including, of course, smell—something that would have been at odds with the Jain view of plants as possessing only one sense: touch. Here is the passage from the *Mahābhārata*:

Likewise, by means of good and bad perfumes and also various incenses.
They are free from disease and in flower. Therefore trees can smell.[30]

This particular point might seem extremely scholastic on first examination. Arguing about the sense of smell of plants might seem like the Indian equivalent of counting angels dancing on a pinhead. But this account of the senses of plants has two implications. First, if plants have all five senses, then the Jain classification of beings according to the number of senses they have (plants only have one sense according to Jains) is incorrect, and the Jain order of the senses, discussed later, which correlates to this classification of sentient beings, has no valid basis. Second, if plants have all five senses, then presumably they are able to experience as much pain and suffering as higher animals. In practicing (selective) vegetarianism and only eating plants—beings that only have one sense (touch)—Jains are able to keep the harm they impose on sentient beings to a minimum. If, however, plants have all five senses, then they can feel as much pain via as many senses as animals can, and there is, therefore, little advantage in being a vegetarian if your goal it to avoid causing sentient beings to suffer. Indeed, if plants have five senses, eating vegetables is arguably as harmful as sacrificing animals in some types of Vedic sacrifices. If you accept the argument in this passage, not only is the Jain vegetarian lifestyle deluded, but also criticisms of the killing of animals in some Vedic sacrifices are entirely hypocritical.[31]

The Mahābhārata

In the *Mokṣadharma* section of the *Śāntiparvan* of the *Mahābhārata*, a discussion of the senses in a dialogue between Bhṛgu and Bharadvāja is one of the earlier sources that provide a technical account of the nature of odor.[32] The exact date of this text need not concern us here, but estimates of the date of this epic place it sometime in the centuries around the turn of the Common Era. But what is a discussion of the fundamental nature of odor doing in this vast epic poem? When the Kuru-Pāṇḍava war at the heart of the epic *Mahābhārata* is over, and victorious Yudhiṣṭhira has been made king, on the advice of Kṛṣṇa, he returns to the battlefield, Kurukṣetra, to listen to the advice of the dying Bhīṣma. While discussing the many philosophical matters treated in the *Mokṣadharma* section, at one point Yudhiṣṭhira questions Bhīṣma about the material nature of the world, the elements, the castes (*varṇas*), the soul, and so on. In response to his query, Bhīṣma relates the dialogue between Bhṛgu and Bharadvāja. And in that dialogue, when describing the nature of the elements, Bhṛgu relates a list of the varieties of the special quality of earth: odor. Thus, it is talk of elements that leads to talk of odors.

I will relate the qualities, named in detail, of that odor:
desired and undesired odor, sweet and pungent,
diffusive, compact, smooth, rough, and pure
The array of odor, connected to earth, is thus known to be ninefold.[33]

As in an account of taste provided in the same passage, the qualities (*guṇas*) of odor seem to fall into relatively neat pairs. The first pair is the most significant: desired and undesired (or "pleasant" and "unpleasant"). The terms attribute a value to odors. In the light of other discussions of odor, the question arises whether these qualities apply to all odors, or whether they are just two out of nine qualities of odor. Considering later presentations of the qualities of odor, it might seem these qualities apply to all odors; although, perhaps it is best to be cautious about interpreting this passage in that way. Nevertheless, these two evaluative qualities are listed first, suggesting they are important members of the list.

The next pair of qualities, "sweet" and "pungent," *madhura* and *kaṭu*, are qualities of taste, and they are given in the list that follows the odors, which enumerates six tastes (*rasas*):

> Sweet, salty, bitter, astringent, sour, also pungent. This sixfold enumeration of taste, made of water, is taught.[34]

I have translated the next pair as "diffusive and compact."[35] Both these terms describe not so much *olfactory* qualities as the first four terms do, but rather they refer to the physico-chemical properties of the odorant. They refer to how odors behave in relation to time and space. It would seem that this passage reflects an attempt to capture as many aspects of odorants as possible.

The next three terms pose more of a challenge. Given that the preceding terms ("sweet and pungent," and so forth) appear to be listed in pairs, then *snigdha* (oily, smooth) and *rūkṣa* (rough, harsh) can also easily be read together as a contrasting pair: "smooth and rough." We should note that just as the terms "sweet" and "pungent" primarily refer to taste, these terms may also refer to the objects of the sense of touch. And the term *snigdha* does indeed occur in this dialogue, when the twelve qualities of touch are described, but the term *rūkṣa* does not occur there. The passage concerning touch is also worth quoting:

> hard, glossy, smooth, slimy, soft and harsh (*dāruṇa*),
> warm, cool, pleasant, painful, smooth and pure.[36]

In this dialogue touch is the only other sense-object that, like odor, has qualities that are value terms: pleasant and painful, *sukha* and *duḥkha*. But how can an odor be smooth or rough? The work of the seventeenth-century commentator Nīlakaṇṭha might be of some help here. I should add that Nīlakaṇṭha wrote many centuries later than when this passage was first composed, or inserted, in the *Mahābhārata* and in a very different cultural context. Nevertheless, he was an extremely well-informed scholar of Sanskrit, and, in addition to what his commentaries tell us about Nīlakaṇṭha and his times, I believe that his comments may (cautiously) be read with a view to augment understanding the text. For "rough" *rūkṣa*, Nīlakaṇṭha gives *sarṣapatailādau*, "mustard oil, etc.," which refers to what the modern study of olfaction refers to as a *trigeminal* stimulus. The effect of sniffing substances such as mustard, pepper, chili, and ammonia is connected to a separate nerve than that used to smell such items as jasmine and corpses. As with "sweet" and "pungent," these classes of odors might be placed together in this manner in order to reflect their shared origins in the terminology of the other senses. Moreover, in distinguishing trigeminal qualities, we can appreciate the unique scope of this examination of the qualities of odorants—a breadth of thinking about the aspects of odorants not matched anywhere in the Western classical world.

But if the rough odor is to be understood as something like mustard oil that stimulates the trigeminal nerve, then what is a smooth (*snigdha*) odor? *Snigdha* could well refer to the odor of oil, because in the play called *The Little Clay Cart* (*Mṛcchakaṭika*) of Śūdraka there is mention, in Prakrit, of a *siṇiddhagandha* (*snigdhagandha*) at the point when the stage director, *sūtradhara*, goes home hungry to find food being prepared: "As if inflamed by the oily odor, hunger torments me all the more."[37]

This is further supported by the example Nīlakaṇṭha chooses: *sadyastaptaghṛtādau*, "recently heated ghee, etc." Here *snigdha* refers to the odor of fat, which makes less of a contrasting pair with *rūkṣa*. In that case, one could possibly understand *snigdha* in the context of odor as meaning something like "fatty," bearing in mind that this Sanskrit term has the positive and pleasant connotations of an English term such as "buttery," which, unfortunately, is too narrow to use.[38] Although this pair of terms originated in touch terminology, it appears that in the play, and also for Nīlakaṇṭha, the term *snigdha* suggests more the odor of a fatty odorant than a smooth odor.

The final and challenging term, *viśada*, primarily means "clear," "clean," "bright," "pure," and so on. Nīlakaṇṭha gives the example of the odor of boiled rice.[39] As noted, this term is also present in the list of touch qualities in the passage. Unlike "desired" and "undesired," this term is not contrasted with a term meaning "unclear," "impure," or something along those lines. The Sanskrit dictionary of Böhtlingk and Roth cites this very occurrence of the term as applied to an odor, and includes this in the sense of this word as *weich anzufühlen*, "soft to the touch." The dictionary also states that when applied to *food* the term is contrasted with *khara*, "sharp/hard," which is noted by the grammarian commentator Patañjali in his *Mahābhāṣya* (on Pāṇini's *Aṣṭādhyāyī* 7.3.69), where the distinction would appear to be between solid-hard and solid-soft foods.[40] This also implies that the application of the term *viśada* to food is quite early. This sense, applied to *food* seems therefore to mean "soft," but as applied to *taste*, it is not quite so clear; perhaps it refers to the taste of foods classified as soft, or perhaps there is an extension in meaning to imply "mild." Although Nīlakaṇṭha wrote a very long time after this passage was composed, nevertheless, the odor he cites here is quite mild. This term, therefore, probably means something along the lines of a "mild" or "clean" odor.

Considered together, this list of odor qualities is varied and ingenious. A series of pairs of qualities is applied to odors. Note that none of these terms are unique to odor:

a contrasting pair of value terms,
a contrasting pair of descriptive taste terms,
a contrasting pair of terms describing the physical/diffusive properties of odors,
a contrasting pair of descriptive touch terms,
a single somewhat ambiguous term, also included in the list of touch qualities, and which is also applied to food elsewhere, and which may well attribute a delicacy or cleanliness to an odor.

Finally, the passage explains that odor (*gandha*) is related to the element earth (*pārthiva*). This is significant because it connects the account of the objects of the senses with the idea that the senses and their objects correspond to the elements, and this explains why of all the objects of sense, smells are dealt with first. I will return to this point in detail later.

This classification of odor constitutes a sophisticated and significant analysis—perhaps the most interesting we have from the premodern world. Yet, I am not claiming that the classification is remarkable because it postulates an "objective" classification of odors, as opposed to "subjective" and evaluative classifications taught by later South Asian philosophies. Nor am I judging this classification in comparison to some standard benchmark of achievement in the classification of odors, be it classical, scientific, or otherwise.[41] Rather, this analysis of odor is remarkable in terms of the extensive range of perspectives on odor and the variety of intellectual resources it draws on. This classification includes the aesthetic and/or hedonic aspects of odors, as well as their physical characteristics.

Nyāya-Vaiśeṣika

In later texts of what is often known as the Nyāya-Vaiśeṣika philosophy this correlation of the senses with the elements is retained. I now look at some of the Nyāya-Vaiśeṣika sources, in which the hierarchy of the senses, based on the order of the elements, also remains characteristic. What I call the Nyāya-Vaiśeṣika school is, in fact, a grouping of two philosophies that came to be associated with each other. The Nyāya school of philosophy excelled in the field of logic and became closely associated with the atomistic and realist Vaiśeṣika school of philosophy. The early, normative texts of these systems do not provide a classification of odor, and, for the most part, it is later commentators that furnish this information.

The normative text of the logical Nyāya school, the early *Nyāyasūtra* itself does not discuss odor qualities,[42] but Vātsyāyana's early (third to fifth century CE) commentary on it gives "desired," "undesired," and "disregardable":[43]

> Odors are desired, undesired and disregardable.[44]

This commentary is probably the earliest Nyāya-Vaiśeṣika text to list the qualities of odor. The *Mahābhārata* list has been reduced to evaluative categories only. Odors are no longer described using the terminology of other senses, nor is there any reference to what we call the physico-chemical properties, just to the aesthetic value of the odors. Yet, a third quality, "disregardable," has been added. This term could refer to a neutral odor, neither good nor bad. Alternatively, it could mean an odor that is overlooked because it is so faint. This latter option may seem strange, but in the light of some other sources considered later, this possibility may make sense. The translation "disregardable/overlookable" could imply both—the odor is disregarded because it has no aesthetic impact, or because it is not even smelled in the first place. This interesting threefold classification of odor is not unlike one of the Buddhist classifications of odor we shall consider later.

Vaiśeṣika, with its strengths in ontology, is, along with Sāṃkhya, the school of thought most strongly associated with the theory that the elements and senses are connected. The element earth is special with regard to smell in that earth alone possesses odor. A binary, evaluative (and subsequently standard) classification using terms specific to smell appears possibly for the first time in surviving works of this school of thought in the *Praśastapādabhāṣyam/Padārthadharmasaṃgraha*, composed by Praśastapāda,[45] and which is the source of what Potter calls "standard old Vaisesika," dating possibly from the sixth century CE.[46] Praśastapāda provides a direct definition of odor: that which is grasped by the sense of smell. He explains that it exists in earth, and we are given the qualities: "fragrant and unfragrant." The third term meaning either "neutral" or "unnoticeable" disappears. Moreover, the terminology no longer consists of a general value term such as "desired/pleasant" (*iṣṭa*), which could be applied to the other categories of object such as flavors, and instead an odor-specific terminology, "fragrant" (*surabhi*), is adopted. The account of odor in these schools of thought is becoming both more succinct and more specific:

> Odor is grasped by the sense of smell. It is present in earth. It is the associate of the sense of smell. It is fragrant and unfragrant. Its origin etc., is explained as above.[47]

But if earth has smell, what of materials that are clearly earthy but have no odor such as stones? In the *Kiraṇāvalī* of Udayana, a major Vaiśeṣika work of the eleventh century,[48] we encounter an argument about such odorless (earth-based) stones. Here the notion of "cooking," *pāka*, used to explain the color change on heating earthy substances, is brought in to explain the problem that some earth-made substances have no odor. The argument is that in the process of "cooking," not only do some earth substances change color, but they also give off an odor. By inference, we can assume there was an odor present previously, but we did not perceive it, just as we do not perceive the odor of the earth element which must be present in the organ of smell. The question arises, who might make an objection regarding earth objects with no odor? Of course, it could easily be a general and rather obvious objection—stones are made of the element earth and do not usually smell unless broken, heated, or moistened. Yet, given that odor and earth mutually define each other, odorless earth objects constitute a serious problem. Maybe smell is not inherent in the element earth after all? One solution to the problem of odorless stones would be to accept the threefold odor of Vātsyāyana—and posit a real third type of odor—the odor with no odor, a zero odor. Indeed, it may be to tackle this problem that Vātsyāyana introduced this third class. However, such an "odorless odor" is something Udayana seems to want to avoid, since he says there are two types of odor: fragrant and unfragrant.[49]

Kiraṇāvalī of Udayana (with translation by Tachikawa):

> Objection: Smell does not pervade the whole of the earth, because it is not found in jewels, diamonds, etc., which are to be spoken of later. Therefore, how can smell be the cause of our setting up [the subcategory earth]?
>
> Reply: No, [smell does not fail to pervade the whole of earth]. If the original color [of an earth substance] disappears and another color appears on account of "cooking," the [latter] color produced by "cooking" is always accompanied by smell. Therefore, in that also which possesses the original color we may infer the existence of smell. If we do not perceive it, this is simply because it is not manifested there, just as it is not manifested in the olfactory organ. This is the intention of the author.[50]

[On the varieties of smell, replying to an objection that the (presumably numerous) subordinate varieties of smell enable one to differentiate one substance from another:]

> Reply: [The text says:] There are two types of smell: GOOD AND BAD. One should supply "in earth only," that is, "not in other substances." As smell of different sorts occurs in one and the same substance at different times due to "cooking," it cannot serve to establish the existence of one substance or another.[51]

By now is should be clear that the binary classification of odor became standard in these texts as of the mid-first millennium CE. This particular understanding of odor lasted for quite a long time. In a very popular early-to-mid seventeenth-century manual of the so-called "new," *navya*, style of logical philosophy, a text called the *Bhāṣāpariccheda*, it is not surprising to find the following definition of odor. (A definition first recited to me several years ago by Dr. Bhat, who teaches traditional Indian medicine in the Sanskrit College at Mysore in South India.[52])

> It is proclaimed as twofold: fragrant and unfragrant.[53]

The *twofold definition* of smell that most Hindu Sanskrit knowledge systems agreed on in the early centuries of the Common Era was still used in the early modern period, as it is indeed still used today, along with the close association of odor with the element earth.

In this examination of a trend in Indian scholarship that holds there is a strong connection between the senses and the elements, we can see a distinct development in the classification of odors. In the passage from the *Mahābhārata*, the sense of smell is closely associated with the element earth, and, moreover, we are given a complex and detailed account of the nature of odors—an account that first notes the pleasant and unpleasant aspects of odor, and, also, using a variety of imported terminology, describes several other aspects of odors. The *Nyāyasūtra* and the *Vaiśeṣikasūtra* do not provide a classification of the objects of the senses, but their later commentators do, from around the mid-first millennium CE.[54] Vātsyāyana presents an entirely evaluative, but *threefold*, classification to compliment the *Nyāyasūtra*, and Praśastapāda presents the twofold version, which later became standard in all Vaiśeṣika and Nyāya texts, and perseveres until the present day.

Unlike the objects of the other senses, odors are from the outset classified using evaluative terminology by this school of thought. For much of the history of this school of thought, there are said to be two of these values, one good and one bad, and these are said to cover all odors. The objects of the sense of smell are the most consistently classified in this manner—the colors perceived by sight and the flavors perceived by taste might well have been subject to evaluation, but the basic elements of these sense-objects (red, salty, and so on) are not intrinsically pleasant or unpleasant.

Jain

I now turn to some Jain sources which deal with the nature of smell. I present these materials next because, as noted earlier, in their preoccupation with the nature of the world and of matter, they could be said to belong to Frauwallner's "nature-philosophical" category of Indian philosophy, to which the schools of thought already discussed belong. However, unlike the previously examined schools of thought, they do not connect the senses with the elements. Yet, as we shall see in the analysis of the order of the senses, the principle by which they order the senses possesses one interesting similarity to that used by the schools of thought I talked about in the previous section.

The first two sources are from what are believed to be possibly the earliest Śvetāmbara Jain texts: the *Ācārāṅgasūtra* and the *Sūtrakṛtāṅgasūtra*,[55] dating from approximately the second or third century BCE. These passages do not directly describe the nature of matter. Rather, in stating what the *jīva*, the soul, *is not*, they indirectly reveal a very early definition of the nature of insentient matter.[56]

Before I go any further, I present the passages themselves. The passage in the *Ācārāṅgasūtra*, discussing the liberated soul, is as follows:

> (The liberated) is not long nor small nor round nor triangular nor quadrangular nor circular; he is not black nor blue nor red nor green nor white; neither of good nor bad smell; not bitter nor pungent nor astringent nor sweet; neither rough nor soft; neither heavy nor light; neither cold nor hot; neither harsh nor smooth; he is without body, without resurrection, without contact (of matter), he is not feminine nor masculine nor neuter; he perceives, he knows, but there is no analogy (whereby to know the nature of the liberated soul); its essence is without form; there is no condition of the unconditioned. There is no sound, no colour, no smell, no taste, no touch—nothing of that kind. Thus I say.[57]

In the *Sūtrakṛtāṅgasūtra*, people who hold some sort of materialist philosophy, who teach that the soul is entirely co-extensive in space and time with the body, describe what they see as a flaw in the ideas of those who believe the soul is different from the body. Thus, these are the words of the materialist:

> Those who maintain that the soul is something different from the body, cannot tell whether the soul (as separated from the body) is long or small, whether globular or circular or triangular or square or sexagonal or octagonal or long, whether black or blue or red or yellow or white, whether of sweet smell or bad smell, whether bitter or pungent or astringent or sour or sweet, whether hard or soft or heavy or light or cold or hot or smooth or rough.[58]

If we accept that these lists are indirect statements of the nature of *ajīva* matter, then, like the *Mahābhārata* passages, they constitute a very early source for views on the nature of odor.

In both passages, the soul is described as neither "fragrant" nor "dis-fragrant," to give a more literal translation than that of Jacobi in the earlier passages.[59] These terms are similar to the later, odor-specific, and very common Nyāya-Vaiśeṣika formulation *surabir asurabiś ca*. Odor is described only in aesthetic terms, and no other descriptive terms are applied. Moreover, the terms used are not general, like the "desired and undesired" used in the earlier Hindu descriptions of odor, but rather specific to odors.

Scholars have paid close attention to these passages, usually with the aim of establishing early Jaina views on the nature of the soul. And these scholars have been especially concerned with a point Malvania made: in these passages, the soul is (among other things) "neither long nor short," which appears at odds with "the Jaina theory, found in the later texts, that the soul is the size of the body in its mundane existence, and occupies, when liberated, two thirds of the extent of the last body." Bronkhorst, when analyzing the possible influence of Buddhism on Jainism in forming the Jaina notion of the body-sized soul, refers to Malvania's point to show that early Jainism did not have such a notion.[60]

Those insights are valuable. However, I suggest that in addition to reading this passage as a negative description of the soul, it is also useful to observe that, in listing a large number and variety of qualities of insentient matter, the passage has a rhetorical force to the effect that "the soul is not in any way whatsoever like insentient matter: it is not big or small or . . ." Moreover, neither of the two texts is written in an analytic style, and both deal with varied material: ethics, cosmology, and so on. Although these passages are interesting from the point of view of the history of the concept of the soul, we should not forget that the contrast here is between soul and insentient matter in general, and thus we should perhaps not take the details about the length or shortness of the soul too literally—what they tell us about matter is just as interesting.

The second passage, taken from the *Sūtrakṛtāṅgasūtra*, is particularly interesting because the list is presented as part of a disproof of another philosophy: the numerous qualities are mentioned incidentally as part of the rhetoric of a non-Jain teacher. Yet ironically, although these words are in the mouth of a non-Jain, they show several distinctive Jain features: the typical Jain order of the senses and the absence of the taste "salty." Thus, in describing an opponent of Jainism, the Jain writers present him with uniquely Jain features. In this way, the passage raises a very important point (to which I will return later in the chapter)—in the context of a debate on a certain contested topic, other parts of a system, which are not especially contested, are laid open to public scrutiny. Should these background, minor aspects of the system, the nature of odor for example, be noticeably different, they are likely to be challenged if brought up in a debate. In that case, one either requires a good defense of that minor part on hand or, to save the effort of justifying that part of the system, one adopts a less contentious account for this less central part of the system.

Not only is the definition of odor here typically Jain, but so is the order of the objects of the senses: visible form, odor, taste, touch.[61] This typically Jain-ordered list of sense-object qualities is at odds with the order generally given by Nyāya-Vaiśeṣikas and Buddhists, as I discuss later. In this rhetorical context, admittedly fictional, composed by a Jain opponent of the view expounded, we can imagine how the ordering of the sense qualities, an issue entirely incidental to the topic at hand, might jar the ears of a Nyāya-Vaiśeṣika or Buddhist. Indeed, the Jain principle behind the order of the senses is the classification of beings according to the number of senses they possess; itself part of the wider Jain description of the universe and its contents. Thus, the Jain order of the senses hints at the rest of the scheme, as do the distinctive orders of the senses and their objects used by the Nyāya-Vaiśeṣikas and the Buddhists. It is notable that the Jains have the same element order as the Vaiśeṣikas, as well as a similar range-of-senses theory to the Buddhists,[62] yet still choose to order the senses hierarchically according to their occurrence in sentient beings.

In Umāsvati's famous fourth- or fifth-century CE Sanskrit systemization of Jain doctrine, the *Tattvārthasūtra*, we find a more explicit statement on the qualities of matter (*pudgala*).[63] It appears that this *sūtra* refers to *pudgala* in the sense of "ultimate atom of matter," whereas later ones refer to the more complex qualities of aggregates of atoms.[64] This definition is in turn expanded by the sixth-century CE Digambara commentator on that text, Pūjyapāda, and we again find many of the same qualities of matter that were denied the soul in the earlier passages.[65] Neither Umāsvāti nor Pūjyapāda use the term *guṇa* to refer to these "qualities" of matter. Here is the text with Pūjyapāda's commentary:

> 5.23 *pudgalas* possess touch, taste, odor, color.
> *Sarvārthasiddhi* commentary:
> Odor is (that which is) smelled, or merely (the act of) smelling. It is twofold: fragrant and not-fragrant . . . These here are the root divisions, and each becomes numerable, innumerable and infinite divisions.[66]

Here, the nature of odor does not change. For Pūjyapāda this remains twofold, yet there is a small change in terminology, from "fragrant odor" (*surabhi-gandhe*) and "bad smelling odor," (*durabhi-gandhe*) to "fragrant" and "unfragrant" (*surabhir asurabhir*). In this later text, the bad odors are now defined as negations of the good ones, using the very same words (and the very same language: Sanskrit) as the Vaiśeṣika philosopher Praśastapāda, also writing around the sixth century CE. Pūjyapāda also makes very clear that these are only the most simple "root divisions" (*mūlabhedāḥ*) and they go on to produce infinite variations.[67]

It seems that this formulation essentially reproduces the classification of odor in the *Ācārāṅgasūtra*, which appears to be an earlier statement that odor is simply fragrant and nonfragrant than found in the extant Hindu or Buddhist sources. From the start, the Jains are only interested in classifying the basic odors with two opposing evaluative terms. This is particularly important because, at least from the surviving textual record, it seems they came to this conclusion (or expounded it in surviving texts) before the Nyāya-Vaiśeṣika and Buddhist schools of thought.[68]

Unlike for the Vaiśeṣikas, all the sensed properties mentioned in the commentary on the *Tattvārthasūtra* 5.23 are attributable to all material atoms, not just to those of certain elements, and unlike in the discussions of the Vaiśeṣikas, the quality of sound is set apart, not included among the most basic qualities of any sort of matter/element. Sound is instead discussed in the next *sūtra*, where Pūjyapāda informs the reader that Umāsvāti is explaining the variations in the rest of matter.

The Jain classification of odor, unlike that of the Nyāya-Vaiśeṣikas and that of the Buddhists, does not appear to have changed over time. From the start, it would seem the Jains had a simple twofold classification of odors as fragrant and unfragrant, which was common in other schools of thought by the early-mid first millennium CE. Nevertheless, it is not clear whether the Jain account of odor was actively taken up by other schools or not; certainly their "salt-less" account of taste did not catch on elsewhere. When discussing the sense of smell with Jain scholars in India today, what strikes them as most significant is not the classification of odors, but rather that smell is possessed by beings that have three senses or more; that the sense of smell, therefore, falls in the middle of the order of senses.[69] Indeed, it was when talking about this matter with Jain scholars in India that I was first struck by the importance of the order of the senses as a reflection of the wider Jain worldview.

Buddhist

Finally, I turn to some Buddhist analyses of the nature of odor. As noted, the principles according to which the Buddhists order the senses are quite different to those of the preceding two schools of thought. Not only do the Buddhist sources differ in this respect, but they also contain a greater diversity of classifications of odor than other schools of thought. Some Buddhist sources provide an interesting glimpse into the process by which the classification of odor was negotiated through discussion. In general, the history of the Buddhist classification of odors and of the order of the senses is the most complex. I address my sources chronologically, as far as is possible.

Although, as I explain later, there is some uncertainty about the classificatory principle behind the order of the senses in some Buddhist doctrinal texts, nevertheless, the Buddhist analyses of the senses do tend to share the same distinct sense order, common to both Pāli texts and the Sanskrit *Abhidharmakośa*. The same sense order is reflected in other Buddhist examinations of the senses, such as the descriptions of the perfected senses found in chapter 18 of the *Mahāyāna Lotus Sūtra*. Uniquely, the earlier Buddhist accounts of odor, in addition to mentioning two or three aesthetic properties (fragrant and so forth), also define odor in terms of its source, and this is predominantly, though not exclusively, expressed in terms of the parts of plants.

I begin with a passage on smell from the *Dhammasaṅgani*, an early Pali text presenting an analysis of the world. This text probably dates from before the Common Era and forms the first part of the Pali *Abhidhammapiṭaka*.[70] Here, in the section on form, *rūpakaṇḍa*, the form of the sphere of odor is presented.[71] Though ultimately the ontological and phenomenological status of odors, matter, and so forth differ from that in a school such as Nyāya-Vaiśeṣika, nevertheless, this passage, in enumerating the components of the objects of the senses, shares much with the other analyses I discuss in that it classifies odors in an attempt to list the ultimate elements of the world/experience:

> What is the form that is the sphere of odor?
>
> That odor, which, derived from the four great elements, with no attribute, producing a reaction, root-odor, heart-wood-odor,[72] bark-odor, leaf-odor, flower-odor, fruit-odor, raw-meat-odor, putrid-odor, good-odor, bad-odor or whatever other odor, derived from the four great elements.[73]

Quite unlike the analyses of odor examined so far in this chapter, this list is dominated by odors of classes of particular objects, and especially the odors of plant parts. First are the odors of roots, heart-woods, barks, leaves, flowers, and fruits. The next two odors are more challenging. *Āmagandha* is defined in the Pali Text Society (PTS) dictionary as the odor of raw flesh. I was at first tempted to interpret *āma* as implying "raw and rotten," yet I think this misses the point: today, we do not always think of the odor of raw meat as unpleasant. In ancient India, not only did raw meat no doubt have a less deodorized, sterile presentation then in an American supermarket, but also the odor may well have been particularly unpleasant. I witnessed piles of very fresh, recently slaughtered chickens in Indian markets; it was not a pleasant smell. Moreover, the term seems to encompass all noncooked flesh, in varying states of freshness, as suggested from another term given in the PTS dictionary, *āmasusāna*, referring to a cremation ground. In the Pali *Suttanipāta*, there is a text known as the *Āmagandhasutta* in which *āmagandha* is equated with a variety of bad deeds.[74] This ethical turn in the language of smelling is an issue I will return to.

"Putrid odor" (*vissagandha*) is another notable term. The PTS dictionary states that it is cognate with Sanskrit *visra* and furnishes the meaning "a smell like raw flesh." Monier Williams' dictionary defines *visra*: "musty, smelling of raw meat." According to the fifth-century commentator Buddhaghosa's explanation, whereas *āmagandha* refers to raw meat and vermin, *vissagandha* odor implies fetid pungent odors such as rotten fish and meat. Nevertheless, the exact distinction between these terms is not clear.

Finally, there is a somewhat familiar looking pair: "good odor" and "bad odor." They are mentioned last and, unlike the other odors, they are general or abstract categories.

Apart from these final two terms, this account of odor does not focus on classifying odor abstractly. Instead, it describes the varieties of odors by means of concrete examples—prototypical cases rather than by general abstract categories. The list makes no claim to be complete and mentions "whatever other odors."

In Buddhaghosa's fifth-century commentary on that passage, the *Atthasālinī*, we can see a familiar development in the Buddhist analysis of odors. Having glossed the various examples of odors, he goes on to emphasize that, in fact, all odors are covered by the terms "good odor" (*sugandho*) and "bad odor" (*duggandho*), which he glosses as "desired" and "undesired" odor respectively. Leaving behind this uniquely Buddhist classification of odors according to examples, by cases as opposed to abstract categories, Buddhaghosa seems to align the classification of odor with those classifications by then found both in Hindu and Jain traditions in India. It is both a move away from explanation in terms of examples and toward conformity with the wider intellectual world on this relatively small point, regarding which the Buddhist texts had previously taken a radically different and peculiar line. By the mid-first millennium CE, no one in South Asia seems to have wanted an idiosyncratic classification of odor. Note also Buddhaghosa's explanations of the terms *āmagandha* and *vissagandha*, which were clearly in need of explanation by his time:

> In the descriptive exposition of the odor-function: "root odor" (means) an odor existing on account of whatever root. It is this same sense in the case of "heart-wood-odor" etc. "Raw-meat odor" is the odor of the uncooked or badly cooked, of lice etc. "Putrid odor" is the odor of bits of fish, putrid meat, foul ghee etc. "Fragrant" (means) desired odor, "bad-smelling" (means) undesired odor. All odor is exhausted by this pair of words.[75]

I now turn to the *Abhidharmakośa* of Vasubandhu, a Sanskrit compilation of doctrine also composed in the fifth century CE. This text presents an interesting and complex case, giving two different classifications of odor, and provides a unique window into the active debate on the nature of odors. The primary definition in the text is that odor is fourfold; an account of odor we have not so far encountered in this study, yet which is not unknown in other Buddhist texts:[76]

> 1.10 Odor is fourfold.
>
> *Auto-commentary:*
>
> Because of the evenness and unevenness of the odor of good odor and bad odor. But in one *śāstra* it is threefold: "good odor, bad odor, even odor."[77]

Vasubandhu explains in his auto-commentary that the fourfold nature of odor is due to the "even-and-uneven odor" (*samaviṣamagandhatvāt*) of good and bad odor. According to his own explanation, "even" (*sama*) and "uneven odor" (*viṣamagandha*) are really two subclasses of good and bad odor. Thus, he ultimately reduces the fourfold definition to a twofold definition of odor. What "even" and "uneven" means in this context is another matter—one that I have not entirely been able to resolve—but before I turn to that, I should mention the second definition Vasubandhu gives in his auto-commentary. Having discussed the fourfold definition, he says that in one technical treatise (*śāstra*) it is said to be threefold: "good odor," "bad odor," and "even odor."

What are we to make of this "even odor"? The only other threefold definition of odor we have seen so far is that of Vātsyāyana—"desired odor," "undesired odor," and "disregardable odor." That classification might have been produced to respond to the fact that some earth materials, such as stones, have no perceptible odor: a zero odor, which allowed that school of thought to keep earth as the locus of odor, even when some earth objects seemingly have no smell. Yet, given that the Sanskrit term *sama* means "even, equal," it seems reasonable in the context of this threefold division to assume that *samagandha* means a "neutral odor" balanced between the two value poles of good and bad odors. But if we go down that path—if the term *sama* ("even") means "of neutral aesthetic value"—presumably *viṣama* ("uneven") means "not of neutral aesthetic value." However, if we interpret the term in this sense, Vasubandhu will run into problems in explaining the use of these same terms in his fourfold definition of odor. In his auto-commentary, he suggests that the terms "even" and "uneven" apply to both good and bad odors. If these terms actually mean "of neutral aesthetic value" and "not of neutral aesthetic value" applying them to the categories "good odor" and "bad odor" would be contradictory or redundant: a good odor that is also a neutral odor is not possible, and to say that a good odor is "not of neutral aesthetic value" is redundant.

How might an interpreter of Vasubandhu avoid these difficulties in making sense of the terms "even" (*sama*) and uneven (*viṣama*) in these two classifications of odor? The answer is by a rather creative reading of his terminology. When discussing the case of Vātsyāyana's threefold definition of odor, I noted that his term "disregardable" (*upekṣanīya*), might be understood as both "neutral" and "unnoticeable." If one were, likewise, to interpret the third value, "even odor," in Vasubandhu's threefold definition of odor to mean "disregardable" in the sense of "unnoticeable," then its opposite *viṣama* may well be taken to mean "very noticeable," rendered into English as "faint" and "strong." In this reading, the two terms "even" (*sama*) and "uneven" (*viṣama*) in the fourfold definition would make perfect sense as viable and nonredundant subcategories (namely "faint" and "strong") of good and bad odor.

I believe the line of reasoning I outlined is precisely what leads the commentator Yaśomitra to gloss "even odor" as "faint" (*anutkaṭa*) in his commentary on Vasubandhu:

> "Because of the evenness and unevenness of both good odor and bad odor." This means because of faint (*anutkaṭa*) and strong (*utkaṭa*) odor. By this account, you opt for a twofold odor. "But in one *śāstra* is it threefold." This means that the extra third one is even odor. However, others explain that "'even odor' is just part of both of them." The meaning is just the same but the word itself is different.[78]

Thus, Yaśomitra explains that these terms "even" and "uneven" refer to low perceptibility (or low intensity), and high perceptibility (or high intensity) respectively. As he rightly observes, this effectively creates a twofold definition of odor, well-known to us from elsewhere. He then discusses the threefold definition, noting first that in this definition the third type of odor is "even odor." He adds that some others—who, no doubt, interpret the term not to mean "neutral" but rather "faint" in the manner he just glossed—believe that this third term actually applies to both good and bad odors. These people seem to be saying that *sama*, understood as "faint," is therefore a part of and/or belongs to both good and bad odor. Reading the term *sama* as "faint," and therefore as a subcategory of both good odor and bad odor (and splitting the application of the word in the process) allows these "others" to produce yet another essentially twofold definition of odor from a threefold one. Such, it would appear, was the drive to have a twofold definition of odor. This is despite the fact that "faint" seems to be an extremely strained reading of the word *sama* in the context of the threefold definition. Indeed, if one were to consider the threefold definition alone with no commentary, it would seem quite sensible to take *sama* in this context as meaning "neutral, even, equal"—an odor-value between good and bad odors.

Fortunately, we are in a position to see where this threefold definition may have come from. In his translation of the *Abhidharmakośa*, La Vallée Poussin notes that one text referred to by the term "*śāstra*," from which the threefold definition might come, is in fact a text called the *Prakaraṇa* of Vasumitra,[79] which may date from the second to fourth centuries CE.[80] This text of the Sarvāstivāda school of Buddhist philosophy, also known as *Prakaraṇagrantha* and the *Prakaraṇapādaśāstra*, now survives only in Chinese. Frauwallner surmises that it is a compilation, somewhat unsystematic, of "the most important achievements that had been made up to his [Vasumitra's] time."[81] In his commentary on the *Abhidharmakośa*, Yaśomitra mentions this text, presumably as one of the sources of Vasubandhu's great compilation.

The same threefold definition also appears in the *Dharmaskandha*, another Sarvāstivāda text that Frauwallner believes to be even earlier than the *Prakaraṇa*. Indeed, Frauwallner believes this text, which has similarities to the Pali *Vibhaṅga*, to be particularly early, deriving from a common source shared with the Pali *Vibhaṅga*.[82] Greiner and Potter believe it to be the "earliest of the seven canonical Abhidharma works of the Sarvāstivādins" and suggest it was composed around 300 BCE.[83] The complete *Dharmaskandha* is now only extant in Chinese and contains a threefold definition of odor, yet this is embedded in a familiar looking, somewhat more extensive description:

> Root-odor, stalk-odor, branch-odor, leaf-odor, flower-odor, fruit-odor, good-odor, bad-odor, neutral-odor.[84]

It may also be useful at this point to repeat the list from the *Dhammasaṅgani*:

> Root-odor, heartwood-odor, bark-odor, leaf-odor, flower-odor, fruit-odor, raw-meat odor, putrid-odor, good-odor, bad-odor.

As can be easily seen, the lists have much in common. The *Dharmaskandha* list, like the *Dhammasaṅgani* list, contains a majority of terms referring to exemplary odors, namely, the odors of parts of plants. Where the *Dhammasaṅgani* list also contains two terms referring to bad odors, most likely of animal origin, the *Dharmaskandha* list omits those, and next states general values of odor. Yet, interestingly, where the *Dhammasaṅgani* list contains only two values, the *Dharmaskandha* list contains three: "good odor," "bad odor," and "neutral odor."

The passage is remarkably similar to that in the *Dhammasaṅgani*, except that it contains the term translated as "neutral odor," possibly from the term *samagandha* or some cognate form in the source language of the Chinese translation. In translating this, the Chinese appear to have understood *sama* to mean "neutral" and not "faint." Although Frauwallner asserts that this text shows marked similarities to the *Vibhaṅga*, the *Vibhaṅga* does not give this classification of odor, but rather it has the same classification as the *Dhammasaṅgani* discussed earlier: the one that does not mention "even" odor.[85] Despite my lack of knowledge of Chinese, I very tentatively suggest that, just as Buddhaghosa makes the various examples of plant and animal odors redundant in his commentary, so by the time of the *Prakaraṇa*, the Sarvāstivāda school had likewise cleaned up its definition of odor, leaving only the (three) most general categories. This in turn was interpreted as a twofold definition by some "other" scholars, possibly under the pressure to align with the near universal South Asian binary definition of odor.[86] It seems there are two forces at work here in the development of Buddhist classifications of odor: a drive for internal systematic coherency, revealed in Yaśomitra's consistent interpretation of the term "even" (*sama*) in the threefold definition; and, secondly, a drive for external intersectarian uniformity—both uniformity in the type of category used for definition (thus removing the definition by example, i.e., "root-odor") and uniformity of the actual definition of odor ("twofold").

The earliest Buddhist definition of odor we considered included evaluative categories but was dominated by exemplary sources of odors, especially by plants, the odors of which are far more numerous than the (bad) odors associated with animals and animal products. This proliferation of (generally good) plant odors, as opposed to a far more limited number of (often bad) animal odors, is something we often see in other South Asian sources. But, by the early centuries CE, the Buddhists have "cleaned up" this complex account, and thenceforth they propound definitions which consist only of general categories. Yet, unlike the other schools of thought examined so far, the diverse "Buddhisms" failed to agree on just one account.

The Order of the Senses

I now turn to the issue of the place of the sense of smell in the given lists of the senses (*indriyas*) and the order of the senses in general. The given order of the senses/sense-objects is quite significant, as it reveals one factor to which a school of thought attributes importance as a classificatory principle. I have deliberately chosen the term "order" as opposed to "hierarchy" for two reasons. First, the orders of the senses are reversed in some contexts, whilst still maintaining the internal relations between the listed senses (i.e., ABCDE, EDCBA), and, furthermore, we should not from the outset assume that the senses are being ranked by these systems as progressively superior to each other in a general manner. Rather, they differ only according to one chosen principle. In addition to looking at the orders of the senses according to the schools of thought already considered, I examine some materials that are associated with another school of thought, called Sāṃkhya; a school that, like the Nyāya-Vaiśeṣikas, would be classed as a Hindu philosophy.

First, let us look at the order of the senses in the systems we have explored so far. For the Nyāya-Vaiśeṣikas, the order of the senses (smell, taste, sight, touch, hearing) is aligned with the given order of the substrata of the objects of the senses.[87] That is, the order of the senses is the same as the order of the elements. For the Jains, the order of the senses is based on a hierarchy of types of sentient being ordered according to the number of senses they possess. Thus: one-sensed beings possess touch; two-sensed beings possess touch and taste; three-sensed beings possess touch, taste, and smell; and so on for sight and hearing. It is not perfectly clear exactly what the Buddhist order (sight, hearing, smell, taste, touch) is based on, though it may well be the spatio-temporal relation between the perceiver and perceived. Thus, the order of the senses indicates sectarian affiliation and also suggests early theoretical concerns: for the Nyāya-Vaiśeṣikas, matter and qualities; for the Jains, the hierarchical structure of the contents of the universe and the sentient natures of various beings; and for the Buddhists, the phenomenological description of the world.

Two of these classifications nevertheless share one striking similarity: for both the Nyāya-Vaiśeṣikas and the Jains the senses are ordered according to the sensory "richness" of their respective concerns: sensed *object*, and sensing *subject* respectively. The Nyāya-Vaiśeṣikas order the senses according to how many types of sense data are found in the *object* perceived. Thus odor is a special quality of earth, the element that is most rich in sensory properties. The other elements are ordered according to a decrease in sensory potential: water has no odor, but you may taste, see, touch, and hear it; fire can be seen, touched, and heard but not tasted or smelled; wind may be touched and heard; and, finally, the element I translate as "space" (*ākāśa*) is only associated with sound. The Jains order the senses according to how many types of sense perception are found in the *subject* perceiving; thus, hearing is found only in five-sensed beings, and so on down to plants, earth-beings, and fire-beings etc., which only have the sense of touch. The Nyāya-Vaiśeṣika classification is object centered, and the Jain classification is subject centered. The above does not apply to any of the possible Buddhist classificatory principles.

For the Buddhists, the classificatory principle is most probably based on an analysis of the nature of perception, on the theory of perception, which may reflect a central concern with the nature of experience. Yet, there was some uncertainty about the classificatory principle of the order of the senses, and this uncertainty led the Buddhists to produce some of the most explicit discussions of this issue. In the *Abhidharmakośa*, Vasubandhu gives two possible explanations of the given order of the senses, which shows that the order itself was an area of interest. Having clarified why the senses precede the "mental organ/sensorium," or *manas* (because their objects are always temporally present) and why touch comes last of the senses (unlike the other senses, its objects are both the primary and secondary matter), he first explains that the other four senses are ordered according to the distance and rapidity of their operation:

> The rest are according to greater distance or speed of action.
>
> *Auto-commentary:*
>
> The eye and hearing have a distant field, so are mentioned before the (next) two. And of those two, the operation of the eye is at a greater distance: though you can see a river from a distance, you cannot hear it. Thus that one is mentioned first. There is no operation at a distance of the sense of smell, or of the tongue. Because of a more rapid operation, the sense of smell is mentioned the first of the two: because you can perceive the odor of food that has not yet reached the tongue.[88]

Following this, Vasubandhu offers another explanation—that the senses are ordered according to the position of the sense organs on the body, starting from the top down:

> Or else the sequence is according to their position.
>
> *Auto-commentary:*
>
> Or else: in this body the site of sight is located uppermost, below that (the site) of hearing, below that (the site of) of smell, (below) that (the site) of taste, for the most part (below) that (the site) of the body (i.e., the organ of touch).[89]

In the twelfth-century Sri Lankan Pali *Abhidhammatthavibhāvinī* of Sumaṅgala, a commentary on the *Abhidhammatthasaṅgaha*, we encounter this discussion again, and here it seems that the Theravāda school held that the order of the senses is based on the nature of their operation, not on their position on the body:[90]

> The *eye-sphere* is that which is the eye and also a sphere, and similarly with the rest. Herein, of the internal spheres, the eye-sphere is clear since it has objects that have appearance and are resistant, and so is stated first. It is followed by the other spheres, which have objects that are invisible and resistant. Of these, because in common with the eye-sphere it has objects that are not [actually] reached, the *ear-sphere* is stated next.
>
> Of the rest, since it has the ability to take its object quickly, the *nose-sphere* is stated first—for the smell of food etc., that is merely placed in front [of one] strikes the nose consequent on the air.[91]

Although there was some confusion as to the reason for the order of the senses in Buddhist schools of thought, given that two of these passages explain that the order of the senses is based on their spatio-temporal relations to their objects, it appears that this was a particularly well-known rationale. Moreover, this order is consistent with and reflects another Buddhist classification of the senses in terms of being contact senses or noncontact senses. I might add that the Buddhist order of the senses appears to have most in common with the most influential order of the senses in Western philosophy: the Aristotelian order of sight, hearing, smell, taste, and touch.[92]

The position of smelling and odors in these orders is significant. In Nyāya-Vaiśeṣika thought, it is at the extreme—generally number one, and this reflects that it is the defining characteristic of the element earth, the most "coarse," the most laden with potential sense data. To sense an odor, according to this system, one also requires an earth-containing body, and one needs to inhabit a world where there are earthy things to smell, which is not inevitable in this system. Indeed, beings that find themselves in this predicament are fortunate (or perhaps unfortunate), in that their bodies and world enable them to experience all five senses and sense-objects. The opportunities for sensual temptation and karmic retribution are the most varied for beings able to smell. Whereas, in the case of elements, odor characterizes earth, for sentient beings the sense of smell could be said to characterize those beings who have the richest world of senses—a world of experience that, like the objects of the sense of smell itself, can be both good and bad.[93] Yet, where the beings who experience odor have the greatest potential for varieties of sense experience, odors themselves are the most restricted sense-objects, in that odors are limited to occurring in earth alone. Odor therefore has the smallest scope of substratum. In this respect, odor is quite the opposite of sound which has all-pervading space, sometimes translated as "ether" (*ākāśa*) as its substratum.

The Senses and the Evolution of the Universe: Sāṃkhya Philosophy

This is a good moment to look at some materials associated with the Sāṃkhya philosophy. As Larson explained, there are several "Sāṃkhyas," but, nevertheless, the different accounts of this type of philosophy share much in common.[94]

Sāṃkhya is a dualistic philosophy, teaching that there are two independent existents: consciousness (*puruṣa*) and materiality (*prakṛti*). The entire experiential and phenomenal world consists of the subdivisions of materiality. Mental entities such as the intellect, "egoity" and the sense capacities, as well as, more obviously, material entities such as the gross elements are merely subdivisions of materiality. Sāṃkhya philosophy goes to great lengths to enumerate these subdivisions and, indeed, the word *sāṃkhya* means "enumeration."

I pause to note an interesting aspect of this philosophy that provides a very clear example of exactly how the meticulous analysis of the senses, their objects, and other components of the world might relate to concerns of ultimate salvation. The text that is generally considered a normative expression of the classical form of the philosophy, the *Sāṃkhyakārikā*, provides an explicit statement of the purpose of materiality—thus the purpose of the mind, the senses, their objects, and so forth. Materiality functions for the sake of the liberation of consciousness, in that it is materiality (including mental entities such as the intellect, as well as the senses, and the elements) that provides both the, often frustrating, experiences and intellectual discrimination that together encourage and allow consciousness to be isolated and/or liberated from materiality:

> As the unknowing (or unconscious) milk functions for the sake of the nourishment of the calf; so the *prakṛti* [materiality] functions for the sake of the release of the *puruṣa* [consciousness].[95]

Studying the enumerations of the Sāṃkhya school itself, and thereby understanding the nature of materiality also presumably aids this process of the gnostic isolation of consciousness. The senses and the world have a purpose: they help consciousness to be liberated, and the technical analysis of the world of materiality is also a vital part of this process. And, although for other schools of thought materiality—or the world of things and matter in general—might not always even have a substantial existence, never mind a purpose, such a soteriological rationale for the project of enumerating and understanding the things in the world (the senses, elements, and so on) arguably applies in a general manner to many of the other systems examined in this chapter.

Returning to the order of the senses in Sāṃkhya, in the course of their enumerations, the Sāṃkhya school teaches the same correlation between the generic sense qualities (the "subtle elements" or *tanmātras*) such as odor, and the elements (*mahābhūtas*), such as earth. In individual texts there is no consensus on the precise nature of the relation between these three types of entities: the sense capacities (*buddhīndriya*), such as smelling; the subtle elements (*tanmātra*), such as odor; and the gross elements, such as earth (*mahābhūta*). Some sources taught what Larson calls an accumulation theory "according to which each subtle element combined with the preceding ones in order to generate a gross element . . . the subtle smell element with the subtle sound, touch, form, and taste elements generate the gross earth element."[96] Other sources argue that the subtle elements (e.g., odor) generate the gross elements (e.g., earth) singly; thus, the subtle element odor alone generates earth. The first account at least—the accumulation theory—makes good sense of the order of the senses as hearing, touch, sight, taste, and smell. As with the Nyāya-Vaiśeṣikas, in that account, the elements are ranked from the least to the most sensory rich, and the order of the senses correlates with this order.

Some earlier texts, describing what has been called proto-Sāṃkhya, give the ordering of the basic principles a cosmological turn.[97] In these sources, the order of the basic principles (*tattvas*), including the order of the senses, reflects the order of their creation in the periodic creation and dissolution of the world. These "emanation" accounts, meticulously studied by Paul Hacker, are found in several *Purāṇas*, in the *Śāntiparvan* of the *Mahābhārata*, and also at the beginning of the *Law Code of Manu*, the *Mānava Dharmaśāstra*.[98] There are, in fact, two creation accounts at the beginning of the *Law Code of Manu*. The first one uses recognizably Sāṃkhya terminology and would count as an instance of "proto-Sāṃkhya," whereas the second passage (similar to a passage in the *Mahābhārata*) has no Sāṃkhya characteristics.[99] Hacker suggests that this second passage is derived from another, earlier, source outlining a non-Sāṃkhya evolutionistic cosmogony.[100] Setting aside such questions of the respective age and so forth of these passages, what is interesting is that in both these early accounts the senses and the elements are lined up, and moreover this is connected to the temporal order in which they were created.

The first account in the *Law Code of Manu*—the one that shows Sāṃkhya features—relates the following concerning the creation of the elements:

> From the subtle particles of the physical frames of these seven males of great might,[101] this world comes into being, the perishable from the imperishable. Of these, each succeeding element acquires the quality specific to each preceding. Thus, each element, tradition tells us, possesses the same number of qualities as the number of its position in the series.[102]

The second account, that likewise places the order of the elements in an evolutionary cosmogonic scheme but without Sāṃkhya terminology, is as follows:

> At the end of that day and night, he [Brahmā] awakens from his sleep; and when he has woken up, he brings forth the mind, which is both existent and non-existent. The mind, driven by the desire to create, transmutes the creation. From the mind is born ether, whose distinctive quality is said to be sound. From ether, as it is being transmuted, is born wind—powerful, pure, and bearing all odors—whose distinctive quality is thought to be touch. From the wind, as it is being transmuted,

> is produced light—shining, brilliant, and dispelling darkness—whose distinctive quality, tradition says, is visible appearance. From light, as it is being transmuted comes water, with taste as its distinctive quality; and from water, earth, with smell as its distinctive quality. That is how this creation was at the beginning.[103]

Both these accounts have a lot in common with the Sāṃkhya accumulation theories mentioned, yet in these versions the accumulation theory is explicitly linked to the very temporal order of creation. In these cosmogonic accounts, the first element (*ākāśa*) and thus also sound, are both prior to odor and also closer to the creative force, be this the subtle particles of the seven somewhat enigmatic males in the first account, or the mind of the Creator, Brahmā, in the second. Undeniably these orderings of the senses (and the others like them that Hacker describes) could be described as hierarchies, because the elements become progressively denser in sensory qualities and more removed from the originating principles. One might argue that in this sort of account sound is more refined, more primordial, and even closer to "the divine," whereas odor and earth are newer, grosser, and at a greater remove from an ultimate originating principle. In this case, we do see something approaching a hierarchy of the senses in early South Asia. And, as I observed near the beginning of the chapter, although Hacker and other scholars rightly observe that the first account in the *Law Code of Manu* is a very early version of what became the fully fledged systematic expressions of the Sāṃkhya philosophy, these passages and others like them were still in circulation in later periods. Indeed, such ideas about matter and the senses as found in the *Law Code of Manu* might well have loomed large in the intellectual worlds of many scholars not regularly engaged with more systematic materials.

Order or Hierarchy?

So, are these orders of the senses hierarchies or not? And, what do the orders tell us about smell? In the Nyāya-Vaiśeṣika and Sāṃkhya schools, smell is placed at the extreme, associated with the element earth, and thus always found in a context that is the richest in other sense properties. Smell and its objects are earthy, and the least aetherial of senses. Certainly in the proto-Sāṃkhya sources sound appears to be more primordial and closer to an ultimate principle, something that accords with the Brahmanic reverence for the sacred sounds of the recited Vedas. For the Jains, the sense of smell falls in the center, indicating a certain level of advancement in the karmic universe, but only half of what can be achieved. According to this view, it is nothing special, relatively primitive, yet there are still many types of sentient beings, including all plants, that are not able to smell. It also reflects the Jains' detailed interest in and concern about the perceptions, experiences, and natures of beings other than humans.[104] For the Jains, hearing appears to be the sense that characterizes those beings who are the most sensorily advanced in the universe. This does not, however, necessarily imply that hearing is superior.

In the Buddhist classification, smell also falls dead-center, yet for entirely different reasons. This sense is not really long ranging like sight and hearing, yet it does permit a certain amount of remote experience of the world, especially compared to taste. Odor comes to one via wind; it is unlike sight, which one can range at will. Like touch, it does allow actual contact with objects, not the source objects themselves, but rather particles of them (as articulated earlier).[105] This also allows odorants in one place to release their odor to a perceiver in another place and consequently to attract or repel the perceiver. The sense that has the most extreme ability in the order of the senses is sight, functioning over a greater distance than other senses, and this might arguable imply that it is superior, at least in certain contexts.

Additional Observations

One might justifiably ask whether I have exaggerated the importance of these orders of the senses, as well as their consistency within a school of thought. Also, aside from what the analysis of these orders can tell us about the senses, can these observations be of use in other contexts?

To tackle the latter question first, I suggest that an awareness of these different orders may be of practical use in reading some South Asian texts. For example, in addition to the standard evidence produced to argue that Amarasiṃha, author of the famous lexicon called the *Nāmaliṅgānuśāsana*, or *Amarakośa*, was a Buddhist,[106] I should note that this text also contains a list of the sense-objects in the order typically found in many Indic Buddhist sources:[107]

> Visible form, sound, odor, taste and touch: these are the sense-objects.[108]

In the next chapter, we will see another text, in reading which our knowledge of the sectarian sense-orders will prove quite revealing. I am not suggesting, of course, that a single incidence of a list of the senses can definitely prove the sectarian identity of a text, but rather that this is another useful tool for the close reader of Sanskrit and other texts.

Returning to the first question: have I exaggerated this? Did South Asian intellectuals really care about or even notice these things? To answer the question, I return to the Sāṃkhya materials. In particular, I examine what is often considered the earliest normative formulation of this philosophy, the *Sāṃkhyakārikā* of Īśvarakṛṣṇa (350–450). As noted earlier, the Sāṃkhya philosophy, like the Nyāya-Vaiśeṣikas, correlates the elements with the senses, sometimes along the lines of an accumulation theory, where earth is the most sense-property rich of the elements. Therefore, when presenting a list of the basic principles (*tattvas*) enumerated by

Sāṃkhya, a modern author such as Larson, for example, lists the sense-capacities (*buddhīndriyas*) in the order one would expect in this context, namely: hearing, touching, seeing, tasting, and smelling.[109] However, when these sense-capacities are presented in the *Sāṃkhyakārikā* the order in which they are listed is something of a surprise:

> The sense organs (*buddhīndriyas*) ("organs of the *buddhi*" or "organs of ascertainment") are called eye, ear, nose, tongue, and skin.[110]

In this normative and important text, the sense-capacities are in fact listed in the order one would tend to associate with Buddhist sources, an order that moreover appears to be quite possibly based on the spatio-temporal relation between subject and object. It is not possible to know the reason Īśvarakṛṣṇa listed them in this manner; although, in a context of such meticulous enumeration such an ordering would most likely not be codified at random. However, it is possible to see what sort of reaction this apparently anomalous ordering of the senses produced from two early medieval South Asian scholars who wrote commentaries on this text.[111]

Although there is much scholarly debate regarding the history of early commentaries on the *Sāṃkhyakārikā*,[112] it seems that the earliest commentary available today is Paramārtha's Chinese translation of the *Sāṃkhyakārikā* together with a prose commentary called the *Suvarṇasaptati*.[113] This text was translated into Chinese between 557 and 569 CE. In the commentary on *Sāṃkhyakārikā* 26—the stanza containing the senses given in the "Buddhist" order—there is no discussion of the reasons for this order, but then in the commentary on the next verse (*Sāṃkhyakārikā* 27) dealing with the nature of the mind (*manas*) this commentary notes (translated from the French of Takakusu):

> Amongst the organs there are those that apprehend close objects, whilst others perceive things from a distance. Their purpose is twofold: 1) to avoid danger; 2) to protect the body. "To avoid danger" (refers to the eyes and the ears, which) by seeing and by hearing from a distance, avoid danger. "To protect the body" (refers to the eight other organs, which) perceive the eight types of object as soon as one of these objects approaches the corresponding organ; that allows us to arrange our bodies according to objects.[114]

These remarks are a response to an opponent who asked why the location of the "organs" varies, referring both to the embodied sense-capacities and also to what Sāṃkhya philosophy calls the five "action-capacities," such as grasping (with the hand: *pāṇi*). For example, the eyes are placed high and are able to see from a distance. "Who" asks the opponent "arranged all that in this manner? Was it the soul, or Īśvara ("God"), or a special Being?" The answer given to the opponent is that it is by means of the three qualities (*guṇas*, a key feature of materiality, *prakṛti*, according to Sāṃkhya) that the organs have been allotted these respective places. Indeed, according to the commentary that would be the very point that the second part of verse 27 of the *Sāṃkhyakārikā* makes:

> The variety of external things and the variety (of the organs) is because of the specific modifications (or transformations) of the *guṇas*.[115]

According to this early commentary, the spatio-temporal capacities of the senses implied by the ("Buddhist") order they are given in *Sāṃkhyakārikā* 26 is evidence of the operation of the three qualities (*guṇas*) in the world of materiality. One is supposed to take notice of the distinctive and surprising order of the senses given in this text precisely because it is this aspect of the senses and their relation to the external world (as opposed to their relation to the elements) that is explained in the next stanza (i.e., in *Sāṃkhyakārikā* 27). Note that the spatio-temporal explanation of the ordering of the senses here is not dissimilar to that given in the *Abhidharmakośa*. What is unique here is the emphasis on avoiding danger, and clearly sight and hearing are in fact superior senses. Finally, this account is harmonious with the teleology of materiality taught in the *Sāṃkhyakārikā*.

For the author of this commentary, the *Suvarṇasaptati*, the apparently anomalous order of the senses given in *Sāṃkhyakārikā* 26 makes perfect sense within the system as a whole: in the context of the teleology of matter (the fact that matter has a purpose), and most important, in connection with the content of the subsequent sūtra.

A later commentary, dating possibly from between the seventh and ninth centuries CE is the *Jayamaṅgalā*.[116] This commentary was possibly composed by a Buddhist—indicated by the benedictory verse: "having paid homage to the sage who knows the *Lokottaravāda*."[117] This commentary also notes the anomalous order of the senses in the *Sāṃkhyakārikā*, but unlike the other commentary we examined, the author(s) of the *Jayamaṅgalā* suggests that the order is simply a mistake:

> On account of sound an absence of order has been created. Rather, the order is: hearing, touch, sight.[118]

I take this to imply that it is on account of the primary position given to sound in this system more generally that hearing should have been placed first. The corrected order here brings hearing, touch, and sight back into line, but it does not mention smell and taste; though perhaps it is assumed that they too should be corrected to line up with the order starting with "sound." It quite clear that the author of this text picks up on this anomaly in the order of the senses, points out that it is disorderly, and offers a correction. If the author (or authors/editor/compiler) of this text was indeed Buddhist, it seems doubly remarkable that he saw fit to criticize the normative text of Sāṃkhya philosophy for using an order of the senses that would presumably have been quite familiar and respectable from Buddhist sources. Then again, perhaps, it was precisely for those reasons that he found it so jarring and disorderly in a text belonging to this different system.

Taking these two commentaries together, it seems reasonable to suggest that scholars were aware of the order in which the senses tended to be listed in philosophical contexts. It was possible for the order of the senses to be simply wrong, or in other cases a strange looking order of the senses could be assigned an appropriate rationale.

Indisputable Differences and a Common Background

In addition to what the study of the South Asian theoretical discourse on smell reveals about the understanding of smelling and odors, the previous materials refine our understanding of the manner in which sectarian doctrine was formed in early South Asia. In a series of essays, the scholar of religious studies John Clayton outlined a theory of the manner in which the culture of public debate (*vāda*) in South Asia was a major force in developing the boundaries, and thus the very form, of sectarian philosophical doctrines. Being obliged to face a variety of opponents required a school of philosophy to clarify exactly what the issues were on which they differed. "The lines separating the emerging *darsanas* [philosophical schools] were firmed up by a gradual sharpening of the points of difference that distinguished them." And this process helped give form to the traditions themselves: "Philosophical debate was thus tradition-*constituting*. Through contesting and being contested, so to say, rationality constructed itself." It is indeed only through the Other that the Self constructs itself.[119]

Clayton suggests this Indo-Tibetan tradition might be a good model today, with a goal of "publicly defensible difference" replacing the ideas of public reason espoused by classic liberal theory. The *vāda*-inspired model is the best way to deal with the radical religious diversity that confronts the world today.[120] But what sort of model would this *vāda* model replace? Clayton contrasts the South Asian tradition with the "Jeffersonian" model of public religious discourse: the "Enlightenment model." This model excludes difference. Anything sectarian or tradition specific is excluded from public rationality as being fundamentally irrational. Instead, only "universal reason" is welcome in the public arena, and it is assumed that all rational debate will eventually result in consensus. As Clayton explains, the great irony of this project is that "the vision of universal, tradition-free natural religion, which is supposed to be above all particularities and attain through reason a kind of objectivity, is in fact none other than a secularized form of Christianity and more narrowly in this case of liberal Protestantism."[121]

These ideas have not left us, and the intellectual and social quest for common ground, the idea that religions are "just different paths to a same goal" is still with us today. Such an approach to public religious and sectarian discourse might have worked in a context where the vast majority of people were Protestant Christians, but it is not currently suitable. According to Clayton, the quest for common ground should be replaced with a culture of defensible difference, where "seeing the difference is the beginning of understanding."[122]

I suggest that close examination of the debate on smell reveals some consequences of the South Asian debate tradition that it might be useful to add to Clayton's account. The previous analysis of the history of the classification of odor might have seemed a little dry at times to some readers. But it is precisely by examining this topic in such detail that we were able to ascertain the complex and gradual manner by which most schools of thought abandoned awkward and complex classifications of odor and for the most part agreed on a simple and (generally) binary classification of odor as good and bad. Even amongst those Buddhists who had a threefold definition of odor, some appear to have thought of a way of making this definition binary. I suggest that this is because the fundamental classification of odor was never a central question for any of these systems, and it was, in this case, preferable to adopt an uncontroversial account of odor, possibly even by emulation of other systems.

At the outset of this chapter, I suggested that it might be interesting to study the history of minor ideas. In following the history of this minor idea, we see that the South Asian tradition of debate led to similarity. But there are similarities and there are similarities. "Similarity" need not be a dirty word: the similarity in classification of odor that early South Asian intellectuals arrived at is not so much a (dubious) universal truth as a carefully considered and expedient compromise. Here the debate tradition led not to convergence but to neutrality: the sort of uniformity that is, in fact, necessary to highlight difference. Moreover, this neutrality presumably somewhat shortened the agenda for debate, which is always a good thing. In this particular case, intersectarian debate did not lead to a common ground, but it did at times clear a common background. And, of course, in the event that a group of doctrinal traditions that had developed such a common background might meet an entirely new and different school of thought, this neutral background might find itself standing out more as a *shared difference*.

With the order of the senses, it is a different story. Even though at times some systems were not sure of the rationale behind the order of the senses typically used in their tradition, the order was never abandoned. Yet, the order of the senses is not so much an argument that could be defeated in debate. Instead, the order of the senses reflects certain principles that are important in a given system. When a system was confronted with an anomalous order of the senses within its own texts it could still cope quite well, but this does not mean that systems of thought were not attached to the more typical orders. Unlike a question such as the existence of a permanent soul, the order of the senses was not really the sort of thing one system would dispute with another. The order could be discussed, but no, doubt, it was often simply reeled off in other contexts. Yet these lists, redolent of other parts of their respective systems, constituted distinct sectarian markers. A particular order of the senses was more of a banner of allegiance than an actual weapon to be wielded: a difference indeed, but, for the most part, an indefensible difference, a sectarian style or colour, as were many other issues, such as certain terminologies and even certain languages. At times, some of these differences were highly relevant to the debate at hand and had to be defended, but I imagine that in most instances the order of the senses simply sounded alien and jarring to the ear of the philosophical other, an irritating moment of intellectual bad etiquette that, no doubt, had some rhetorical impact both on the opponent and on the audience to the debate.

In addition to Clayton's valuable observations on the manner in which the South Asian tradition of debate led to the public clarification of difference, this study of the debate on smell showed that at times public contestability led to uniformity, especially on minor matters, thus permitting the debate to focus on more crucial issues. Yet, the classification of odor still remains one small part of the systems of doctrine, and the fact that odors are very similar in some Hindu, Buddhist, and Jain systems is not because they all started out the same—this uniform feature of doctrine appears to have developed when messier, earlier classifications were dropped and streamlined. Although this seems not to have worried the scholars mentioned, nevertheless, it did mean that this topic was more or less permanently removed from the forum of debate. In considering Clayton's suggestion that South Asian debate traditions might be a good model for interreligious dialogue in a pluralistic society, this latter fact should not be forgotten: debate can neutralize certain themes and silence discussion on certain questions. The practice of public contestability also showcases differences that might not be defensible, such as the order of the senses. Such a difference is more a matter of sectarian style than a point of doctrine; yet, these rhetorical, stylistic differences still play a vital part in the texture of the overall debate.

The Theory of Smell

Where does this leave the sense of smell? Odor is the quality of sensed objects that is most consistently described in evaluative terms in South Asian philosophy.[123] Given the peculiar nature of odors (the objects of smell), the sense of smell is therefore presumably understood to be an affective sense. Although the classifications of odor vary, especially in the earlier sources, at all times they included two terms that indicated that they were good or bad. At least in regard to smell, all the sources agree that the experienced world always has a value of some sort.

The sense of smell itself is ambiguous. Like sight and hearing, it can detect things at a distance, yet it requires actual, and potentially polluting, contact with particles of the odorant smelled. Smell, therefore, also requires another element to function: the tactile wind that carries the particles to the organ of smell. For some Hindu philosophies, odorous objects are by definition potentially audible, visible, palpable, and tasteable—things that have an odor therefore also tend to have many other properties.

These accounts of smell are perhaps a little too tidy. For example, surely not all good smells are the same? In what other ways were odors classified in traditional South Asian thought? It is to these other, less tidy and more complex understandings of odor that we turn in the next chapter.

PART TWO

SMELLS IN THE WORLD

3

Lotus, Fish, and Cows

The Smellscape of Traditional South Asia

> . . . the bottles were empty and our praise of them wilder and more exotic.
> " . . . It is a little, shy wine like a gazelle."
> "Like a leprechaun."
> "Dappled, in a tapestry meadow."
> "Like a flute by still water."
> " . . . And this is a wise old wine."
> "A prophet in a cave."
> "And this is like a necklace of pearls on a white neck."
> "Like a swan."
> "Like the last unicorn."
>
> —Evelyn Waugh, *Brideshead Revisited*

Charles Ryder and Sebastian Flyte are describing wines. This is an example of a flamboyant style of wine description in English. The wine writing we are accustomed to today tends to use a more sober terminology, such as "blackberries," "butter," "oak," and so on. There are a number of Sanskrit texts that describe odors for various practical reasons, for example, the evaluation of sandalwood or the diagnosis of illness. In some ways, like contemporary reviews of wines and coffees in a publication such as the *New York Times*, these Sanskrit texts were written for an educated elite class, and they draw on a descriptive vocabulary based on notable odorants—a vocabulary that assumes a shared knowledge of both odors and odorants. In recent times, a rich language of gustatory and olfactory connoisseurship has increasingly flourished in Europe and North America.[1] The smells and odorants people typically talk about today are in many cases different from those that stood out in medieval India. As an example, the menu at my local coffee shop uses the following terms to describe coffee: swiss chocolate, butterscotch, apple, caramel, marmalade, and almond. In medieval Indian Sanskrit texts, some typical smells used to describe other smells would be fish, lotus, goat's urine, sandalwood, and ghee (clarified butter).

In the previous chapter, I discussed the manner in which philosophers analyzed odors in attempting to describe the fundamental aspects of the world and of experience. In these analyses, odors were quite commonly said to be of two types: good or bad, and sometimes neutral. In this chapter, we will see what sorts of actual odors were important—what constituted these good and bad odors—in exploring the smellscape of traditional South Asian texts. This smellscape is presented, not in sophisticated literary or poetic descriptions of smells, but rather in technical treatises on such matters as medicine, elephants, divination, and the examination of aromatics. This is a notable contrast with the coffee and wine talk of today. To say or write that coffee smells like marmalade and butterscotch is a language of connoisseurship, sophistication, elite consumption, and social distinction. Whilst there are South Asian texts, mainly on perfumery, that take part in a discourse of olfactory connoisseurship and elite consumption, the texts in this chapter do not, being concerned with more mundane matters such as diagnosing illness and classifying elephants. Unlike the olfactory and gustatory connoisseurship of today, in medieval South Asia the connoisseurship of perfumes was not a matter of flamboyant, subjective verbal expression. As we shall see in a later chapter, a medieval South Asian Sebastian Flyte would display knowledge of the correct combination of perfumes according to an erudite "olfactory grammar," as well as an ability to play with the poetic and linguistic aspects of the perfumes: their charming names and sometimes elaborate textual formulae. Being able to describe odors in detail ("like lotus," "like cow's urine") is more the domain of the physician, the merchant, and the treasurer, but, of course, being able to describe odors in Sanskrit still requires a familiarity with elite discursive practices.

It is essential to note that in examining this smellscape, I am not attempting to "draw up an inventory of the sensations that were present at a given moment in history in each social milieu."[2] The smells in this chapter are not simple catalogues of what was "out there" to smell in medieval South Asia, rather, these are the smells that people most often wrote about in Sanskrit texts. As Corbin says of the early work of Guy Thuillier, a project of merely cataloging sensations (with a focus on sounds)[3]

> is based on a questionable postulate, it implies the non-historicity of the modalities of attention, thresholds of perception, significance of noises, and configuration of the tolerable and the intolerable. In the last analysis, it ends up denying the historicity of the balance of the senses which is here my theme. It is as if, in the eyes of the author, the habitus of the Nivernais villager of the nineteenth century did not condition his hearing, and so his listening.[4]

Yet, we should also note that Corbin does not reject this sort of project outright, and, indeed, he believes such work can be revealing when the approach is refined.

It is the complexity of the situation that is interesting: the fact that these smells were part of the world, and that they, of all the thousands of smells in any lived environment, were picked out to be mentioned in various texts. The smells in this chapter were what intellectuals consciously chose to discuss; the odors that they wished to present as their olfactory benchmarks. These odors are not a given smellscape, but an idealized, conventional, respectable, and rather conservative smellscape. Therefore, in addition to noting the contents of this special smellscape, it is vital to consider why these smells were worthy of note. Perhaps, the most important way to approach this is to consider the manner in which these smells were connected to a material smell-source (an odorant), and the manner in which these materials were in turn associated with a variety of concepts, such as pure and impure, that were part of several South Asian classifications of the objects in the world. For instance, odors could be associated with various types of divine being, and with various social classes (*varṇas*). Also, certain odors seem to be associated with the time of year and types of terrain.

Put simply, things smelled differently in early and medieval South Asia than they do today: not only were there many different odorants to smell (more elephants and sandalwood for example, at least in certain circles), but, more important, things smelled differently because of what was in people's heads when they smelled things. This chapter, and much of this book, is an exploration of the latter point: the smelling act is not only a natural event but a cultural one.[5] This culturally informed "smelling act" was not only different for people, but also for other sentient beings *as they were imagined and represented* in early and medieval South Asian texts, including, of course, gods and enlightened beings as found in narratives and in temples.

I will not discuss in detail every odor and odorant encountered in this chapter—there are far too many—but I will pause to focus on some of the most significant smells and the more revealing broader contexts. Moreover, given the number of odors and odorants in this chapter, and the complexity of the variables informing the smelling act, it is impossible to present one single thesis or linear argument here. Instead, this chapter is somewhat encyclopedic in nature, introducing and discussing many odorants, and much of this material will be useful in understanding the materials in the remainder of the book. For example, I think it quite likely that many readers have little idea what costus root is, and before proceeding any further it is necessary to address some of these matters.

I have arranged the sources chronologically as far as is possible, given our meager knowledge of some of the dates. This is in order to consider whether there is any historical change in the smellscape of South Asia. As it turns out from this small sample, "natural" features of the smellscape, such as cows and lotuses, seem to remain stable over long periods, but what does change is the range of aromatics mentioned in the smellscape, which I discuss both here and in later chapters on perfumery and aromatics.

Describing a Smell in Sanskrit

In Sanskrit texts, odors are frequently described by means of either general adjectives, for example, pleasant, sweet, stinky, and so forth, or by what I call *ostensive definition* relating to particular objects, e.g., "lotus-like"; the latter method of description is common in both English and Sanskrit.[6] Odors in Sanskrit are not, from what I have read, commonly described by reference to a wider class of objects, i.e., floral, fruity, woody.[7] This is in striking contrast to the modern attempts to classify and describe smells, particularly those produced by perfumers.

It is one thing to say, "After Brad ate his lunch, the office cubicle smelled of orange," when one's data-entry colleague has just eaten an orange, but this is simply the naming of a smell: the smell of an actual orange. This sort of reference to a smell is very common in Sanskrit literature, especially in poetic texts (*kāvya*). When I talk in this chapter of the description of smell, I mean the description of an unknown smell in terms of a familiar one, like "cyanide smells of bitter almonds" or "bitter almonds smell like marzipan," or even, "James, today my orange has a strange marzipan-like smell." This sort of description assumes a shared reference vocabulary of odors from which one can choose terms. The smell of bitter almonds is not so well known these days, so it might be best to talk of marzipan (or amaretto) instead. This sort of vocabulary for describing smells, the sort contemporary wine and coffee tasters use, is, to a large extent, contingent to a certain time and place and culture, as we can see if we imagine describing something in terms of the smell of Spanish leather, or the smell of a *champak* flower, which were/are quite well-known smells in certain times, places, or cultural contexts.[8]

Ostensive definition of smells assumes that we share with those with whom we communicate not only a common knowledge of our language but also a common knowledge of our world of experience, both natural (lotus) and man-made (ghee, alcohol). Such discourse about smells appears to assume a world of experience outside the text. As we have seen, in South Asian thought this is a world where these real smells are understood to have fundamental aesthetic qualities that are independent of our judgment ("good smell" and "bad smell"). We may all know thousands of smells, yet in these descriptive contexts it is quite notable that we choose to use certain smells as benchmarks: smells that are seemly to mention and derive from objects that are culturally relatively familiar; smells about which one could say that "we know where we stand with that smell and its source." These latter factors might also derive heavily from what people have encountered in texts and educated conversation: "bitter almonds" is an odor found quite often in English texts of a certain era (as is "new mown hay"). The notion of this material as a smell benchmark is by no means forgotten, even though most people nowadays are not familiar with bitter almonds. As for seemliness, someone writing about coffee today is far more likely to talk of an aroma of crushed fig leaves with all its connotations of leisurely exploring Tuscan Villas, than they are to refer to the gamey tang of a lactating pit bull's nipples.

It is commonly believed that we have difficulties talking about smells—I do not believe this to be true, but the idea certainly sits comfortably with the discourse of smell as primitive and unconscious. We may have to use what I call ostensive descriptive language to talk about smells, but, in fact, the same applies to most of the objects of the other senses. Although we lack anything comparable to the specific vocabulary of color in the case of smell, nevertheless, if we need to describe a color precisely (though not scientifically), we go about doing so in much the same manner as for smells. If, for example, we wish to describe a particular color we have to resort to the same ostensive description as with smells: "She painted her bedroom a sort of custardy yellow." Here, the basic color category "yellow" does a crude job of conveying the color in question—indeed, you could replace the word "yellow" with the word "color" and the meaning would not change much. What we lack for smell in both English and Sanskrit are general smell-specific adjectives that cover the basics of most smells, and which might therefore be considered the main types of smell. If we compare this with the case of color, where in both English and Sanskrit there is a richer, color-specific lexicon, we see why it proves difficult to produce a workable system that classifies smells into "primary smells" and contains broad and comprehensive categories of smell—this is the problem that the theoreticians addressed in the previous chapter, and, as we saw, they mostly opted for a simple, twofold evaluative classification.[9]

Unlike those metaphysicians, the people involved in producing and using the texts we examine in this chapter were not consciously attempting to create an ultimate classification of smells but rather describe smells for pragmatic reasons. Or, more precisely, they produced formal textual treatises describing an ideal version of such practical olfactory evaluation. In doing so, they reveal how South Asian scholars over a long period wrote, and quite possibly talked, about smells in a nonphilosophical *śāstric* context. This is interesting, because it is these very same people, and others of a similar background and milieu, who were, no doubt, the producers and consumers of many other Sanskrit texts. In describing smells by ostensive definition, by naming sources of smell deemed prominent, typical, and mentionable in the world of their experience, they reveal their preferred olfactory lexicon. These smells are presented with a view to describing the varieties of elephants, the smell-symptoms of children's diseases, and so on—they are not describing a luxuriant, royal pleasure garden or an ideal, pure land. Nevertheless, these writers do important things with smells that go beyond pure description, and they sometimes use smells to give an olfactory expression to correlations between features of the world and their larger intellectual universe, such as a typology of elephants based on divine and human hierarchies.

Source I

Evaluation of the Aromatics in the Treasury According to the *Arthaśāstra*

The first passage occurs in the *Arthaśāstra*, an early text devoted to statecraft, of uncertain date but possibly from around the first century BCE with additions until the first century CE.[10] In a description of the contents of the ideal royal treasury, the different varieties of sandalwood, aloeswood, and other aromatics stored there are mentioned. Although some of the names of the varieties of the aromatics in this passage are of interest, I will not be able to discuss these issues here, and instead I concentrate only on the smell-descriptions this passage contains:

> *Sātana* sandalwood is red and **smells of earth**. *Gośīrṣaka* (Ox-head Sandalwood) is dark copper (color) and **smells of fish**. *Haricandana* (Green sandalwood) is the color of a parrot feather and **smells of mango**, as is *Tārṇasa* (sandalwood.) *Grāmeruka* (sandalwood) is red, red-black, and **smells of goat urine**. *Daivasabheya* (sandalwood) is red and **smells of *padma* lotus**[11] as does *Jāpaka* (sandalwood) . . .
>
> (On aloeswood:) That from over the sea is mottled and **smells of vetiver**[12] **or navamālikā jasmine . . .**[13]
>
> (On other precious substances[14]:) *Tailaparṇika*,[15] *Aśokagrāmika* is flesh color and **smells of *padma* lotus**. 62. *Joṅgaka* is red-yellow, and **smells of *utpala* lotus or of cow's urine**. *Grāmeruka* is glossy and **smells of cow urine**. *Sauvarṇakuḍyaka* is red-yellow and **smells of citron.** From *Pūrṇa* island **smells of *padma* lotus or fresh butter** . . . And both **smell of costus root**.
>
> Thus the precious substances.[16]

There are two points of particular interest in this passage. First, the colors of most of the varieties of sandalwood seem somewhat strange.[17] But we must leave that problem aside for now; in chapter 8, I discuss the complex question of the nature of "sandalwood" and the properties it was valued for.

The second point, perhaps of greater interest here, is that some of the varieties of aromatic mentioned had a somewhat unpleasant smell, at least to us: fish, goat urine, and cow urine. If an expensive type of aromatic smells like goat urine, then why not simply use goat urine? It cannot, of course, be taken for granted that those smells were not good smells in that cultural context. However, it is clear, even at this stage, that these are not smells that would have been highly desired and valued on the body or in the environment in the same way that perfumes were. Goat's urine and so forth, are not ingredients in any of our perfumery manuals nor are they traded as aromatics. Here, I think a comparison with today's culture is helpful. In describing wine, all manner of odorants are mentioned, many of which (e.g., "sauvignon blanc smells like cat's pee") are far from appetizing in their own right, yet, as an element of the aroma of a wine, they can be considered quite pleasant. Also, we should not lump these smells together simply because they do not appeal to us—the role of the smell of fish and the smell of cow urine may well have been quite different in early South Asia, just as the smells of horse "manure" and dog "dirt" are treated quite differently in our own culture. Finally, we shall see later in the book that sandalwood was not simply a perfume but its color and tactile qualities were highly valued, so these less than perfumed odor qualities might not have been a problem here. The red sandalwood available today is not, for example, primarily valued for its odor.

Unlike the exotic, rare, and expensive aromatics described here, all the odorants used to describe them would have no doubt been common in South Asia. An exception to this tendency, the one odorant with a distant origin, was costus root, but this was a culturally established product, traded since very early times. The others, such as fish and cow urine, were (and still are for the most part) familiar features of many South Asian village and urban settings. We should note the prominence of domesticated animals in this passage, because we will see them again, and we should observe that given the high status of the cow in South Asian culture, and the use of cow urine in several contexts,[18] this may well not have been perceived as a bad smell.

In thinking about the history of the smellscape of Sanskrit texts, we would also do well to remember that this quite early passage is, above all, concerned with the evaluation of sandalwood and aloeswood, plus some other unidentified aromatics. I explore the imagined exotic origins of these sorts of products in chapter 7, but here it is notable that their olfactory qualities were made accessible by referring to common South Asian objects—things easily available and universally familiar. The smell of the exotic and unfamiliar is defined in terms of the local and mundane.

Before moving on, I will discuss four of the more important odors mentioned in the passage in more detail.

Odor Discussion

Costus Root

Kuṣṭha, or "costus root" (also known as *pachak*), is generally identified as the root of *Saussurea lappa*, a plant that grows in the Himalayas, chiefly around Kashmir and Sikkim. Costus has a goaty, animalic smell. This root has been a key aromatic also in Europe since classical times: Pliny, in his *Natural History*, notes that exquisitely scented costus root is highly valued in India.[19] It is still used in many perfumes and incenses in South Asia and beyond. Along with *guggulu* resin, this root has been a valued aromatic in South Asia from quite early times; both aromatics are mentioned in Vedic texts. Indeed, it would appear that *Kuṣṭha* and *guggulu* are the most notable aromatic materials in Vedic sources (excluding odorous materials, such as ghee). *Kuṣṭha* is mentioned in the *Atharvaveda* especially as a cure for fever, *takman*. Kenneth Zysk usefully summarizes what the *Atharvaveda* tells us about this plant, and such is the importance of this aromatic herb that the passage is worth reproducing here (without Zysk's footnotes):

> *Kuṣṭha* was considered to be the principal medicine for one suffering from fever. He was known to be a divine, aromatic plant with all-pervading strength, the medicine for all diseases, and the choicest amongst herbs. He was said to be thrice-born from various divinities and known by ancient venerable men. Most importantly, he was closely connected with Soma, even being called his brother. For his consecration, the healer quite insistently relied on mythological events concerning his origin. He is said to have been born and acquired by the gods from the divine place where there is the appearance of immortality. This place was said to be in the third heaven from here, where there is the seat of the gods, the *aśvattha*-tree. It is where golden boats with golden rigging sail about and where there are the highest peaks of the Himavant, the birthplace of eagles. We are told that the golden boats with golden oars, traveling on golden courses, transported the plant to the mountain . . .
>
> He is given the epithet of the embryo of the herbs, of the Himavant and of every being. We are also informed that he was a valuable item of trade brought from the mountains in the north to the people in the east where the choicest types were bartered.[20]

It is interesting that, as with *Soma* and gemstones, there is an origin myth for this plant, something that we also have for *guggulu*, as I show in chapter 10. *Kuṣṭha* is not, however, derived from the body of a divine being as *guggulu* and gemstones are, but rather, like *Soma*, it appears that *Kuṣṭha* himself is divine.

Although *Kuṣṭha* continued to be a well-known and important aromatic in later sources, the root seemed to lose the prominent place it occupied in the *Atharvaveda*, as well as that suggested by the reference in the *Arthaśāstra*. As an aromatic of prominence in these early sources, the reference to *Kuṣṭha* as a benchmark odor in the relatively early *Arthaśāstra* is not surprising at all.

Citron (Mātuluṅga)

This is the fruit of *Citrus medica* L. This is a large fruit known as a "citron" (*cédrat* in French), and it is the same fruit known as the *etrog* used in the Jewish holiday of Sukkot.[21] This fruit was probably far more culturally prominent in the ancient world than today, no doubt as an important source of citrus scent prior to the ubiquity of oranges, lemons, and other fruit. The citron is somewhat like a large lemon with thick pithy skin, scant internal flesh, and many seeds. The peel (*tvac*) of this fruit has a lemony citrus fragrance and was used as a mouth freshener. It is mentioned as such in the *Kāmasūtra*[22] where citron peels (*mātuluṅgatvacas*)[23] are said to be part of the ideal man-about-town's domestic paraphernalia. As well as the *mātuluṅga*, it is also known as *bījapūra*, "full of seeds," and it is a common element in certain iconographies, for example, Jaina sculptures of *yakṣīs*. A stylized and elongated version of the same fruit is held by the female attendants who adorn the famous Hoysala temple of Somnathpur near Mysore. On these elongated fruits, the knobbles and ridges that are found on some citron varieties are carved in a very regular manner (as is the case for stouter depictions carried by Jain *yakṣīs*), and the fruit, therefore, somewhat resembles a rather pointy, de-husked ear of maize. On the basis of these sculptures, it has been mistakenly suggested that maize was present in India prior to its introduction from the New World.[24] The great irony of this claim is that it obscures the significance of South Asia as the origin of many citrus species.

Earth

One smell we should note in this passage is the odor of earth (*bhūmigandha*). As we saw in the previous chapter, odor is the special quality of earth in some philosophical systems. In the passage, we see that the specific odor of earth itself is noted. In South Asian culture, there appears a deep connection between the earth and smell—a connection not limited to philosophy alone and found as far back as the *Atharvaveda*.[25] In the passage quoted, a highly valued aromatic is described as smelling of earth. The smell of earth is mentioned in Sanskrit poetry also. A very striking example occurs in Kālidāsa's poem, the *Raghuvaṃśa*. In this account of the origin of the line from which Rāma descended, at one point king Dilīpa, longing for progeny, is delighted when he realizes his wife is pregnant. He ascertains that she is pregnant because of the smell of clay on her breath, which indicates she has pregnancy cravings to eat clay, and his joy is compared to that of an elephant in the rains:

> The lord of the earth, in private, smelling at her mouth that was fragrant with clay could not be satisfied,
> Like an elephant at the end of the hot season [smelling at] a forest-grove pond sprinkled with drops from rain-bearing clouds.[26]

Here the smell of earth is produced by the moistening of clay/earth, either by eating it or rain falling on it. In the case of rain falling on the earth, this is associated with the end of the hot season and a sense of relief at the arrival of the cooling rain—thus, here, the smell of earth seems associated with a time of year and also with feelings of relief and coolness. The love of the smell of the earth after the rains is not limited to classical texts, and even today a traditional perfume (attar/itr) called *miṭṭī* or *gil* (from the Persian for "clay" or "mud") is distilled from fired earth and sold in India, a product that is attested from the early nineteenth century.[27] This fragrance very successfully recreates the fragrance of the cooling rain falling on the earth and is quite possibly the product of the ongoing and complex Indo-Persian aromatic synthesis that took place in the late medieval and early modern periods. Gabriella Eichinger Ferro-Luzzo also notes the importance of this smell in more recent Tamil culture and literature, observing that a phrase meaning "local color" more literally means "the smell of the earth."[28] Here, we see how two thousand years of philosophy, literature, technical treatises, and even the technology of traditional distillation in contemporary India all reflect a deep cultural preoccupation with a smell that is not commonly acknowledged in Western culture.[29]

Lotus

Another smell mentioned in the passage is the smell of lotus (*padmagandha*)—a particularly important smell in many Sanskrit texts. The passage also notes another type of lotus smell (*utpalagandha*), but we will focus on the former smell. This is not the place to embark on a full study of the cultural significance of the lotus in South Asia, so I limit myself to investigating the *smell* of the lotus and aspects of the lotus that seem most relevant to its aromatic nature.

Before I continue, I mention two difficulties in studying the lotus. First, as anyone who has studied Sanskrit for any length of time will be aware, there are a large number of words in Sanskrit translated as "lotus" in English. Therefore, we first need to be clear about which plant we are talking about.

This leads me to the second problem: having ascertained the type of lotus that we are dealing with in the case of *padmagandha*—most likely the typical large, often pink lotus[30] that most people think of when they hear the word "lotus"—I have noticed on several occasions that this species of lotus has a rather faint perfume, somewhat heady and medicinal, quite unlike, for example, the perfume of the various species of jasmine that are valued in Indian culture. Why then is this quite mild perfume (certainly an *anutkaṭa* odor) of the *padma*-lotus so highly valued?

In several passages, we see that lotus-smell appears to be an especially desirable smell when found in the mouth. As we will see in the chapters on perfumery, sweet-smelling breath was a concern in South Asia, and various products were used to perfume the mouth, including citron peel. In its enormous concern with fresh breath, it seems that contemporary North American olfactory culture equals or perhaps even exceeds classical Indian olfactory culture; thus, this is an area that some might find easier to relate to. But breath perfumes aside, the ideal was to have fragrant breath with no intervention, and where this is admired, it seems the best breath may be lotus-smelling breath. As mentioned, the *padma* lotus does not have a very strong fragrance, and I suggest that it is the other associations of the lotus that motivate writers to attribute its mild smell to breath. The pink/red visual beauty, the purity, shape, and the fragrance of the lotus altogether make it an ideal subject for comparison to the mouth. Also, to encounter the smell of a lotus one needs to get close to the flower, suggesting a certain intimacy. Again, in the *Raghuvaṃśa*, when king Dilīpa and his wife Sudakṣiṇā are traveling to the hermitage of Vasiṣṭha they smell cooling lotuses, which are compared to their breath:

> They could smell the fragrance of the lotuses[31] in the pools, cool from being agitated by the waves, imitating their own breath.[32]

Lotus breath is not limited to humans: in Hemacandra's twelfth-century account of the Jain elders, the *Sthavirāvalīcaritra*, there is a description of a mouth as fragrant like a lotus, only, in this case, the mouth belongs to an auspiciously marked horse:

> He has breath with the fragrance of lotus, a glossy coat, voice of a cuckoo, he is the type of horse with white eye-spots, he has slightly stiff ears, he has a long mane.[33]

These are just two examples of the extremely numerous references to lotus breath found in Sanskrit literature. What other connotations might this fragrance have aside from its associations with appealing mouths? The lotus is aquatic, cooling, and attractive. In addition to the close association with the mouth, presumably it is also a seasonal smell because of the seasonal nature of the flowers. While the smell of the earth sprinkled with rain is most associated with the cooling effects of the rainy season, it appears that the *padma*-lotus may be associated with the lakes of autumn (*śarad*) and also with the spring season (*vasanta*).[34] We should bear all this in mind when we see the smell of lotus later. Nevertheless, I very tentatively suggest that it is the general cultural importance of this flower and its spectacular visual appearance that raise the profile of its rather faint smell—a smell that is certainly not very "diffusive" (*nirhārin*). As with the case of the smell of earth, we see again a case of the cultural conditioning of olfactory discourse, and possibly also olfactory attention, in South Asia. The faint scent of the lotus in medieval Indian literature is perhaps somewhat like the song of the nightingale as we know it today: a little disappointing when experienced, yet enduringly famous as the most beautiful birdsong. Borges's observations on the nightingale might well apply to the fragrance of lotus: "Poets have exalted it to such an extent that it has come to be a little unreal, less akin to a lark than to an angel."[35]

The smells of earth and of lotus are prominent in a variety of contexts. It is possible that there was a circle of influence: that these discourses of smell both directed attention to these smells, and this in turn led to the production of further materials (textual and aromatic) in which these particular smells were prominent. Unable to become true anthropologists of the senses in the lived reality of medieval South Asia, we can nevertheless follow these textual traces and at least gain some insight into the ideal representations of the modes of olfactory attention of the educated elite.

Source II

Ominous Fragrance in the *Carakasaṃhitā*

Texts on traditional medicine, *Āyurveda*, contain notable passages where odors are described. One of the oldest foundational texts of traditional South Asian medicine, *Caraka's Compendium*, the *Carakasaṃhitā*, a text with a complex history and uncertain date (second/third century BCE—fourth/fifth century CE), contains a particularly important passage describing smells.[36] In the *Indriyasthānam*, the fifth division of this text, the olfactory characteristics of a terminal decline in health are described. The person whose imminent death may be ascertained in an olfactory manner is known by the appropriate term "bloomed/flowered" (*puṣpita*), a professional medical euphemism that refers also to the impending fatal fruit:[37]

8. He who, day and night, gives off a **smell like various flowers, like that of a forest of various trees and creepers in bloom.**
9. The wise call that man bloomed with the marks of dying, it is certain that that man will leave his body after a year.
10. And he, whose smell **thus becomes the same as flowers, individually, whether they are desirable or undesirable**, is said to be bloomed.
11. The doctor should recognize that one as bloomed, in whose body he should smell inauspicious smells, combined or else individually.
12. And he is said to be bloomed, in whose body, bathed or not bathed, there are alternately auspicious and inauspicious smells, with no cause.
13. **Thus for instance: sandalwood, costus, *tagara*, aloeswood, honey, a garland, urine and excrement, and dead corpses**.
14. And those other smells, of various natures, and various origins are also to be understood by inference as diseased.
15. And, for the purpose of analogical reasoning, we will relate this mark, related to smell, having recognized which, the doctor may predict death.
16. In whose body there is produced a smell without origin, that is permanent, whether desirable or undesirable, he will not survive the year.[38]

There is quite a lot to note in this passage. In the passage from the *Arthaśāstra*, the flowers lotus and a variety of jasmine were mentioned, and here more flowers are mentioned. Indeed, the smells of various flowers remain prominent throughout this book, and it is something I return to frequently. The fragrant scene described at the beginning of this passage—a forest full of trees and creepers—is typical of much Sanskrit poetry, and it also very much resembles one of the scenes from the *Mahābhārata* considered in the next chapter. Yet, in this text it appears that a pleasant smell is not always a good thing. This passage is really quite sinister and uncanny: should someone have the smell of an idyllic, woodland, floral scene, then they are "flowered" and will undoubtedly die in a year.

The manner in which the fateful floral odors are introduced is notable: "he whose smell thus becomes the same as flowers, individually, whether they are desirable or undesirable, is said to be bloomed." These smells are said to be desirable/pleasant or undesirable/unpleasant (*iṣṭair vā yadi vāniṣṭaiḥ*), a twofold classification of the smells of flowers that should by now look quite familiar. This stereotyped formula is reminiscent of that used in the *Mahābhārata* classification of odors. The occurrence of this smell classification further suggests that the sorts of materials described in chapter 2 were probably in dialogue with other texts, be it lexica, such as the order of the senses in Amara's lexicon, or medical texts such as the one quoted.[39] Not only does this assumed twofold classification of odor reflect some of the ones we saw previously, but the order of the senses as given in this chapter is the same as that commonly used by the Buddhists, which might point to the complexity of the development of this text.[40]

Exemplary Good Odors and Bad Odors

The next verse I highlighted in this passage is especially noteworthy:

> 12. And he is said to be bloomed, in whose body, bathed or not bathed, there are alternately auspicious and inauspicious smells, with no cause.
> 13. **Thus for instance: sandalwood, costus, *tagara*, aloeswood, honey, a garland, urine and excrement, and dead corpses.**

Here, we are given an explicit statement of exactly what constitutes a good/auspicious (*śubha*) or bad/inauspicious (*aśubha*) smell. These terms are significant, for they not only imply "good" or "pleasant" but can also relate to notions of auspiciousness. We shall explore this possible correspondence of fragrance and auspiciousness (and the converse) later in the book.

The following list contains some examples of odors that are typical of the categories of good smell and bad smell for some educated South Asians of the early first millennium CE. The first six odorants are clearly the fragrant ones: sandalwood, costus root, *tagara*, aloeswood, honey, and garland. Above, sandalwood held pride of place in the aromatics section of the treasury as described in the *Arthaśāstra*. As noted, costus root is an important aromatic in some quite early sources. *Tagara* is worth some discussion in its own right.

Tagara

Along with costus, *guggulu*, sandalwood, and aloewood *tagara* is an aromatic that appears to be prominent in older sources, dating from a few centuries before and after the turn of the Common Era. As is frequently the case with plants, there is some confusion regarding the actual identity of this material, possibly the root of some fragrant Indian valerian species (*Valeriana wallichii* D.C. = *Valeriana Jatamansi* Jones) or the root of the Indian rosebay (*Tabernaemontana coronaria* Willd).[41] In the case of this plant, the definite identity and thus also the regional origin elude us. Just as we see in European languages ("musk rose," and the etymologies of "nut*meg*" and French "*mug*uet" that are derived from terms for musk), prominence in perfumery might have led to several fragrant plants, both flowers and dried products, being named after *tagara* in various times and places. We will see similar complexities in the case of sandalwood later in this book. Nevertheless, whatever *tagara* was (and not forgetting that it may well have been different things to different people at different times), the fragrance of an aromatic called *tagara* was particularly highly valued in several early sources. It is, for example, mentioned in the large, encyclopedic, and somewhat challenging Śvetāmbara Jain Prakrit text called the *Viyāhapannati/Vyākhyāprajñapti* (also known as the *Bhagavaī*) where we find a passage, placed apparently rather randomly after a section on the import of dreams, in which it is stated that if someone moves a vessel of perfume around in the wind, one does not smell the vessel nor the perfume but only the fragrant particles (*poggalā*).[42] One of the odorous materials mentioned as placed in a vessel is *tagara* and also possibly costus.[43] This is, of course, a very similar theory of smelling to that seen in the previous chapter.

There is also an early reference to *tagara* as a superlative aromatic in the Buddhist *Dhammapada*. Here, *tagara* along with sandalwood, *mallikā* jasmine, and *utpala* lotus are listed as excellent sources of fragrance that are nevertheless surpassed by the fragrance of virtue:

> The smell of flowers does not go against the wind, nor that of sandalwood, *tagara*, or *mallikā* jasmine,[44]
> But the smell of good people goes against the wind: the good man diffuses scent to all directions.
>
> Sandalwood or *tagara*, *utpala*-lotus and *vassikī* (jasmine)[45]: amongst these types of perfumes, the perfume of good character is unsurpassed.
>
> This perfume is slight, namely *tagara* and sandalwood,
> But the perfume of people of good character is supreme (and) blows amongst the gods.[46]

This passage exploits the essential role of wind in transmitting odors and is another example of a sense-conceit. No normal odor can escape the power of the wind, which therefore controls and limits the diffusion of pleasing fragrances from aromatics and flowers. However, the fragrance of virtue knows no such limitations. This Buddhist metaphorical use of fragrance is appropriate because the sense of smell and the nature of odors lend themselves to being a model of the epistemology of values in general. As the scholar Gregory Schopen noted, in many early sources the relics of the Buddha are said to be "infused with" (*paribhāvita*) the good qualities of the living Buddha, or I might translate this as "steeped in the fragrance of" qualities. Moreover, certain people are also steeped in the perfume of virtue.[47] Robert Brown suggested that the use of perfume boxes as relic containers in Gandhāra might have resonances of the same metaphors.[48] Odors are good and bad, pleasing and displeasing, just like ethical actions and intentions, and *dharma* and *adharma*. Unlike the several types of flavor for example, their qualities diffuse out in the world to be perceived by others who are then inevitably affected by them. Somewhat on the same lines, one Sanskrit term for "fragrance," *saurabhyam*, can also mean "fame" or "reputation." A similar idiom is also found at the beginning of the *Daśakumāracarita* of Daṇḍin, where king Rājahaṃsa is said to be "reputed/perfumed all round by fame."[49]

Fragrant odorants have other qualities of note: flowers are transient and sandalwood is precious and rare. Thus, virtue is fragrant and evil stinks. Although, in this example, the fragrance of virtue is superior to that of fragrant materials, we should not assume this implies that in all contexts the ethical-metaphorical associations of odors are more important than the aesthetic, auspicious, and so forth. Indeed, as we shall see throughout this book, in a karmic universe good people often smell good and evil people often smell bad. According to some texts, it is arguably the inevitable sensory consequences (stinky, painful, fragrant) of ethical actions that render them desirable and undesirable.

The dry aromatics mentioned in this Pali text, in the *Arthaśāstra*, in the passage from *Caraka*, and in the Jain *Viyāhapannati*, namely, sandalwood, aloeswood, *tagara*, and costus feature in many earlier South Asian texts. It does not seem excessive to suggest that these aromatics are typical of early South Asian olfactory culture—a period in which musk, for example, had yet to be added to the mix.[50]

Plants and Animals

Honey is a smell we will see again, and both from that context (the Brahmin-elephant smells of honey amongst other things) and from the earlier passage, we can conclude this was a highly valued smell. I will discuss garlands at some length in chapter 6 on perfumery, and I discuss flowers in the next chapter, but I briefly note that garlands were valued as much for their scent as for their appearance. Apart from honey, all the good smells in the passage from the *Carakasaṃhitā* about the odorous signs of impending death are parts of plants: heartwoods, roots, and flowers.[51] This is reminiscent of the earliest Buddhist classification of smells by their plant-sources and reinforces the notion that plants were seen as an especially important source of smells. The stinks, on the other hand, are all animal derived, and this connection of stinks and animals/humans is something we examine later. Not only are these stinks animal derived, but they are also ritually impure substances (assuming human urine is meant here). The nonplant substances: urine, excrement, and corpses are foul-smelling, inauspicious, and impure.

In the very final chapter we will explore these dimensions of smells more, when we read a text that locates stinks and fragrances within a cosmogony that accounts for their various properties.

Source III

The Smells of "Seized" Sick Infants in the *Suśrutasaṃhitā*

A passage in another important early medical text contains a particularly ripe description of stinks. This passage occurs in the *Uttaratantra*, the sixth and final division of the *Suśrutasaṃhitā*, again of uncertain date, though it appears that this section was added some time before 500 CE.[52] In the *Carakasaṃhitā*, those doomed to die were fragrant and said to be "bloomed,"; here sickness stinks. A rather vivid and disturbing passage gives the signs, including olfactory ones, of childhood diseases arising from possession by the nine childhood-disease-causing demons, the nine child-snatchers or *bālagrahas*, beings who themselves are in many cases stinking:[53]

8. (The child) with swollen eyes, **the same smell as blood**, disliking the breast, with twisted mouth, with eyes dead on one side and moving on the other, who recoils, with eyes rolling a lot, who cries little, with firm feces compacted into a ball, is afflicted by Skanda.

10. With limp body, trembling with fear, **with the smell of bird**, greatly tormented all over by oozing wounds, covered with pustules, roasted by fever: (this) child is understood to be hurt by Śakunī (Bird).

12. The boy with limp body, who sleeps happily in the day, but not at night, excretes loose feces, and **has the same smell as a crow**, is afflicted by vomiting, who has goose-flesh, and is very thirsty is seized by Pūtanā (Stinker).
13. He who dislikes the breast, and is tormented by diarrhea, cough, hiccups, vomiting together with a fever, who is a bad color, who lies always face-down, **with a sour smell**—doctors in this case say he is afflicted by Andhapūtanā (Blind-Stinker).
14. The one who recoils, and trembles excessively, who howls, who sleeps stuck to the bed, and whose intestines gurgle, **whose body smells putrid**, and has excessive diarrhea: in this case, doctors say he is afflicted by Śītapūtanā (Cool—Stinker).
15. He whose body wilts, whose hands, feet and face are very beautiful, who eats a lot, whose stomach is covered with foul veins, who is agitated, and who has **the same smell as urine**: in this case the child is to be known as afflicted by Vaktramaṇḍikā[54] [Face-Ornament?].

> 16. He who vomits foam and is bent in the middle, and who wails with agitation looking upwards, who constantly has a fever, and who **smells of (animal or human) fat**, and who is unconscious—he has been visited by Naigameṣa.[55]

The repulsive world of demonic childhood disease is a particularly stinky place in several respects. Unlike in the case above where the fragrant "flowered" patient is doomed to die, these ill children smell bad: they smell of blood, bird, impure, carrion-eating crows; or they smell sour, putrid, of urine, or of animal fat. With perhaps the exception of "sour" these are smells of animal or human origin; they are the smells of dismemberment, decay, and excretion—the impure odors of body tissues and fluids "out of place" in the manner described by Mary Douglas in her famous analysis of the concept of impurity.[56] These smells are those of impure substances, and they are repellent.

The smells constitute one of the signs by which one may recognize the species of child-snatcher responsible for the sickness, and then consequently the doctor can treat the disease, by a combination of massage and (stinking) demonifuge fumigation of the child in addition to worship of the child-seizer.[57] To give an example of the stinking fumigations, for a child possessed by Skandāpasmāra the fumigation consisted of vulture and owl excreta, hair, elephant nails, ghee, and hair from a bull.[58] There are two things to note about these sorts of fumigations. First, they appear to rely, in part, on the literally repellent nature of bad smells, as opposed to the literally attractive nature of good ones. Second, they highlight the complexity in the category of bad smells, and they show that the simple philosophical discourse of fragrances and stinks is far more differentiated in other contexts. Presumably these fumigations stink, and these stinks repel the demons. Yet, ironically these demons often appear to have sensual appetites that are contrary to those of humans, and it is sometimes their tastes for impure body fluids (that would presumably count as bad smelling), that leads them to attack pregnant women and children in the first place. Given these unorthodox appetites, reflected also in the materials used in some tantric rites, one would not necessarily think that these beings would be so repelled by stinking materials. Indeed, their olfactory preferences in this particular respect do not differ from those of humans, including Brahmins, who are presumably not supposed to smell burnt vulture dung if the prohibitions on smelling noted in the previous chapter are taken into account. Significantly, these fumigations do not consist of human body fluids—the sorts of things some of the sick children smell of. Rather, a key ingredient in some fumigations is a variety of solid or dry animal parts, including the animals of the village, the (royal) elephant, as well as birds of prey (owl) and carrion birds (vulture). Both in this fumigation and in one described by Smith, animal hair and nails feature, and Smith suggests that the connection with the animals in question might play a role in the action of these fumigations because "they were feral and could thus overpower the afflicting *graha*."[59]

A particularly extensive and fascinating description of such fumigations is also found in a medical text on childbirth and pediatrics (*kaumārabhṛtya*), the *Kāśyapasaṃhitā*, dated possibly from around the seventh century CE.[60] There, following a list of forty incenses and/or fumigations, two classifications are mentioned. First, there is a threefold classification as *dhūpa*, *anudhūpa*, and *pratidhūpa*, ambiguous terms that the translator P. V. Tewari translates as "principal fumigation," "associated fumigation," and "subsequent fumigation."[61] How might these fumigations have differed? We might understand the *anu-* prefix in *anudhūpa* to suggest that those incenses are somehow functionally "after," "subordinate," or "conformable"—in general they are "supporting-incenses." The *prati-* incenses, on the other hand, might be understood in general as somehow "counter-," "against-," or "return-incenses." The examples of *pratidhūpas* in the text (there appear to be no *anudhūpas*) seem to bring good fortune, so possibly that type of incense is indeed more apotropaic and preventative than the *dhūpas* that drive out demons. The second classification of fumigations is twofold, according to whether the incenses are based on animals (*jaṅgama* "moving") or plants (*sthāvara* "stationary"). As we have seen, animal products are a striking feature of such fumigations and throughout this chapter this division between plant odorants and animal ones will be quite noticeable. The text then relates a brief origin myth of these fumigations, and it is worth pausing to present this:

> When the children of sages were taken by *rākṣasa* demons over and over again as they were born, all the great sages sought refuge with Fire (Vahni, i.e., Agni). They were possessed of oblations, recitation and austerity and so then Agni, being satisfied, said, "Offer these incenses offered by me [or "to me"] and use them. You will no longer have fear of *rākṣasas*, *bhūtas* and *piśācas* . . .[62]

This intuitive connection of incense with Agni, the sacred fire and god of fire is something we shall see again in chapter 10, where the body of Agni is described as the source of certain aromatics. Here, however, he only provides fumigation incenses to save the children of sages from demons, and it is clear in the context that these are based on animals and plants, not divine body tissues.

To return to our passage, as Smith notes, when pregnant women and children are possessed by child-snatchers (*bālagrahas*), the possession is manifested in disease or miscarriage. This is unlike the case of the possession of adults by types of *grahas*, or *bhūtas*, which is related to mental illness, and the canonical medical texts acknowledge this distinction.[63] Analyzed in an olfactory manner, one can draw another contrast here. The child-snatchers produce illness and this is partly manifested in terms of smells and stinks. The possession of adults, on the other hand, is not so frequently, or so dramatically, manifested by bodily odors, but equally by changes in the person's inclinations toward certain smells. As with the passage we will examine on the "character types" (*sattvas*) of elephants, this can reveal something about the odors and odor preferences of various divine beings.

Considering together the passages Smith assembles and quotes on the possession of adults, it appears that in general, people possessed by *devas* (gods)[64] and *gandharvas* (heavenly musicians)[65] have a sweet scent, whereas those possessed by a *piśāca* (flesh-eating demon) can smell foul.[66] A taste for perfumes, garlands, and so forth is a sign that one is possessed by a *gandharva*[67] or a *yakṣa*.[68] People possessed by both *gandharvas* and *yakṣas* sometimes have a preference for red items. Additionally, in one important medical text, the *Aṣṭāṅgahṛdayasaṃhitā* as quoted by Smith, those possessed by *devas* (gods) also like white garlands,[69] and those possessed by *vetālas* (corpse-animating spirits) are also fond of fragrant garlands, possibly because of their presence in the cremation ground.[70]

The olfactory nature of child-snatchers is different. Not only do the sick children stink of body fluids and so on, but three of the child-seizers in this passage, Pūtanā, Andhapūtanā, and Śītapūtanā, have smell-related names, meaning something along the lines of "Stinker," "Blind-Stinker," and "Cool-Stinker" respectively. Possibly, the stinky nature of these beings was believed to give rise to particularly stinking diseases.[71] Or, perhaps, the repulsive olfactory aesthetics reflects a visceral cultural dread of childhood sickness in a world of frequent infant mortality. Also, sickness in early South Asia must have been a far fouler smelling affair than in a modern hospital.

Pūtanā might be familiar to some because she is an important figure in other texts—indeed two of these child-seizers have a close connection with the childhoods of religious figures. Pūtanā is associated with the childhood of Kṛṣṇa, and Naigameṣa (as Hariṇaigemeṣin) is associated with the embryo-transfer of the Jain Fordmaker Mahāvīra. The episodes show that the figure in question (Kṛṣṇa or Mahāvīra) has either a dominance over or an alliance with a certain child-seizer, and therefore possibly childhood sickness in general.[72] It is important to note that these child-snatchers are not all female, and the narratives promote the virtues of Kṛṣṇa and Mahāvīra more than those of the child-snatchers.

The story of Pūtanā ("Stinky") as related in the *Bhāgavata Purāṇa* is especially pertinent to the analysis of smell in South Asian religions for what it reveals about the effects of stinks and fragrances, about embodied evil, and the aesthetically modifying power of devotion. Whilst Kṛṣṇa was an infant living in the region of Vraj (Bryant's translation):

> The dreadful Pūtanā, slaughterer of children, had been dispatched by Kaṃsa, and was roaming about devouring infants in towns, villages and pastures.[73]

Having taken on the guise of an attractive woman, she approaches the infant Kṛṣṇa and offers him her poisoned breast, whereupon Kṛṣṇa sucks out her very life:

> The dreadful ogress placed Kṛṣṇa on her lap there, and gave the infant her breast, covered with deadly poison. Squeezing it tightly with both hands, the furious Lord sucked it, along with her life breath.[74]

When she was thus killed she assumed her original, enormous, and horrible form. The people of Vraj then dismember the corpse and burn it, at which point:

> The smell rising from the burning body had the pleasant smell of aloe; its sins had been instantly destroyed when suckled by Kṛṣṇa.[75]

Even though the breast she offered Kṛṣṇa was poisoned, nevertheless, by means of this offering, for which she has was suckled to death by the infant Kṛṣṇa, her huge repellent body is no longer "Stinky," but rather gives off the perfume of aloeswood, the extremely costly and rare aromatic wood that was frequently burned in incenses.

The passage conveys how unpleasant a figure Pūtanā must have seemed. That by offering her breast (even with evil intent) to Kṛṣṇa, her body took on the fragrance of such an elite aromatic must have seemed all the more remarkable to a medieval audience. Not only is the smoke from her pyre fragrant, but, as with some other fragrances we consider later in the *Mahābhārata*, this aloeswood fragrance diffuses, and it attracts the people of Vraj who, curious to find the source of the smell, perform rites for the infant Kṛṣṇa. Diffusion and attraction are essential to what fragrant odors effect in many classical Sanskrit texts. Here, not only has association with Kṛṣṇa made a repellent and evil demoness called "Stinky" fragrant, but it has also made the smoke from a corpse (one of the most bad-smelling things) in a cremation ground (one of the most bad-smelling places) attractive:

> When the people of Vraj smelt the fragrance of the smoke from the cremation ground, they approached Vraj, saying: "What is this? And from where does it come?"
>
> After hearing the description of the arrival of Pūtanā, her subsequent acts and her death from the *gopīs* [female cowherds] there, they were struck with great amazement and performed rites of blessing for the baby.[76]

Returning to the smellscape of these texts, what sort of things stink in the passages seen so far? Stinks are mostly animal products, impure substances that are in some cases produced from excretion, dismemberment, or death, but in other cases they are simply the smells of certain animals, such as crows, that eat impure carrion: materials that are often also ritually impure. Plants, it seems, are more often said to be the sources of fragrances. Where people or animals are naturally fragrant, they are even compared to plants (lotus breath), whereas impure animals and impure animal parts stink. Although some plants may smell bad, these sorts of plants are not generally mentioned in these foul contexts.[77]

Source IV

Prognostication by the Smells of Semen in the *Bṛhatsaṃhitā*

In the *Great Compendium*, the *Bṛhatsaṃhitā* of Varāhamihira, dated to the sixth century CE there is another instance of smell description.[78] The *Great Compendium* is an extremely important text that mainly focuses on prognostication, but it also contains some early materials on perfumery, so this is not the last we will see of this source. In the rather striking context of prognostication by the examination, mostly olfactory, of a man's semen there are some more descriptions of odors:

> The Signs of Men:
> 14. With shriveled fore-bellies, they are devoid of wealth and understood as unlucky. With semen that has the **same smell as flowers**, they are to be known as kings.
> 15. When it **smells of honey**, they have much wealth. When it **smells of fish**, they have many offspring. A man with meager semen is a begetter of females. With (semen) the **smell of flesh** he will be very prosperous.
> 16. When it **smells of alcoholic liquor**, he is a sacrificer. When his semen has **the same smell as a caustic substance [lye?]**, he is poor. He who has sex quickly is long lived, and [different] from that, his life is otherwise [i.e., short.][79]

It is quite notable in this passage that there appears to be no correspondence (or an exact inverse correspondence as sometimes found in texts on oneiromancy) between the associations of the smells and the outcome of the man's life. Some of these odors (alcoholic liquor) are the sorts of thing that Brahmins were forbidden to smell, but, of course, not everyone was forbidden to smell these things. Such observations regarding the social relativity of olfactory aesthetics are very important to bear in mind reading the next passage on the smells of elephants. But the crucial aspect of this short passage is that these smells by now look quite familiar. From the small sample of passages discussed so far, it seems that the odors of honey, flowers, fish, and meat/flesh were prominent smells over a long period in Sanskrit textual cultures, along with earth and aquatic plants such as the lotus. This contrasts to the stock list of aromatic materials (costus, *tagara*, and so on) noted in the early sources, which in later texts we will see replaced by another "canon" of aromatics. In this text, in the medical texts, and also in the text on elephants, the important role of the sense of smell in the evaluation of people and animals by experts is also noteworthy: to find out certain things about the world you had to use your sense of smell, and this investigational smelling was also to be informed and articulated according to such technical discourses found in this chapter.

Source V

Smells and Elephant Types in the *Mātaṅgalīlā*

In the world of Sanskrit texts, elephants have a good sense of smell. Elephants are also described as odorous animals. A particularly esteemed type of elephant is called the scent-elephant (*gandhahastin*). This type of elephant is called this because of the effect it has on other elephants when they smell a scent-elephant: according to various sources they are frightened, calmed, or excited by its odor. This would, of course, be viewed as helpful when the elephant was used in warfare:

> When they smell his scent, hostile elephants do not stay:
> truly he is called a scent elephant, bringing the king victory.[80]

> Springtime is said to produce lust/musth for all beings, and especially so for elephants. Therefore those begotten in the spring are scent-elephants. And from smelling their sweat, excrement, urine, and musth liquids other elephants instantly become intoxicated. These scent elephants make victory for kings.[81]

The second quotation above mentions the musth (*mada*) of elephants. Sometimes translated as "ichor," or "rut" this secretion from the temples of elephants was not only deemed affective to other elephants but also to bees, which are often depicted in Sanskrit poetry as crowding around the musth-dripping temples of elephants. The production of musth was not limited to scent-elephants and was generally associated with elephants in rut (as well as with bees and with Ganeśa) in poetry. South Asian scholars were quite right to observe that the odors of elephants are a form of olfactory communication, and recent research has shown that the varied, odorous musth secretions of elephants do play complex and important roles in elephant "society."[82]

Given the importance of odors and the sense of smell in the traditional understanding of elephants in South Asia, it is not surprising that a detailed classification of elephants would highlight the olfactory aspects of these animals. The following text is called the *Play of Elephants* (*Mātaṅgalīlā*) and is ascribed to a certain Nīlakaṇṭha.[83] This text is probably a lot later than the others I have examined so far; it was possibly composed in sixteenth-century Kerala, and it will be a good source to search for any changes in the smellscape.[84] This text provides first an account of the mythological origins of elephants, followed by chapters dealing with the physical characteristics and classification of elephants, the prices of elephants, the phenomenon of musth, the keeping and capturing of elephants, as well as the characteristics of elephant drivers. The classification of elephants in terms of character type (*sattva*) has close parallels to similar classifications of humans, such as found in several medical texts (e.g., "*gandharva*-type," "*rākṣasa*-type").[85] These character types, both human and elephant, correspond to a hierarchy of divine and semi-divine beings, and in this respect they also share much, both in name and character, with the hierarchies of beings (*bhūtas/grahas*) that cause adult possession in the form of mental illness.[86]

The human character types (*sattvas*) do not manifest themselves by means of odors, rather by actions and inclinations, and the possession of adult humans by the corresponding *bhūtas* only manifests itself through odor in a few cases.[87] For elephants, it is quite a different matter. Given that elephants were said to be both odorous and also able to communicate to other elephants through odor, it is not surprising that one of the more important indicators of the character-type (*sattva*) of an elephant was its smell. This text thus tells us a lot about both elephants and divine (and human) beings. In the case of elephants, we learn that their odor profile was deemed, at least in this text, to be an index of their general natures. Perhaps more unique is what this text reveals about the divine beings and social castes which provide the basis for this particular typology. When describing the *rākṣasa* character type of humans, authors and compilers of texts told us quite a lot about the personality traits associated with *rākṣasas*, at least as they were imagined in certain times, places, and contexts. As Smith notes in the case of medical texts: "Many of these *sattvas* correspond in both character and name to the various *grahas* listed in the *bhūtavidyā* sections [of medical texts]. From this, we must assume that *grahas* or possessing entities may be viewed as substantialized or reified collocations of personality attributes." These possessing entities are in turn said to derive their natures from their "respective masters," the gods and so forth.[88]

If the texts on human character types and symptoms of possession arguably reveal the natures and behaviors that were attributed to various types of divine beings, then this text on the character types of elephants appears to provide an account of the sorts of odors that would be associated with gods and so forth, at least as imagined by a traditional scholar in sixteenth-century Kerala. I can hardly emphasize enough that this is only one source in the vast world of South Asian texts, and therefore what it implies about the imagined odors of various beings should not be taken as universally applicable. Nevertheless, it is a particularly rich and rare glimpse into how a wide range of divine beings and social castes were represented in olfactory terms in one South Asian case:

1. One should distinguish the gods (*deva*), enemies of the gods (*dānava*), celestial musicians (*gandharva*), semidivine protector demons (*yakṣa*), dangerous demons (*rākṣasa*), human, and the flesh-eating demons (*piśāca*) and serpent character type by their respective characteristics.[89]

2. The one that is charming, **has the same smell as *kumuda* lotus, sandalwood, seven-leaf,**[90] **orange, *padma* lotus and four-finger,**[91] with beaming face, who forever possesses the eagerness of a young elephant, is worthy of respect, with the cry of an Indian cuckoo—he is of a god (*deva*) character type.
3. Intent on the contemptible, excessively delighting in fighting, with a base nature, not in the least compassionate, **with the smell of the *sinduvāra*,**[92] **aloeswood or fish**, this elephant, who is a killer, has the character type of an enemy of the gods (*dānava*).
4. They call celestial musician (*gandharva*) one who has the **same smell as *atimuktaka*,**[93] ***yūthika* jasmine,**[94] **lotus, *puṃnāga*,**[95] ***nāga*,**[96] **or *haricandana* green-sandalwood**, who is fond of singing, with a fine gait, with beautiful tusks, eyes, temporal bosses, head, trunk and trunk-tip and has small spots.
5. Pure and of an impatient nature, lovely, of attractive appearance, energetic, and with erect ears is an elephant with the semidivine protector demon (*yakṣa*) character type.
6. He who has **the stench of a crow, monkey, donkey, camel, cat, urine or excrement,**[97] kills elephants, is violent at night, who desires sour food, flesh and blood, badly behaved, ungrateful, (and) acts perversely is by character type a dangerous demon (*rākṣasa*).
7. Fond of solitude, with **the same smell as a corpse or of blood,** who roams confused at night and has a deep voice, who gets extremely angry on the days of the moon change, and who is stupid, the sages declare that elephant to have a flesh-eating demon (*piśāca*) character type.
8. He who has **the smell of fish, *śaivala* waterweed,**[98] ***phanijjhaka* basil,**[99] **and mud, also with the same smell as rice wine and butchered meat**, who is frightened hearing even the sound of clouds, who is angry at night, (and) delights in water and dust is a serpent (*bhujaṅgaḥ*).
9. The brahmin is pure, **has a body perfumed with the same smells as honey, milk, milk-rice, molten ghee,**[100] **or mango blossom**, is fond of Vedic sung recitation, and friendly to all elephants, peaceful, fond of bathing, with a virtuous mind, (as) named by princes of sages.
10. He who is the **same in smell as sandalwood, ghee,**[101] **yellow orpiment and realgar**[102] and also the **same in smell as *guggulu* resin,**[103] skillful in the work of a war elephant, and fearless in battle, is a *kṣatriya* elephant, heroic with regard to the assaults of various cutting weapons.
11. He who is with **the smell of the *bandhūka* plant,**[104]**rice, sesame (plant or seed), *ketaka* flowers,**[105] ***mālatī* jasmine,**[106] and a highly ornamented palate and tongue, enduring distress, an eater of butchered

meat, and fond of kind words, though angry he quickly calms down, he is a *vaiśya* type (*jāti*).

12. Thrilled by left-overs, all of a sudden he is fearful, with **a smell that is sour, acidic, or of a he-goat, bones or crab**, angry, corruptible, miserable, ungrateful, by nature that one is a *śūdra*, the lowest of elephants.
13. Destroying trust, cruel, with a crooked step when moving, who does not eat excessively when in musth is thought to be an elephant with the character type of a serpent.
14. And those with the character type of gods, kṣatriyas, celestial musicians and Brahmins are *sattvic*. The *vaiśya* and the *śūdra* are *rājasic* and the others are *tamasic*.[107]

This complex passage deserves a far more extensive commentary than I can give here. It is also a challenging passage; my translations of some of the odorants are tentative, and it is also difficult to ascertain the broader cultural associations of many of these odorants. Using somewhat broad strokes, it is however possible to discuss some parts of this passage in greater detail. If indeed it was composed in the sixteenth century, then it is remarkable how conservative in some respects the Sanskritic olfactory world has remained over time.

The different types of elephant are classified according to three schemes, namely, a hierarchy of divine beings, a social hierarchy of castes (*varṇas*), and finally all the elephants are classed according to the scheme of the three qualities (*guṇas*) that I mentioned in the discussion of Sāmkhya philosophy: *sattva*, *rajas*, and *tamas*. These are difficult terms to translate, but approximately: *sattva* is pure and good, *rajas* dynamic and passionate, and *tamas* inert and dark. In all cases, these hierarchies are listed from "highest" to "lowest."

Starting at the top, the *deva* (god) elephant "has the same smell as *kumuda*-lotus, sandalwood, seven-leaf, orange, *padma*-lotus and four-finger . . ." As one might expect, these are all presumably good smells. It is notable that the cool aquatic *padma*-lotus as an ideal body (mouth) smell occurs again, as does cooling sandalwood, which is another exemplary and prestigious fragrance. The elephant with the character of a *deva* smells mostly of cool aquatic flowers, terrestrial flowers, as well as of a fruit and a fragrant wood: one of the most the prestigious aromatics, sandalwood. This is the only time that we will see the smell of orange mentioned in Sanskrit sources in this book. In contrast to the god (*deva*) elephant, the elephant with the nature of the enemies of the gods (*dānava*) smells of aloeswood amongst other things. Like sandalwood, this is a prestigious aromatic, yet where sandalwood is cooling and light (or ruddy) in color, aloeswood is black and heating. Sandalwood and aloeswood (*candanāgaru*) are frequently mentioned together in many contexts as a somewhat contrasting pair (white versus black; cool versus hot; smeared versus burnt) of superior aromatic woods. Prestigious but opposite, this would appear to be an appropriate aromatic to associate with the "anti-gods."

The elephant that has the character of those people at the top of the human social hierarchy is the Brahmin elephant that "has a body perfumed with the same smells as honey, milk, milk-rice, molten ghee, or mango blossom . . ." As with the godlike elephant, these are all doubtless good smells, yet unlike the case of the *deva* smells that are mostly flowers, these are mostly food smells, and not only that, but in many cases these are smells of the sorts of food that are offered in orthodox sacrifices—thus the ideal olfactory association of Brahmins is predominantly with pure sacrificial foods, especially the sweet and fatty products of the cow. In fact, these foods are all derived from animals, but unlike meat and blood, they are ritually pure. Most important, these foods are also rich, sweet and no doubt generally desirable.

The only exception to this list of foods is the smell of mango blossom. This smell is important in Sanskrit literature; it is associated with descriptions of spring. Indeed, it is "the prominent representative of the Spring and the agent-in-chief of the God of Love."[108] And it constitutes one of the god Kāma's lust-inciting arrows. Also, this flower gives rise to a *fruit*.[109] As S. R. Sarma states, "Its fragrance is such that the black bees leave every other flower in its favour."[110] Sarma also quotes an unknown poet who declared, "Neither camphor, nor sandalwood, neither musk, not any other kind of flower or fruit, has such fragrance as the mango does."[111] The anthology in which that verse is quoted dates from the fourteenth century, and although the verse itself might well be older, it makes a good contrast with the Buddhist verses on the perfume of virtue discussed earlier. Both these verses note the superiority of a certain odorant (virtue, or mango blossom) with respect to other superlative aromatics. In the earlier Buddhist passage, the superlative aromatics surpassed only by the fragrance of virtue were *tagara*, sandalwood, lotus, and types of jasmine. Likewise, the exemplary good smells in the *Carakasaṃhitā* were sandalwood, costus, *tagara*, aloeswood, honey, and a garland. Here, in a text that is most likely later than those two texts, *tagara* and costus are not mentioned, and camphor and musk have been added. Again, this very much reflects the development in the formal "canon" of aromatics, no doubt in dialogue with changes in a practical "canon" of aromatics, something I discuss later in the book.[112]

To return to the Brahmin elephant that has the perfume of mango blossom, in this caste context, it may be that he smells this way because this is the supremely attractive and fruitful fragrance for the most arousing season. Thus the Brahmin elephant, who otherwise smells of universally pure, rich, sweet, and sometimes sacrificial food, also has an attractive and arousing bodily perfume according to the author of this treatise.

At the other end of the spectrum of divine beings, the elephant that has the same character as a ghoulish flesh-eating demon, the *piśāca*, has "the same smell as a corpse or of blood"—the animal-based stinks of impurity. The elephant that corresponds to the *śūdra* caste, an animal that is said to be the lowest of elephants, has a "smell that is sour, acidic, or of a he-goat, bones or crab." Presumably, these are deemed unpleasant smells, and again they suggest decay and intrinsic impurity from a brahmanical point of view and may provide an insight into the class-based smell prejudices of upper-class sixteenth-century Kerala.

Yet, this catalogue of smells does not only reflect a hierarchy of pure and impure substances; it also reflects the sort of territory associated with various beings. For example, the elephant with the nature of a serpent, often associated with underground watery realms, smells, amongst other things, of waterweed and mud.

The manner in which certain smells are associated with certain divine beings and castes is complex. These smell associations seem to reflect, in some cases, the status, activities, and purity of the caste, as well as the typical imagined diet of that rank of divine being or caste (e.g., goat and crab, or corpses). These smells may also reflect the sort of terrain one inhabits, as in the case of the serpents. In general, the higher one is in a hierarchy, the better one smells, but this is not absolutely the case, for the *dānava* elephant smells both of aloeswood and fish, and the *kṣatriya* one smells both of sandalwood and of the garlicky, yellow pigment, orpiment. The significance of such odorants as orpiment is quite complex, and a full account of this passage would require much further research. From the few odors I have examined, it is clear that the author of this text did not choose these smells at random, so it is likely that his other choices also reflect olfactory associations available to a scholar steeped in traditional Sanskritic learning, as well, of course, as vernacular and folk traditions.

What of the types of beings who in other texts are associated with odors and smelling in one way or another? The *gandharva*, who in texts on the possession of humans is associated with the love of fragrance, is suitably fragrant in this passage, but the *yakṣa*, who in the context of human possession is also inclined toward fragrance, is not characterized by odors in any way here. Is there a hierarchy of divine odors? If so, fragrant flowers, including the lotus, seem to be at the top: god-elephants smell of flowers including two cooling, aquatic flowers, and Brahmin-elephants smell of arousing springtime mango blossom. Finally, god-elephants also smell of ever-prestigious, cooling sandalwood, the South Asian aromatic par excellence, as do those elephants with the nature of pleasure-loving *gandharva*s, and the nature of regal *kṣatriya*s.

Discussion: The Smellscape of Sanskrit Texts

We have encountered a lot of odors in this chapter. Certain beings appear to be especially odorous: sick children and the demonesses that possess them, *gandharva*s, *yakṣa*s, and possibly also *piśāca*s, and of course elephants. Bearing in mind all the caveats I stated at the outset of this chapter with regard to the concept of a smellscape and the limitations of my sources, it appears that in extremely broad terms, the more "natural" odors, such as fish, lotus, meat, earth, and so on appear to remain relatively constant over time. The most noticeable change in smell-descriptive vocabulary in such technical contexts as these is the typical range of aromatics: an evolution from *tagara* and costus, to musk and camphor, with sandalwood and aloeswood remaining constant.

The prominent smells in these texts are for the most part what we would call organic, derived from animals and plants, with the exception of the mineral smells of earth, orpiment, and realgar. Amongst the smells of animal origin, there are the smells of animals themselves, such as the smell of camel, as well as the smell of animal and human bodily products. Within these animal products, some are natural secretions and excretions of the animals, being either pure, such as milk, or potentially impure, such as urine. Other smells of animal products are smells of the animal body which has undergone some damage or even death, such as smell of blood and the smell of corpses.

The plant smells also show a great variety, being dominated by flowers, but nevertheless, several roots (costus), woods (sandalwood), and leaves (basil), as well as fruits (citron) are present in the various sources. The vegetable foodstuffs rice and sesame are also mentioned, as is honey, regarded as a product of bees. There is then the final category of odorous substances that are human preparations, derived from both plants (alcohol) and animals (ghee).

With the exception of some of the smells given in the *Mātaṅgalīlā*, especially the smells of the *rākṣasa* type of elephant, the reader will notice the category of smells that shows the greatest extension is the smells of plants and their parts. This would seem to reflect what we saw in the early Buddhist analysis of smells:

> What is the form that is the sphere of smell?
>
> That smell, which, derived from the four great elements, with no attribute, producing a reaction, root-smell, heart-wood-smell, bark-smell, leaf-smell, flower-smell, fruit-smell[113], raw-meat-smell, putrid-smell, good-smell, bad-smell or whatever other smell, derived from the four great elements . . .

Plants in this passage are a very productive source of smells, and animals less so, associated with only two unpleasant smells. It would appear, therefore, that both in practice and also in some theoretical analyses of smells, plants dominate, and most plant smells would have been classed as fragrant smells (jasmines, sandalwood, mangoes, and so forth.)[114] Also remarkable is the extent of the assumed knowledge of plants and plant smells when compared to the knowledge of a large number of even highly educated present-day inhabitants of North America. Such a knowledge of plants is not limited to sources like medical texts—composers of much poetry in classical Sanskrit also assume this familiarity with a large number of plant species, their sensuous properties, and conventional associations. This can make translation at times difficult, not only because the plants in question may not be known to a Western reader, but also because many readers simply do not have an easy familiarity with the plant kingdom as a whole, and they might well be tempted to pass over these important passages more quickly than they should. The writers and readers of these texts, though they may have been urban, nevertheless inhabited, both bodily and intellectually, a world which was far richer in plants than we do, and they seem to have been more aware of that aspect of the world than we are, for the most part, today. We tend not only to be somewhat ignorant of perfumes but also of plants. In terms of the animal smells, there is far less of a contrast: I am familiar with the smells of all the animal products (milk, urine, etc.), and I am also relatively familiar with the smells of a number of animals: cat, dog, cow, goat, sheep, horse, skunk, and so forth. The same applies to minerals and foodstuffs, where our present-day knowledge would appear to be not unlike that of those composing and reading these texts.

Animal smells are less numerous and varied in most of these passages, and those most commonly occurring are the smells of animal *products*. Aside from pure and good smelling dairy products, for the most part, these are what one would probably classify as bad smells, as seen in the passage from the *Suśrutasaṃhitā* on childhood diseases. This, of course, excludes the long list of animals in the *Mātaṅgalīlā*, which includes only animals that would probably be found in an urban setting, though not all are domesticated (monkey-smell).[115] A particularly striking smell is the smell of the impure carrion-eating crow, which occurs both in the *Mātaṅgalīlā*, as well as in the passage from the *Suśrutasaṃhitā*. Until reading these passages, I never considered that a crow would have a particularly remarkable smell—I have never smelt a crow, nor do I know anyone who has, not in North America or in South Asia. The perfumer Christophe Laudamiel notes of the smell of pigeons, doves, and magpies that they smell "a bit dusty, a bit acidic, a bit of flour, dry, and a bit of fish food without the fishy smell (like dry protein, but not smoked of course)."[116] No doubt, the crow with its diet of rotting, dead animals was viewed as a particularly impure bird. Maybe people did have occasion to smell crows' bodies, though it seems relatively likely that they did not, and, as with the smell of lotus, this might be a case of a certain odor being mentioned, not so much because it was often smelled, but because it was considered innately significant, even if most people had not smelled it.

Not only is an understanding of these smell-values revealing in reading many South Asian texts, but also these aspects of smells and smell-sources contribute to the construction of the other sorts of values. For example, that sandalwood was believed to have the very real and useful values of being cool, generally pure, and very fragrant created a demand for it that contributed to its high exchange value. There is an inseparable relation between the discourse and practice of smells and aromatics. I hinted earlier in the case of the passage from the *Play of Elephants* that some of the significance of certain odors might be derived from practices and discourses outside the realm of Sanskrit texts. It is likely that this is the case for many of the other sources mentioned. But that does not mean that the world of Sanskrit texts exists at all times in an artificial and elite bubble of unreal smells—quite the opposite. Perhaps, ultimately, what I find most notable about these particular sources, these highly academic treatises composed in

Sanskrit, is that the sweet smells of the kitchen, the sour stinks of the unpleasant sick room, the varied odors of the market place, and the cow urine on the street all diffuse into the world of Sanskrit *śāstric* textuality, a world that is so often assumed to be elite, universalizing, and utterly removed from dung and rotten fish.

Smelling in these texts is a way of knowing things about the world. People can use smells in order to tell whether a particular source of smell is pure or impure, cool or warming, aquatic, related to the springtime, and low caste or high caste. Additionally, the sense of smell can be used to tell if sandalwood is good quality, if a person is dying or a child is possessed, if a man has good fortune, and if an elephant is any good or not. In these ways, smells play an important and complex role in epistemology, and given the assumed affective nature of smells, this role is especially pronounced in the epistemology of religious values, be they ethical, aesthetic, auspicious, or purity related.

In addition to informing you about the nature of an odorant, what else might an odor do? The analysis of matter produced by the Nyāya-Vaiśeṣikas is not without use today as an analytic tool. Smell-sources, or odorants, are not just pure and impure, but also, according to their analysis, odorants contain the element earth, and they therefore must display the qualities of all the other sense-objects. At least in everyday life, this is generally the case.[117] Take a little dark brown grain of musk for instance: in addition to the smell of the musk, it also has taste, color, shape, texture, and temperature; and, I suppose, the potential to make a tiny sound. These are all sensible qualities above and beyond a value quality such as purity. As understood in South Asia, smells always have sources, and smell-sources always possess several other sensible qualities. If a fragrance diffuses, anyone smelling it can be sure there is an odorant somewhere, and as with the people who came to find the source of the fragrance released by the burning body of the demoness Stinky (Pūtanā), when they arrive, they might find that the odorant is somebody or something significant.

4

Flowers and Fish in the *Mahābhārata*

Along with ghee, lotus, and cow urine, the smells of flowers and fish were prominent in several sources we saw in the previous chapter. But what did such smells make people do in the imagined world of Sanskrit narratives? When smelling acts occur, what happens to the smeller and the object smelled? We saw a few examples of the effects of smells, but now I focus on two particularly important episodes involving these types of smells in the Sanskrit epic, the *Mahābhārata*. I choose this particular text because it is well-known, even today, and both of the episodes have enduring popularity. This is a short chapter, and I simply want to emphasize a certain role that smells can play in Sanskrit narratives; this will help us understand other materials we will see through the book. As well as highlighting one of the important things that smells make people do in these texts, I also wish to compare what we learn about smells here with an important aspect of smells in modern Western discourses—that of smells as evoking memories.

When discussing my work on smell with people in India, with scholars, perfumers, and others, on many occasions, what first came to the mind of the informant was a smell-related episode from either the *Mahābhārata* or the *Rāmāyaṇa*, and the episodes described in this chapter stood out more than most. Not only have these two epics been read and recited for hundreds of years, but also the Sanskrit versions are simple and accessible, and they were available in many vernaculars. Therefore these epics are, and possibly always were, one of the more important ways in which people have encountered traditional textual reflection on the powers of smell in South Asia. These episodes are not the only references to smelling and odors in the *Mahābhārata*, but it would require an entire book to explore smell in the *Mahābhārata* as a whole. Some readers might feel that the passages I examine have a wider significance in the text, in terms of the greater narrative, as well as the development of certain characters. I will have to leave the exploration of such topics to other more qualified scholars, for here I am only interested in noting the most basic and immediate effects that odors have on people in this type of text. Although epic narrative has its own conventions, we have already seen in the episode of Pūtanā a motif very similar to some of those in this chapter.

The Fragrance of Flowers and the Divine *Saugandhika* Flowers in the *Mahābhārata*

The role of the smell of flowers in South Asia is enormously important, and a study of this topic could quite easily fill a whole book. Therefore, I will try to limit my discussion to certain aspects of flowers that make them unique among sources of smells, focusing on how these qualities are exaggerated or inverted in some narratives and on the results of these exaggerated smells.

Flowers as odorants have some qualities that are distinct from other sources of smells. Although flowers, roots, and other plant parts have been exploited as aromatics for their fragrance, flowers are in many ways unlike other aromatics, such as sandalwood and camphor. Some of the following may seem obvious to the point of being banal, but, in fact, these are all important distinctions to bear in mind:

1. Flowers come from plants, such as trees, shrubs, and herbs and they may be smelled whilst still on the plant, as well as plucked and separated from the plant.
2. Flowers, strung on a thread, are the principal components of garlands.
3. Flowers generally are subject to certain *spatial limitations*.
   - In classical India they tend to be *native species*, not exotic. This is quite unlike the situation in England or California today, for example.
   - In early and medieval South Asia flowers were not (in their fresh state at least) traded long distances, so they were *local produce*.
4. Flowers are also *temporally limited*.
   - They are *seasonal*—a certain species is often available at a certain time of year and associated with other aspects of that season. Were a certain flower to bloom (or be caused to bloom) unseasonably that would be remarkable.
   - They also have the temporal limitation of *fading rapidly*, lasting often only a day or even less. The transience of flowers allows them to be a metaphor for transience more generally; were one to encounter flowers that were not transient in this way, it would be remarkable.
5. Flowers often cost nothing, and sometimes they are not traded at all. Where they are traded they are not so expensive as they are generally not rare—one would not stock a treasury with fresh flowers as one would with aromatic woods. Nevertheless, a permanent supply of flowers might require the endowment of a special garden and the allocation of labor. A gift of flowers costs far less than a gift of sandalwood: they are a *terminal commodity* and cannot be re-traded because they do not last long enough to do so.[1]
6. Flowers very often have an odor: if a flower had no smell this would be notable, and as for those flowers that do have a smell, not surprisingly, they smell either pleasant or unpleasant.

7. As well as fragrant, they are often visually beautiful, which is less universally the case for dried aromatics (e.g., costus root); although, the visual appearance of some dry aromatics (camphor, saffron, sandalwood, musk-ink, aloeswood smoke) is highly admired.
8. The fragrance of flowers also tends to attract bees, as well as people.

Given the above qualities, were one to encounter a rare flower, retrieved with difficulty from a great distance, this would be most remarkable, as we shall see below. Some readers might notice that I have indirectly alluded to several other incidents in Sanskrit literature involving flowers with remarkable properties, but as these do not involve the smell of the flower I will not be able to discuss these here.

All these factors have an impact on what fragrant flowers signify in South Asian culture. For example: How is a flower-bower different to a sandalwood pavilion? In this section, and in the remainder of the book, I will explore some of the issues that will allow me to begin to answer just this sort of question.[2]

Some of the aforementioned qualities of flowers were deliberately exaggerated or inverted in narratives, which would have been quite striking to the reader. Indeed, this theme, of exaggerating one aspect of a sense and/or sense-object, or inverting, exaggerating, or perverting the normal action of a sense and/or sense-object is something we have encountered already. These sorts of sense-conceits seem to have particularly fascinated, charmed, and impressed those who composed and appreciated texts of many varieties in early and later medieval South Asia.

Flowers—local, not exotic, and liable to fade—were probably not expensive items in ancient and medieval India. This is borne out by various statements in *dharma* literature. In terms of theft, which in *dharmaśāstra* texts is punished according to the type of object stolen, flowers are classed together with objects of relatively low value, such as food, water, plants, and small quantities of unhusked grain.[3] The same applies to taxation, where flowers are not classed with livestock and gold but rather with a variety of things that were of lesser value, such as roots, medicine, and firewood.[4] In the *Dharmasūtras*, we are told quite a lot of other things about flowers, including that they are free to gather, like grass and firewood;[5] that Brahmins may not trade in them;[6] and that flowers (and fruit) of trees growing in impure places are not themselves impure.[7] In general, whilst free to gather (presumably from the wild, not from a special garden), flowers do have an exchange value, though it is quite low. Trading flowers was not considered a respectable job for Brahmins, and flowers do not take on the impurity of the location where they grow, at least according to these sources. Yet, this does not mean that flowers themselves cannot become impure, suggested by regulations forbidding wearing other people's garlands.[8] Indeed, that Brahmin householders can wear fresh garlands suggests that flowers themselves are ritually pure. However, the *brahmacārin* celibate Vedic student cannot wear flowers or other ornaments,[9] though no doubt this is because they are sensuous luxuries, avoidance of which increases his "ascetic toil."[10] This is the same reason for which these items are renounced by Buddhist monks, and, indeed, we will see later just how affectively powerful contact or adornment with flowers could be.

Generally speaking, flowers were not rare, not very expensive, not exotic, pure unless tainted, as well as sensuous and unsuitable for ascetics. Turning to the smell of flowers, this perfume (or bad smell) may be carried by the wind away from the flower, allowing a remote experience of this aesthetic aspect of the flower. Typically the smell of a flower travels only a relatively short distance, but as seen with the Buddhist perfume of virtue, and as we shall see shortly, the notion of a perfume that diffuses a great distance seems to have fascinated people. Like the narrative of Satyavatī (discussed later), another narrative concerning a remarkably pleasant fragrance occurs in the *Mahābhārata*, and in this case the source of the smell is a flower, a particularly rare, divine flower, obtained only with great difficulty. More than the diffusiveness of the perfume of this flower, what is emphasized in this episode is the desire the fragrant object creates, not an erotic desire, but a desire to possess the object to permit more experience of the perfume. Good smells in South Asian literature make people move from one place to another, and in this case, I argue that the fact that the wind is involved in the process seems particularly significant.

In the section called the *Āraṇyakaparvan* of the epic *Mahābhārata*, the recently exiled Pāṇḍava brothers are traveling. Arjuna has gone to visit Indra to collect some divine weapons, which will be useful later in getting vengeance on their enemies, the Kaurava brothers. The rest of the Pāṇḍavas, together with their shared wife Draupadī and a significant retinue, are informed by a sage called Lomaśa that they should undertake a pilgrimage to the sacred bathing places. One day, whilst wandering about the beautiful fragrant woods in the vicinity of the hermitage of Nara and Nārāyaṇa near Mount Kailāsa, the wind carries an amazing flower which Draupadī collects. Desiring more, she entreats one of the Pāṇḍava brothers, Bhīma, to go to the source of this highly fragrant flower, the Saugandhika[11] Forest on Mount Gandhamādana ("intoxicating with perfume") where these flowers grow in a pond in the pleasure garden of the god Kubera. In the course of this journey, Bhīma encounters his half-brother (by their father Vāyu, the god of the wind), Hanumān, an intrusion from another epic, the *Rāmāyaṇa*. This episode appears to have proved particularly intriguing to later audiences, for at least two dramatic renditions of this episode exist.[12]

> In that place the **wind blew, with a good smell and pleasant feel**,
> Gladdening all the Pāṇḍavas together with Kṛṣṇa and bulls of sages.
> Then, unexpectedly, a clear wind from the north-east carried
> a thousand-petalled, sun-like, divine lotus.
> Pāñcālī saw that lotus, of divine perfume, and pleasant,
> brought by the wind, pure, fallen on the ground.
> The beautiful one, having found that beautiful, excellent, white water-lily,

> Being extremely joyful, oh king, then said to Bhīmasena:
> "See, oh Bhīma, the divine, very radiant, most excellent flower,
> **Endowed with perfume and form, delight of my mind.**
> But I will offer this one to King Dharma, oh enemy burner,
> For love of me, you should take this one back to the Kāmyaka hermitage.
> If I am dear to you, oh Pārtha, fetch many of these,
> I want to take them back to Kāmyaka hermitage."
>
> **Facing that very wind whence that flower came,**
> Desirous to fetch other flowers, swiftly he went.
>
> He, of great vigor, **smelling that unfettered perfume produced of flowers of all seasons,**
> Unfettered in the forest, like an intoxicated elephant
> His body hair was greatly thrilled; his tiredness removed by his father, with the **wind** on Gandhamādana mountain, **cool with the touch of his father.**[13]

There are several points to note about this passage. First of all, there is the prominent role of (the god of) wind, Vāyu, who also happens to be the father of both Bhīma and Hanumān. While Bhīma travels to find the fragrant lilies, his father the wind soothes and cools his tired body. The wind does this by touching his body, and we are also told at the beginning of the passage that the wind is pleasant to the touch. This should remind us that touch is indeed the special quality of wind according to the schools of thought that associate the elements and the senses. Not only does wind caress and cool his son's body, but also I believe it is not entirely implausible to suggest that wind quite deliberately brings his two sons together in this episode. This task is achieved by means of another of the abilities of the wind—carrying things—in this case the golden, perfumed water lily. The wind also provides what may well be a scent-trail for Bhīma to follow, as he sets out facing the wind that carries the amazing perfume of the flowers of all the seasons. The wind is instrumental in bringing the flower to Draupadī, but it is the perfume and beauty of the flower itself that create in her the desire for more flowers, and it is the subsequent desire of Bhīma to please her that leads him to his brother: wind, perfume, desire, and union.

The flower itself has an especially beautiful smell, as well as a radiant form. As mentioned, in the case of many flowers, perfume and visual beauty are combined, creating particularly attractive objects. Draupadī goes to the flower, and her appreciation of the flower is quite chaste, and she is said to be joyful. Unlike in the case we shall see later, she is in no way stated to be erotically aroused by the flower, nor does she want to keep it for herself, but rather she wishes to offer it to King Dharma.[14] Nevertheless, the flower does create in her a desire to possess more of the same flowers, to have them brought to her—the perfume causes the smelling subject to be joined to the source of the smell, in this case via two instruments: the wind that carried the first flower to her, and Bhīma, who she sends to collect more flowers. But Draupadī does not, at least initially,[15] intend to go to the odorant herself, her union with the odorant is mediated by the wind and the son of the wind. As so often is the case, the perfume-carrying wind is the ultimate go-between where smells are involved. Although in chapter 2, smell was analyzed as good smell and bad smell, again the picture becomes more complex beyond the realm of philosophy: there are different types of fragrant smell, which have different effects on the person who smells them. These fragrances have their source in an object that is possessed of other qualities, and this further complicates what happens when people smell fragrances in the world of Sanskrit literature.

The Smell of Fish in the *Mahābhārata*

There were several references to the smell of fish in the previous chapter. The smell of fish is very strong and distinctive, and not necessarily very pleasant, especially when the fish is not fresh. It is also a smell that one would associate with the sea, or with fishing communities living by rivers. As to the ritual purity of fish in traditional Hindu religious law, *dharmaśāstra*, as Kane notes, "About fish there is no unanimity."[16] In the *Āpastambha Dharmasūtra*, some fish are forbidden, whereas *Manu* initially forbids the eating of all fish but subsequently makes some exceptions.[17] As fish was not clearly prohibited, it was presumably not universally regarded as an impure or disgusting substance prohibited to be smelt by Brahmins according to the sorts of prohibitions seen in chapter 2. Nevertheless, as with the smell of fried onion in our own society, even for those who ate fish, it was most likely not considered desirable outside the context of the preparation and consumption of food, thus a fishy body smell would probably not have been considered fragrant.

This leads us to perhaps the most well-known reference to the smell of fish in Sanskrit literature, and indeed one of the most well-known South Asian narratives in which smell plays a central role. This is the episode in the *Mahābhārata* concerning Satyavatī, the great-grandmother of the Pāṇḍavas and the Kauravas. Satyavatī for a while had a body that smelled of fish, which was clearly distressing to her—as soon as she got a chance to do something about it, she asked for a boon to smell fragrant instead.

First we are told that Satyavatī smells like this because of her association with the fishermen, who presumably always smell of fish.[18] In addition to these social connotations, the smell has obvious aquatic associations, but unlike the lotus, these are not pleasant. When, in the passage, Satyavatī receives a boon, and the sage changes her body smell to a fragrant one, we are told little about the character of this fragrance, but we are told that it is very diffusive, and the diffusiveness of this smell is really quite remarkable: her perfume is said to travel a *yojana* (about nine miles). As discussed in chapter 2, the diffusiveness of a smell is one of the variables of smells which Indian thinkers analyzed, and here this property of a smell is exaggerated to an enormous extent. One of the suggested rationales for the "Buddhist" order of the senses was the spatio-temporal relation between perceiver and perceived, and in this respect, smell fell behind vision and hearing. Yet in this case, the fragrance of Satyavatī is so remarkable that it excels them both, because it is not likely in normal circumstances that someone could be seen or heard at a distance of nine miles:

> . . . which girl, the daughter of the female fish, who smelled of fish, and who was possessed of beauty and goodness, and furnished with all good qualities
> was given then by the king to the ferryman, saying "May she be yours."
> But she, "Truthful" by name, with a bright smile, smelt of fish for some time because of the connection with the fishermen.
> And Parāśara, wandering about on a pilgrimage to sacred bathing places saw her leading a boat in the water in order to be obedient to her father.
> And having seen her, excessively endowed with beauty, desired even by the *siddhas*,
> That wise one, knowledgeable, dutiful, a bull amongst sages,
> desired her of fair appearance, the maiden, the descendent of Vasu.
> She said "Look sir! There are sages standing on the near and far banks,
> While we can be seen by them, how might we have intercourse?"
> Thus addressed by her, that holy master, created a mist
> By means of which it was as if the whole land became dark,
> And then when she had seen that mist created by that most excellent sage
> She was astonished, and that maiden, abashed and intelligent said:
> "Sir, know me to be a maiden, always following the desires of my father,
> and, oh blameless one, my maidenhood would be spoiled by intercourse with you,
> and with my maidenhood spoiled, oh best of twice-born,
> how will I be able to go home, and how could I bear to stay at home, oh wise one?
> When you have reflected thus, sir, do whatever follows."
> And when she had thus spoken, the delighted best of sages said to her:
> "When you have done my favor you will still be a virgin
> And, oh shy one, choose that boon which you desire, oh radiant one!
> My grace has never before been fruitless, oh lady with a bright smile!"
> Thus addressed, she chose a boon: the most excellent fragrance of her body.

And that holy master bestowed (upon her) her heart's desire.
Then, when she had received her boon, delighted, adorned with the qualities of womankind, she had intercourse with that sage of extraordinary actions.
Therefore her name "Fragranced" was renowned on earth,
And men could smell her fragrance from nine miles (a *yojana*) on earth.
Therefore her name "Nine-mile-fragrance" was famous
And as for the holy Parāśara, he went home.[19]

But this is not the end of the role of smell in the narrative concerning Satyavatī, nor is it the beginning. For, although Satyavatī has the smell of fish because she was born from a fish's belly and thus lives with fishermen, the manner in which this fish came to conceive in the first place involves smell, in this case a fragrant smell which has an erotic effect. In the following interpolated passage[20] from the *Mahābhārata* concerning the origin of Satyavatī, King Vasu[21] was obliged to go hunting for deer to provide for the ancestral offerings, just when it was his wife Girikā's fertile period. Wandering, frustrated in his desires, in a forest abounding in the romantically arousing features of springtime, he accidentally ejaculated, and this semen ended up being swallowed by a fish, who conceived Satyavatī. In the critical edition, simply being in the pleasant forest, frustrated, and thinking of his beautiful wife causes the spontaneous ejaculation; in the relatively commonly interpolated passage we are told more about the forest, in particular we are given a detailed list of flowering plants, as well as descriptions of the sounds of springtime. But, it is at the end of the passage, when the king inhales the perfume of the flowers carried by the wind that he becomes joyful and ejaculates:

That king, not transgressing that order of his ancestors,
Wandered hunting, lustful, thinking only of Girikā,
who was excessively endowed with beauty, as if another Śrī in the flesh
[interpolation starts:]
Filled with *aśokas*,[22] *campakas*,[23] mango trees, *tilakas*,[24] and *atimuktakas*,[25]
With *punnāgas*,[26] *karṇikāras*,[27] *bakulas*,[28] with divine trees,
Jackfruit trees, coconut palms, sandalwood trees, as well as *arjuna*[29] trees,
With these and other great trees, pleasant and with tasty fruit
Noisy because it was filled with cuckoos, buzzing with intoxicated bees,
Seeing that forest in the springtime, which was like the divine *Caitraratha* forest of the god Kubera,
Then, he was seized by the god of love, (but) he did not see (his wife) Girikā.

Then, wandering at will, inflamed by lust, that king saw
A delightful place, where the tips of the branches were entirely covered by blossom,
Which was beautified by young (red) shoots, covered with clusters of *aśoka* blossom,
Then, comfortably seated on a branch under a tree,
The king, having smelled a delightful perfume from the flowers, mingled with sweet smells, carried along by the wind, attained joy,
[interpolation ends]
Wandering in the pleasant forest, his semen sprayed forth,
As soon as that semen was sprayed, the king
Collected it with a leaf, (and) that lord (thought): "My semen should not be sprayed in vain,
Nor should my wife's fertile period be fruitless."[30]

Here we see the connection between a fragrant smell, in particular springtime flowers, and the erotic physical response, something we will explore at greater length in the next chapters on perfumery.

Where, in the previous narrative passage, the flowers on Mount Gandhamādana were of all seasons, here they are the natural flowers of only one season, a season that is especially arousing, both for people and for elephants, as noted earlier. For a sexually pent-up man to spontaneously ejaculate when he smells the fragrance of spring flowers while reflecting on his beautiful wife may sound strange to a modern reader, but in this literary context it is quite normal, for the fragrant flowers have a real quality of good-smell, and, not only that, but a good smell is normally automatically attractive and in some cases sexually arousing. The fragrance of spring, responsible for the character of the scent-elephant, puts all beings in rut. Draupadī was also made joyful by the flower and desired to possess more of the remote and exceptional flowers, but she was not said to be erotically excited. Here, the question of possessing the flowers does not arise, because the flowers are in abundance, they are not unusual nor remote, so the king has no need to seek them out. Here, an incidence of fragrant smell, the smell of spring flowers, produces both joy and contributes to sexual arousal. Not all fragrant smells produce the same effect on the agent—the state of the agent, the time, place, and nature of the smell and smell-source all play a complex role in producing a particular effect. We ought also consider whether gender plays a role; it is the male, King Vasu, who is aroused by the smell of springtime, whereas Draupadī merely enjoys the beauty of the smell. On the basis of these two cases alone, it seems difficult to decide whether responses to smells are gendered. But, in the following chapters, we will see many more deliberately arousing smells and perfumes. It would appear in those contexts, at least, that the use of perfumes is equally arousing and pleasing to both males and females.

Returning to the narrative, once Satyavatī has received the boon from the sage, she loses the fishy smell—a problem that started when the fish swallowed the semen ejaculated when King Vasu smelled the flowers—and she thenceforth smells very pleasant.[31] This new smell in turn leads to another development in the narrative. Since this innate bodily perfume is so exceptionally fragrant (and therefore potentially attractive and arousing) and diffusive over a large area, inevitably in the world of Sanskrit literature, someone smells it and consequently desires to find the source of the pleasant and remarkably strong smell. This person is King Śaṃtanu, the father of Bhīṣma:

> One time, that king came to a forest by the Yamunā river
> And he smelled an excellent fragrance which he could not specify.
> Searching for its source, he wandered all around,
> Then he saw the fisherman's girl with divine beauty.
> When he had just seen her, he asked the dark-eyed girl
> "Whose are you, who are you, and what, oh shy one, do you desire to do?"
> She said "I am a fisherman's daughter, I conduct a boat according to righteousness and profit
> By order of my father the great king of the fishermen. Prosperity to you!"
> King Śaṃtanu, having looked at that fisherman's daughter,
> Who was endowed with beauty, sweetness, and fragrance, a beautiful divine image, desired her.[32]

Here we have another erotic smell: Śaṃtanu is attracted, not by the sight of Satyavatī, but by her smell. It is solely this fragrance that is instrumental in leading him to her, where he can see that she also has the qualities of beauty and (sonorous?) sweetness. Just as with the episode of the *saugandhika* flower, and the burning of Pūtanā's body, this smell causes the person smelling it to go to the source, and in this case the source of the smell proves to have other sensual qualities that render her attractive. The wind as an instrument of smell-carrying is not mentioned in this passage. Indeed, the fact that the perfume of her body travels so far is not just a result of the wind, but rather this extreme diffusiveness of the smell is a more likely to be a quality of the body of Satyavatī, which is emphasized as the agent of attraction far more than the wind.

There is a complex play of smells in this narrative. There is the springtime flower-smell that excites the king and gives rise to Satyavatī; the unpleasant fishy smell of Satyavatī, which makes her unhappy and causes her, when given a boon, to ask for her heart's desire: an exceptionally good smell. This exceptionally diffusive fragrance in turn attracts King Śaṃtanu. Smell operates in two places in this narrative by attracting, and also by (creating a fear of) repelling.

Conclusion

Although in the second chapter we saw a narrow and simple philosophical account of all smells, smells in other Sanskrit texts are far more complex. In this brief chapter, we have examined two famous odor-episodes—one involving a fragrance and one a somewhat bad smell—noting some factors that influence the effect of these odors on a person who smells them. Many of these factors relate to the nature of the source of the smell, which is endowed with other qualities aside from smell—additionally time (e.g., springtime); place (e.g., alone in the forest); and the state of the agent (e.g., aroused) played their part in the response to the odor.

One effect of smelling a *fragrant* smell seems to be quite prominent in the *Mahābhārata* (and possibly elsewhere): that a fragrance causes the smeller to desire the source of the smell and frequently impels the smeller to seek out the smell's source. Smells in the *Mahābhārata* do not bring back memories of the past, as they often do in more recent European literature. They do not make people who experience a smell recall a moment in their lives from another *time*. Rather, as we have seen, smells, fragrances in particular, seem to have the result of uniting people and smell-sources (flowers, people) in space: kings navigate dark gardens; half-brothers are united; kings meet their wives; disease-demons are expelled by foul incense; and devotees arrive to worship baby Krishna. The perfect model here is the bee that flies to a fragrant flower in search of nectar.

This highlights a major difference in the treatment of smells in Sanskrit literature when compared with the motif of the odor that evokes memories so prominent in many Euro-American discourses. An odor carried to you by the wind can be perceived apart from the source of that odor. Someone perceiving a fragrance could, in fact, remain apart from the odorant, simply savoring the odor with no interest in the source of that odor, for example, when someone walks past a baker's shop and enjoys the smell but does not enter. The enjoying of an odor separate from any other experience of the odorant is well described by what Mark Johnston calls the "pornographic attitude," by which terminology he wishes "to highlight the error of mentalizing affect. Instead of affect being a way in which the appeal and repulsiveness of other things and other people makes itself manifest, the affective states themselves become the focus of attention, as if affective engagement were an interior, private sensation detachable from one's being taken with or repelled by things."[33]

In these South Asian narratives, such solitary enjoyment of the affective powers of the diffused odor is never enough, and the person smelling the odor wishes unite with the odorant, by going to it or having it brought to them, in order to experience the rest of that other thing or other person. The result of an act of smelling is thus spatial: smellers subsequently move toward or away from the odor, as well as relational: smellers are not just interested in the subjective experience of the odor, but are in some manner concerned with the source of that odor. I do not wish to suggest, however, that this model of smell is not present in modern Western discourses, but rather the register at which this idea is prominent differs. In talking about my research on smell, it is not uncommon for people to tell me a personal anecdote about how a certain smell once evoked a memory of a time or place, whereas no one has ever related a story of how wearing a certain perfume caused someone to pursue them down the street—for us, that story is typically limited to the domain of perfume commercials, and quite often lower-end fragrance products at that.

The model of smell as memory-evoking, which commands middle-class respect in our society, is different from the Sanskrit model. First, the affective powers of an odor are not central to the phenomenon: a stink as much as a perfume can transport your memory. The aesthetic qualities of the odor and odorant at the time of memory may be incidental; even the "pornographic attitude" is not necessarily present. Furthermore, the odorant is of no intrinsic interest; the odor is needed to evoke memories. The subject that smells the odor is not necessarily interested in the affective quality of the odor or in the nature of the odorant. The greatest importance of a memory-evoking odor lies in its instrumental power to connect a person with the self at a former time: smells connect self with self across time—a solipsistic and internal experience. Of course, the memory can be of another place—"that smell reminds me of when I was in India"—but it is still memory that frames the thought of another place, and the smell does not literally and materially transport the person in space. This is a vast contrast with the South Asian model where: (1) A necessarily affective fragrance (2) draws the subject to the odorant, the Other, that the perceiver is very interested in meeting. A larger contrast is harder to imagine, and this understanding of smelling as spatial and as relating the smeller to another person or thing explains the importance of the manipulation of smells in many contexts: human-divine relations, human-demonic relations, subject-monarch relations, and, of course, erotic relations. Smell is above all social, connecting people to other people and to the things in the world.

On the latter note, we saw that in some cases smells can have a powerful erotic impact on the person who experiences the smell. In the case of King Vasu in the forest this was accidental, but in the next chapters we will see how these affective and attractant powers of smell were consciously (and quite understandably) exploited in traditional Indian culture, and that the consequent quest for effective aromatic materials and formulae created a sophisticated and cosmopolitan culture of perfume connoisseurship.

PART THREE

SMELLS IN PRACTICE

5

Moon Juice and Uproar

Perfumery Texts

> Owing to early European interest in Indian Philosophy an impression has been created in European countries that ancient Indians were more concerned with the things of the spirit than the things of this mundane world, which contribute to the enjoyment of the pleasures of life. An English writer defined the ideal of happiness in his country as the possession of "a big boiler and a bull's neck." Though ancient Indians regarded spiritual values with utmost veneration and planned their lives on the basis of these values in accordance with a graded course of spiritual development, they gave due attention to the enjoyment of the pleasures of life so called, for which "a big boiler and a bull's neck" are, of course, necessary.
>
> —P. K. Gode

Whether to please the gods, to project the fragrant fame of the king, or to control other peoples' erotic desires, in a world where odors were understood to be so powerfully affective it makes sense that people would exploit and manipulate smells, primarily by means of the art (*kalā*) of perfumery.[1] South Asia was uniquely well placed in the world in terms of access to varied and exceptional aromatic substances, and from a very early period the wealthy urban population could refer to a remarkable number of woods, roots, flowers, and so on with which to create complex, beautiful—even erudite—perfumes. These aromatics and aromatic creations would not only have been an important feature of everyday (elite and royal) life and religious practices, but they also crop up in many texts, from courtly poetry to manuals of temple ritual.

Perfumes and perfumery are discussed in a remarkably large, diverse, and possibly unique variety of genres: liturgical, prognosticatory, medical, literary, erotic, and encyclopedic. Less technical references to this art are also abundant in many other genres, and the study of perfumery might therefore enrich our reading of many texts. Most important, perhaps, reflection on the nature of the world in which some of these texts would have circulated will also enliven our view of early and later medieval South Asian educated and elite culture, drawing attention to the fact that material culture was every bit as sophisticated as textual culture, and that the two were at times inextricably linked. For us, perfumery is linked to the fashion industry ("Chanel No. 5"), and sometimes to the entertainment industry ("Beyoncé True Star"), but as we shall see, for medieval South Asians perfumes were redolent with the conventions of literature ("Southern Wind"), religion ("Pride of Kāma"), history ("made by [King] Bhoja"), and even sometimes with political theory, as we shall see in the next chapter.

There is a large amount of material here, and I have chosen to discuss it in two chapters that reflect different perspectives on perfumery. In the present chapter, I examine the history, the more literary features, and the structure of *texts* on perfumery. In the next chapter, I explore what the texts say about the perfumes themselves. Perhaps more than any other part of this book, the material here could easily have been the subject of a very long and detailed study in its own right. However, in the interests of presenting a more rounded account of the sense of smell in South Asian culture and religion, I limited myself to a general survey of this particular aspect of smell.

Texts on Perfumery

Such was the importance of perfumes in South Asia that the quest for aromatic materials led merchants to undertake dangerous sea voyages to remote regions, and in chapter 7 I discuss representations of such trade. Back at home, these materials were often very costly, and they were transformed into pastes, incenses, and other products to be consumed at court, in temples and monasteries, as well as in the houses of the wealthy. The processing of aromatics into perfumes and incenses was not always simple, and the knowledge of how to prepare perfumes—one of a conventional list of sixty-four or seventy-two arts (*kalās*)—formed a part of the ideal education of the elite. The texts in this chapter present this knowledge of perfumery in various contexts and in various forms, but the existence of these texts in Sanskrit and Prakrit suggests that this art was taken quite seriously in South Asia at certain times.

What is implied by the word "serious" is another matter. Today, we tend to oppose applying terms such as "serious," "necessary," and "useful" to concepts associated with luxury and pleasure—unless, of course, an aspect of pleasure/luxury is seen as somehow related (by legitimizing, expressing, etc.) to a category we take seriously, such as power. In early South Asia the situation was different, and there was a well-established and explicit discourse that valued pleasure (*kāma*) as an *end in itself*. Thus, such terms as "frivolity" or "luxuria" (or their inverse) are not appropriate for discussing the "importance" of perfumery in South Asia as it was understood by South Asians, at least in the context of worldly life—in the discourses of asceticism, things were more complicated. When, in this book, we see perfumes used in the temple or in the bedroom, we should not think of them as empty fun, as superficial, or, on the contrary, as an instrumental (yet empty and redundant) expression of power or some other principle that we take seriously. Even if we were to insist on reducing these sensuous enjoyments to another factor such as power, the sheer fact that these particular materials were the instrument of choice in achieving another more "serious" goal would require explanation.

We possess a large number of textual sources dealing with the art of perfume blending in South Asia, most of which date from the mid-first millennium CE to the mid-second millennium CE. Despite the relative abundance of sources, only three texts survived that are entirely devoted to this art, the *Gandhasāra* and *Gandhavāda*, preserved together in one manuscript, and another related text called the (Anup) *Gandhasāra* preserved in one manuscript in the Anup Sanskrit Library in Bikaner. We know, however, that there were other such treatises, now lost, and I discuss them below and in the appendix. Aside from these three perfumery texts, the rest of our sources are sections and chapters devoted to this art included in other texts. The variety of texts that contain materials on perfume blending is quite remarkable; it reveals the diverse contexts in which perfumery was deemed relevant.[2] There are discussions of perfumery in works on medicine,[3] erotics,[4] astrology/omens,[5] alchemy,[6] *tantras/āgamas*,[7] *purāṇas*;[8] as well as in encyclopedic works[9] (including the eleventh-century CE *Lōkōpakāra* composed in Kannada);[10] and in one famous verse-anthology, the *Śārṅgadharapaddhati*.

These multiple genres reflect the diverse understandings and uses of perfumes and aromatics in South Asia. Like food, aromatics were believed to interact with the constitution of the body and thus were treated in medical texts. Perfumes were believed to be important accessories to lovemaking and the elegant life of the man-about-town, and therefore they were discussed in texts on erotics. Perfumes were also essential materials in several forms of ritual worship, and thus they are discussed in scriptures and manuals describing such rites. Finally, as perfumery was one of the sixty-four (or seventy-two for the Jains) arts (*kalās*), any text claiming to present an encyclopedic survey of knowledge, especially pertaining to royal life, ought to contain a section dealing with this topic. To summarize: perfumes were indispensable to the goal of pleasure (*kāma*), and the informed consumption of them was a vital part of what it meant to be a cultivated person. These odorous substances mattered: association with them and the possession of expertise concerning them played an essential role in "fashioning" the ideal man-about-town, the successful ruler, not to mention a great many representations, both textual and material, of gods and semi-divine beings.

The different genres of text also present varied perspectives on the goals of perfumery. In erotic texts and in the complex perfumery texts, perfumery is a sensuous and erudite pleasure, almost a high-class game, as perfumery was in medieval Japan.[11] In texts on courtly life, accounts of perfumery display how well the ideal king fulfils his worldly functions and how well he "enjoys the world" (even in private), to use an important metaphor from medieval South Asia.[12] In medical texts and astrological texts, perfume recipes are given to balance the humors and as part of a generalized discourse on the meaning of materials pertaining to the body. In liturgical texts, their function is, in part, practical, that is, giving instructions on how to prepare various materials; yet, these texts also authorize, clarify, and disseminate knowledge of the olfactory splendors of the icon in the temple.

The History of Writing on Perfumery

The earliest texts that mention aromatic preparations in any detail appear to be medical texts; some *purāṇas*; and then, at a later date, an important text on omens, the *Great Compendium*, *Bṛhatsaṃhitā*. Only at a later stage, from approximately the late centuries of the first millennium CE onward, do we see significant materials on perfumery incorporated into texts on erotics and courtly life.[13] It is also around the same period, possibly a little later, that we start to hear of texts that deal entirely with perfumery.

As R. T. Vyas discusses, and as we shall see later in certain cases, there are considerable overlaps in several of the texts: sometimes the same verse is found in several texts, and sometimes the style of a passage about a certain topic is very similar from one text to another.[14] Vyas tries to make use of this in dating the texts, but I am less inclined to do so because some of what were apparently the most important texts on perfumery were lost, and thus we are definitely missing the whole picture of textual interactions. Also, I think that some of this material may have been a floating perfumery tradition that may have repeatedly been used in numerous texts over a long period, rendering inadvisable an attempt at a rigorous textual history. I should also add that it is not my intention here to list every text that treats of perfumery in some form, rather I wish to theorize the textual culture of perfumery based on a few important examples.

Before turning to look at the texts entirely devoted to perfumery, I shall spend some time thinking about two of the earlier texts that contain passages on perfumery. In one case, the *Great Compendium*, *Bṛhatsaṃhitā*, the text is relatively well-known; I reflect on why such a text deals with perfumery and why it does so in such a distinctive way. In the second case, the *Haramekhalā*, the text is not so well-known, and I highlight the importance and interest of this unusual text.

Perfumes in *The Great Compendium*, the *Bṛhatsaṃhitā*

Varāhamihira's huge book on omens, dating from the mid-sixth century of the Common Era: *The Great Compendium*, or *Bṛhatsaṃhitā*, contains, perhaps, our earliest substantial text on perfumery. As with many other materials on perfumery, this account is embedded in another text, and that may be why it survived so long, especially given the enduring popularity of the *Bṛhatsaṃhitā*. Although the perfumes described are, in some cases, said to affect people in various ways, they are not actually treated as omens—so what is a detailed account of perfumery doing in this text? The section on perfumery (chapter 77 in Bhat's well-known translation) appears in a part of the text dealing with erotic matters, following a chapter on aphrodisiacs (chapter 76) and preceding a chapter on sexual union (chapter 78).[15] The latter chapter in turn is followed by a chapter specifying auspicious and inauspicious types of beds and couches (chapter 79), and chapters on gemology (chapters 80–83), that mention the auspiciousness of these materials—both beds and gemstones are regarded as useful accessories to lovemaking. The chapter on perfumes also follows soon after the lengthy sections dealing with the meaning of bodily signs of men (chapter 68) and girls (chapter 70), including prognostication by means of the smell of semen. This places the chapter squarely in the domain of the investigation of things human and corporeal, the prognosticatory "reading" of the body, yet this is an expanded account of that science and perfumes are placed at the erotic, practical, and material end of the spectrum. Although perfumery is not directly connected with prognostication, Varāhamihira must have thought this was an appropriate place to include such useful information, and he uses the subject matter of this chapter to demonstrate his mathematical expertise in the field of combinatorics. As we shall see later in the book, mathematical expertise was closely associated with both the learning of the astrologer and the evaluator of precious commodities.

Varāhamihira famously provides a number of perfume formulae in which, from a given number of ingredients placed in a grid, numerous combinations can be made, leading in some cases to a vast number of potential perfumes. Not only does Varāhamihira provide these formulae, but he also gives an early, rather complex, algorithm for calculating how many perfumes one can make from a given number of ingredients.[16] In one case, up to 43,680 perfumes can be made.[17] As Wujastyk notes, this would have been of commercial importance, yet I wonder to what extent these mathematical exercises in perfumery may have been a source of intellectual delight for the educated connoisseur of perfume, a intellectual-aesthetic delight not unlike the complex mathematical style of church bell ringing popular in England, known as "change ringing," or the pleasure that Baxandall suggests trained Florentine merchants might have taken in observing and analyzing paintings containing figures of perspective and volume.[18] Later perfumery texts additionally contain sophisticated verbal puzzles that seem designed to entertain and impress the cultivated makers and users of perfumes. As we will see, another text contains the same sorts of combinatoric formulae Varāhamihira gives, taken still further in their magnitude; thus, I suggest that pleasures of perfumery were not entirely olfactory but also included the clever delights of combinatorics and word games.

To translate and discuss in full one of the more complex combinatoric formulae would take far too much space, so I present a less complex formula, still of a mathematical nature, a perfume formula which takes the form of a pandiagonal magic square, in which the aromatics are to be placed in cells of a grid (*kacchapuṭa*) in proportions such that, when combining any four ingredients in a row (including the diagonals, hence "pandiagonal"), they always produce eighteen parts of the desired aromatic mixture.[19] (See table 5.1) The quantities in the grid range from one part to eight parts. As Hayashi suggests, were a grid containing the numbers 1–16 used "the ratio, 16:1, of the largest to the smallest of the numbers used in that square would have been too large for his purpose."[20] The combined aromatics are then also finished with two of the common processes of perfumery that we shall discuss later (rousing and fumigation). I have retained the use of the special number terminology in Sanskrit whereby certain numbers are indicated by objects that famously are found in that number, so, for example, moon = 1:

> Two, three, senses [i.e., five], or eight parts aloeswood, *patra*,[21] frankincense and *śaileya*;[22]
> sense-fields [i.e., five], eight, sides [i.e., two], or fires [i.e., three]: of *priyaṅgu*,[23] *mustā*,[24] *rasa*,[25] *keśa*.[26]
> Of *spṛkkā*,[27] cinnamon, *tagara*, and of *māṃsī*,[28] *kṛta* [i.e., the side of the die marked "four"], one, seven, or six parts;
> Seven, seasons [i.e., six], Vedas [i.e., four], moon [i.e., one] of *malaya* sandalwood, *nakha*,[29] *śrīka*,[30] or *kundurūka*.[31]
>
> When four raw materials are mixed in whatever way in a sixteenfold grid
> They, the blended perfumes and so on, [are] then eighteen parts.
> Mixed with *nakha*, *tagara*, and frankincense, roused with the powder of nutmeg, camphor, and musk
> They are to be censed with *guḍa* mollases and *nakha*, [and thus] are to be made the perfumes [called] Auspicious in All Directions (*sarvatobhadra*).[32]

The perfumes made in this manner are called by the word *sarvatobhadra*, meaning "auspicious in all directions" and sometimes referring to a certain type of diagram. Possibly perfumes made in such a manner were actually held to partake in the auspiciousness of the figure used to create them, again linking the auspicious

Table 5.1 **Diagram of the Grid of Perfumes**

aguru 2	patra 3	turuṣka 5	śaileya 8
priyaṅgu 5	mustā 8	rasa 2	keśa 3
spṛkkā 4	tvac 1	tagara 7	māṃsī 6
malaya 7	nakha 6	śṛīka 4	kundurūka 1

to the aesthetically pleasing. Earlier I suggested that, in addition to being of use in creating combinations of perfumes, and in thinking about the mathematics of combinatorics, the use of such a grid could have been a source of intellectual pleasure. Later we will see several formulae for perfumes that are, in their own way, just as intellectualized as the above grids, and it seems more than likely that manipulating their clever features also constituted a pastime for the highly educated.

Girdle of Hara, Haramekhalā

Along with the perfumery texts, perhaps the other most extensive source on perfumery is the *Girdle of Hara* (that is, Śiva), the *Haramekhalā*. This fascinating text, which deserves further study, was composed in Prakrit by a certain Māhuka (Mādhuka in Sanskrit) and dates most probably from the ninth or tenth centuries of the Common Era.[33] It is difficult to categorize because it discusses a variety of matters: the 1,500 verses are divided into seven chapters dealing with curiosities and wonders, methods to defeat enemies, subjugation of people, medicine, and perfumery.[34] The final two chapters deal with arboriculture and food, and minerals respectively.[35] There is also a Sanskrit gloss (*chāyā*) of variable quality, together with a Sanskrit commentary of uncertain date and authorship. This latter commentarial text is in itself a useful source of materials on perfumery. In terms of our chronology, the *Girdle of Hara* is somewhat later than the *Bṛhatsaṃhitā* and probably earlier than the *Gandhasāra*.

The use of Prakrit for this text is notable as the author, Māhuka, was evidently a Śaiva and one might think a Śaiva scholar writing in this period would compose such a text in Sanskrit.[36] It is perhaps significant that a fragment of one of the lost texts devoted to the science of perfumery, the *Gandhayukti* of Īśvara, quoted by the Kashmiri Bhaṭṭotpala in his commentary (966–969 CE) on the *Great Compendium* of Varāhamihira, is also in Prakrit.[37] Furthermore, in the *Complete Man-About-Town*, the *Nāgarasarvasva*, a text on erotics and lifestyle that I shall discuss more fully, the author mentions a text by a certain Lokeśvara as one of his sources on perfumery. Is Bhaṭṭotpala's Īśvara as mentioned in his commentary on the *Great Compendium* the same author of a text on perfumery as this Lokeśvara? If this is indeed the same work, we might conclude that this work was particularly prominent at the time, approximately from the tenth to twelfth century CE. Could it be that texts on certain technical/material matters such as perfumery—the very sorts of material that were starting to be included in texts more explicitly devoted to pleasure—were, for a period prior to or around the tenth century, sometimes composed in Prakrit? The *Haramekhalā*, together with a small fragment of the *Gandhayukti*, raise the possibility that there was a body of non-Jaina *śāstric* technical literature in Prakrit at this time.

I will discuss the structure and framing of the *Girdle of Hara* again, but for now, I mention some more interesting features of this text, which is arguably more "ornamented" than the *Great Compendium* (*Bṛhatsaṃhitā*), yet considerably simpler in form than the *Essence of Perfume* (*Gandhasāra*). For reasons of space, I decided to focus my attention in this chapter on the latter text, the *Essence of Perfume*, but I emphasize that the *Girdle of Hara* is a very important source on perfumery.

As with the *Great Compendium*, and as with most, if not all, Sanskrit texts on perfumery the names and descriptions of perfumes in the *Girdle of Hara* are poetic and playful, a phenomenon that is perhaps most well developed in the *Essence of Perfume*. Like in the *Essence of Perfume*, the terminology for aromatics in this text is idiosyncratic and at times suggestive. Frequently, in the *Girdle of Hara*, the cooling and erotic associations of perfumes are highlighted, a typical description being: "this oil, cool as a row of moon rays, is dear to the bodiless [i.e., god of love, Kāma]."[38] But the most interesting formulae correlate the ingredients of preparations with parts of the body of a bird and an elephant.[39] The formula for the "bird incense" is perhaps the most interesting in the light of the lengthier commentary provided. The unusual suggestive vocabulary and form of this recipe, of course, make it rather challenging to translate, especially because the ingredients that constitute the "body" of the perfume evoke other meanings (for example, *māṃsī* = "flesh"/"jatamansi root"). Here is a modest attempt at a translation of the "bird incense" in which I have tried to convey the strange, suggestive terminology (we should also bear in mind that the Sanskrit might not accurately reflect the original Prakrit).[40] Translations of aromatics are provisional and based (for the most part) on the glosses in the commentary:

> Dense (nutgrass rhizome) head,
> *tagara* eyes,
> wavering (Indian frankincense) throat,
> body made of *kaṅku* (a grain? *priyaṅgu*? N.B. *kaṅka* means "heron"),
> wings made of fingernail (fragrant shell operculum),
> a mouth of flesh (Indian spikenard),
> feet made of goddess (*spṛkkā*, fenugreek?),
> this is an incense called "*kalahaṃsaka*" [a type of aquatic bird], that is pleasant (or juicy) with the sweet sound that is honey, and whose luster is increased by association with the Lake Mānasa that is a cultivated, beautiful woman.[41]

The commentary, in addition to providing synonyms for the aromatics explains that this incense, when considered as a *kalahaṃsa* bird, "has a beauty increased by association with the lake Mānasa,"[42] a conventional annual abode of this bird. The word *mānasa*, however, also means "mental, related to the mind." Thus, the incense itself when used is said in the commentary to have "a beauty distinguished by contact with the lake-that-is-the-heart [i.e., the mind] of beautiful women."[43] Thus, the two readings are explained. At the end of the commentary we are told that "there is the imposition of a multipart metaphor on the beautiful ingredients for the poetry to be striking, but the measure of all of them is equal parts."[44] The verse does not appear to take full advantage of the strange terminology in this text, however, since "fingernail wings" and "goddess feet" are striking but not especially appropriately matched terms, though some of the other terms seem to work a little better, for example "flesh mouth," which is, admittedly, not perfect for a bird. The elephant formula is also a mixed success, though maybe it is the difficulty of these texts that obscures our full appreciation. It is possible to imagine a more thoroughly worked out verse of this nature, and a clearer one, where all the punning names of aromatics (e.g., jatamansi root = flesh) match the metaphorical context somewhat better—and indeed that is what we shall see in the *Essence of Perfume*. But we should set aside the wonderful *Girdle of Hara* for the moment and turn to other texts on perfumery.

Lost Texts on Perfume Blending and Perfumery

Texts devoted entirely to describing the technical art of perfumery, *gandhaśāstra*, appear to be a relatively late genre because they are not attested until the tenth century.[45] I discuss a few of the lost texts on perfumery, but for a more linear presentation of all the lost texts we know about, see the appendix.

As I briefly noted, it appears the earliest attested reference to a text devoted to perfumery is in Bhaṭṭotpala's tenth-century CE commentary on the *Great Compendium* of Varāhamihira, where he mentions and quotes from a text called the *Gandhayukti* ("Perfume Blending") by a certain Īśvara, which, like the *Girdle of Hara*, was composed in Prakrit:

> It is stated by Īśvara in his own *Gandhayukti*:
> "The moist placed in the moist is called 'piercing' (*vedha*);
> moreoever 'rousing' (*bodhaḥ*) is powder in the powdered, [and] it is clear-smelling."[46]

As I noted, this text may also be mentioned by the author Padmaśrī in a text on erotics (*kāmaśāstra*) called the *Complete Man-About-Town*, or *Nāgarasarvasva*; a text that shows some Buddhist features and which was composed sometime between 800 and 1300 CE.[47] Here Padmaśrī mentions a text by a certain Lokeśvara as one of his sources on perfumery.[48] If this is indeed the same work we might conclude that this work on perfumery, the *Gandhayukti*, by Īśvara/Lokeśvara was particularly prominent at the time.

A number of lost works that appear to deal specifically with perfumery are mentioned in an important commentary on the mid-to-late eleventh century CE *Cikitsāsaṃgraha* of Cakrapāṇidatta: that is to say, the commentary called the *Ratnaprabhā* of Niścalakara which was probably composed in Bengal in the late twelfth century CE.[49] Niścalakara quotes a number of works though it is not always clear whether some of these are different designations for the same work or references to authors as opposed to titles. Texts on perfumery Niścalakara quotes are a *Gandhaśāstra* by Bhavadeva,[50] the *Gandhaśāstranighaṇṭu*,[51] the *Gandhatantra*,[52] and the *Gandhatantraśāstra*, as well as verses attributed to Pṛthvīsiṃha and to *gāndhikāḥ* (perfumers).[53] To confuse matters still more, it is not clear in every case whether these are actual titles of texts (*The Treatise on Perfume*) or merely generic types of text ("in his treatise on perfume . . ."). For a clearer presentation of this material see the appendix.

By far the most intriguing of these lost texts is the *Gandhaśāstra* attributed to a certain Bhavadeva. Now, a man named Bhavadeva was an important Bengali author who composed several works, some of which survived and some of which were lost.[54] This Bhavadeva appears to have flourished around 1100 CE. His surviving works treat various topics of *dharmaśāstra*: judicial procedure, the rites of Sāmavedin brahmins, and religious penances. He also wrote a treatise on the *Pūrvamīmāṃsā* philosophy (the *Tautātitamatatilaka*)[55] and a text on purification in the case of impurity from a dead body.[56] We possess an inscription from Orissa that appears to praise the accomplishments of this same Bhavadeva. This inscription records his endowment of a reservoir as well as a temple and sacred images of Nārāyaṇa and other Vaiṣṇava deities.[57] The inscription also relates that he was a Brahmin, descended from the minister of peace and war of the king of Vaṅga, and that Bhavadeva himself was a minister to King Harivarmadeva. In addition to describing his lineages and endowments, this important inscription also praises his scholarly achievements—thus we possess for Bhavadeva surviving works and a medieval representation of his scholarly prowess. He is said to be a master of philosophy; astrology ("another Varāha[mihira]"); law; *mīmāṃsā* hermeneutic philosophy; as well as "proficient and unmatched in all the arts of poetry, *āgama*s, texts on statecraft, medicine, the science of weapons and so on" (*sakalakavikalāsv āgameṣv arthaśāstreṣv āyu[r]vvedāstravedaprabhṛtiṣu kṛtadhīr advitīyo*).[58]

It is very tempting to think that this well-documented Bengali Bhavadeva from around 1100 is the same person who is quoted as an authority in the late twelfth-century commentary of the Bengali Niścalakara. If we do accept this, then for the first time here we have quite a good glimpse at the sorts of people and institutions that fostered the production of texts on perfumery in medieval South Asia. Bhavadeva was a wealthy and well-connected Bengali Brahmin able to fund the construction of a reservoir and a temple, including endowing sacred images. Following the family tradition, he was engaged in service to the king. He was a renowned scholar of law, astrology/horoscopy, and *mīmāṃsā* philosophy, as well as medicine and other topics. And he appears to have authored a text on perfumery, though only the sections on evaluation and purification of aromatics survive, so we do not know what sorts of formulas the rest of this text might have contained. Not long after Bhavadeva was working, Niścalakara, also working in Bengal, had access to this treatise on perfumery, which he regarded as an important authority on aromatic substances. If we accept the identity of the two Bhavadevas, we can see the study of perfumery was a highly respectable activity for some educated, wealthy, and well-connected Brahmins at the turn of the second millennium CE. Not only was composing a treatise on perfumes a respectable endeavor but one also assumes there was an audience for such texts.

There are also some materials concerning perfumery in the fourteenth-century *Śārṅgadharapaddhati* composed by Śārṅgadhara of Śakambharī.[59] This anthology is remarkable in that it not only contains verses dealing with the usual subject matter found in such anthologies—poetry, women, love, dharma—but it also contains more typically encyclopedic material on numerous other topics, including perfumery. In this text, the verses on perfumery are contained within the section on secret signs of lovers and so forth (*saṃketādivivṛti*). This places the material in a very similar context of erotic urban intrigue as the section on perfumery in the *Nāgarasarvasvam* (which is, in fact, quoted in this text), as well as in a similar context of material accessories to the erotic we see in the *Great Compendium*, *Bṛhatsaṃhitā*.[60] Here also, in addition to the verses quoted from the *Nāgarasarvasva*, the *Complete Man-About-Town*, we find a verse from a lost text, which from the title appears to have been devoted solely to perfumery, the *Gandhadīpikā* (*The Illuminator of Perfumes*, or *The Perfumed Lamp*):

> One part camphor, *nakha*, *giri*,[61] musk, *jatāmāṃsi*, lac, two parts of *malaya* sandalwood and aloeswood. The clever man should cense clothes and house and so forth with [the above] mixed and ground with *guḍa* molasses.[62]

This reference to the *Gandhadīpikā* brings me to another source of information on lost perfumery texts. The *Ṭoḍarānanda* is a massive Sanskrit encyclopedic text commissioned by the emperor Akbar's finance minister, Ṭoḍaramalla, and prepared for him by several scholars in Benares sometime in the late sixteenth century. In the medical part of this encyclopedia, in the section on disorders of wind, the compilers quote passages from at least three other lost texts on perfumery: the *Light on Fragrance* (*Parimalapradīpa*), the *Document on the Light on Perfume* (*Gandhapradīpapatrikā*), and the *Treatise on Perfume* (*Gandhatantra*).[63] These titles might now sound somewhat familiar, and indeed some of these passages are extremely similar to some of the passages from lost perfumery texts quoted by Niścalakara in his commentary. For example, in discussing the *evaluation* of fragrant shell operculum (*nakhī*), the *Ṭoḍarānanda* quotes a passage very similar to one on this topic attributed to Pṛthvīsiṃha by Niścalakara. And the passage on the *purification* of shell operculum in the *Ṭoḍarānanda* would seem to correspond to that from the *Treatise on Perfume* (*Gandhaśāstra*) of Bhavadeva quoted by Niścalakara.[64] Thus the works of Bhavadeva and Pṛthvīsiṃha, as well as the *Gandhatantra* (assuming these are all three distinct texts) appear to have been important authorities on perfumery, cited in late sixteenth-century, as well as in late twelfth-century, Bengal. Of course, some of the passages given in the

Ṭoḍarānanda might be lifted from another compiled text, one that might have possessed a title on the lines of "perfume treatise"—this is, after all, what we see with the two texts called *Essence of Perfume* (*Gandhasāra*), which are different yet share some materials. And those texts mentioned by Niścalakara might also have borrowed from other sources that were later available to the compilers of the *Ṭoḍarānanda*. If Bhavadeva was indeed the author and not the compiler of his perfumery treatise, then we can see that his writings circulated for several centuries. It is even quite possible that parts of the surviving two texts called *Essence of Perfume* (*Gandhasāra*) and also the *Lore of Perfume* (*Gandhavāda*) contain passages that were in the texts of Bhavadeva, Pṛthvīsiṃha, and so on. It is also noticeable that these three latter texts, which survive in their entirety, are not cited or quoted in the sources already discussed. Are these texts, which I shall presently discuss, perhaps later? Or were they composed in a context that had little contact with the places where the previous compilations and commentaries were produced?[65]

Considering this somewhat fragmentary information, it appears that some of these lost *Gandhaśāstra* texts may have been first produced prior to, or around the tenth century. After this time, Sanskrit texts dealing specifically with perfumery appear to have been produced and cited in certain circles until the sixteenth century and possibly beyond.

This loss of many of these texts in the present day is noteworthy. In reflecting on his own early historical researches E. H. Carr noted, "It never occurred to me to enquire by what accident or process of attrition that minute selection of facts, out of all the myriad facts that must have once been known to somebody, had survived to become *the* facts of history."[66] In the case of the texts dealing only with perfumery, it seems fair to say that, for the most part, the "facts" have *not* survived, and that what little has survived did so almost by accident. We possess only two manuscripts containing a total of three complete texts on perfumery, and the other materials we possess are fragments, or short sections contained within texts of other genres, such as texts on medicine, prognostication, general anthologies, and rites of worship. These latter are texts that people did choose to copy and retain over many centuries and therefore survived. Although, around the turn of the first millennium CE, it appears that Sanskrit texts devoted to perfumery were deemed important, evidently by the mid to late second millennium they were no longer in demand and were no longer copied and preserved, even though from the references to them it appears they were previously relatively readily available to people with access to good manuscript collections. Yet, this is not a case of the voice of the subaltern remaining unrecorded or being suppressed—these are very elite texts, for the most part in Sanskrit, dealing with the luxury lives of the wealthy, educated, and, above all, powerful. Many of the other texts associated with such milieux have survived and, after all, people in South Asia have continued to use perfumes until the present day, so what happened to these texts and to this perfumery culture?

A detailed answer to this question lies outside the scope of this book, though I believe it likely that this courtly perfume culture was displaced by Islamic and Persianate perfume culture and practices (which were themselves inflected by Indian perfume culture), and ultimately by European perfume culture—as we shall see, exoticism and novelty were part of the South Asian perfumery scene from early times. This is not to say that traditional "Sanskritic" perfumes did not continue to be made in some contexts, but rather that they ceased to be what the elite generally wrote about in their various technical discourses of luxury.

The picture is quite complicated. A perfumery text called the *Gandhavāda*, which Gode dates from 1350 to 1550 is provided with a Marathi commentary,[67] and also contains two sections composed in Hindi *dohā* couplets.[68] One of these sections refers to frankincense as *lobāna* (ultimately from Arabic *lubān*), and the Marathi commentary on the same section appears to introduce an extra ingredient: ambergris (*ambara*) associated, above all, with Islamic perfumery.[69] The section of Hindi couplets also refers to a certain Siṅghaṇa as the creator of a fragrant powder, and Gode suggests this might be the Yādava King Siṅghaṇa (1210–1247).[70] These Hindi verses with Marathi commentary, and what turn out to be quite common references throughout the text to *lobāna* and ambergris, along with references to *tavakṣīra* (*tabashir*), perhaps give a taste of a textual expression (and practice) of perfumery that was becoming increasingly vernacular, local, and at the same time somewhat Persianate in aroma.[71] Included here, in the mostly Sanskrit *Gandhavāda*, the Hindi verses also demonstrate the manner in which the primacy of Sanskrit as a medium for the discourse (and terminology) of perfumery was starting to fade or at least becoming somewhat mixed by the mid-second millennium CE.

Similar in contents to the *Gandhavāda* is another surviving perfumery text in Sanskrit also called the *Essence of Perfume* (*Gandhasāra*) that exists in the form of one manuscript in the Anup Sanskrit Library in Bikaner.[72] To distinguish between this latter text and the text described by P. K. Gode in the Bhandarkar Oriental Research Institute (BORI) in Pune, I shall call the one in Bikaner the "Anup *Gandhasāra*." I was briefly able to examine this manuscript in summer 2010, and I will present some preliminary observations. Broadly, the text begins with some passages also found in the BORI *Gandhasāra*, and then much of the rest of the text appears to be formulae given in (and similar to) the *Gandhavāda*, and thus there are also references to ambergris and so on.[73] The opening verses can even be read as stating that this is an abbreviation of the *Gandhavāda*, and in places the text appears to directly cite the *Gandhavāda* (for example, *iti Gandhavādaḥ*). The perfume formulae appear better preserved than in the extant *Gandhavāda*, and there is a Sanskrit commentary which, like the Marathi commentary on the *Gandhavāda*, relates the quantities of aromatics to be used. In the opening verses, we are told that all the formulae are stated in Sanskrit, which suggests that this might not always be the case in perfumery texts or possibly in one of the sources of this text. Toward the end of the text, there are a number of formulae for *covā*, a perfume that is mentioned in Indo-Persian sources, as well as formulae for rose/pink pills (*gulālaguṭikā*—*gulāla* being from the Persian).[74] The text is evidently compiled, and I would suggest that the formulae for *covā* were composed between the fifteenth and seventeenth century CE.

These two texts seem to show the "Sanskritic" perfumery tradition blending with a more Indo-Persian style and vocabulary of perfumery. However, in cases where courtly Sanskritic culture was later encouraged, new texts of a more traditional sort could still be produced. In a text that I have not yet mentioned, the late seventeenth century/early eighteenth century vast encyclopedia called the *Śivatattvaratnākara*[75] by the Vīraśaiva king, Basavarāja of Keḷadi,[76] we find some very late Sanskrit material on perfumery.[77] In a format possibly modeled on another Southern courtly encyclopedia, the *Delight of the Mind* (*Mānasollāsa*), this text also discusses the enjoyment of perfumes (*gandhānām upabhoga*). Yet, unlike in the *Mānasollāsa*, where the various aromatic preparations are described in different sections scattered throughout the other daily pleasures of the king, this text groups all aromatic preparations together in one place. Not only does the encyclopedic format and structure emulate the *Mānasollāsa*, but the *Śivatattvaratnākara* also contains many perfume formulae taken from that source.[78] In addition to deriving materials from the *Mānasollāsa*, the chapter on perfumery incorporates much material from the section on perfumes in the *Bṛhatsaṃhitā*—our oldest and apparently most enduring source.[79] Indeed, when compared to the highly complex, playful BORI *Gandhasāra*, this later text, although it attempts to resurrect Sanskritic courtly perfume culture in a textual form, in fact bears witness to the loss of the flourishing and evolving "Sanskritic" perfumery culture that preceded it by only a few centuries. The text also suggests an evolving concept of a "classical" Sanskrit perfumery, found only in such texts as this, in temple rites, and in the descriptions found in *kāvya* literature. This text does not so much reflect the perfumes of the times as create an archive of Sanskrit perfume classics.

One final point to bear in mind in surveying the variety and history of perfumery texts is the number of specialized glossaries of materials (*nighaṇṭus*) that accompany the perfumery texts and chapters. Bhaṭṭotpala provides one for the *Bṛhatsaṃhitā*; there is one in the *Haramekhalā*; and the final chapter of the *Gandhasāra* provides an extensive glossary of perfumery terms, in addition to advice on the examination of aromatic materials.[80] Evidently these texts were difficult to read when they were produced, owing to the idiosyncratic vocabulary often used for aromatic substances in them. In many cases, as we have seen, all that now survives from perfumery texts is the technical discussion of aromatics and their purification as quoted in medical sources. That contemporaries of these texts needed assistance in reading them should perhaps make us feel somewhat better in the face of the difficulties we encounter today in understanding them—some of the perfume formulae are incredibly puzzling and in some cases deliberately so.

A More Ornate Textual Culture of Perfumery—The *Gandhasāra*

We now turn to the *Gandhasāra* (a title meaning both the "*Essence of Perfume*" and "*Sandalwood*"), one of the three surviving treatises on perfumery, of which it is perhaps the most complete and arguably the most complex. Composed by a certain Gaṅgādhara, about whom we know nothing, the text is very difficult to date, though the editor, R. T. Vyas suggests a date in the latter half of the twelfth century CE.[81] Although the words used for aromatics in this text are not as heavily influenced by Persian (or possibly Urdu, or Arabic) as the *Gandhavāda*, the *Lore of Perfume*, nevertheless, there are references (notably confined to one small section) to a substance and preparation named *javādi*.[82] I shall not provide the details here, but I believe this word is ultimately derived from the Persian or Arabic *zabād* and refers to the perfume ingredient called civet. Cognate forms of this word (such as *javādi*) start to appear in Indic language sources from the late thirteenth century CE and are relatively common by the fourteenth and fifteenth centuries CE.[83] Thus, I would tentatively date the text in its attested form a little later than Vyas does—maybe to the fourteenth century or after, though some parts could well be earlier.

The *Essence of Perfume* is a rich source of information on many aspects of perfumery, consisting of three sections: the first on the processes and theory of perfumery, the second providing formulae, and the third a glossary and guide to the examination of raw materials. In this part of the chapter, I focus on the second section containing formulae, in particular on the literary aspects of this text. But before discussing the possible significance of this phenomenon, I think it best to see exactly what I mean by literary perfumery.

The *Gandhasāra* not only contains some introductory benedictory verses (that I examine in the next chapter), but also contains simple poetic verses at the commencement of several sections, especially in the second section (*prakaraṇam*), which contains the formulae. This section, for example, starts as follows, with a rather simple piece of *kāvya*, and, interestingly, the verse makes no immediately obvious reference to anything particularly aromatic:[84]

> Deserving of the honor of bowed gods and *dānava*s, possessed of water from the jars that are the breasts of Gaurī,
> With supreme ornaments of the best of snakes, may Hara, moon-possessing, provide joy.[85]

Further verses are also found preceding the section on *udvartana* (rubbing paste), addressed to Kṛṣṇa, Rāma and Hariścandra,[86] and also there is a verse to Ganges water preceding the section on *snāna* (bathing preparations), this verse being more suited to the context than the previous:

Mixed with the juice of part of the digit of the moon; pierced by the fingernails of Gaurī,
May the Ganges bathing water of Lord (Śiva), purify you.[87]

Likewise, at the beginning of the section on water perfume we find another well-placed verse invoking the purification of "water that is pure from the confluence with the river of the world of the gods" (*suralokanadīsaṅgaśuddhaṃ nīraṃ*).[88]

Another verse to the god Śiva occurs at the outset of the incense section,[89] whereas toward the beginning of the section on incense rolls (*varti*), the incense rolls themselves are praised in several clever and tricky verses with double meanings, which might possibly be like the "bird incense" in the *Girdle of Hara*, or maybe they are bitexual in a more straightforward manner,[90] comparing their powers of seduction to those of beautiful women, for example:

Incense reading:
Possessing points with glittering eyes, and dense with the [smoke] produced from aloeswood (*agurujaghanā*),[91] with thick hard tips [literally "teats"], delightful, adorned with color, whom do [incense] sticks not overpower?

Erotic reading:
Their faces with tremulous eyes, with heavy thighs, with large firm breasts,
Like beloved ones in the grip of passion, whom do [incense] sticks not overpower?[92]

Again, at the head of the section on powders and ashes (*uddhūlanam*) we find a verse addressed to Kṛṣṇa, also relatively well suited to the context, in its reference to flower pollen:

In the middle of a vine-pavillion, ornamented by flower pollen,
wearing a forest garland, may Kṛṣṇa grant you joy.[93]

The verses add a pleasant poetic note to the long lists of technical formulae, sometimes appropriate to their context, and in one case the verses directly praise the aromatics in bitextual, poetic language.

The presence of the verses is not, however, particularly surprising, because such verses are found in many genres of text, including many technical ones; yet, we should bear in mind that these poetic touches do set this text apart from many of the others we have seen so far—texts that are generally somewhat less ornamental, at least in the manner they treat perfumery. But these verses are not the most striking literary features of the *Gandhasāra*; in some cases, the formulae themselves are infused with literary features of some complexity—features that we may be quite surprised to see in such a technical context, transforming the already complex compounding of perfumes into a verbal and olfactory tour de force for the cultivated elite.

Riddles, Puns, Scandalous Perfumes, and Erotic Suspicion

In this text, at least one formula can be read in two ways (bitextual): a complex pun. Or I might say that it is tritextual, because it is a riddle combined with a set of puns. Additionally, this is the formula for an incense—an olfactory artifact—so I might say that the text can be experienced on potentially four separate levels. We will linger on this verse at some length, in part because it is complicated and needs some space to explain clearly, but also because reflection on this verse will reveal much about the ideal readers imagined for such texts in medieval South Asia. This verse also occurs in another perfumery text we possess, the *Gandhavāda*, with a slightly different reading, and, thanks to the old Marathi commentary in the *Gandhavāda*, we can get an idea of how the double meanings work. Making the best we can of the two versions, it superficially reads as follows, as noted by Kulkarni and Wright:[94]

> Decoration is the shame of a respectable woman, stealing others' wealth is produced from evil, incense is not right in the doctrine of the Jina, indeed it is a fracas.[95]

However, the very first time I read these lines, placed as they are amongst so many incense recipes I read them as follows, expecting them to be another recipe, and this reading hints at another rather unusual way of reading it:

> Decoration,[96] the shame of a respectable woman, stealing others' wealth, evil-production, the thing that is not right in the doctrine of the Jina—the incense named Fracas (or "Uproar").

Taken on face value this verse consists of a somewhat random list of phenomena that are in one way or another transgressive in a medieval South Asian context, such as stealing wealth. But is that all there is to this text? It is merely a rather vague observation on morals that mentions that incense is undesirable to Jains (not something I found unless one perhaps means for the personal censing of ascetics). Without the Marathi commentary to the version of the text in the *Gandhavāda* it is unlikely that anyone would have ever fathomed what is going on here.[97] I should note in passing that Kulkarni and Wright, in their review of the edition of the *Gandhasāra*, were inclined to think, in fact, nothing is going on here. They did not take kindly to the reading of this verse suggested by the Marathi commentary and preferred to read this verse as a straightforward moral maxim.[98] However, given the placement of this verse amongst other rather unusual "novelty" verses in the *Gandhasāra*; given also the nature of the other playful verses such as the "bird incense" in the *Girdle of Hara*, and given the fact that this verse *was* interpreted in a certain manner by the *Gandhavāda* commentary, I think it entirely reasonable to accept that this verse-as-attested in the *Gandhasāra* and the *Gandhavāda* was supposed to be read in a peculiar and playful manner in those contexts. I am unable to say, however, whether the verse ever had a chaste single-significance life as a rather dull moral aphorism prior to being seduced by reading communities of eroticizing perfume experts, and thus rendered clever, saucy, and fragrant.

The Marathi commentary gives the common names of the perfume ingredients that make up the alternative reading of this punning (*śleṣa*) puzzle (though, thus far, I have still to make perfect sense of all of these readings.) Even with the commentary, however, we will have to rely on our understanding of Indian culture and religion to make the connection between the riddle and the ingredients. I should note that fine points of grammar have also come second in my reading, owing to a desire to make sense of the verse—given that the two versions differ substantially, the text is clearly quite corrupt, possibly because it has always been an extremely confusing verse. I explain the perfume reading of the verse as well as I understand it:

"decoration/armour" = cloves. I have been unable to extrapolate the connection between the terms here, which differ greatly in the two versions of the verse we possess. Also, the manuscript here appears to be especially corrupt according to the edition. However, the word *śṛṅgāra* ("ornament") is a synonym of "cloves." Might this synonym be the link between "decoration" and "cloves"?

"the shame of a respectable woman" = *nakha*, meaning *unguis odoratus*, aromatic seashell operculum, as well as "fingernails" that are responsible for the scratches of, presumably extramarital, lovemaking.

"stealing others' wealth" = *kacorā* according to the commentary, a term that does suggest the word for thief (*cora*). *Kacora* is an aromatic, possibly zedoary root.[99]

"evil-production" (or the *Gandhasāra* version has "produced of evil," *pāpasaṃbhūtam*) = *kus̩t̩ha*, meaning costus root, as well as a type of skin disease that could be produced as the result of bad deeds.[100]

"the thing that is not right in the doctrine of the Jina" = *jaṭamāṃsī*, *Valeriana jatamansi*, or spikenard.[101] This root is also called *māṃsī*, a word suggesting *māṃsa* "meat" which was forbidden to vegetarian Jains.[102] This plant is also known by a number of hair-related synonyms.[103]

To make this clear, the three readings of this verse are now presented, as well as a tabular presentation of the information (see table 5.2).

Moral aphorism

Decoration is the shame of a respectable woman, stealing others' wealth is produced from evil, incense is not right in the doctrine of the Jina, indeed it is a fracas.

Incense riddle

Decoration (or "armor"), the shame of a respectable woman, stealing others' wealth, evil-production, the thing that is not right in the doctrine of the Jina—the incense named Fracas.

Halfway solution to the riddle

Ornament (?), fingernails, a thief, a skin disease, meat: the incense named Fracas.

Aromatic puns on the solution to the halfway solution to the riddle

Cloves, fragrant shell-operculum, zeodary, costus root, spikenard: the incense named Fracas.

These ingredients are also very typical incense ingredients, and the resulting incense appears to be quite a standard one, probably smelling somewhat like modern Tibetan incenses, which often seem to contain such Himalayan roots as *Valeriana jatamansi* and costus root. In surveying the whole of the *Gandhasāra* in order to analyze the names of the perfumes, I came across a number of other verses which may also be of this nature, though in the absence of a commentary it is a challenge to translate them.[104] Even some of the verses quoted previously could plausibly have an "aromatic reading":

> Mixed with the juice of part of the digit of the moon pierced by the fingernails of Gaurī
> May the bathing water of the Ganges of Lord (Śiva), purify you.[105]

Table 5.2 **Reading the Aphorism as a Riddle and as a Recipe**

Riddle	*Riddle solution*	*Pun/ingredient*
decoration (or "armor") →	ornament (=*śṛṅgāra*?) →	cloves (=*lavaṅga* also called *śṛṅgāra*)
shame of a respectable woman →	fingernails (= *nakha*) →	fragrant shell operculum (= *nakha*)
stealing others' wealth →	thief (= *kacora/cora*) →	zedoary (= *kacora*)
evil production →	a skin disease (= *kuṣṭha*) →	costus root (= *kuṣṭha*)
nondharmic thing in Jainism →	meat (= *māṃsa*) →	spikenard (= *māṃsī*)

Here *gaurī* could also mean turmeric; "fingernails" could be *nakha* or unguis odoratus; "moon" is a common word for camphor in the *Gandhasāra*; "juice" (*rasa*), possibly meaning simply "liquid" or "water," could also be a number of aromatics according to the *Gandhasāra* glossary; and, of course, "mixed" are all terms that may refer to aromatic ingredients. Furthermore, the word I translated as "pierced" (*bhinna*), could perhaps be a synonym for the perfumery process mentioned known as "piercing" (*vedha*), referring to adding moist ingredients to moist. Moreover, turmeric water with some camphor would seem a likely formula for bathing water. This may sound farfetched, but I think given that we have an explicitly bitextual formula, and given that after reading hundreds of perfume formulas and acquainting myself with the somewhat esoteric language of perfumery,[106] this formula and several others seem to me eminently suited to such a reading—I think the conjecture reasonable. But my reading is uncertain, and at one point I wondered if I was becoming paranoid that every verse might have an aromatic double meaning. Then it struck me that this may even be the intention of these verses: to create a sense of hidden aromatic-erotic intrigue and suspicion. Much of the terminology of perfumery in these texts is rather esoteric ("moon" = "camphor"), and this may be to protect the formulae or to remove the language of perfumery from the standard terminology associated with texts on pharmacology and medicine. Or maybe this special terminology was in part popular as it pushed these recipes, potentially rather dull reading, in the direction of poetic bitextuality as we saw developing in the *Girdle of Hara*. The glossaries of such obscure synonyms for aromatics also aid this tendency in reading.[107] Although in literary texts camphor is valued as cool and white like the moon, such consistent use of this terminology seems to be peculiar to perfumery texts. This unique terminology gives the *Gandhasāra* a poetic and enigmatic tone at times.

Although the "Fracas" (*kolāhala*) verse is not in the form of a question, it also shares some features with riddles. The question format of conventional riddles often makes it clear that they are puzzles, yet these verses are much more enigmatic in form. Riddles imply "the other": as Galit Hasan-Rokem and David Shulman state: "The riddle's form is dialogic, requiring the interaction of self and other. Two levels are joined in the question, only to be disentangled in the answer."[108] We know that there existed large numbers of riddles (*prahelikās*) in Sanskrit, but as Richard Salomon notes "despite their evidently extensive cultivation in literary circles, *prahelikās* and some of the related riddle-like genres never attained full acceptance as legitimate literary devices." This may be because of their "frequently erotic or pseudo-erotic content."[109] In the case above, the dialogue of riddle and solution demands a lot of those involved: a knowledge of literary Sanskrit, of religious and literary conventions, as well as a good knowledge of the equally, if not more, specialist language of perfumery. Moreover, the *kolāhala* (ethical and dharmic chaos) described in the riddle and the *kolāhala* (erotic chaos) that is no doubt supposed to ensue from the burning of this incense, are both expected to be a source of elite literary *and* sensuous delight for those playing this riddle game. Solving a riddle "can reveal in a brief flash an excluded cosmos, a non-world or topsy-turvy world lurking just beneath or within our properly ordered and familiar one."[110] In this case, solving the *kolāhala* riddle not only shows how clever you are, but it also requires you to reveal your nature—both to yourself and to someone puzzling you with this verse. And you are ultimately revealed to be someone who is quite comfortable with the *kolāhala* side of life, with a mind that is delightfully tainted by the constant suspicion of erotic intrigue. As Daud Ali astutely notes, in early medieval India "courtship was posed as a contest."[111]

It appears that the solving of riddles was associated with a certain type of person: the "cultivated man" (*vidagdha*), who we will consider in more detail in the next chapter, though needless to say *vidagdhas* were also quite fond of perfumes. Two of the surviving works on riddles even contain the term *vidagdha* in the title: *Ornament of the Mouth of the Cultivated Man* (*Vidagdhamukhamaṇḍana*)[112] of Dharmadāsa,[113] and the recently described *Surprise for the Cultivated Man* (*Vidagdhavismāpana*).[114] The latter text, like the erotic *Complete Man-About-Town*, *Nāgarasarvasva*, seems to have been composed in a Buddhistic milieu in the tenth or eleventh century.[115] As Michael Hahn says, the *Surprise for the Cultivated Man*, along with the metrical works such as Ratnākaraśānti's *Chandoratnākara* and Jñānaśrīmitra's *Vṛttamālastuti* "give us a very good idea of what courses of study [were available] at a Buddhist university in the first half of the eleventh century and the predilections of the professors there." In considering what sort of people used manuals of riddles, Hahn notes that he "would like to classify these texts as a kind of pastime and exercise for the erudite, the really clever ones, the *vidagdhas*."[116]

Not only do we know something of the ideal user of such riddles, but we also have some idea of the ideal context for solving riddles. As Nalini Balbir notes in the case of Jain texts "riddles are here clearly an element of private life, even of intimacy . . . the preferred moment for the riddle is the first night of lovers or of a married couple; the first exchange before carnal love."[117] These lovers "are for the most part young people of good family, whether princes or not, who are well-versed in the sixty-four or seventy-two arts and techniques (*kalā*) that define their education."[118] In addition to this erotic context, it would seem riddles were associated with the literary gathering, the *goṣṭhī*.[119]

It seems that certain types of disguised language and social intimacy go hand in hand. In addition to sections on perfumes, gemstones, and more standard erotic subjects, the medieval *Nāgaravarvasva* or *Complete Man-About-Town* contains sections on the secret codes and signs (*saṅketa*) used by lovers to communicate their illicit meetings.[120] Accounts of the use of these same secret lovers' codes are also found in narrative literature.[121] Coded language was not limited to erotic contexts, and, as Ronald Davidson notes, in esoteric tantric Buddhist texts a coded language (*sandhyā-bhāṣā*) was used, in which overt talk of costly perfumes, amongst other things, could disguise references to tantric rites and substances normally forbidden, at least by norms of brahminical purity: where, for example, musk (*kastūrikā*) could refer to urine and camphor (*karpūraka*) to semen.[122]

These observations may help us better understand the anticipated audience for this riddling, punning, and scandalous perfume recipe. The solving of riddles is associated with the bedroom, as well as the lifestyle of the cultivated man, and this particular riddle is a natural extension of the cultivated, poetic, and suggestive terminology of this perfumery text as a whole. The riddle, and perhaps others like it in this text and in lost texts, creates a sense of suspicion that any innocent-looking verse might, in fact, be read as a recipe, possibly even a recipe for a powerfully arousing perfume. Po-faced moral aphorisms might be unmasked as smoldering aphrodisiacs at any moment. Yigal Bronner suggests that one Sanskrit literary theorist Mammaṭa is worried "that under the influence of *śleṣa* [bitextual writing, punning], literature will turn into a wild costume party in which the true poetic identity of verses or works will never be certain."[123] The "fracas" verse and reading appears to celebrate this very possibility, uniting the world of puns with the world of riddles and the bizarre and rarified nomenclature of aromatics in order to promote, not just a costume party, but erotic chaos. I might repeat here that although the revealing commentary on this verse appears only in the *Gandhavāda*, this verse is given in the *Gandhasāra* in part of the text that contains other rather playful verses, so it seems reasonable that it was to be read in a saucy manner there also. This sophisticated and delightful sense of erotic readerly suspicion makes life more interesting and appears perfectly consistent with the more widespread notion that the erotic life of the man-about-town was filled with playful bedroom riddles and secret lovers' codes, where a poetic verse could be a recipe for a bedroom incense, and a mere slap on the back could be a coded invitation to an illicit romantic tryst.[124]

Other Erudite and Literary Features of the *Gandhasāra*

In addition to this formula, several of the aromatic preparations in the *Gandhasāra* are given in various literary meters, and the name of the final aromatic product is the same as the meter. It is as if you had a formula composed in iambic pentameter for fragrant *Iambic Water*, except the names of Sanskrit meters are typically quite evocative in themselves, so, for example, *vasantatilakā* means "Ornament of Spring." "Metrical" perfumes given in this text are a *Vasantatilakā* mouth freshener and *udvartana*; *Drutavilambita*, *Vasantatilakā*, and *Śālinī* incense rolls (*varti*); *Aupacchandasika*, *Upagīti*, *Skandha*, *Pathyā* (*ārya*), *Vaitālīya*, and *Udgīti* lamp wicks, the latter being part of a small roll call of *jāti* meters.[125] As S. R. Sarma has noted,[126] outside the context of texts on poetic meter (where this phenomenon is not uncommon), the phenomenon of the inclusion of names of poetic meters within a verse written in that very same meter is also found in the mathematical treatise called the *Gaṇitasārasaṅgraha* by the Jain Mahāvīra of ninth-century Karnataka.[127] In this treatise, some of the chapters conclude with a verse written in a meter (for example *utpalamālikā*: "garland of *utpala* lotuses"), and these verses also contain the name of that meter as used in a poetic context.[128] For example, "after adding these according to the rules which are strung together in the manner of a *garland of blue lotuses* made up of fractions, give out, O friend, (what the result is)."[129] Possibly then, these metrical perfume formulae were composed in a milieu such as that in which Mahāvīra lived and worked, a place and time where such metrical ornamentation of technical literature was practiced, namely South India toward the latter half of the first millennium CE (and later joined to a more compiled *Gandhasāra* that we have it today).[130] This particular feature of the *Gandhasāra* is not suggestive of erotics, but it nevertheless explicitly connects perfumery with poetry: the *metrical ornament* of poetic language has an evocative nomenclature that is shared here with the *aromatic ornament* of the body of the cultivated (and no doubt literary) person. Later, when we consider other perfume names, we will see that the nomenclature of perfumes was developed far beyond these metrical names.

Not only could the educated and wealthy connoisseur of perfume take pleasure in a fragrance that was a clever punning riddle, as well as in an incense both described in and named after a complex, charmingly named, literary meter, but one could also wear a perfume composed by the historical paragon of culture and taste, King Bhoja. In the *Gandhavāda*, that slightly later (or, at least, more Persianate) perfumery text that mentions ambergris etc., we find a formula attributed to King Bhoja who was, in the imagination of the later Sanskrit cosmopolis, the "ultimate arbiter of grammatical correctness, rhetorical propriety, and literary good taste."[131] Clearly Bhoja was not only deemed to be the arbiter of literary taste but also of olfactory taste, as this recipe for a preparation of civet (*javādi* = probably Persian *zabād*) is clearly attributed to that king: "the *javādi* made by Bhoja," "made by Bhoja."[132] A short treatise on personal hygiene, the *Cārucaryā*, or *Attractive Conduct*, is also attributed to King Bhoja and this text contains substantial materials on perfumery, but not, however, the formulae for civet attributed to Bhoja in the *Gandhavāda*.[133] Again, we see the convergence of Sanskrit high literary culture with the textual culture of perfumery, and we can begin to imagine the sort of wealthy, educated, and pleasure-seeking elite audience that would have been able to patronize the author of such a text as the *Gandhasāra*, and who were at once able to appreciate its subtleties, as well as able to afford the exotic, expensive ingredients required to realize these beautiful and arousing perfumes.

Another interesting feature of the single manuscript, approximately two hundred years old, of the *Gandhasāra* is the eight tables incorporated into the text.[134] Seven of these clearly list various aromatic ingredients, and they are placed throughout section two of the text, which contains the aromatic formulae. These are grids (*kacchapuṭas*), seen also in the *Bṛhatsaṃhitā*, that are used for creating perfumes. For example, the final and largest table, comprising sixty-four squares (eight rows by eight columns) gives sixty-four different aromatics, numbered 1–64.[135] As with the combinatoric grids in the *Bṛhatsaṃhitā*, these tables are to be used in actually preparing perfumes described in the text, though we have no idea at what stage this tabular presentation became part of the text. Such tables of aromatics are not incorporated in the other perfumery text that is part of the same manuscript, the *Gandhavāda*. One might think that tables in one text and not in the other, in the very same manuscript, suggests that they cannot have been added by the copyist in order to clarify the text, but this is not necessarily the case, because the *Gandhavāda* contains a Marathi commentary clearly explaining the proportions of the ingredients, so additional tables were not as necessary for this text. The final table in the *Gandhasāra*, found at the very end of the text, after the *nighaṇṭu*, is rather different. This confusing table appears to be a tabular presentation of a verse concerning the goddess Parvatī, and it is possible that these terms are also synonyms for aromatics. The text thus finishes with a table, with the implied combinatoric and mathematical associations of such figures. But the contents of this table also possibly suggest the bitextual poetics of aromatics seen elsewhere: a benedictory flourish perfectly in line with what we have seen so far in the text.[136]

In the *Gandhasāra*, the *Essence of Perfume*, dating most likely from the early- to mid-second millenium CE, and to a certain extent in the *Haramekhalā*, the *Girdle of Hara*, we see a very noticeable literarization of perfumery, to use Pollock's term for the process of achieving conformity with the literary paradigm: technical literature (*śāstra*) and material culture merge with poetry (*kāvya*).[137] While the *Bṛhatsaṃhitā* does contain some interesting and evocative perfume names and poetic features, as well as the marvels of combinatoric formulae, that text seems rather straightforward in its treatment of perfumery, when compared to the highly complex *Gandhasāra*.[138] Of course, given that we have lost most of the older texts on perfumery, it is not possible to say whether they too contained materials like those found in the *Gandhasāra*. It is quite possible that the *Gandhasāra* is not an entirely original composition but a compilation (like the Anup *Gandhasāra*), and indeed we saw that the *Kolāhala* riddle-pun verse also occurs in the *Gandhavāda*.[139]

Above I alluded to the fact that the very names of the perfumes are often quite poetic. These evocative names are a feature of all the perfumery texts we have discussed, though they are particularly abundant in the *Gandhasāra*, and it is to these poetic perfume names—texts that you can wear—that I now turn.

Perfume Names in Medieval South Asia

In reading medieval South Asian texts on perfumery, and especially the *Gandhasāra*, I was struck by many of perfumes' names, especially by how similar they were to the names we give our perfumes, yet also by how much they resound with the conventions of Indian literature.[140] To a certain extent, the study of these names is a history of the imagination, because they reflect the culture and values of the creators and users of the texts; yet, I think it reasonable to say it goes beyond the text into the world of material culture, because the names were tied to substances that people must have used: smearing them on their bodies, burning them in the bedroom at night, and chewing them before kissing. Just as with perfumes today, these bodily experiences were, no doubt, supposed to be enhanced and transformed by the knowledge that a certain smoldering incense was called, for example, "Southern Wind" or was said to "destroy the morals of a respectable lady." As we will see in the next chapter, in a literary account concerning perfumery, it seems to have been a feature of the medieval Indian imagination that the name of a perfume was deemed a valid and interesting subject for reflection, discussion, and the potential object of wordplay, like the formulae we saw previously.

The perfume names in the *Essence of Perfume* fall into several categories, some being simply compared to other odorants, particularly flowers, for instance, "the same as the smell of the *campaka* flower" (*campakagandhasamāna*).[141] Some are described as beloved of a particular god, e.g., "beloved of Hara" (*harapriya*),[142] or as beloved of a certain type of person, such as the cultivated *vidagdha* or the king: "beloved of the cultivated man" (*vidagdhadayita*).[143] Although it might seem that these terms such as "beloved of the capturer of the three cities" (*tripuraharavallabha*)[144] merely indicate the gods to whom these incenses should be offered, (not being an actual name of the product) this is not necessarily the case. First, we are told in some cases that these incenses are "called" by that term,[145] and second, "beloved of the capturer of the three cities" is mentioned by this very name in other formulae where it is to be used to cense other products.[146]

Perhaps the most important category of perfume names alludes to erotic matters. These can refer directly to the god of love, Kāmadeva, himself, for example, the alliterative "Pride of Kāma" (*kandarpadarpa*);[147] or to the potency of the perfume to increase lust, for example "Arouser of Kāma" (*smaroddīpanaḥ*).[148] These erotic names can be more suggestive in tone, referring to the cooling nature of the incense, which in addition to a seasonal and humoral value, would have probably been most suggestive of the need to allay the fevers associated with unrequited desire, for example, "Southern Wind" (*dakṣiṇapavana*).[149] Similarly suggestive of coolness are names related to the moon and its cooling rays, e.g., "Moon-juice" (*candrarasa*).[150] Several of the names are related to bees, e.g., "Bee Attractor" (*bhramarākarṣaṇa*),[151] suggesting that the perfume will make the wearer, like a fragrant, nectar-filled flower, attractive to bees, who, amongst other things, form Kāmadeva's bow string. Also, indirectly related to Kāmadeva, there are several perfumes called "arrow" and its synonyms, e.g., "(Iron) Arrow" (*nārāca*),[152] probably referring to the flower arrows with which Kāmadeva shoots his victims of love.

Finally, there are a number of names that one might describe as novelties or conceits. These include the names associated with the bitextual verse discussed, as well as with the metrical perfumes. Perhaps of all the perfumes in this book, the name of the following perfume is the most delightful. This perfume is described only three verses after the bitextual *Kolāhala* (Fracas) perfume, in a part of the text which seems to contain a relatively high number of these more imaginative and clever names. Like the *Kolāhala* perfume, this name suggests the turmoil that will follow in the wake of such a powerfully attractive perfume:

> [When] the man who has censed his entire body [with this], is walking,
> it is said by people "Who goes there?" therefore this incense is called
> "Who Goes There?"[153] (*kogacchati*)[154]

As we have seen many times, the "cultivated man" often pretended to aspire to be at the heart of a storm of erotic social instability, and our texts depict perfumes as particularly potent inflamers of such heady chaos.

Not only are there several distinct categories of name, but also the distribution of names, and of types of name, amongst the different varieties of perfume is striking. Half of the perfumed waters, for instance, are compared in fragrance to flowers: "with the same perfume as *kamala* (= *padma*) lotus" (*kamalagandhasama*).[155] The mouth fragrances have more erotic, Kāma-related, names such as "Fame-wave of the *Makara*-Bannered One," (i.e., Kāma) (*makaradhvajakīrtikallola*),[156] whereas the perfumed oils are again compared to flowers: "with the perfume of *campaka* flowers" (*campakāmoda*).[157] As we shall see in the next chapter, these oils were indeed sometimes perfumed with actual flowers, not by distillation, but by *enfleurage* (*vāsana*) of sesame seeds or other oily materials with flowers. Several of the perfumes for water have cooling associations, with names such as "Frost-Rayed" (i.e., the cooling moon) (*himakara*).[158]

When we leave behind the bathing perfumes and water perfumes, and consider the perfumes that would have been either worn all day or used later in the day, namely perfumes (*gandhas*) and incenses (*dhūpas*), the names take on a noticeably more erotic tone. Indeed, two of the "arrow" perfumes are found in the section on incenses. There is also a group of incenses clearly intended for divine worship, since we are told that they are "for (the goddess) Śrī" (*śriyai*),[159] and so forth. Toward the end of the list of the incenses we find the "novelty" formulae such as "*Kogacchati?*" ("Who goes there?"); these are followed by incenses with other applications—ones that repel insects, control elephants, and so on.[160] Following the incenses, which occupy by far the longest section, we have the incense sticks (*dhūpavartti*) and perfumed lamp wicks (*dīpavartti*), and here we see the major part of the so-called metrical perfumes. As with the incenses, the nature of these products, and also their place at the end of the list of aromatics, suggests they were used at night, quite possibly in the erotic context of the bedroom.

In general, it seems that the cleansing substances used earlier in the day tend to be compared to flowers, with descriptions that are pleasant, though not necessarily erotic, and they are not assigned names per se. The products that are used, not to cleanse, but to produce a lingering perfume are more likely to have literary names associated with erotic phenomena (both arousing and cooling), as well as clever names, playful in a manner reminiscent of the many courtly love-games of the king and his queens described in the latter part of the *Mānasollāsa*. An exception is the mouth perfumes that also have erotic names, but which are listed toward the beginning of the text together with the bathing substances and so on. Yet the mouth, being the locus of the kiss, plays an important role in lovemaking, so it is not at all surprising that the perfumes for this area have erotic names.

As with the riddle perfume, the perfume names in the *Gandhasāra* suggest a mingling of literary, olfactory, and religious culture, such that the world of perfume making, perfume use, and perfume texts is far more complex than one might expect. It is possible that we have only scratched the surface in this short analysis, though, hopefully, we now understand enough to begin to produce more complex and subtle readings of other texts in which perfumes and perfumery are mentioned. Another significant aspect of this and other perfumery texts is the principle of internal organization, and I now turn to this issue, the study of which will reveal more about the Indian understanding and practice of perfumery.

Internal Organization of Texts

It appears that most of the texts dealing with perfumery are organized according to the time of day when the aromatic preparations were used. There is an explicit statement to this effect in the *Haramekhalā*, the *Girdle of Hara*:

> Just as they are always used every day in a [particular] order,
> In that same way I briefly relate those perfumes for clever people.[161]

The order of preparations described in the *Haramekhalā*, sequentially as they are used through the day, is summarized by the commentator in the following passage. We should also note that following the aromatics of the daily routine, other preparations of a more general application, in particular, artificial versions of expensive aromatics such as artificial musk, are described:

> This collection of the applications of the fifth [chapter] is composed:
> There [is found] the preparation of water fragrance, as well as the preparation of tooth sticks,
> The preparation of beeswax [for the lips], as well as kohl to decorate the eyes,
> Mouth fragrances, etc., oils, as well as the preparation of rubbing unguents,
> Then [there are] the practice of bathing, bathing materials, and the bath accessory materials,

> Fragrant clothes powders, [incense] sticks/wicks, and the preparation of perfumes, etc.
> The artificial manufacture of musk and the method of the extraction of various perfumes,
>
> And [artificial][162] camphor, saffron, *nakha*, aloeswood and Indian olibanum [from *Boswellia serrata*],
> And the manufacture of mango [oil], as well as the manufacture of camphor oil,
> The [artificial] manufacture of cloves, cardamoms, and costus root respectively.
> The means for mango-stability[163], as well as the fluids of all flowers,
> And also the fluids of *ketakī*, *campaka*, and so on separately.[164]

The chapter on perfumery in the *Nāgarasarvasva*, the *Complete Man-About-Town* of Padmaśrī has some similarities to the *Haramekhalā* in how it is organized, consisting of a number of aromatic formulae respectively for the hair (*keśapaṭavāsa*); armpits (*kākṣikavāsa*); dwelling (*gṛhavāsa*); mouth (*mukhavāsa*); water (*jalavāsa*); betel-nut (*pūgaphalam*); bathing powder (*snānīya*); for a perfume called *catuḥsama* (consisting, according the commentator, of one part musk, two parts camphor, four parts saffron, and sixteen parts sandalwood);[165] massage unguent (*udvartana*); powder (*cūrṇa*); incense sticks (*dhūpavarti*); and lampwicks (*dīpavarti*). As we can see, mouth perfume again precedes bathing substances and the final aromatics; presumably used at the end of the day are the incenses and fragrant lamp wicks. Thus, it appears that the formulae in the *Nāgarasarvasva* are listed more or less according to their daily use. I might add that this order of use of aromatics is similar to that used in many *pūjā* rites, because in the *pūjā*, the deity is bathed, clothed, fed, and later put to bed, like a respected and important person, such as a king.[166] Likewise, in the *Kāmasūtra*, we are told that in the morning the man-about-town uses unguent, incense, and garlands,[167] and in the evening his bedroom is censed with fragrant incense (*vāsagṛhe saṃcāritasurabhi-dhūpe*).[168] The *Gandhasāra* follows a similar scheme—indeed this text is organized in a very similar manner to the *Haramekhalā*. The *Gandhavāda* contains two tables of contents at the end of the text. This text appears to be organized less rigorously than those described so far. At the beginning of the text, a large number of formulae are given for a fragrant powder called *bukā*.[169] These are followed by some formulae for artificial musks and so forth, as well as some perfumed oils and incenses, in that order. Apart from the inclusion of the artificial musks toward the beginning, this approximates the order of products in the other texts, though there is much less variety of products, and the text is generally less tightly structured.

Another scheme by which one text is organized is according to the "pleasures" (*bhogas*). This is the explicit organizing principle behind the discussion of a variety of aromatics described in a text we have already seen: the *Delight of the Mind*,

Mānasollāsa attributed to King Someśvara III. This extensive encyclopedic manual of courtly life contains a considerable section devoted to the royal "pleasures" (*bhogas/upabhogas*). These are all courtly pleasures that contain a strong element of sensual pleasure: the pleasure of the bath (*snānabhoga*), of clothes (*vastropabhoga*), of food (*annabhoga*), of beds (*śayyābhoga*), and so forth. These courtly pleasures are described at length and are followed by an account of the royal "sports/entertainments" (*vinoda*), also a source of pleasure but not primarily sensual. Although the *bhogas* taken as a whole address the needs of far more of the senses than the preparations in the perfumery texts, nevertheless, their order seems to share the same temporal logic. Thus, after the enjoyment of a bath, a betel wrap, and the application of unguents, the king puts on clothes, garlands, jewelry, after which the author describes the seats and fly-whisks, food and drink, and finally beds, incense, and the enjoyment of women.[170] In the *Vikramāṅkābhyudaya*, a prose work also attributed to Someśvara III, that describes the reign of his father, when describing the moment when the king goes to bed with the queen, Someśvara notes the use of incense at this time of day; he describes the bed as "perfumed with the fragrance of incense made of camphor and aloeswood."[171] By placing perfumes in a temporal context, together with other varieties of sensory pleasures, the *Mānasollāsa* enriches our understanding of what was involved in the use of aromatics more broadly, as we shall see when considering the perfumes themselves in more detail.

Conclusion

In this chapter, we studied texts written to describe how one should go about manipulating the world of smells through perfumery. The earliest surviving texts to treat this subject in any detail appeared in South Asia around the middle of the first millennium CE. Liturgical texts aside, in these texts, perfumery is discussed in the context of matters of the body and the bedroom. By around the turn of the first millennium CE, we have evidence of texts devoted entirely to the art of perfumery, and we have seen one especially elaborate perfumery text dating from the early to mid-centuries of the second millennium CE. The technology of the manipulation of smell was increasingly deemed important enough to include in texts that articulated the nature of several aspects of life, as witnessed by the variety of Sanskrit and Prakrit texts that deal with perfumery. Although we learned in previous chapters that smells are complex in nature, being both good and bad in a variety of ways, nevertheless, the production of pleasure was a dominant theme in the discourses considered in this chapter. This pleasure might be erotic, intellectual, olfactory, all these things, and more. But, whatever the nature of the pleasure of perfumes, smell was certainly considered a powerful affective modality of experience that needed to be mastered in the bedroom, palace, and temple (and regulated in the monastery). The discourses of perfumery were often erudite, demanding a lot from the audience. Sometimes the audience (possibly astrologers) was expected to understand complex mathematics; sometimes they were simply required to recognize the specialist names of plants and processes; and, in some cases, the audience was expected to engage in a bewildering, yet pleasurable, contest of intellectual, olfactory, erotic riddles. Such is the nature of texts on perfumery in early and later medieval South Asia. After having considered the history, literary features, and organization of these texts, we turn, in the next chapter, to see what the texts say about the perfumes they describe.

6

Allies, Enemies, and *Yakṣa* Mud

Perfumes

> Little by little the arcana of this art, the most neglected of them all, had been revealed to Des Esseintes, who could now decipher its complex language that was as subtle as any human tongue, yet wonderfully concise under its apparent vagueness and ambiguity.
>
> To do this he had first to master the grammar, to understand the syntax of smells, to get a firm grasp on the rules that govern them, and, once he was familiar with this dialect, to compare the works of the great masters . . . to analyse the construction of their sentences, to weigh the proportion of their words, to measure the arrangement of their periods.
>
> —Huysmans, *A rebours*

Des Esseintes, the decandent protagonist of Huysmans' *A rebours,* is preparing to study the art of perfumery. First, he must master the language of odors, and only then can he produce a perfume that is both "grammatically" correct and pleasing. Such close attention to the rules of olfactory propriety is what we also find in South Asian texts on perfumery: not only is the language of these texts at times very literary, but, arguably, the odorous "language" of the perfumes themselves is also highly developed. The medieval South Asian perfume connoisseur is an expert in both the application of the rules of perfumery and in the articulation of the literary terminology of perfumery. But he does not flaunt his exquisite subjective experiences of perfumes through flamboyant and evocative descriptions, which is in notable contrast to much taste and smell connoisseurship today. In the chapter's epigraph, Huysmans uses a linguistic metaphor to describe the rule-bound aesthetics of French perfumery, whereas South Asian perfumery draws on a variety of other discourses and metaphors: from medical theories of humoral balance to the language of texts on statecraft. In this chapter, I continue to explore texts on perfumery, only *not* with a view to examine their textual and literary features but to see what they say about the perfumes they describe.

Investigating these perfumes is important for two reasons. First, it allows us to understand the categories that animate many other texts that deal in one way or another with perfumes, be they liturgical, literary, erotic, or in other genres. Second, we may find some materials that are not just of historical interest, but that may also help expand our limited contemporary discourse about smells and perfumes. I am interested in the possibility of reviving these categories, not because I am possessed by "a morality of regard for local interpretations,"[1] but rather because of the relative dearth of serious theoretical reflection in the humanities about smells and perfumes, especially the aesthetics of perfumes. Theory of smell aesthetics by intellectuals living in a society with an especially rich olfactory culture might, with some careful translation, be directly useful to some scholars today.

Perfumes in medieval South Asia were manufactured in a variety of manners for a large number of purposes, as can be seen from the many varied preparations mentioned so far. As with so many aspects of the world in traditional South Asia, this variety was in many cases theorized: perfumes and raw materials being classified and organized according to analogies and correlations with other South Asian intellectual categories. What in the wider scheme of things is the point of perfumery? For whom is the cultivation of expertise in perfumery appropriate? Many of the materials in this chapter echo the contexts I mentioned when discussing the anticipated audience for perfumery texts. The complex literary pleasures and reading competencies I noted in the previous chapter were inseparable from the sophisticated and intellectually informed olfactory pleasures of the cultivated man. Akin to the contemporary culture of wine connoisseurship, this elite practice was complex; it required knowledge of correct perfume combinations; informed perception of complex aromas; and fluency in certain types of specialized, articulate conversation. The appreciation of perfumes also involved using elegant paraphernalia; produced physical intoxication; and, lest we forget, required plenty of money. All these things are integral parts of an elaborate practice that we should not attempt to reduce to one aspect alone. And, as I have emphasized before, it was not only humans who appreciated these perfumes in medieval South Asia, but also gods, demons, and other beings, in temples, rituals, and as represented in texts.

Aromatic Variables

In Sanskrit texts, aromatic preparations (as opposed to raw materials) come in a number of varieties with several generic names: perfumed pastes (*vilepana*), incense (*dhūpa*), and so forth. They can be used to adorn certain parts of the body with fragrance or they can fill a space, such as a temple or bedroom, with perfume. As noted in the previous chapter, the use of certain preparations was often associated with certain times of the day, and, in many cases, they are also especially suited to certain times of year. This can be seen from the following instructions taken from the twelfth-century encyclopedic *Delight of the Mind, Mānasollāsa,* in the section on the type of preparation known as *vilepana*: a perfumed paste, an unguent, applied to the body and left on to render it fragrant. In this respect, *vilepanas* are somewhat closer to our idea of perfume, unlike, for example, *udvartana* which is an exfoliating, fragrant, oily, scrubbing paste which functioned more like soap and washcloths do today. Note that the stated purpose of *vilepana* is to remove the bad odor of sweat; thus, it also works like what we could call a deodorant, and after the bath, it was to be applied to the armpits and other crevices found at the joints of the body. This particular *vilepana* is also associated with a certain season, and following this section different *vilepanas* are described that are appropriate for other seasons. Thus, the passage below is followed by a section on the qualities of sandalwood (cooling), and in the section on *vilepanas* for the cooler seasons we are given the qualities of musk (heating). Finally, the pleasure-giving nature of this substance is stated: *vilepanas* are pleasurable to the body, presumably to the sense of *touch*. This particular type of aromatic, with a specific function and nature (pleasurably cool/warm, fragrant, and deodorizing) is restricted in use by time (season and time of day) as well as by place (armpits, etc.). Moreover, the perfume also has an evocative name: *Yakṣa* Mud:

> Here the pleasure-of-unguents is related, beloved of the voluptuary.
> Anointing with unguent is clear, pleasant and gives pleasure to the body,
> Therefore the king should practice [it] in a manner that is pleasant with the hands of his beloved [lady or ladies]
> Containing sandalwood, aloeswood, camphor, musk, saffron
> added to *granthiparṇa*[2] mixed with *surabhī*[3] and *kesara*[4]
> with nutmeg, and *pūtiphala,*[5] very fine and repeatedly censed,
> In spring he should make the best *Yakṣa* Mud ointment.
> He should practice the anointing called "for joints."[6] In the armpit area, where the ears join, on the navel and also on the crotch, in order to remove the smell of sweat.[7]

We possess a number of formulae for *Yakṣa* Mud, whose name refers to the type of supernatural beings called *yakṣas*—for whom this perfume is evidently like mud. This perfume would have been a dark-ruddy color, very fragrant, and, no doubt, a very costly paste. The *Dhanvantarīnighaṇṭu*—an important medical glossary of early but uncertain date[8]—tells us that it is cool; removes skin disease, headaches, and poison; and is an ornamental perfume.[9] Along with musk, camphor and so on, an aromatic spice called cubeb pepper (*kakkola*) is often included in recipes for *yakṣa* mud, which would have given this paste a very distinctive peppery odor. The formula is provided in several texts: including the extremely popular lexicon, the *Nāmaliṅgānuśāsana* of Amarasiṃha (*Amarakośa*),[10] and also the later Jaina *Abhidhānacintāmaṇi* of Hemacandra.[11] A formula is also found in the large *dharmaśāstra* compendium, the *Caturvargacintāmaṇi* of Hemādri.[12] Given its occurrence in the these texts, *Yakṣa* Mud is the one blended perfume whose playful name and luxurious, yet nontechnical, formula would have probably been quite familiar to almost every educated medieval scholar of Sanskrit, be they poet, courtier, logician, or monk. Given the fame of this fragrance, it is not surprising that the author Budhasvāmin chose to play on the name in a humorous manner in a passage we shall examine later in this chapter.

Not only might a certain perfume be correlated with a location on the body, the time of day, and the season, but a perfume should also complement the constitution of the wearer, thus linking the practice of perfumery closely to the theory of medicine. In the *Gandhasāra*, at the end of the first section, which deals with the processes of perfumery, the following verses explain that the expert in perfumery needs to be able to evaluate the bodily constitutions of those who will wear his perfume:

> He who blends perfume materials should be known to be the most expert in perfume,
> Having ascertained the nature of living beings as chiefly wind, bile or phlegm,
> Then he should apply *udvartanas* (rubbing-pastes), and so on that calm the humors.
> For windy: a fiery substance. For bile-related [constitutions]: a cool one is best,
> And he should blend a pungent, bitter, [or] astringent one for the man who has phlegm.[13]

This is the system of savors and humors that Zimmermann has so eloquently described.[14] I would argue that, as with the medical systems Zimmermann describes, the full catalogue of distinctions is by no means always foregrounded in any given context, and, as we see throughout this book, in the case of perfumery, it is perhaps most commonly the binary qualities of hot (e.g., musk) and cold (e.g., sandalwood) that are applied to aromatics. In addition to these diverse effects on the wearer, perfumes could please and erotically arouse other people who smelled it, and arguably this is one of the most important effects. In the passage quoted from the *Mānasollāsa,* the emphasis was, above all, on the pleasure of the person to whom the perfumed *vilepana* was applied, for whom it would smell and (importantly) feel pleasant. The removal of the smell of sweat was no doubt a good thing for the king and also those around him, but this effect is negative—the removal of a bad smell—and there is nothing in the text to suggest for whom the removal of sweat smell would be desirable. But this is not always the case, and a great many aromatic preparations are explicitly intended to affect people other than the wearer, often inducing sexual desire in them. In this passage from the *Complete Man-About-Town* (*Nāgarasarvasva*), we see this aspect of aromatics stated quite explicitly:

> Various sophisticated (*vidagdha*) perfumes are celebrated as eminent inflamers of lust,

> The best lover should be carefully instructed at the start from perfume texts.
> Having collected the essential part of the perfume texts, which are difficult to understand by those who are not clever, [and] which are by Lokeśvara, etc., I set [it] forth with very well-known words.[15]

Perfumes here are not merely pleasant but absolutely vital in creating an erotic ambiance. The author even states that the "best lover should be carefully instructed" in perfumery. In the passages from the *Mahābhārata* on the smells of flowers and fish, we saw the attractive and arousing nature of fragrances, and in the previous chapter, we reflected on the sophisticated perfumery wordplays associated with the erotic life of the cultivated man-about-town, and no doubt also the women he associated with.

As one might expect, as well as arousing perfumes, there also existed bad-smelling preparations designed to repel certain beings, though these preparations would appear to be fewer in number than the pleasant ones. In chapter 3, I noted the use of stinking fumigations to drive away demons responsible for childhood diseases. The *Essence of Perfume* (*Gandhasāra*) also contains some formulae for incenses designed to drive away various beings (insects, snakes, and demons), and the following formula is for an incense that presumably drives away possession-causing beings:

> Incense made with *guggulu*,[16] mustard seed, sloughed skin of a snake, neem leaves,[17] removes possession by *bhūtas* and the harm of the *ḍākinī*.[18]

In addition to the attractive and repellent properties of smells, some preparations have other functions, such as the following incense that calms the royal (or perhaps royal-directed) anger. This recipe, together with its interesting name, is found in the earliest substantial text we have on perfumery, the section on perfumery in the *Great Compendium*, *Bṛhatsaṃhitā*:

> Four parts of sugar, *śaileya*,[19] *Cyperus rotundus*, two parts [each] of resin of *Pinus longifolia* Roxb.,[20] *sāla* tree resin,[21] and *nakha* [unguis odoratus] and *guggulu*
> With the addition of powder [i.e., the perfumery process called *bodha*, "rousing"] of camphor, made into a ball with honey—this incense for the king is called Anger-cover.[22]

Thus perfumes have a large number of qualities and functions. Some aspects of perfumes (tactile qualities such as coolness) primarily affect the wearer, and some others, such as the fragrance of incenses and perfumed unguents, affect anyone who smells them. It was understood that the maker and user of perfumes required instruction to become an expert in all these complexities, that is to say, in order to gain the knowledge that would enable him (and so far it seems it is indeed a male of whom we speak in these texts) to take full advantage of all the effects that smells and aromatic substances have on others. But what exactly did the cultivated man need to learn? What was believed to be involved in making perfumes, and what was their purpose in the wider scheme of things?

Processes and Theory of Perfumery

The discussion so far covered many of the varied qualities and functions of aromatic preparations, yet the raw materials themselves and the processes of perfumery are also quite diverse, and we should not be surprised, in the context of South Asian intellectual culture, to see that these too were carefully classified. The entire first section of the *Gandhasāra* is concerned with such perfumery processes. The extent of this text is unique, for although this sort of material occurs elsewhere,[23] this is the only such lengthy and detailed exposition of this sort of material we possess. Presumably, the lost perfumery texts may have also had such sections, which is suggested by the fact that Bhaṭṭotpala, in his tenth-century CE commentary on the *Bṛhatsaṃhitā* of Varāhamihira, referred to one of these lost perfumery texts in order to elucidate a technical point concerning perfumery processes. The *Gandhasāra* begins by listing and then explaining the processes of perfumery:

> Steeping (*bhāvana*, steeping dry matter in fragrant liquid and then drying it), cooking (*pācana*), rousing (*bodha*, adding powder to powder), piercing (*vedha*, adding moist to moist),[24] censing (*dhūpana*),[25] and *enfleurage* (*vāsana*). Thus six processes for materials are related here by experts.[26]

Amongst these six processes perhaps the most important and well-known is what I have here translated as enfleurage, *vāsana*, and I will pause to discuss this in a little more detail. A very similar term to this, namely *vāsanā*, with a long "*ā*" is of some importance in certain South Asian philosophical discourses, where it refers to latent dispositions or "karmic habits" responsible for future tendencies.[27] I translated *vāsana* in the passage as *enfleurage* because the latter term is a perfect translation in a perfumery context. The French term *enfleurage* is also employed in the specialist language of English perfumery for the process by which certain flower extracts were produced, though the process is little used these days because it is labor intensive, less effective, and usually brings significant contamination.It has been replaced in modern perfumery by several types of solvent extractions. In *enfleurage*, as in *vāsana*, quantities of flowers are placed in contact with the material to be perfumed—in Europe this was often purified lard spread on sheets of glass, and in the *Gandhasāra* it can be any (generally oily, like sesame oil) material that needs to be perfumed.[28] In *enfleurage* and *vāsana*, by contact alone the perfume of the flowers diffuses into the fatty material to be perfumed, the spent flowers are discarded, and the fragrance-charged oily matter ("pomade" in technical perfumery English/French) is processed. The perfume in the perishable flowers is retained in another medium to be appreciated at later times: the actual perfume of the flowers is "recorded."

The process is described at length for making perfumed oils in *Gandhasāra*.[29] There, three methods are given, using sesame seeds, oiled cloth, and a bowl of oil. The sesame seed method—placing flowers amongst sesame seeds that are then crushed for oil—is still used in India today to produce hair oils.[30] It appears that this practice may be quite ancient, because in the Pali Vinaya, Buddhist nuns are forbidden to bathe with scented sesame-seed paste (*vāsitakena piññākena*), which might have been perfumed in this manner.[31]

Vāsana is one of the main ways in which the perfume of a certain object such as a flower can reach the nose of a person smelling it. Normally, the smell of a flower is brought to the nose by the wind, crossing space, but in the case of *vāsana* the smell also traverses time, being located in an intermediary object which the smeller then smells. What sets the process of *vāsana* apart from the other perfumery processes is the use of ephemeral fresh flowers (as opposed to camphor, sandalwood, etc.), and the fact that only contact, not admixture, is involved. Also, unlike in the case of censing, the flowers are not destroyed to release the fragrance that will perfume the material to be treated; instead, they release the perfume spontaneously by the laws of physics or diffusion between two substrates. Christophe Laudamiel explains it very clearly: "a bit like osmosis, or like making a tea in sesame oil instead of water."[32] Nevertheless, the flowers will wilt, die (as is their nature), and be discarded when they have diffused their quality of fragrance into another appropriately absorbent material.

The sources on perfumery that provide these details of the process are later than many key philosophical texts that use the related term *vāsanā*, nevertheless, the clarification of this term as used in perfumery may be of interest to scholars in considering the philosophical uses of the related term.[33] In philosophical contexts, such as the Buddhist Yogācāra philosophy and the Sāṃkhya philosophy, *vāsanā* refers to the phenomenon—sometimes translated as "perfuming"—of the production of certain characteristic, latent dispositions in a person (or apparent person) by which future states are generated for that person. If we understand the essential process of *vāsana* in perfumery to consist of the diffusion of a particular *quality* from one independent entity to another, contiguous, independent entity to be experienced at a later time, this would explain why it would make a good model for the transfer of dispositions across time in various more metaphysical contexts. If the previous is the main import of this particular metaphor, then we should also remember that the fact that the sense of smell is invoked here is merely incidental, or at the most secondary. There is nothing to suggest that *vāsanā* as "karmic memory" is related to or reflects the Euro-American discourse in which an important function of odors is to evoke (sometimes unconscious) memories. *Vāsanā* is more of a technical term than an experiential one, more like "osmosis." It is simply a very good metaphor for the irreversible and progressive transfer of qualities from one thing to another across time. That the term also evokes the idea of fragrance might have added to its significance—somewhat like "the stain of sin" works on several levels or "osmosis" might evoke a scientific discourse—but, as we noted, smell is never singled out as particularly evocative of memories in the discourses of early and medieval South Asia. Of course, if, as outsiders, from an etic perspective, we wish to explore an *unconscious* connection we are proposing between smells and memories, then *vāsanā* and memory is a fruitful topic for exploration.[34]

In addition to classifying the processes of perfumery, the aromatic raw materials themselves were also classified in a manner related to their use in perfumes. In the *Gandhasāra*, this is presented after the processes of perfumery have been fully described. The striking metaphor used in classifying these materials is derived from texts on statecraft (*arthaśāstra*), an olfactory taxonomy that charmingly uses South Asian political theory in the description of a well-blended perfume as analogous to a harmonious kingdom:

> He who, not properly knowing enemies, neutrals, and allies according to texts, performs the blending of perfumes is not an expert in perfume.[35]

> Materials are of three sorts: allies, neutrals, and enemies,
> they are to be blended by the wise at the right times according to the advice of texts.
> The ally-material is to be added in the same amount; the neutral: half of that,
> and the enemy material: a quarter—it is instructed in the blending of perfumes.[36]

To illustrate the theory, the author names examples of the raw materials belonging to three classes (*gaṇa*),[37] of which some better-known aromatics are:

> ***mitragaṇa*** (ally class) examples: mango flower (*cūtapuṣpa*), costus root (*kuṣṭhaṃ*), jatāmāṃsi (*māṃsī*).

> ***udāsīnagaṇa*** (neutral class) examples: *Cyperus rotundus* (*mustaka*), a variety of aloes wood (*kākatuṇda*), zedoary (*kacoraka*).

> ***śatrugaṇa*** (enemy class) examples: camphor (*karpūraṃ*), *Commiphora mukul* (*guggula*), lichen/bitumen/benzoin (*śailaja*), sulphur (*gandhaka*), asafoetida (*hiṅgu*).

At least with the enemy class it is very clear that these are particularly strong smelling substances: camphor, asafetida, and so on. One also wonders what sulfur is doing in this list, because I have not yet seen this strong-smelling mineral in any perfume compositions; although, perhaps the inclusion of this material is more to illustrate what is meant by an "enemy" ingredient as well as for completeness. Nevertheless, the system is quite clear and, as with the "arrow" perfumes, the choice of metaphor might reflect the association between the technology of erotics and the metaphor of warfare. At the very least, we see a theory that evokes some tendencies of early Indian medicine. As Zimmermann astutely notes for both the case of early India and ancient Greece "ideas about justice and political harmony were associated with the idea of health . . . Medicine is a form of politics."[38]

Finally, aromatics are classified in terms of their origin from roots, fruits, leaves, and so forth, as seen both in the early Buddhist classification of odors, as well as in the organization of the glossary of the *Gandhasāra* perfumery text.[39]

There is not enough space in this chapter to relate all the details of the numerous variables involved in both the production and the use of perfumes. But, I hope that in addition to the important general tendencies explored earlier (for example, perfumes are erotic, seasonal, made of different classes of aromatics, and so forth), I made clear the extent to which the blending and use of aromatics was a highly complex art that required substantial skill and knowledge on the part of both the perfume maker and the perfume user. This notion, of the skill involved in both making and consuming perfumes is something we will see later in a narrative context. Not only was the skill of deciphering the puzzles of the *Gandhasāra* probably a sign of the accomplishments of the cultivated man or woman, but so was the ability to compound and apply perfumes correctly.

The Purpose of Perfumery

I now turn to the more general theory of the purpose of perfumery as presented in these texts. What do these texts suggest about the purpose of perfumes considered most broadly? Who are perfumes for, and what will the perfumes do for them? Perhaps the most useful sources here are the *Nāgarasarvasva*, the Prakrit *Haramekhalā*, and the later *Gandhasāra*, all of which contain passages on the goals of perfumery.

The *Nāgarasarvasva*, or *Complete Man-About-Town*, is a text on erotics produced in a Buddhistic context that we have encountered several times so far. This text places the use of perfumes in an erotic context: like gemstones, perfumes are one of the necessary accessories for the love life of the man-about-town, the *nāgara* of the title of the work, as we saw in the verse quoted earlier:

> Various artful perfumes are celebrated as eminent inflamers of lust,
> The best lover should be carefully instructed at the start from perfume texts.[40]

Perfumes in all their variety are here said to be well-known for their power to incite erotic desire, and thus someone who would be the "best lover" needs to learn to control these materials from the very start. This is achieved by the study of perfume texts. Technical materials on perfumery and gemology have now been fully incorporated into the texts on erotic pleasure, *kāmaśāstra*. This text is far more encyclopedic than an earlier text on erotics, the famous *Kāmasūtra*: the man-about-town is now provided with details of all sorts of knowledge he will need to be a successful lover and man-about-town. Indeed, the very title of this work shifts the focus of the text from the pursuit of *kāma* toward the all-around perfection of the lifestyle of the man-about-town. In this respect, the *Nāgarasarvasva* somewhat resembles the section on perfumes in the *Haramekhalā*, where the qualities and goals of the *vidagdha* likewise frame the discourse on perfumes, as we shall see below.

The *Girdle of Hara* (that is, the god Śiva), the *Haramekhalā*, may date from approximately the same period as the *Nāgarasarvasva*, and although the lifestyle of the sophisticated man is prominent in the chapter on perfumes in this text, the section as a whole is less focused on erotics than the *Nāgarasarvasva*. Instead, the focus is very much on the generally sophisticated qualities of the *vidagdha*; a term that I have translated as "cultivated man." The *Haramekhalā* provides a definition of the *vidagdha*:

> Those who are solely intent on perfecting lives of righteousness, wealth, pleasure, and fame are called cultivated men (*vidagdha*)—however, those who are hungry to cheat others are not [so called.][41]

This passage tells us that the *vidagdha* pursues the three goals of life: the familiar "set of the three" (*trivarga*) of righteousness (*dharma*), wealth and power (*artha*), and sensual pleasure (*kāma*), as well as a fourth goal. This goal is not liberation (*mokṣa*) from the cycle of rebirth—an extra, fourth goal listed in some contexts—but instead fame/glory (*yaśas*). Thus the *vidagdha* is an ideal worldly, wealthy citizen who has his eye on his reputation, though he is not in anyway unpleasantly ambitious. He is a sophisticated, well-to-do, pleasure-loving gentleman, and a socialite. The *vidagdha* is the ostensible intended reader of this text—the person for whom the perfumes are apparently made, as we are told at the very beginning of the section:

> Having looked at numerous technical books on perfumery composed by very clever people, now [there is] the fifth book, the section that is *Beloved of the Cultivated Man*.[42]

In a manner flattering to certain readers of this text, we are thus told that this fifth book on perfumes is dear to the *vidagdha*, which suggests that he is particularly fond of this sensuous pursuit. We are given further comments to this effect—that the purpose of perfume is to please the *vidagdha*—at the end of the section. At the end of the glossary of terms (*nighaṇṭu*) we are told that:

> Here those synonyms of the things that have increased the joy of cultivated men [are related], such as are employed in the *Girdle of Hara* (*Haramekhalā*) book.
>
> Here is completed this *Girdle of Hara*, luminous with the arrangement of gold [also "with the arrangement of good syllables"], of beautiful form, marked by another name: The Production of Passion for the Cultivated Man.[43]

Perfumery materials are said to have "increased the joy" of *vidagdha*-folk (*vidagdhajanavardhitānandāḥ*) and indeed the whole chapter is also known by an alternative name: "The Production of Passion for the Cultivated Man" (*vidagdhānurāgakṛti*) for the first time, suggesting the erotic use-value of these materials—something emphasized from the start in the *Nāgarasarvasva*.

In these two texts, the ideal user of perfumes is a society gentleman, an upright, well-known, and sophisticated pleasure-loving man, who has a particular interest in the pleasures of the senses, and for whom the delights of perfume also have an erotic use, since these substances can arouse amorous desire. The *Gandhasāra* shares these ideals, although there is a little less emphasis on the man-about-town (*nāgaraka*) and the cultivated man (*vidagdha*). If anything, this text is slightly more royal in orientation, and the author presents both the text and the science of perfumery as having more universal goals, including ones of a religious nature. Here are the introductory benedictory verses of the text, which set the tone of the introduction, in which the full *trivarga* is presented as the purpose of perfumery:

> Homage to Ganeśa! Homage to the Teachers!
> 1. May the one attended on by the immortal gods with Brahmā and Viṣṇu at their head, by *apsarases, gandharvas, yakṣas*, and by the king of snakes,
> Who is adorned with the vines that are the arms of the daughter of the mountain, may Sky-Haired [Śiva] provide us with joy.
> 2. I worship him, whose ear-flapping is filled with garlands of restless bees greedy for the sweet perfume flowing all around,
> The elephant-faced one, born of the body of her who was born of the mountain, the obstruction-cutter, honored by the crowd of ageless [gods].
> 3. Having paid homage to the goddess who is the royal goose to the lotus of Brahmā's mouth, and to the Perfume-*yakṣa*, and to experts in perfume-texts, I will briefly relate, together with its essence, the auspicious *Essence of Perfume*.
> 4.–5. So, this treatise, instructive in good and auspicious perfumes is related here by a mere indication, [this treatise that] provides for a rite of worship of the gods with incense and auspicious perfumes; makes men thrive; provides the results of the *trivarga*, and removes one's own misfortune; that pleases kings, and delights the mind of the cultivated lady.[44]

In addition to the well-known gods (Śiva, Ganeśa, and Sarasvatī) mentioned in the benedictory verses, the author also mentions the *gandhayakṣa*, the "perfume *yakṣa*." As far as I am aware, this is the only reference in Sanskrit literature to this being—the *gandhayakṣa* could be a tutelary deity of perfumers,[45] or the term could be a poetic invention for the purpose of these verses, though we might note that the almost identical verse at the start of the Anup *Gandhasāra* reads "lore of perfumery" (*gandhavādam*) in place of "perfume *yakṣa*" (*gandhayakṣam*). This name is not to be found in the long list of *yakṣa*s given in the Buddhist protective text known as the *Mahāmāyūrī*.[46] However, in chapter 3 I noted that people possessed by a *yakṣa* show a preference for fragrances, and in this chapter I noted the famous perfume called *Yakṣa* Mud (*yakṣakardama*)—both these observations suggest a possible association between this type of being and fragrances, something I discuss in the final chapter. I also note that in describing the god Ganeśa the writer mentions the bees swarming round his temples which are perfumed with the sweet fluid produced by elephants in rut: this is an especially appropriate image here in the context of a perfume text, to remind us of the fragrant and literally attractive nature of a poetic vision of Ganeśa, who shares the olfactory eminence typical of elephants.

These Sanskrit benedictory verses frame the whole text in a somewhat standard medieval, Hindu manner. Having invoked the blessings of several appropriate gods, we are then told the purposes of the text and, by implication, of perfumery in general: First, it aids in the worship of the gods, and it also makes men thrive, presumably both physically and in prosperity. Importantly, perfumery provides the fruits of the *trivarga* of *dharma, artha,* and *kāma*, and removes one's own misfortune. By providing materials for the worship of the gods, perfumery provides the results of *dharma*. The next two benefits related are satisfying kings and delighting the minds of the cultivated (*vidagdha*) lady (or "the *vidagdha*'s lady"); two benefits that are connected to the goals of *artha* and *kāma*. The passage as a whole makes far more ambitious claims about the text and about perfumery than we saw in the two texts discussed previously. Perfumery no longer remains exclusively in the realm of the erotic life of the cultivated man, associated primarily with the goal of *kāma* (though, as seen, the distribution of perfume *names* in the *Gandhasāra* suggests otherwise at times), and instead the purposes of perfumery are connected to all three aims of worldly life. The *dharmic* use of perfumes in worshipping the gods is given pride of place, and the text is located in the general *trivarga* scheme of the purposes of life, in which it is of universal use. Although this might seem like hyperbole, in the case of perfumery this really was accurate in the context of traditional South Asia. Perfumes were important in worship; they also formed an indispensable part of royal daily ritual, and, finally, they were of great use in erotics. Although perfumes are stated to be almost universally useful—at least in the context of worldly life—arguably both the application to the goal of *dharma* and *artha* presuppose the pleasure-producing qualities of perfumes implied by their use in the pursuit of *kāma*—after all both gods and kings (generally) like pleasure. In premodern South Asia, perfumes and other adorning materials and technologies associated with *kāma* are not frivolous and unnecessary; rather they are necessary because they make things complete.[47]

Returning to the typical users of perfumes, not only are a variety of people said to appreciate perfumes—the king, the gods, the *vidagdha*—but elsewhere we also see that a certain ethnic and regional group was understood to be expert in perfumery, perhaps producing regionally distinct products. The *Haramekhalā* mentions that *yavanas*, northwesterners under Hellenic influence (or perhaps, by this period, "Arabs") made a particular type of perfume, and the unknown commentator notes that *yavanas* were particularly skilled at perfumery:

> molasses,[48] honey, black aloeswood, *sal* tree resin, crystal sugar in equal parts
> An incense for a *bhājana* vessel for perfumed oil is related by *yavanas*.[49]

The commentary here notes that:

> "by *yavanas*" who are without exception experts with regard to blending perfumes.[50]

This awareness of the regional nature of the production of luxury materials is something to which we shall return in the next chapter on trade and economics of aromatics.

The first two texts we examined in this chapter presented the use-value of perfumes as preeminently erotic, and the later, more comprehensive *Gandhasāra* makes a claim about perfumery almost as universal as one could find in the traditional scheme of brahmanical thought.[51] Apart from one ambiguous reference (to the "*vidagdha* lady"), in cases where humans are concerned, in all three texts the goal of these perfumes is to please *men*. The texts do not so much suggest a "male gaze" as a "male nose." This is something we shall see again in literary accounts of perfumery, and something which is in marked contrast to popular conceptions about the use of perfumes in our society.[52]

A Literary Account of Perfumes in Practice

I will now discuss a literary account of the nature of perfumery and perfume connoisseurship in early India, taken from the early Sanskrit version of the now lost Prakrit *Bṛhatkathā*, the *Bṛhatkathāślokasaṃgraha* of Budhasvāmin.[53] This is to my knowledge the richest and most detailed account of perfume connoisseurship in a Sanskrit literary source.

The *Bṛhatkathāślokasaṃgraha* is an early Sanskrit version of the famous lost Paiśācī Prakrit collection of tales, the *Bṛhatkathā*. Thus Lacôte notes the title should be translated as the "*Bṛhatkathā* abridged in *śloka* verses."[54] The date of this text by Budhasvāmin (probably not a Buddhist—the name is *not* Buddhasvāmin) is uncertain; it may date from some time in the first millennium CE.[55] We can very cautiously say that the text reflects the perfumery culture of that approximate period, a perfumery culture also reflected in the perfumery sections in the *Nāgarasarvasva* and the *Haramekhalā*: both texts that emphasize the cultured and sensual life of the urban cultivated man (*vidagdha/nāgaraka*).

In the nineteenth canto of this text, Gandharvadattā, one of the new wives of the protagonist, Naravāhanadatta, has her jealousy aroused by her husband's interest in a forest girl he noticed on the way to a festival. Therefore she relates the following story, to explain to him the fate she fears for herself in these circumstances. The story related by Gandharvadattā takes up the major part of this canto and begins as follows:

> On the shore of the Western ocean, there is a city (called) Forest Island, whose people have good conduct and wealth—the mirror-image of the city of great Indra.
> There was there a king, who did not have the qualities of Indra, [but] who was loved by his subjects. He had a charming son, who was even "Charming" (*Manohara*) by name.
> Though he knew all [types of] knowledge, he was especially fond of the science of perfumery—amongst the beings with various tastes there is somebody desirous of anything.
> As if he were springtime, he had two friends: Bakula and Aśoka (also names of trees associated with spring). Their affection never left him, like (Bakula and Aśoka trees never leave) springtime.
> Once, the doorkeeper, having saluted the prince, who was in the princely quarters with his friends, announced:
> A man called Sumaṅgala ("very auspicious"), learned in the precepts of perfume, not vulgar, and of composed speech, desires to see you for some reason.
> Manohara, having told the doorkeeper "Go, have him enter!" quickly applied some perfumed paste (*vilepana*) and burnt some incense.
> And Sumaṅgala, given leave [to enter], entered from the direction of the door, pressed his head with his hands, contracted his body and drew back.
> And said "This incense I smell, disagreeing with the perfume and garland, has given me a sharp headache."
> And when he had pulled out a double painting board[56] from his own bag, constantly looking at Manohara, he blended his own incense.
> Then, he bowed and said to Manohara: "Please burn this incense that agrees with the flowers and perfume."

> Then Manohara, together with Bakula and Aśoka, satisfied with that perfume, honored Sumaṅgala as someone who knew the science of perfumery. And thus favored, the clever Sumaṅgala completely satisfied the prince for three or four days.[57]

Following this meeting, Prince Manohara falls in love with a beautiful painting of a female *yakṣa*, a *yakṣī* that he sees at a festival. He even tries to seduce the painting, and then it turns out that the *yakṣī* depicted in the painting, called Sukumārikā, was only trapped in the painting by a curse. When the prince attempts to seduce her, this curse is broken and at last she is freed. The prince falls in love with her, but she instantly vanishes to her home on the mountain *Śrīkuñja*. Eventually the prince manages to sail to the mountain to find her and at that point there is the following description, in which we again see one of the main fragrance motifs in Sanskrit narratives where, blown by the wind, they often attract people to places:

> And suddenly there blew a fragrance brought by the wind from the North, and, methinks, the world became all-nose to smell it.[58]
> We, with curious eyes, trying to see its source, saw from a distance a mountain with *kiṃnaras*[59] on its jewel peak.
> I asked the ship's pilot "What is this?" and he said "This peak is *Śrīkuñja* (blessed bower) that old folks have reported."[60]

Unfortunately, prince Manohara is not able to remain there with her for longer than five days and has to return home where the *yakṣī* will instead visit him. In preparation for her arrival, the perfume-addicted Manohara asks that some especially excellent perfumes be prepared:

> When he had returned to his own palace, he said to Sumaṅgala "Please mix an incense that is the most precious result of the science of perfumery,
> Today my girlfriend is coming, together with friends for you—
> They say that a perfumed woman is the most important thing for perfect sex.
> That Yakṣa Mud that is declared to be our greatest perfume is equal to mud for them—that's why it is (called) Yakṣa Mud.
> Therefore, make an effort and show your learning today, for of the whole of the science of archery, the greatest skill is in piercing to the core."
> Urged on in this way, as well as by his own business, Sumaṅgala mixed incense, bathing materials, perfumes, and so forth as instructed.
> But Manohara, making the fuss that lovers make, together with his friends, resorted to his bed of suffering that was devoid of his lover's presence.

> Then, that perfume, of such qualities, perfected with such effort, was however driven out by another [perfume] as a rain cloud by the wind.
> As if, by means of her glory, rendering pale the moonlight on the moonstone and so forth, Sukumārikā entered suddenly, and sat down on the bed.
> Then, smiling she looked at Bakula and the others and said "I have come with my companions, go and please relax."
> They bowed, and when they had left, the prince and Sukumārikā passed the night in the manner they had yearned to do.
> On the morning Bakula and the others communicated the events of the night to the prince by means of [the mere sight of] their bodies which were pleasant from sexual enjoyment.
> United every night and divided every day—thus a year passed unnoticed by them.[61]

At the end of the year, Sukumārikā is obliged to return home, and the grieving Manohara tries to sail back to her mountain home to find her again, but unfortunately he is shipwrecked. Eventually, he is taken to a great city where he is welcomed by the king, where he is surprised to meet again the perfume expert, Sumaṅgala. Sumaṅgala explains that he had been sent on a mission to find a suitable husband for the daughter of the king of this land, so he found a way to meet Manohara and examine him:

> And having become aware from the people that you are addicted to the science of perfumery (*gandhaśāstra*), I then made it come to your attention that I was knowledgeable in the science of perfumery.
> For dependents with equal knowledge quickly delight the hearts of their masters, though devoid of qualities.
> And when you burned the incense that did not agree with the perfumes and flowers of the garland—you and your friends were testing me.
> And when I mixed the incense that agreed with the perfumes and flowers of the garland, I looked at the princess painted on the board.[62]

Manohara is therefore united with the king's beautiful daughter, Nalinikā, but then one day the *yakṣī* Sukumārikā finds him again and takes him away—this being the very fate that Gandharvadattā feared and which prompted her to relate the tale.

There are several points we should note in this episode. First, it is very clear that a full knowledge of perfumery, both in terms of making perfume and connoisseurship of perfume, is represented as relatively uncommon, impressive, and possibly a little unusual or eccentric. The prince who has this obsession is shown to be a sensitive and sensuous person, who falls in love with paintings and retreats to his private quarters suffering from love sickness. This prince and his friends "tested" Sumaṅgala for his expertise, and then commissioned him to make especially good perfumes for the visit of the *yakṣī*. The perfume addict and the perfume expert are both male, and though the perfumes are also made for the visit of the *yakṣī*, this world of blending and connoisseurship of perfumes is presented as mostly male. Also, the prince's interest in perfumery covers a variety of preparations—incenses, pastes, and unguents—showing that the connoisseurship of perfume was not limited to one product alone, and it is this same variety of preparations that is seen in the actual texts on perfumery. Related to this variety of perfume preparations is the fact that the fragrant items in one context, in one place and time, all have to "agree" (*saṃvādin*) with each other. The perfumes are not judged in isolation but as part of a whole, and it is partly relative to other aromatic preparations that a certain incense can be considered bad. A bad combination is not only aesthetically unpleasant, but also Sumaṅgala claims to have an intense headache on smelling the disharmonious combination of smells. This reflects the beliefs we saw earlier concerning the possible physical effects of perfumes, and the importance of using the right perfume at the right time and in accordance with the constitution of a person.

Again, the culture of perfumery described here reminds me of the culture of fine wine connoisseurs in our society. In wine culture, we see the possible cause of a (sometimes slightly affected) obsession, involving the sensory connoisseurship of rare and expensive materials from all over the world. The appreciation of wine requires not only knowledge of the wine itself but also knowledge of the appropriate combinations with food. Also, as with wine, the name is of importance, though, as we have seen, the names of perfumes tend to reflect literary, erotic, and even (suggestive) military culture. In this respect, the names of cocktails (Torpedo, Maiden's Blush Cocktail, The French 75)[63] are similar to medieval Indian perfumes. Here we witness an imaginary scenario where perfume enthusiasts discuss a name, and even joke about the name, "*Yakṣa* Mud," which is appropriate when actual *yakṣa*s are coming to visit—and this reflects the playful and complex nature of perfume names in medieval South Asia.

The passage does indeed reflect many of the ideas about perfumery we deduced from the perfumery texts themselves, yet it also highlights something I did not consider previously. A considerable part of the aesthetic value of the individual perfumes depends on the other preparations in a given context, and one very important source of fragrance in these urban and domestic contexts that, we have so far utterly failed to discuss, is flowers and garlands: fragrant items that, according to this passage, play an important role in this wider olfactory structure.

Visual and Fragrant Delights

Given the importance of the garland, it seems appropriate to look at a text on garlands. There are not, to my knowledge, as many Sanskrit texts specifically about garlands as there are about perfumes, but there is a passage in the *Mānasollāsa* where we are told of the different types of garland that the king should wear after putting on clothes, prior to putting on jewels and ornaments:

> Now the delightful pleasure of garlands is fully related:
> Having done the decoration with clothes, then he should arrange the garland—
> *campaka*[64] joined with *mallikā,*[65] *campakas* with lotuses,
> *campaka* joined with *surabhī,*[66] *campaka* linked with *pāṭalas,*[67]
> *mallikā* joined with *pāṭalas, mallikā* joined with *surabhī,*
> *mallikā* mixed with *bakulas,*[68] *mallikā* joined with lotuses,
> *mālatī*[69] furnished with *mallikā, mālatī* linked with *pāṭala,*
> *mālatī* furnished with *bakula, mālatī* joined with *pāṭala,*
> the delightful *śatapatra* (lotus) combined with the oleander
> *śatapatra* with *maruka* (peacock?), *śatapatra* with *pāṭala,*
> the *mālatī, mallikā, yūthī*[70] joined with globe amaranth[71]
> *kurabaitī*[72] as well as *yuthī* and *nevalī* (?) is likewise esteemed
> The king wears the garland on his head according to his own custom,
> and in his hair and on the neck—the enjoyment of garlands is declared.[73]

In this passage, we see a meticulous listing of numerous *combinations* of flowers; combinations that would produce various different perfumes as well as patterns of colors. Indeed, similar to perfumes, garlands were also subject to mathematical speculations on combinatorics.[74] We should remember that garlands, more so than the other perfume items, would have been seasonal, and thus the related aromatic whole must have been seasonal not only by choice (for example, making warming musk-based pastes in the cold season) but also by necessity.

This understanding of the importance of the whole aromatic context not only applies to their human use, but also to their use in divine worship, by means of *pūjā* rituals in which the icon in question is treated very much like an honored person. In the *Varāhapurāṇa*, we see the following in a list of offenses that may be committed in performing the ritual, presumably the smell equivalent of only serving dessert at a dinner party:

> But he who, not having given perfume and flowers, offers incense—
> I consider this as the thirty-first offense, oh wise lady.[75]

The previous literary description of perfumery confirmed most, if not all, of what we had found before in the technical texts on perfumery, and it also highlighted one aspect of perfumery we had not noted before, perhaps because it was so obvious in actual practice in medieval South Asia—the importance of the *combinations* of garlands, perfumes, incense and so forth: the structurally relative nature of olfactory aesthetics.

Visible Fragrances

Garlands are not only perfumed, but they are also colorful and beautiful. Now we should think about the visual aspects of other perfumes in South Asia.[76] Contemporary perfumes are invisible: although the bottle may be attractive, the perfume itself leaves no visible trace. This is not the case for someone wearing many of the perfumes in the texts we have been reading.

A paste such as *yakṣa* mud would have been an intense color. I have made such pastes myself, and the combination of the colored woods with musk and saffron make an intensely dark-golden paste. The visual appearance of many of the more important aromatics is regularly described: sandalwood is white, reddish, or yellow; aloeswood is black; musk is black; camphor is bright white; and saffron is red. In the next chapter, we will read a poetic description of a tribute to King Harṣa, and there the visual beauty of many of these aromatics is quite prominent, as they are in many poetic texts. The fact that aromatics were in many cases highly visible effectively permitted a form of conspicuous consumption: were we to witness a medieval South Asian king in procession we would *see* the rich, fragrant pastes smeared on his body. This also applies to the icons of the gods in the temple. Even today, one of the most famous images of a Hindu icon is that of Venkateśvara, whose highly noticeable white forehead mark consists of a considerable quantity of (borneol) camphor[77] molded onto the face of the image and divided in the center by a striking, bamboo-leaf shaped streak of dark musk (which is mixed/diluted with sandalwood paste).[78] Arguably, this is the most famous adornment of any image worshipped in Hinduism today, and although a "perfume," it is most well-known as a visual image.

The use of aromatics could not only be intimate and private, but it could also be a public performance, and the display of perfumes could, and can, be an important public aspect of state and temple rituals. Yet, there might well have been a noticeable class-based difference in the reception of such visible fragrances. Although most people seeing the saffron-smeared arms of the king or the musk stripe on the temple icon would have perceived the same colors, if people observed these adorned beings from a significant distance it would take imagination to have an idea what the king or the icon actually smelled like. We can never know how many people in medieval South Asia were familiar with the scent of a costly musk paste—presumably not everyone was. Some people would be familiar with wearing the materials themselves. Other people, engaged in certain relevant professions—such as aromatics traders, perfumers, doctors, priests, and personal servants—might have had a good idea what many aromatics smelled like. Still other people might well have had no personal experience of the smell of some of these aromatics and perfumes, and thus their ability to imagine the smell of distant yet visible aromatics would have been quite different from those who knew them firsthand. Of course, this also applies to the reception of textual descriptions of perfumes, including those described in texts as used by the gods.

Conclusion

We have established that any given perfume might be associated with a part of the body, a time of day, and the time of year. An aromatic product might also be cooling or warming, attractive, and associated with a particular bodily constitution. Perfumes could also be repellent, erotic, and sometimes even calming. Perfumes sometimes had admired visible qualities. Perfumes often had names, and these names often provided a strong indication of the supposed qualities of the perfume. In the early centuries of the second millennium CE, it appears texts on perfumery were becoming increasingly literary on a number of levels. Furthermore, there were rules for the production of perfume, and a product could be well made according to various processes with ingredients in the correct proportions, or they could be badly made by an ignorant perfume blender—for example overcooked and overbearingly camphoraceous. Finally, the individual preparation itself needed to be carefully matched to the other aromatics in use at the same time. In terms of gender, the production and appreciation of perfumes was presented as the domain of men; although, perfumes were believed to affect women, adorning them, attracting them, and pleasing them in an erotic context. The story of the perfume-addicted prince helped us appreciate certain other variables of perfumery, yet the actual perfume mentioned was a particularly well-known preparation, *Yakṣa* Mud, knowledge of which was by no means limited to the sorts of perfume experts described in the story. Thus, in literary narratives perfumery is presented in an accessible manner that requires only the most basic level of knowledge, not unlike the presentation of cocktails and wines in films and television. This tendency to simplify expertise to engage and even flatter the reader (or hearer) in literary narratives is also something we shall see later.

In medieval South Asia the cultured and educated elite carefully combined and processed certain aromatic materials for a number of ends, ends which were in many respects consistent with the understanding of smell that we saw in the earlier chapters. Not only did people make these perfumes, but, for approximately one thousand years starting around the fifth century CE, they wrote about how to make them in both Sanskrit and Prakrit. How did this sort of very unique perfume culture come into being? Sheldon Pollock, writing about the place of Sanskrit and culture in South Asia, notes with respect to the *Delight of the Mind*, the *Mānasollāsa*:

> An encyclopedia of royal conduct from early-twelfth-century Karnataka, the *Mānasollāsa*, demonstrates how literary-theoretical competence (*śāstravinoda*) was as central to kingliness as military competence (*śastravinoda*). Episodes of grammatical and literary correctness such as these are not idiosyncratic tendencies of the persons and places in question. They point toward an ideal of proper rule and proper culture being complementary—an ideal in evidence throughout the cosmopolitan age, from the earliest recorded evidence in the second century, and beyond

into the vernacular epoch, when so many cosmopolitan values of culture and power came to find local habitations and names.[79]

It is vital to note that in addition to these two competences Pollock mentions from the *Mānasollāsa*—competences whose importance in society we recognize today—many others are described. These are in some cases competences that we might not expect of the educated and powerful today. These include numerous sensual enjoyments (*bhogas*) which involve the use of perfumes and aromatics. By the mid-to-late first millennium CE these practices, including perfumery, were codified and presented in Sanskrit—just as grammar, logic, and statecraft were. Along with literary-theoretical competence and military competence, competence in the creation, use, and connoisseurship of aromatic materials was also evidently a vital part of cosmopolitan social status—for the king, the wealthy townsperson, and the icon in the temple. Indeed, the *Mānasollāsa* itself is a statement to the effect that the court of King Someśvara had mastery over all these matters—from appreciating luxurious sandalwood shoes, to directing scholarly disputations.

Perhaps it will be helpful to consider exactly how the contents of the encyclopedic *Mānasollāsa* relate to the three goals of a person (*trivarga*). What exactly does the *Mānasollāsa* contain, and how is it organized? The *Mānasollāsa* is ostensibly organized into five main sections of twenty parts (*viṃśatis*), dealing with:

1. The attainment of the kingdom (*rājyaprāptikāraṇa*).
2. The maintenance of the kingdom (*rājyasya sthairyakāraṇa*).
3. The pleasure of the king once the kingdom is stable (*sthirarājyasya bhūbhartur upabhogāḥ*).
4. The entertainments (or sports) that delight (*pramodajanakās . . . vinodā*).
5. The games that produce happiness (*sukhopapādikā krīḍā*).[80]

I suggest that behind this more obvious fivefold structure the text also reflects, less obviously, the *trivarga* of *dharma*, *artha*, and *kāma*.[81] Thus, the contents of the first short section dealing with the attainment of the kingdom are all very much within the fold of *dharmic* duties: from avoiding untruth, to worshiping the ancestors. Moreover, the second section, on the maintenance of the kingdom, is like a small example of a text in the genre of *arthaśāstra*: describing, among other matters, the qualities desired of various officials, the contents of the treasury, and the nature and activities of the army.

The remainder of this work, indeed the greater part of the *Mānasollāsa*, is devoted to what the king of a stable kingdom does next—enjoys the world. The third section, on the pleasures (*upabhogas*), corresponds most closely to what one might expect to find in a *kāmaśāstra*, including a (no doubt temporal) ideal sequence of adornments, from betel and unguents to jewelry, and culminating in the evening pleasures of bed, incense, and women. It is here that we see the enjoyment in the form of jewelry of the many types of gemstones already described in the discussion of the contents of the treasury, where they are raw commodities. The two sections that follow also treat sources of pleasure very broadly conceived: entertainments and games. Examples of royal games are described in another text attributed to Someśvara III, the *Vikramāṅkābhyudaya*,[82] as activities connected with the third *puruṣārtha* (*kāma*) that the king would pursue once the stable kingdom was placed in well-established and in capable hands.

The *Complete Man-About-Town, Nāgarasarvasva,* similarly expands on the competences required of the wealthy cosmopolitan man-about-town, introducing chapters on gemology, perfumery, and the secret language of lovers' signs. It is also during the same period, in the centuries surrounding the turn of the second millennium CE, that we find evidence of the earliest treatises devoted entirely to perfumery. The same cosmopolitan cultural momentum that produced the *Mānasollāsa* may have led to the creation of these manuals, whether they were used at court or at home by wealthy citizens: more people than ever felt they needed to be up to speed on these sorts of competences. As we saw in the episode from the *Bṛhatkathāślokasaṃgraha*, it was the prince, as well as his courtly friends *and* the traveling sophisticate who had a mastery over the science of perfumery.

In the *Nāgarasarvasva* and the *Mānasollāsa*, we see the increasingly encyclopedic nature of certain texts devoted to aspects of the "world of *kāma*" (including perfumery) during the latter centuries of the first millennium CE and the first centuries of the second millennium CE. This appears to indicate a greater inclusiveness in the Sanskritic *śāstric* fold where technologies of pleasure are concerned. Earlier texts might well mention the importance of the study of the sixty-four arts and other technologies of pleasure, but only now do we see them described in such a literary and detailed manner in Sanskrit. The move to discuss perfumery in greater detail in *kāma*-related contexts that emphasize their consumption, along with their various affective powers, would suggest that Sanskritic, codified expertise in the materials associated with *kāma* was becoming increasingly important and respectable in South Asian high culture. Possessing these things, as well as knowing about them, was an essential part of being a sophisticated man-about-town, or king, or, indeed, god in the form of a king or a man-about-town. No longer was it enough to know how to examine these materials in the treasury (as seen in the *Arthaśāstra*): one needed to know how to consume them correctly. People could write and read about these luxurious, intoxicating materials in Sanskrit, and conversely, the world of Sanskrit texts increasingly embraced a specialized and extensive discourse about pleasure-giving things. Quite often, these were strange things with strange names brought from the margins of the imagined domain of Sanskritic culture, as we shall see in the next chapter.

PART FOUR

AROMATIC MATERIALS

7

The Incense Trees of the Land of Emeralds

Exotic Aromatics in Medieval South Asia

> All of a sudden the serpent prince released that [bile] on the lowlands of the mountain that is the Lord of the Earth, which possess frankincense trees anointed with their own resin, and which are perfumed with the fragrance of *nalikā* forests.
>
> Right at the time immediately after it fell down, on account of that, the place that is beyond the abode of the *barbaras*, near the desert, [and] by the land on the ocean shore, became the source of emeralds.
>
> —*Ratnaparīkṣā* of Buddhabhaṭṭa

Buddhabhaṭṭa, in his treatise on the examination of gemstones, the *Ratnaparīkṣā*, writes about the origin of the source of emeralds in remote lands. This writer, possibly a Buddhist, dating from perhaps the mid to late first millennium CE,[1] chooses to describe this exotic land almost entirely in terms of its aromatic products: it both abounds in the fragrance of *nalikā* forests and is filled with trees dripping with valuable, fragrant frankincense resin.[2]

This passage is particularly striking but not unique—certain key aromatics were often perceived to be exotic as well as fragrant, and this contributed significantly to their charms. Indeed, the most important aromatics in medieval South Asia were both exotic and expensive, not unlike spices in medieval Europe. Perfumes made of such exotica, as well as gemstones and other luxury commodities, were closely associated with the ideal lifestyle of the king and the cultivated man-about-town; and they also adorned the gods, both in literature as well as in the temple.

In this chapter, I explore one aspect of the aromatic materials, namely, the fact that many aromatics such as camphor and aloeswood (often called agarwood) were exotic—they came from faraway places—and an important part of their prestige and significance in many discourses, both textual and olfactory, was a result of these real and imagined origins. Not only were many aromatics actually exotic in practice—that is to say, for many people living in South Asia, a perfume such as musk actually did come from far away—but as the epigraph demonstrates, representations of these materials often described them as originating in foreign lands that were imagined to be filled with sensuous delights, with wild people, and with danger. Mapping the spatial imagination of Sanskrit culture in terms of the represented origins of luxury materials paints a different picture than that produced by focusing on the origins of the texts themselves. Conventional representations of aromatics and the practices associated with them appear to have been relatively universal; yet, the materials themselves were a conceptual benchmark for the intrinsically regional, and rightly so, since musk deer never lived in Ujjain, for example.

A number of genres of texts enrich our understanding of the wider sphere of practice and discourse involving the exotic, sensual luxuries so vital to the pursuit of pleasure, whether divine pleasure or human. For example, texts on gemology and on perfumery, lexicons, as well as literary texts, epics, and Buddhist *avadāna* texts can enrich our understanding both of the nature of these commodities and of the way they were commonly represented in the South Asian discourse of material luxury over hundreds of years. These exotic materials were seen as originating in specific lands and, conversely, certain regions could be characterized in literary texts by their natural abundance of these same luxuries. In the Buddhist monastery, Hindu temple, royal palace, or man-about-town's bedroom, such things as sacred icons, relics, and also people might be ornamented with these prestigious and pleasurable exotics from the margins of civilization, creating an elite and literally cosmopolitan material environment in a local setting.

Luxurious, Perfumed Exotica

It appears that in the Sanskritic literary imagination certain aromatic materials were more important than others, and that there was indeed something like a "canon" of major aromatics, much as there was a conventional list of great gemstones (*mahāratnas*);[3] although these principal aromatic raw materials were not assigned to an explicit and named category. This classic list of prestigious aromatics superseded earlier lists found in texts dating approximately from the centuries around the turn of the Common Era, which tended to include items such as costus root, *tagara*, sandalwood, and aloeswood, as noted previously. Sandalwood and aloeswood remained prestigious aromatics, but costus and *tagara*, though still used in perfumery, no longer seem to have been so prestigious. I first establish what the most important materials were, and I then examine their imagined origins. I do not attempt to provide a history of trade in these items, but rather I examine literary *representations* of some key aspects of trade. My emphasis here is on such representations, but, nevertheless, a basic awareness of some documentary facts (for example: aloeswood was produced in Assam, cubebs produced in Southeast Asia) can make an important difference in the way we read these texts.

Many aromatic substances are described in South Asian texts as exotic and luxurious items of trade and tribute from abroad, and their foreign names and the stories of their marvelous distant origins lent them an aura that contributed to the cultural value of these costly rarities. Tribute and trade in aromatics was perceived to bring the urban elite and the mercantile classes both directly and indirectly in contact with marginal and subordinate groups, and representations of these groups are found in sources associated with both mercantile and courtly milieux. In these discourses, the exotic "other" does not so much smell of anything, as arrive loaded with sacks of the fragrant and expensive materials that abound in their distant homeland. The marvelous earlier chapters of the imaginary biography[4] of the aromatic substances that were being pounded, blended, smeared, and burnt in the palace, temple, monastery, or in the house of the wealthy man-about-town, no doubt, remained a feature of these materials for these wealthy urban consumers, both in discourse and practice.

The "Canon" of Aromatic Raw Materials

First of all, we need to establish what sorts of materials were deemed important in the South Asian practices and discourses of wealth and pleasure (as opposed to medicine). Some aromatics appear to have occupied a more prominent place in the medieval South Asian world of smell: sandalwood, aloeswood, musk, saffron, camphor, nutmeg, cloves, cubebs, and certain resins;[5] the first five items being the most important. I should note that when I refer to aromatics, I am not dealing with fresh flowers and garlands, as discussed above. The nature of the trade in fresh flowers is quite different from the trade in, for example, sandalwood, and it is the latter sort of trade that interests me here (only at a later date does distillation permit the type of commodification of flower-scents that we see at an early date for a material such as camphor).

First, I look at lists of aromatics in two major glossaries. I choose these works, and not the specialized glossaries of *materia medica* and so on, because they represent what must have been standard, much memorized, and frequently used lists of aromatic substances—well-known to a large number of those who received an education in Sanskrit, including those involved in the production of literature. Although medical glossaries classify aromatics in a separate category "Sandalwood and the rest" (*candanādi*),[6] this category includes all aromatics, costly and cheap, local and exotic, from sandalwood to vetiver; that classification does not make the interesting category distinction between exotic "spices" and local products I wish to explore.[7] Here, I am interested in a more literary discourse, linked both to urban consumption and to exoticism, and, in fact, it is precisely against the background of the more comprehensive aromatic lists in pharmacological and perfumery lexica that I wish to highlight the narrower focus on prestigious exotica found in sources more closely aligned with concepts of wealth (*artha*) and pleasure (*kāma*).

In what is perhaps the most well-known Sanskrit glossary, the *Nāmaliṅgānuśāsana* or *Amarakośa* of Amarasiṃha, of uncertain date, possibly around the sixth century CE,[8] aromatics are listed in two places: in the "Section on Wild Herbs" (*vanauṣadhivarga*) in the second part (*kāṇḍa*), and in the "Section on Humans" (*manuṣyavarga*) also in the second part, because both are components of the terrestrial world covered in that part of the work. In the section on wild herbs, Amarasiṃha groups several plants together that produce aromatics in the context of forest plants/forest products.[9] Later in the second part, in the section on humans, some other aromatics are listed, and these are of most interest to us here. These aromatics are not presented in the context of their origins, as in the section on wild herbs, but rather these substances are now removed from the forest and have entered the human world. Following a list of the parts of the body, the glossary moves to matters of ornamentation of the body (*manuṣyavarga* 2.6.99), where, following lists of ornaments, textiles, and garments we move on to massage, bathing, and finally to cosmetics, where saffron (2.6.123–124) is mentioned along with red lac (2.6.125). After these particularly highly colored cosmetics, the glossary lists other aromatics: cloves (2.6.125); an aromatic, possibly a type of aloeswood, that I have not identified with certainty, called *kālīyakam* (2.6.125–126);[10] aloeswood (2.6.126); *sal* tree resin (2.6.127); a resin about whose identity I am not certain called wolf-incense (*vṛkadhūpa*) (2.6.128);[11] frankincense (2.6.128); *Pinus longifolia* resin (*sarala*) (2.6.128-129); musk (2.6.129); cubebs (2.6.129–130); camphor (2.6.130); several types of sandalwood (2.6.130–132); and nutmeg (2.6.132). Finally, Amarasiṃha gives the formula for the famous *yakṣa* mud we saw in the previous chapter, as well as general terms for unguents and so forth. Following this, the glossary remains firmly in the human realm of the ornamented and pampered body, as the text lists synonyms for garlands, beds, lamps, seats, combs, perfumed powder, and mirrors, before completing the section with fans. Indeed, the whole section of the *manuṣyavarga* of the *Amarakośa* reads very much like a glossary of the sorts of luxury ornaments that are important accessories for the lifestyle of the man-about-town in texts on erotics.

The list would appear to have the following structure: highly colored cosmetics/aromatics are followed by aromatics that are primarily burned, and then by aromatics associated with being made into pastes, mouth fresheners, and so forth. Thus, after saffron we have aloeswood, various incense resins, followed by musk, cubebs, camphor, sandalwood, and nutmeg.

Several hundred years later, the *Abhidhānacintāmaṇi*, a twelfth-century lexicon by the Jain Hemacandra, the "uncrowned king of medieval lexicography,"[12] contains a similar list of aromatics. Again, these are listed in part of the work dealing with the human body and its ornaments.[13]

One final, entirely different, source we shall examine in our investigation of the discourse of aromatics, is a highly literary, and again quite typical, description of the merchants' quarters in an idealized royal capital city. These mercantile residences are characterized above all by the commodities with which they are filled. The text in question is the *Vikramāṅkābhyudaya* attributed to King Someśvara III, who was also responsible for the *Delight of the Mind* (*Mānasollāsa*), which we discussed earlier. Here, toward the beginning of the text, the author gives an interesting description of the royal capital city Kalyāṇa,[14] where, amongst other things, there is a depiction of the part of town where the merchants live. In *The Great Cat Massacre*, Robert Darnton analyzed the manner in which an eighteenth-century French bourgeois described the city of Montpellier. This description apparently reflects the fact that "in Montpellier, as in India, *homo hierarchicus* thrived through the segmentation of society rather than from its polarization."[15] Although one might expect the medieval Indian king and scholar, Someśvara III (or whoever actually composed the text), to exemplify some aspects of *homo hierarchicus*, his description of the city of Kalyāṇa, for the most part, shows other preoccupations than the order of society, and if anything, varieties of material wealth rather than *varṇa* appear to be his organizing principle. And, in any case, he only pays detailed attention to those people who are associated with luxury and sensual pleasure, whether wealthy traders in gems or courtesans. After describing the moat and tall, white city wall, he describes the temples (*devāyatana*). These too are very tall and white, and they are filled with boisterous crowds. He then describes the dense masses of tall white mansions (*dhavalagṛha*). Then follows a description of the abodes of the merchants, two-storied and stuccoed; and these are followed by what appear to be market stalls abounding in piles of grain and salt; the paraphernalia of betel traders including many types of fruit; the goods of perfumers; and finally those of garland makers. Someśvara then depicts the city courtesans at some length, following the passage with an interesting description of the market streets that contain cooks preparing all sorts of delicious foods. Finally, he merely lists the four *varṇas*: Brahmins, Kṣatriyas, Vaiśyas, and Śūdras at the beginning of a longer list of all sorts of professions, followed by a shorter list of the various types of people from other regions found in the city. The general impression of the city is not unlike the medieval South Asian model of the terrestrial world: it is encircled by tall mountainous walls, filled with many extremely tall, brilliant-white mountainous buildings housing gods and the most important people. Then, at a lower level, there is an abundance of riches, sensuous materials, as well as people adept in furnishing various sensual pleasures, all of which is, of course, for sale.

Here we are interested in the merchants and the perfumers. The houses of the merchants are described almost entirely in terms of the rare (*durlabha*) luxuries they contain. The first category of luxury product mentioned is aromatics, after which are described gemstones and then textiles—all common categories of luxury products. Like the lexicons mentioned, this text describes what were evidently the most important aromatics in early and later medieval discourses. This particular prose style abounds in the punning/bitextual use of language (*śleṣa*), and I have put the "aromatic readings" of the comparisons in parentheses:

> The royal capital, called Kalyāṇa was adorned with merchants' houses: with rows of two-storied, stuccoed houses on both sides, constructed in a uniform style, with abundant groups of things that are rare in the three worlds found in each merchant's house, the very image of hidden treasure made visible. Like days with rain clouds their quintessence is many dense clouds (they possess much camphor); like lowly people they are delighted by small bits of wealth (are brilliant with sandalwood); like the non-orthodox they have houses without spiritual preceptors (have the perfume of aloeswood); like the Ganges' stream they have many paths (possess much musk); like places in Nandana[16] they contain the Haricandana tree[17] (possess yellow sandalwood); like metrical science, like the technical manuals on song, like *smārta* brahmins, and like forests, they possess: the many results of *jāti* meters; the many results of the notes of the scale; the results of many re-births; fruit of many varieties (possess much nutmeg).[18]

Here in an ideal medieval city, rare aromatics take pride of place in the mercantile quarters; listed first amongst all luxury products. The list is by now familiar: camphor, sandalwood, aloeswood, musk, and nutmeg. There is no mention of saffron, clove, cubebs, or of the various resins, though, in other respects, the choice of aromatics is highly typical of what we see elsewhere.

Although this is a highly literary and idealized vision of a city, nevertheless, it is notable that Someśvara makes a clear distinction between the aromatics merchants and those whose business is perfumery. The perfumers in Someśvara's vision of the city are mentioned in the section after that describing the abodes of merchants of luxurious commodities, in the section describing markets full of large piles of grains and salt, of merchants of betel nut paraphernalia, and garland makers. In a passage that presents a few difficulties/corruptions, the city is said to be made delightful

> in other places by perfumer-traders [in stalls?] fruitful with fragrant emblic, unctuous "Masculine" perfume,[19] musk "mud," sandalwood liquid, perfume oil, flower extracts, camphor, crows-beak [aloeswood], deodar cedar, sugar, honey, frankincense . . . [incense?] sticks, mouth perfume, perfumed powder, drinking-water perfume and so forth.[20]

The materials represented in this context are far more numerous than those in the aromatics merchants' abodes, and in many cases they are materials that have undergone some sort of processing: the sandalwood has been made into a liquid paste, the musk appears to have been made into a preparation called "mud"—possibly a term for a thick cosmetic paste perhaps analogous to our word "cream" as in "face cream." This also helps make more sense of the name of the famous *yakṣa* mud perfume—it is quite easy to imagine a product called "fairy cream."

Described as they are in a section after that depicting the wealthy merchants' abodes, it seems that perfumers, like garland makers and betel sellers, are far less wealthy than the merchants. In general, professional perfumers appear not to have had the same social status as aromatics merchants, whose social standing I shall discuss in more detail in the next chapter.

As I noted, in some respects this commonly repeated short list of aromatics recalls the conventional lists of great gemstones (*mahāratnas*) contained in Sanskrit texts on gemology. Yet, unlike gemstones, these aromatics were never explicitly categorized as "the great aromatics." In at least one case, Islamic scholarship did, however, recognize two clear categories of aromatics—the principal ones and the secondary ones. The principal aromatics, as given by Ibn Māsawaih (777–857 CE) in his *Treatise on Simple Aromatic Substances*, are as follows: musk, ambergris, aloeswood, camphor, and saffron.[21] It is notable that sandalwood is absent, being a secondary aromatic substance, and ambergris features as a primary aromatic. Conversely, ambergris is absent from most of our sources. In the course of his prolific writing on cultural history, P. K. Gode wrote an entire paper about the history of ambergris in India—this might seem a somewhat obscure topic, but, in fact, given that this particular ingredient seems a distinguishing characteristic of the Muslim olfactory aesthetic, and it is found in the Indian Ocean, its history in India is of no small importance.[22] Gode suggests that there is only one perfumery text that refers to ambergris in any of the sources on perfumery, the *Gandhavāda*, though it is also mentioned in the manuscript I am calling the Anup *Gandhasāra*. This is despite the fact that the substance appears in a number of Sanskrit glossaries dating from the late first millennium CE. Among the glossaries Gode mentions that refer to ambergris, perhaps the earliest one of a relatively secure date is the *Trikāṇḍaśeṣa* by the Bengali Buddhist Puruṣottamadeva, dating from the first half of the twelfth century.[23] He provides a definition of the word *ambara*: "*ambara* has the sense of 'sky,' and a substance with an intense perfume."[24] Although scholars of Sanskrit knew of ambergris, it is not, as noted, mentioned in many perfumery texts, nor, to my knowledge, are there any references to ambergris in literary texts in Sanskrit. This contrasts with the Mughal description of the preparation of perfumes in the *Ā'īn-I Akbarī*. Also notable in that text is the prominence of roses.[25] It would appear that ambergris is a perfume closely associated with Islamic culture, and that this association continues in Mughal India. Conversely, when Ibn Māsawaih discusses the "secondary aromatic" sandalwood, he states: "It is a sweet aromatic of the Indian people,"[26] suggesting that people were to some extent defined in the eyes of others by the aromatics they favored and vice versa.

Despite the fact there is no explicit category of "great aromatics," for a long period in South Asia, the substances highlighted appear to have been the most prestigious aromatics in the cultural milieux that were also associated with the production and consumption of Sanskrit texts. They are a feature of discourse, and no doubt they were also an important feature of practice. Of course, perfumery texts mention many other substances, such as vetiver (*uśīra*) and costus root, not mentioned here. These sorts of substances are more closely associated with the forest in Amarasiṃha's lexicon, and they are not mentioned in the description of the merchants' houses above. Only the most expensive aromatics, the ones that were important commodities, became part of this list of aromatics. What matters to us is that these more important aromatics were all obtained by long-distance trade, both within South Asia and beyond. These aromatics were costly, prestigious, and exotic; and, in this respect, they have many of the same characteristics as materials falling into the category of "spices" in European medieval discourses. Such relatively cheap and local items as vetiver, listed by Amarasiṃha in the forest section, and by Hemacandra in the plant section, might then be compared with the category of "herbs." As Paul Freedman notes:"In the Middle Ages in Europe, spices were aromatic items of commerce with a high unit cost (that is, price per pound) imported from distant lands . . . Herbs . . . were above all familiar, literally part of the European landscape."[27] It seems that the "land of spices" itself classified certain materials in a manner quite analogous to the European category of "spice," even if there was not an actual term to designate these items. Texts in Sanskrit most often do not locate themselves at the center of the production of gems and aromatics. Although some materials such as sandalwood are indeed found in South India (and therefore in a region of Sanskrit textual production) these materials are virtually always represented as coming from remote places.[28] These lists of sandalwood, aloeswood, musk, and so on are arguably a somewhat "formal" canon of aromatics, an idealized stock list of the best fragrant materials, and the reality of perfumery involves a lot more materials. However, these aromatics were used in actual practices, and inclusion on this list would have raised their prestige in real-life situations. Plus, the perceived prestige associated with the use of these actual materials would, of course, have fed back into the more idealized world of texts, in what was probably a dialectic of real perfumes and ideal perfumes that, no doubt, had an impact on demand and trade. Over time, new aromatics enter the realm of practice and slowly change the canon, as we saw in the change from early lists of superlative aromatics that mention costus and *tagara* to lists that include the exotics camphor and so forth. But, of course, one assumes that when a new aromatic entered the canon, such as when camphor arrived on the scene, it had already been noted as prestigious in another context, be that practical or textual.

The Sources of Aromatics: Marginal Kingdoms and Exotic Tribute

The question that now concerns us is the way people imagined one went about obtaining these aromatics. As we will see, these substances were believed to be produced in a variety of places, and the imagined exotic origins of many aromatics remained associated with them in several contexts. Not only did the aromatics retain the aura of their exotic sources, but conversely certain aromatics would be mentioned in some texts in order to characterize certain regions in a material and sensuous manner; for example, this chapter's epigraph. This literary use of aromatics and other, often luxury, commodities to convey regional character was also consciously theorized in at least one text, which we examine in this chapter. Indeed, it is by the material nature of their world—the products of their land, their clothes, and eating habits—and not in terms of their beliefs or social organization that many marginal groups are primarily characterized, and interaction with these groups is often represented in the form of material exchanges.

There are two principal ways by which aromatics are described as being obtained in South Asian discourses: tribute and trade. In this chapter, I will focus on one of these categories—tribute. In a later chapter, I will consider a narrative concerning trade: the Buddhist *Pūrṇāvadāna*, where we see similar themes to those encountered in narratives of tribute; especially the motif of an abundance of luxury in the hands of marginal and wild peoples.[29] Whilst in trade narratives we often glimpse the land of origin of luxuries, in the case of tribute, the narratives focus on the people bringing the materials and their goods. The people, from a remote region associated with the production of aromatics, are often represented as humbly offering a tribute gift to a ruler to secure an alliance. In a study of early trade, Karl Polanyi calls this a type of gift "trade," creating a relationship of reciprocity.[30] The goods involved in such exchanges are generally luxury items, what Polanyi calls "treasure." Aromatics are included with these luxuries, along with precious metals, gemstones, textiles, skins, and the other items that are described as filling the ideal royal treasury in that early manual of statecraft, the *Arthaśāstra*. Polanyi, arguing that the primary form of trade is external trade, also makes the simple but important point that "from an institutional point of view [as opposed to a market definition], trade is a method of acquiring goods that are not available on the spot."[31] Indeed, whether the main aromatics are given in tribute or traded in a market, it is well-known in all these discourses that they are not available locally, and they are even seen as the specialties of certain regions. In order to obtain these key aromatics, and therefore in order to have the most culturally prestigious odors in one's environment, on one's body, or adorning the bodies of one's gods, it is understood that one cannot avoid dealing with people and places "external to the group."[32] Indeed, the external/exotic origin of musk, for example, is arguably an intrinsic part of its identity in almost all contexts of the Sanskrit cultural sphere: it is an essential component in the construction of the substance's prestige. To those in the know, the possession of these aromatics and the presence of their odors imply either that you belong to a community that has been offered tribute or that you are a wealthy or esteemed member of a community that is a part of a cosmopolitan trading network. And the prestige of these smells really matters: these aromatics, and other luxury materials, were not perceived to be simply frivolous accessories of the social elite, something I have emphasized throughout this book. As Polanyi astutely notes, the term "luxury" (as opposed to "necessity") in the context of early trade can be misleading: "The distinction is, of course, more tenuous than is sometimes realized, for what we term 'luxuries' were no more than the necessities of the rich and powerful, whose import interest determined foreign economic policy."[33]

On that note, we now examine some representations of the arrival of luxuries at the center of a great empire.

Aromatic Tribute

The following two passages describing tributes are from different genres and periods: one is from the *Mahābhārata* epic, and the other is from the seventh-century *Harṣacarita*, composed in elaborate Sanskrit literary prose by the master of that genre, Bāṇa. Despite differences in style, the passages share much in common in the descriptions of an abundance of luxury materials brought from a remote kingdom in order to demonstrate allegiance. In both cases, through the lengthy description of the contents of the tribute consisting of rare and costly items, the text conveys the superior status of the recipient in a material and aesthetic manner. The materials are impressive, and they also provide rich material for sensuous and appealing literary descriptions. Another reason for choosing these passages is that they both deal with a tribute brought from the Northeast: a region renowned for aloeswood, which forms a significant part of both gifts.

In the second book of the *Mahābhārata*, before the fateful game of dice, the Pāṇḍava Yudhiṣṭhira performs a royal consecration sacrifice (*rājasūya*), to which many kings come to pay their respects. The Kauravas also come, and they are all given a role in the proceedings. The Kaurava called Duryodhana, in particular, is assigned to oversee the tribute gifts from the other kings.[34] When Duryodhana returns home from the occasion, humiliated by several accidents involving the marvelous illusions in the great assembly hall (*sabhā*) of the Pāṇḍavas, he is resentful and wishes to challenge Yudhiṣṭhira to a dice match. Duryodhana explains his resentment to his father Dhṛtarāṣṭra by describing the lavish tribute gifts he saw at the sacrifice. When his father Dhṛtarāṣṭra refuses to allow the dice match, he describes again at greater length the wonders brought in tribute to the sacrifice. Duryodhana twice relates what he saw when assigned the role of collecting the tribute at the sacrifice, and it is, above all, the splendid material wealth of the Pāṇḍavas that fuels his resentment—even his humiliation in the assembly hall was the result of his parochial unfamiliarity with the precious and sophisticated trompe l'oeil effects it abounds with. He says for example:

> I had not heard the names of the jewels[35] in front of me, that I saw in that (assembly hall)—and that burns my mind.
> But, listen, oh Bhārata, to that best wealth of the Pāṇḍavas I saw there brought by kings from all over.

> I do not find myself steady having seen that wealth of the enemy, whether it be grown or from the earth. Consider, oh Bhārata![36]

Not only does Duryodhana describe how the various kings brought this enormous quantity of luxuries, but such was the material hubris of the Pāṇḍavas that they refused entry to many of them, despite their gifts. The entire description of the tribute gifts contains much information on peoples and their associated luxury products according to the worldview of the *Mahābhārata*, but here we will concentrate on one small extract. In the following passage, Duryodhana describes the tribute given by the kings from the far Northeast, approximately the modern states of Assam and Arunachal Pradesh. We should note that, in addition to their geographic origin, these people are characterized by what they eat and what they wear. Also, the northeastern region of South Asia was famous for the production of aloeswood, and it is therefore quite appropriate that these kings bring this particular tribute:[37]

> Those kings who are on the other side of the Himalaya, on the mountain behind which the sun rises, and who are the edge of the ocean of *Vāriṣeṇa*,[38] on both sides of the Lohitya river,
> And those *Kirātas* who eat fruits and roots, who have clothes of skins, brought loads of sandalwood and aloeswood, and of *kālīyaka*,[39] as well as heaps of skins, jewels, gold, and perfumes,
> And a myriad of *Kirāta* servant girls, oh lord of peoples! They brought exotic animals and birds that were meant to be a delight.
> Having brought piled-up gold of great splendor from the mountain, as well as all the tribute, they stood held-back at the door.[40]

Though these kings show the signs of a simple life by how they dress and the food they eat, nevertheless, they come from a region rich in luxuries—the list of products (sandalwood, aloeswood, skins, jewels, and gold) corresponds quite closely to the categories of objects in the treasury as described in the *Arthaśāstra*.[41] Marginal and primitive as these people are in the eyes of the narrative, it only is by contact with them that one obtains the luxuries so necessary to a great emperor and his court.

The language used to describe the animals is of note. They are said to be *dūraja*, meaning "originating in a distant place," or perhaps simply "exotic" in its most literal sense. "To be enjoyed" is the "purpose" (*ramaṇīyārtha*) of these exotic animals—they are delightful, exotic animals. At least in the case of these animals, their sheer unusualness—the fact that they are the sort of animals one only finds in remote places—appears to make them a source of pleasure. Thus, we see that the remote origin of a product can in some cases contribute to its cultural value, and it seems therefore reasonable to say that there is a fascination with exotic things in parts of the *Mahābhārata*.

Our next text, the *Harṣacarita* by Bāṇa, is a historical-biographical work concerning some aspects of the reign of King Harṣa (606–649 CE), who ruled over a large empire from the capital, Kanauj. Unlike the relatively simple language of the *Mahābhārata*, this text is written in the most elaborate Sanskrit prose style, and it must have been fully accessible to only the most educated. The passage we examine deals with a tribute brought to King Harṣa by an envoy of the king of a northeastern kingdom (*Prāgjyotiṣa*). The most significant part of this tribute is a luxurious, divinely cooling, white parasol described in the sort of detail that only Sanskrit literary prose style can achieve. Following the presentation of this marvelous parasol, King Harṣa is shown the rest of the gifts:

> And when the king had seen that principal thing, the servants displayed just the rest of the offering (*prābhṛtaṃ*) in sequence. Namely:
>
> . . . and books made up of aloeswood bark containing aphorisms . . .
>
> . . . and very thick bamboo tubes of vine-mango juice and black aloeswood oil, armored with sheaths of *kapotikā* leaves that were reddish brown like a dove, and heaps of black aloeswood the color of pounded kohl, placed in silken sacks, and (heaps) of ox-head sandalwood that destroys intense scorching heat, and camphor, bright-white and chilly like a splinter of a slab of frost, and musk pods, sprays of cubebs with ripe fruit and hairy with matted locks, bunches of clove flowers, and clusters of nutmegs
>
> . . . musk deer who perfume space with their fragrance . . .
>
> He, amazed, thought "What other reciprocal respectful gift is there except for an undecaying alliance?"[42] And at the mealtime he bestowed on Haṃsavega: sandalwood, the remainder of which he had smeared [on himself], enclosed in a silver coconut covered with a piece of white cloth; two garments that had touched his body; a girdle called the "Halo" with parts clustered with shining pearls like autumn stars;[43] an ear-ornament called the "Wave" that reddened the day with the glimmer of its excessively valuable ruby,[44] and abundant things to eat.[45]

As earlier, this tribute includes large amounts of northeastern black aloeswood and books of aphorisms (*subhāṣita*) written on aloeswood-bark (*sāñcīpāt*); a writing material that is the equivalent of birch-bark or palm-leaves for this region.[46] Again, we see how the distinctive material products of a region are used to characterize it in literary discourses. The tribute gift also comprises "vine-mango juice" (*latāsahakārarasa*);[47] cooling sandalwood of the famous "ox-head" variety, which we shall see again; cooling, white camphor; along with musk, cubebs, cloves, and nutmegs—almost the complete roll call of "great aromatics," leaving out saffron (strongly associated with Kashmir and northern regions) and the various resins.

That is not the entire list of gifts—I focus on the aromatics, or items related to aromatics. The rest of the gifts are the usual objects valued in early South Asian culture, including jewels, textiles, skins, areca nuts (notably absent from the list in the *Mahābhārata* passage), chowries, exotic animals and birds, and ivory. Then, in the second passage, when Harṣa actually experiences the cool shade of the parasol, he is said to be amazed and decides to make an alliance with Haṃsavega's master. To show his favor, he offers several gifts; all which have presumably touched the king's own body. As well as jewels and precious garments, he gives him the remains of the sandalwood paste with which he anointed (*vilipta*, as in *vilepana*) his body. Apart from the sense of hearing, these gifts will satisfy all the senses, and now Haṃsavega can present these gifts to his master, so he can satisfy all his senses with beautiful items that have been in contact with the body of King Harṣa. At this stage in the visit, very few words have been exchanged—the transaction has been mostly material (expensive, rare, and exotic) and sensual (delightful). Some of the gifts from the Northeast (aloeswood) are quite typical of the region, and, in other cases, the materials are prestigious items that could be from elsewhere (cubebs). So far we have looked at the social aspect of these aromatics, namely the people with whom they are associated, and the idea that obtaining these aromatics would bring one into contact with marginal people whose worlds abounded in luxuries. Now I turn to idealized representations of the lands where prestigious aromatics were believed to originate.

The Geography of Aromatics

Connected with the social aspects of the origins of aromatics are the regional origins of these substances—they are associated with certain people because they come from certain places. Rājaśekhara, in a manual for poets, the *Kāvyamīmāṃsā* composed around 900 CE, provides an explicit statement of the literary conventions concerning the sources of aromatics and other items. It appears that Rājaśekhara was quite interested in regional variation, and he seems to have composed a now lost geographical glossary.[48] One theory that Rājaśekhara emphasizes in the *Kāvyamīmāṃsā* is the origin of regional stylistic differences in literature, dress, and so forth, for which he presents a mythical origin in the third chapter.[49] The latter half of the text, from chapter 14 to the 18th and final chapter, deals mainly with the conventions a poet should know.

In chapter 17, Rājaśekhara describes the conventional characteristics and contents of the various regions of the world. He calls this section of the work the chapter on the "distinction of place" (*deśavibhāga*). This contrasts with the following chapter on the distinction of time (*kālavibhāga*). He begins the section by stating concisely the usefulness for the poet of the correct descriptions of place and time:

> In distinguishing place and time, the poet is not lacking with respect to expressing his intended meaning.[50]

Rājaśekhara then describes the conventional division of place into heaven, earth, continents, oceans, Mount Meru, and so forth, before describing the mountain at the south of the subcontinent, Mount Malaya. Here he lists the products of the southern region. Thus, when he later describes in more detail the regions, mountains, and rivers of the south, he notes that its products were described previously in the section on Mount Malaya.[51]

Mount Malaya is described as having four characteristics (*viśeṣa*) for which Rājaśekhara provides illustrative verses: the four verses illustrate Malaya as abounding in certain plants, especially sandalwood; as full of gems; as a marvelous and fruitful abode of gods, men, and ascetics; and as the location of Laṅkā, the capital city of Rāvaṇa. The first characteristic is what concerns us:

> That [Malaya mountain] is the birthplace of fine sandalwood trees that are delightful to people, and that are enveloped by cobras from the rootstock, and [also the birthplace] of nutmeg[52] trees joined with cubebs, cardamom, and black pepper.[53]

Sandalwood trees infested with snakes are strongly associated with the mountain; this was a very common motif in Sanskrit literature. Also, the region is said to produce nutmegs, cubebs, cardamom, and pepper—two of which we saw several times in our lists of aromatic "spices."

Following his description of the Malaya mountain, Rājaśekhara provides the characteristics of the regions of the four cardinal points. This he does according to a generally fixed format. First he defines a region (*deśa*) by giving its relative position, that is, "[t]here, beyond Varanasi is the Eastern region,"[54] after which he names the countries (*janapada*) of that region, followed by the mountains, the rivers, and, finally, the products (*utpāda/utpatti*) typical of that region. He describes the regions in the auspicious clockwise order starting from the East, as one would expect in South Asian intellectual culture.

In the eastern region,[55] beyond Varanasi, are found the countries of Aṅga, Kosala, Magadha, Prāgjyotiṣa (whence the tribute to Harṣa was brought), Tāmraliptika, Nepāla, and so forth. The products here are *lavalī*,[56] *granthiparṇaka*,[57] aloeswood, grapes, and musk, among others.[58] Next, he describes the South (*dakṣiṇāpatha*)[59] beyond the Māhiṣmatī River. The products here are the same as the Malaya mountain. The West is defined as the region beyond Devasabhā,[60] including, among several others, the countries Surāṣṭra, Bhṛgukacca, and Yavana, whose products are *karīra*,[61] *pīlu*,[62] *guggulu*,[63] dates, camels,[64] and more.[65] Finally, Rājaśekhara tells us the characteristics of the northern region, beyond Pṛthūdaka,[66] a region including amongst other places, Śaka, Hūṇa, Kāmboja, Bāhlīka, Vahlava, Turuṣka, Barbara, etc. The products of this region are pine,[67] deodar cedar,[68] grapes, saffron, yak-tail fly whisks,[69] antelope skins, *Sauvīra* antimony (for kohl), rock salt, *vaiḍūrya* gemstone, and horses.[70]

Rājaśekhara presents many important aromatics as originating in diverse regions—musk and aloeswood in the East; sandalwood, nutmeg, cubebs, and cardamom in the South; *guggulu*-myrrh in the West; and saffron in the North. He provides these details so that a poet can evoke the character of a region according to the correct literary conventions. This is by no means esoteric knowledge—rather, Rājaśekhara codified what appears to have been quite well-known. Thus the East is conventionally supposed to produce musk and aloeswood, and, indeed, many of the details of the tributes discussed earlier reflect this literary convention. Nevertheless, those tributes contained many other things not necessarily associated with the eastern region, including things that characterize other regions—such as sandalwood. This raises the problem of the extent to which aromatic products would be associated with a certain region: one might associate the East with aloeswood, but one might *not* necessarily associate all aloeswood with the East; just as we nowadays tend to think of tea when we think of Darjeeling, but we do not necessarily think of Darjeeling when we think of tea.

To answer the question whether the association of aromatics with certain regions was reciprocal, we shall now examine some of the synonyms for the aromatics.

Deer Testes and Bactrian Saffron: The Strange and Foreign Origins of Aromatics

Both in the case of the "Turk" frankincense mentioned in the epigraph, and in many of the perfumery formulae, it was not uncommon for aromatics to have names that referred to their place or people of origin. For example the word *malayaja*, "produced from Malaya mountain," is a very common synonym for sandalwood, indicating its conventional southern, mountainous origins. It will be helpful now to present this information in a more systematic manner, though note that we are only interested in those synonyms that have some relation to the origin of the substance, that refer to its role in trade, or its value, and not so much its physical qualities. I will mostly rely on two popular glossaries that I examined previously, the *Nāmaliṅgānuśāsana* of Amarasiṃha, also called simply the *Amarakośa*, and the *Abhidhānacintāmaṇināmamālā* of Hemacandra. As I mentioned, these texts seem to be typical of the glossaries that were widely available to many scholars over a long period.[71] I also add a few terms from the specialist perfumery glossaries in the *Gandhasāra* perfumery text, as well as that found in Bhaṭṭotpala's commentary on the *Bṛhatsaṃhitā*.[72]

Aloeswood (Agaru/Aguru)

kṛmija (produced by worms);[73] *joṅgaka*[74] ("Because of coming from Mount Joṅgaka");[75] *rājārham* (worthy of a king);[76] *anāryajam* (produced in non-Āryan land).[77]

Kālīyakam

jāpakam ("Because of being produced on Jāpaka mountain").[78]

Sandalwood (Candana)

malayaja (produced on Malaya mountain);[79] *tailaparṇika*[80] ("Tailaparṇa mountain is its source");[81] *gośīrṣa*[82] (ox-head, "Because of being from Mount Ox-head");[83] *rohaṇadruma* ("The tree of Mount Rohaṇa");[84] *mahārhā* (of great value);[85] *āheyam* (snake-related).[86]

Nutmeg (Jātiphala)

No synonyms of note.

Camphor (Karpūra)

Most synonyms for this tend to describe qualities of whiteness and coolness, not the origin or value. "Moon" synonyms also often apply.

Musk (Kastūrikā)

mṛganābhi (deer's navel);[87] *mṛgamada* (deer's rut);[88] *mārjārī* (cat-related);[89] *mṛgāṇḍajā* (produced from deer testicles);[90] *mṛgadarpa* (deer-pride/deer-musk);[91] *mṛgodbhava* (deer-arisen).[92]

Saffron (Kuṅkuma)

kāśmīrajanma (of Kashmiri origin);[93] *bāhlīka* (Bactrian);[94] *kāśmīra* (Kashmiri).[95]

Cloves (Lavaṅga)

No synonyms of note.

Cubebs (Kakkola)

dvīpamarīcakam (island pepper).[96]

The names of some of these aromatics clearly reflect their *conventional* sources—especially in the case of saffron (Kashmir, Bactria) and sandalwood (Mount Malaya)—but also in one very revealing term for aloeswood ("produced in non-Āryan land").[97] There is also a synonym for cubebs indicating an overseas origin, and both sandalwood and aloeswood have several names, such as "ox-head," that Hemacandra interprets in every case as referring to the (probably imaginary) mountain that is their place of origin. These names, ox-head (*gośīrṣa*) sandalwood, oil-leaf (*tailaparṇika*) sandalwood, and *joṅgaka* aloeswood are also found in the chapter on the contents of the treasury in the *Arthaśāstra*.

Given the previous, it seems reasonable to suggest that many educated people in this culture, equipped with a good knowledge of the Sanskrit lexicon and literary conventions, would have had a basic awareness, not only that Assam contained aloeswood, but also that aloeswood often came from Assam. Indeed, people in India today tend to associate saffron with Kashmir, sandalwood with Karnataka, and the Assam Government Emporium in New Delhi proudly displays a large piece of rugged, twisted, darkened wood that is supposed to be a priceless piece of (now almost extinct) Assamese aloeswood.

In discourse and practice, aromatics would have retained something of the aura of their exotic origins, which was further culturally supported by the conventions of literature; the very literature that was associated with the same elite who could afford to savor these commodities. The origins of aromatics were also reflected in many of the names of the materials themselves; names that either referred explicitly to their origins (Kashmiri, Turk) or that were possibly suggestive of their foreign source owing to their exotic linguistic opacity (*joṅgaka*).

The list of synonyms of aromatics also hints at another aspect of the manner in which these products were represented in medieval India. The great value of the aromatics is suggested by two terms, one for aloeswood ("worthy of a king") and one for sandalwood ("of great worth"). Indeed, in the *Sabhāparvan* of the *Mahābhārata*, we find another passage, earlier than the one we read previously, describing the tribute gifts presented by Rāvaṇa's brother, Vibhīṣaṇa, to the Pāṇḍava Sahadeva when the Pāṇḍavas have all gone to collect tribute as a prelude to performing the royal consecration sacrifice. It is clear that sandalwood and aloeswood are an important part of a great treasure—indeed, in the following passage, the sandalwood and aloeswood are said to be the most important (*-mukhya*) of the precious items (*ratna*):

> And then he sent forth diverse precious things, the best amongst them being sandalwood and aloeswood, and also divine ornaments, and very valuable garments, and also costly gemstones.[98]

This is an extremely important point. Perhaps above all others, these aromatics, especially the two woods mentioned, were considered extremely valuable substances in Indian culture over the long duration of time that we consider. The raw materials sandalwood and aloeswood were not just perfumes, nor did they just have the status of fine wines in our own society; rather, they were ranked as very important items of treasure, much like gold and ivory in European culture or jade in Chinese culture.

The synonyms suggest also that some of these substances were understood to have strange, unpleasant, or even dangerous origins. For example, aloeswood is also known as *kṛmija* (produced by worms), referring, no doubt, to the fact that aloeswood often looks like rotten wood. Sandalwood is also called *āheyam* (snake-related) referring to the common convention, which we saw in Rājaśekhara's account of Mount Malaya, that sandalwood trees on that mountain are infested with venomous snakes. The medieval Indian aromatic with, perhaps, the strangest connotation is musk, produced in the preputial follicles of the musk deer, which were, no doubt, cut off and traded, as they were until the twentieth century, as small furry pouches (pods) of the strong-smelling brown particles ("grains") of musk.[99] Clearly there was some confusion about exactly what part of the deer's body the musk came from, although it seems to have been generally known that the animal of origin was a deer. One very common, and early, term for musk is *mṛganābhi*, which means "deer's navel," though another term is *mṛgāṇḍajā* "produced from deer testicles." Neither of these deer parts is a particularly attractive source for this costly luxury perfume nor is the "worm-eaten" origin of aloeswood very appealing; and the sandalwood tree in situ was not presented as an entirely enticing object. How did the culture that so valued these aromatics respond to these strange imagined origins? Or, why did they construct them as such?

First, we should note that South Asian culture was not merely aware of these origins, but rather the origins were in some cases celebrated, especially in poetry, as we saw with Rājaśekhara, and also in many collections of aphorisms, *subhāṣitas*. This is the genre of text that was presented to King Harṣa on aloes-bark manuscripts in the tribute gift we described. One way in which the *subhāṣita* sayings exploited the convention of the snake-infested sandalwood tree is exemplified by the following verse taken from the *Hitopadeśa*, a text supposedly intended for the education of princes that is well-known to any scholar of Sanskrit, though a large number of other such verses exist:[100]

> The root is frequented by serpents, the flowers by bees, the branches by monkeys, the tops by bears,
> There is nothing in the sandalwood tree that is not occupied by the very wicked and cruel.[101]

This proverb occurs in the context of a fable about the fickle and dangerous ways of kings. The sandalwood tree, whose virtues are not stated but assumed, is compared to a king, who may be wealthy and important yet is surrounded by vicious people. This is typical of the way the sandalwood tree is depicted in this genre: the virtues of the sandalwood tree are assumed and, though we are informed that it seethes with potential danger, there is no mention of any actual harm to sandalwood collectors; rather, it is a metaphor for something or someone that has obvious importance yet must be approached with extreme caution.[102]

Another important, and quite different, passage that deals with this issue is found in the opening verses of *The Origin of Minerals* (*Dhātūtpatti*) composed in the early fourteenth century by the Jain scholar and treasurer Ṭhakkura Pherū, who I introduce in detail in the next chapter. This short text, composed in simplified Prakrit in fifty-seven stanzas, opens with some interesting verses on the peculiar/unpleasant/impure origins of several substances, many of which are the sorts of luxury materials that one would expect to find in a royal treasury. This translation was kindly provided to me by Professor S. R. Sarma:

1. Silver from the earth, gold from the sand grains of the rivers and mountains. Two noble metals arise also through alchemy (*dhāuvvāo* = *dhātuvāda*).[103]
2. Silk from the worms, musk comes from the deer's navel, *dūrvā* grass from cow's hair, and lotuses, you know, arise out of muddy waters.
3. Know that the bumble bee[104] comes from cow-dung and *gorocana*[105] from the cow's bile,[106] the [royal] fly whisk from the tail of (the mountain) ox,[107] and gems from serpents' heads.[108]
4. Wool [comes from] the sheep, ivory from the lordly elephant, tail [feather] from a peacock,[109] hides from cattle, fire from chips of wood.
5. Bitumen from a mountain, [and] the best civet (*javāi* = *javādi*)[110] from the anus ["excrement entrance"]; although these have a lowly origin, they are pure due to their [good] qualities.[111]

The origins described are a mixture of well-known real origins (silk from worms); misunderstanding (musk from the deer's navel); and pure convention (gems from serpents' heads). Some of these origins, such as the origin of the lotus, would have been locally familiar to many people reading the text; moreover, some of the other origins do not seem particularly lowly, for example, an elephant, a mountain. These inconsistencies aside, the key to understanding this passage seems to lie in the conclusion that, whatever their origins, the fact that they have remarkable innate qualities renders these materials valuable. I might note that, if Professor Sarma and I are correct in taking the verse to refer to civet as called by an Arabic/Persian term (*zabād*), then this is really a very up-to-date set of verses, aromatically speaking. Civet, however, does not feature in the list of aromatics subsequently discussed.

In the *Dhātūtpatti* passage, this moral has been applied by analogy to the value of things. Indeed, this entire passage, placed at the introduction to a short text on metallurgy (and aromatics), may be taking advantage of this subject matter to preach a material-based, metaphorical, moral, and social messages in the place of the usual benedictory verses. Also, whilst the origin of silver and gold is said to be in their various ores, the origin of these two great metals also lies in alchemy (*dhāuvvāo*, Sanskrit: *dhātuvāda*), thus indicating that one needs not only the ore but also the expertise to obtain these precious materials.

The conventions of the dangerous and strange origins of some materials were thus employed in Sanskrit aphorisms and literature to stand as metaphors for the idea that along with good things come bad. These motifs also function as metaphors in a social critique that argues that origins are of little importance compared to innate qualities. The fact that these commodities were so highly valued aesthetically, as well as economically, was especially conducive to the propagation of these conventions in literary contexts.

Conclusion: Spices, Universal Exotica, and Encyclopedias of Pleasure

It seems that aromatics were divided into the local and cheap, such as vetiver, and the costly and exotic, such as camphor and musk. The latter materials were associated with consumption in a cultivated urban setting, and also with their origins in remote lands that might evoke images of danger and abundance. This division of materials, and indeed much of the discourse of these aromatics, has a lot in common with the medieval European discourse of the origins of spices, only here the spices are not just out of the east but from all directions: India is hemmed in on all sides by remote lands of luxury. This emphasis on exotic aromatics also contrasts with the theory of medicinal plants and meats so central to early Indian medicine as described by Zimmermann. In that medical theory, the most valued medicinal meats (for example, antelope) were those produced at or near the preeminent dry *jāṅgala* land, the center where kingdoms were to be established, whereas in the world of aromatics the ideal political center produces little of interest.[112] Moreover, the tribute- and trade-based *commodity-geography* implicit or explicit in the sources in this chapter also forms a strong contrast with the agricultural and ecological vision of the world presented in medical texts as elucidated by Zimmermann.

We should not forget that many of the aromatic materials described in medieval South Asian texts were actually brought by long-distance trade from remote places, for example, emeralds from the Egyptian desert or musk from the Himalayas and China. In addition to the high price and consequent high prestige deriving from their (real) arduous production, these "spices" retained a well-deserved aura of the exotic which was at times quite developed in the South Asian imagination. Not only that, but some substances, such as musk, were at the same time repellent and seductive, providing rich materials for the production of all manner of appealing, allegorical interpretations of these luxuries.[113]

South Asian writers were entirely conscious of these conventions. In an analysis of the South Asian scholarly debate over the nature of regionality in Sanskrit writing, Sheldon Pollock discusses the tenth-century commentary of Ratnaśrījñāna on a key text on literary theory, the *Kāvyādarśa*. In that commentary, we see that sandalwood is the touchstone for the innately native: Ratnaśrījñāna wishes to argue for the innate regionality of poetic style, and states: "Just because sandalwood may be observed elsewhere [than in Malaya] does not make it indigenous to that other place."[114] Presumably, even his opponents cannot argue with that. Although Pollock explains that Ratnaśrījñāna's theory of regional literary style was of the minority, his ideas about sandalwood were evidently universal. Not only were the literary conventions concerning exotic and regional aromatics universal, but the practices that used these materials were relatively universal in the sphere of medieval Sanskrit culture from relatively early periods until the early to mid second millennium. The basic contents of many of the formulae for incense and pastes available to Bhaṭṭotpala in Kashmir hardly differ from those in the *Mānasollāsa* composed in twelfth-century northern Karnataka; though, of course, perfumery texts changed over time, and at a somewhat later date perfumes definitely began to incorporate such materials as ambergris.

For Europeans, spices came from the East, and it would appear that most literary people in the East likewise thought that their spices came from somewhere strange and faraway. Apparently no one wanted to live in the land of perfumes and gemstones, even when they lived relatively close to it.[115] Presumably, living in the land of spices would have significantly reduced the allure of these materials. The king and the man-about-town, not to mention the icons in the temple and monastery, needed their essential luxury materials to come from far away—from places near the edges of the known and beyond the supposedly tamed world of Sanskrit culture. These materials, so vital to the proper pursuit of pleasure, captivating indices of royal competence, indispensible in many religious contexts, and an intrinsic part of the identity of the cultivated man-about-town were thus at once universal and innately regional. The margin both implies the center and materially adorns the center, allowing those at the center to perceive the reach of the power of the kingdom. When these beautiful spices fill a royal capital city they do not simply legitimate power, nor do they merely symbolize power, but rather the presence of exotic wealth goes hand in hand with conquering the world. These aromatic materials were not just regional, but in many cases (aloeswood "produced in non-Āryan land," "Turk-resin," emeralds from remote mountains), they were believed to come from the extreme margins of the sphere of imaginable universal power. When these exotic items were brought as tribute, this demonstrated just how far the reach of royal power and fame had gone. These materials also betray a (universal) desire for the strange world beyond, conventionalized as that world may have been. Consumed in an expert manner in an erotic setting (or described as so consumed), they linked the medieval South Asian urban context to a not entirely imaginary world of bountiful mountains filled with fierce snakes; worm-infested, priceless forests; and regions teeming with deer whose very scrota were irresistible.

8

Sandalwood

Merchants, Expertise, and Profit

In premodern South Asian textual depictions of trade, the figures of the merchant and of the evaluator are particularly important. In this chapter, I will consider representations of the expertise of these people, because it was believed that both familiarity with trade routes and knowledge of the examination (and artifice) of commodities made these people rich. I will concentrate on representations of, arguably, the most important South Asian aromatic—sandalwood—and I consider how the lucrative knowledge of merchants concerning this material was framed in a textual form. Such is the long-term importance of sandalwood in South Asia that I will also take the opportunity to discuss the nature and significance of this aromatic in some detail.

In addition to trading material commodities, such as sandalwood, the merchant, and especially the commodity examiner, profited from trading the commodity of knowledge, and some of the texts in this chapter codified, validated, and even ornamented this knowledge-commodity that was so vital to their communities.[1] In studying this aspect of aromatics, we are especially fortunate in possessing a unique text on the evaluation of aromatics by a Jain who was the assay-master at the court of the Delhi sultans, and we will reflect at some length on this text since it places the discourse of the evaluation of aromatics in a far richer historical context than most of the other sources.

Mercantile expertise was practical and had to be applied to the material world in order to create a profit. This required the evaluator and merchant to use their bodies and their senses. For that reason, I will also consider representations of the use of the senses in these contexts. Unlike in the previous chapters, here the pleasure-giving qualities of aromatics are less important, and what matters is the identification and correct description of authentic materials with a high exchange value.

Knowledge: Quality, Artifice, and Profit

As noted in the passage on the origin of metals in the previous chapter, knowledge of the source alone is not enough to produce some commodities; one also needs expertise to identify, extract, process, evaluate, label, and successfully exchange the luxury materials. In the summer of 2005, I was in India doing research for this project, and, determined to get some more direct experience of the aromatics I had been reading about, I made efforts to buy and examine some of these materials. In particular, I was keen to find some aloeswood/agarwood, because I had not seen or smelled this aromatic. In Mumbai, there are a large number of traders who specialize in selling aloeswood, mainly, it seemed, to buyers visiting from Persian Gulf states, where the wood (*oud*) and oil is still widely used and appreciated. I visited a number of these merchants over a few days, asking them about aloeswood and examining some of their stock. Rapidly, I realized that buying this expensive wood is a difficult business unless you are well-informed. The wood comes in several shapes, sizes, and colors, all at different prices, from different places, and with different smells when burned. Some of the wood looked, even to me, like a variety of palm-tree wood infused with dyes and perfumes; and, in one case, I was kindly informed that a certain dubious-looking quality of wood was good only for a gift but no good for personal consumption. I bought some wood, but to this day, I have no idea whether this is real aloeswood, good aloeswood, or just some suitable wood soaked in various resins and colorants. I became acutely aware that fakery of the wood and adulteration of aloeswood oil was very common. I wished I had been accompanied by a good guide who could explain how to tell fake from real wood and also to evaluate the quality of a given piece of wood. It was not just that I was unfamiliar with the smell and appearance of the wood, but also I was unable to talk about what I saw and smelled—to find the rights words for a certain glossy or streaky appearance that some of the wood had or for a harsher or sweeter odor of the oil. Nor was I sure whether the variations I noticed were in fact pertinent factors in the choice of good wood. The traders, as well as many of the buyers, appeared well-informed regarding these matters, for example, applying all sorts of tests to the materials. No doubt, at some point in the chain of trade, there are also expert fabricators and adulterators. This is not unique to the case of aloeswood; I had similar experiences with sandalwood, which seems even easier to fake, and for which there is a far greater demand within contemporary India.

The traders and experts of medieval India likely dealt with the same problems I encountered; and not only with aloeswood but also with other aromatics, as well as with gemstones, precious metals, and other costly materials. Whether one was buying or selling as an independent merchant or employed to assess products in the king's treasury, knowledge of how to assess, authenticate, and describe aromatics was indispensable to one's livelihood and reputation. Furthermore, the abundance of texts on the examination of various materials, especially gemstones, implies that there were concerns with poor quality and fake materials, which is not surprising given the high exchange value of the materials and the difficulty in obtaining them. Just as knowledge of the authentic was profitable, so was knowledge of fakery.

There is not space here to discuss fully all of the sources dealing with these issues or even to discuss all the aromatics covered in just one text; instead, I will focus on the case of sandalwood—perhaps the most important aromatic substance in South Asia both today and in the past. Not surprisingly, given the expansion in the use of Sanskrit for all sorts of genres of texts in the first millennium CE, those who were involved in the examination and artifice of aromatics, gemstones, and so forth, began to produce and consume texts in Sanskrit (and Prakrit) that codified their expertise. These texts were practically useful, but they also provided an authoritative, and even an ornamented, textual *śāstric* articulation of the knowledge that was a key commodity for those who traded and examined aromatics and other luxury materials for a living. The texts allowed people to write and talk about these materials in the correct way. As we will see later in the chapter, the ideal education of the merchant class involved mastery over a range of these types of knowledge, and, arguably, these texts were analogous to the various texts that Brahmins were supposed to master for their livelihood.

Communities of merchants and experts employed at court to look after the king's wealth would have been relatively wealthy patrons and consumers of other types of cultural products. This is a situation not unlike the patronage and connoisseurship of art in the Italian renaissance by wealthy mercantile families, who would have undergone a very specific type of education. As discussed in chapter 1, Michael Baxandall studied the "cognitive style" of the fifteenth-century patron and viewer of paintings with some success, and he called this way of seeing the "period eye." In this chapter, in addition to highlighting some Sanskrit texts that have been neglected, I will reflect on the "period nose" (and indeed the other senses) of the mercantile class, as well as that of those who aspired to be successful merchants.

Excursus: Sandalwood

Sandalwood is such an important aromatic in South Asia that it is worth pausing to consider this material in more detail. Sandalwood is arguably both the most prestigious aromatic in South Asian culture and the most enduring in importance, having been highly valued from a quite early period until the present day.

What Is Sandalwood?

As with all materials of great cultural importance, the nature, significance, and uses of sandalwood are highly complex and at times confusing. First of all, the terminology for sandalwood is imprecise. It is a good exercise to explore the English word "sandalwood," one we are more familiar with, before looking at the Sanskrit terminology for sandalwood. I should stress very strongly at the outset that in the following discussion I am not correlating scientific names for sandalwood with Sanskrit terms (e.g., *candana*) that we might translate as "sandalwood," connecting Sanskrit terms to those that belong to the God's eye view of science. Whilst I make this qualification, nevertheless, later in this chapter I will relate early Indian terms for "sandalwood" to certain plants as we identify them today, since I believe that, just as the hunt for a fixed and absolute identification of one type of tree that corresponds to the thing referred to by Sanskrit terms for sandalwood is naïve, so a refusal to contemplate any translations from Sanskrit to modern terminology deprives us of some revealing connections to the discourses of the disciplines of archaeology, botany, and geography. Nor does the useful experiment of translating a word such as *candana* into modern languages and discourses imply that we thereby ignore other more cultural aspects of the significance of the word and the substances it referred to in premodern South Asia.

The English word "sandalwood" often refers to the fragrant heartwood of the tree *Santalum album* L., but "sandalwood" also refers to a number of other valuable woods. Other fragrant types of sandalwood that have been exploited include several Australian *Santalum* species, the Fiji sandalwood tree (*Santalum yasi* Seem.); the Polynesian sandalwood tree (*Santalum marchionese* Skottsb.); and the East African sandalwood tree (*Osyris tenuifolia* Engl.). Another entirely different tree called West Indian sandalwood (*Amyris balsamifera* L.) provides a type of oil used in perfumery.[2] Finally, there is a wood called red sandalwood, red sanders, or simply sanders (*Pterocarpus santalinus*) valued for its hardness and red color, though this wood is not fragrant.[3] Thus "sandalwood" can refer to several different species of tree and types of wood that grow in different places. Already, it seems, sandalwood can be a confusing material to talk about in English.

Even if we ignore these other types of sandalwood and focus on what is most commonly called sandalwood—the wood of *Santalum album*—then things are still complicated: this species grows in different parts of the world, and there are numerous different grades of the wood. *Santalum album* grows in dry deciduous forests of the southern Deccan in South India, as well as in Indonesia, where it is found in eastern Java, the Lesser Sunda Islands, and Timor. On the grounds of a biogeographic disjunction—a significant and anomalous break in the distribution of species—it has even been suggested that *Santalum album* was introduced to India from Indonesia. Such an introduction must have occurred at a very early date because Asouti and Fuller report sandalwood charcoal discovered in the "late Neolithic/Megalithic transition levels of Sanganakallu (Sannarachamma hill) dating between 1400 and 1000 BCE."[4] Thus, sandalwood (*Santalum album*) is found in South India and on several islands of what we now call Indonesia.

This one type of sandalwood not only comes from several widely dispersed places, but also the quality of the wood varies. Only the heartwood is fragrant, and the quality of the wood varies according to the conditions under which the tree grows[5] and according to the part of the tree from which the wood is taken—the heartwood of the roots being of a particularly high quality.[6] In a study of Indian timber, Gamble reports a table of values that accompanied a trophy exhibited by the Maharaja of Mysore in the Paris Exhibition of 1900. The table in question lists a total of *eighteen classes* of sandalwood (all derived from *Santalum album*), including three classes of billets, three classes of roots, and sawdust.[7]

To sum up: the English word "sandalwood" can refer to the wood of several different species of tree, though most commonly it refers to the heartwood of *Santalum album*. That particular sandalwood tree grows in several locations (from India to Timor), and the wood from any one place may be classified in numerous quality-grades that all have different names and economic values. Writing about sandalwood in 1939, Fischer confessed to finding the situation quite confusing, and Yule and Burnell noted likewise in the "Glossary of Anglo-Indian Colloquial Words and Phrases," *Hobson Jobson*.[8] A paper by Metcalfe from 1935 shows, perhaps, most clearly how many different woods were traded and used at that time as sandalwood-type materials, and how incredibly confusing their identities and origins could be, even with the help of microscopes and a system of scientific nomenclature.[9] The impressively thorough work of many authors on this topic is a clear testimony to the colonial desire to organize and distribute knowledge concerning this very lucrative but confusing market.

It will do no harm to repeat that my aim is not primarily to identify what sandalwood was in ancient India in terms of modern scientific terminology, but rather to illustrate that even today the English word "sandalwood" is far from straightforward—this is a good preparation for thinking about Sanskrit words for sandalwood. The Sanskrit word *candana* is perhaps the most common word translated as "sandalwood" in English. Perhaps not surprisingly, *candana* is not simply the wood of the one tree, *Santalum album*, but, as with "sandalwood," the word may apparently refer to the wood of several species, obtained from a number of regions, occurring in various grades. The situation is further complicated by the fact that the terminology for types of sandalwood changes over time, and, as is typical of the Sanskrit language, the many varieties of *candana* have a number of synonyms. These complications only apply to real sandalwood—artificial and fake sandalwoods have evidently been an additional complication for many centuries. Unsurprisingly, the historian P. K. Gode has provided by far the most thorough analysis of these complexities.[10]

The Sanskrit word *candana* is likely of Dravidian origin, possibly related to a term *cāntu* meaning "daub, rub into a paste; sandalwood (paste)," suggesting that this material came from, or passed through, a Dravidian-speaking area prior to being introduced into Sanskrit.[11] I noted the archaeological finds of sandalwood (*Santalum album*) charcoal in South India dating between 1400 and 1000 BCE—the charcoals were found in a region of South India where the tree would not normally grow, suggesting the early long-distance transport of and cultural demand for the wood. Thus, for *candana*-as-*Santalum album*, we can extremely tentatively suggest a very early introduction of this wood from Indonesia to South India, with a later exposure of communities who used Sanskrit both to this wood and to this word. However, it might be wiser to take a slightly more cautious approach and suggest that *candana* and related words referred, at an early period, to a valued wood that was ground to a paste, and the wood of *Santalum album* was one type of *candana* available in South India that would additionally have been considered fragrant and lighter (i.e., not red) in color. Perhaps it is helpful to compare *candana* with ivory: though most closely associated in our minds with elephant ivory, ivory is also produced from walrus tusks, sperm whale teeth, and other animal sources. There is also a material known as vegetable ivory, and the use of bone as an ivory substitute is not uncommon, not to mention plastics.

Candana in Early Texts

Candana is not mentioned in the earlier Vedic texts, such as the Ṛg Veda, and first appears in Sanskrit sources dating from several centuries BCE, by which time it appears already established as a fragrant material. Early Sanskrit references to *candana* include a reference in Yāska's *Nirukta*,[12] a text of uncertain date, possibly composed "within the later period of a possible timespan between the seventh and third centuries BCE,"[13] as well as a reference to the odor of *candana* (*candanagandha*) in Patañjali's commentary on Pāṇini, the *Mahābhāṣya*, dated to the second century BCE.[14] This is not just an early attested usage of the term, but, as Gode notes, *candana* is mentioned as a fragrant wood.[15] Even at this early period, *candana* is an exemplary fragrance, suggesting that this *candana* could possibly be *Santalum album*.

Despite enormous problems with the exact dates of many early Indic texts, several centuries before the Common Era, references to *candana* are abundant in Indic sources. In the Sanskrit epics (which may be of a somewhat later date), the *Mahābhārata* and the *Rāmāyaṇa*, *candana* is frequently mentioned as an item of adornment. In the following passage from the *Mahābhārata*, the morning bath of Yudhiṣṭhira is described:

> Having slept well on a most valuable bed he woke up. Then he got up, and went to the bathing room for the purposes of [his] necessary duties. Then, one hundred and eight young bath-servants, who were wearing white clothes and who had bathed, approached with filled golden jars. Well-seated on a throne, he put on a light garment and bathed with water mixed with *candana* that had been consecrated with mantras. He was rubbed with astringent/ointment (*kaṣāya*) by strong, well-trained men, and he was washed with fragrant, perfumed water. The great-armed one, having smeared his body with yellow/tawny (*hari*) *candana*, and wearing a garland, with unblemished garment, stood facing eastwards with his

hands joined in supplication. That son of Kunti muttered prayers in conformity with the way of good people.[16]

Here *candana* is mixed with the consecrated water used for bathing, and Yudhiṣṭhira smears his body after bathing with *candana* that is described as yellow/tawny (*hari*). The only attribute of this *candana* that is noted is the color, not the fragrance. This *candana* has evidently been ground in order to mix it with water and to make it into a paste. Given that this is what a great king uses for his morning bath, along with an auspicious number—108—of bath attendants and golden vessels, *candana* is presumably understood as a very prestigious material.

Candana is not only used to adorn and clean the body, but the material is used to decorate other items. At one point in the *Mahābhārata*, Bhīma's terrible club is said to be "smeared with paste of *candana* and aloeswood like a desired beautiful, young woman."[17] Again, *candana* is mentioned as used in the form of a paste, adorning a great and terrible weapon, but the comparison also suggests that this would be an adornment fit for a young, beautiful woman. Also notable here is the pairing of *candana* with aloeswood (*candanāguru*), an extremely common word-compound in many Sanskrit sources.

A search of the critical editions of the *Mahābhārata* and the *Ramāyaṇa* reveals that *candana* is, for the most part, described in the epics as an adornment smeared on the body (or on a weapon as above), presumably in the form of a paste.[18] *Candana* is also said to be fragrant and cool,[19] and there are also references in both epics to red *candana* (*raktacandana*).[20] Where *candana* wood is mentioned, it is either as an item of tribute (presumably to be made into an adorning paste), as an addition to King Daśaratha's funeral pyre in the *Ramāyaṇa*,[21] where it is used along with aloeswood, resins, pine (*sarala*), and *padmaka* wood,[22] or as the actual tree itself.[23] But nowhere in the two epics have I found a reference to an artifact made of *candana* wood such as a statue or throne—this is a very significant contrast with some of the descriptions of sandalwood we shall see later.

This is not the place to document all the references to *candana* in Indic texts from this point onward—the references are far too numerous, though I do hope that my reflections here will encourage scholars to pay close attention to the terminology, qualities, and, above all, the usage of *candana* (and other aromatics) in other texts, with a view to revealing new distinctions depending on period, region, genre, and sectarian affiliation.

The Qualities of *Candana*

Certain types of text deal quite explicitly with sandalwood—its origins, qualities, and evaluation. These include texts on evaluation of the contents of a royal treasury, texts on *materia medica*, in addition to the texts on perfumery we examined. As we saw, in the *Arthaśāstra*, an early text on statecraft, in the chapter on the royal treasury there is an extensive description of various types of aromatics. There is a description of sixteen varieties of *candana*.[24] According to the passage, *candana* comes in many colors, for example red (*rakta*); reddish black (*raktakāla*); the color of a parrot feather, presumably green (*śukapatravarṇa*); pale red/pink (*pāṇḍurakta*); black like aloeswood (*agurukāla*); and so on. At least according to their visible qualities, these are different types of wood; and, as we saw in chapter 3, these *candanas* have diverse odors, from the smell of earth (*bhūmigandhi*), to the smell of fish (*matsyagandhi*), and the smell of lotus (*padmagandhi*) to give just three examples. These types of *candana* also have various names, which in some cases appear to indicate their places of origin (*kālaparvatakam, māleyakam*), as well as possibly their color (*haricandana*). In the previous chapter, we saw how Hemacandra interpreted the many names of *candana* varieties as referring to a mountain of origin, so for him ox-head (*gośīrṣaka*) *candana* is so called because it comes from Ox-head mountain.

The *Arthaśāstra* not only describes these varieties of *candana*, but this text also contains a statement of the qualities of *candana* in general:

> Light, unctuous, not dry, smearing oil like ghee, of pleasant smell, suitable for the skin, mild, not fading, tolerant of warmth, absorbs great heat, and pleasant to touch—these are the qualities of sandalwood (*candana*).[25]

Thus *candana* is not only pleasant to smell, but it also has a tactile quality, is smooth, and smears in an oily manner like ghee. It is also said to be suitable for the skin (*tvaganusārin*), pleasant to touch, and generally cooling/removing of heat. In this general description of *candana*, rather than color or odor, these tactile qualities are the most prominent.

The *Dhanvantarīyanighaṇṭu* is an important medieval lexicon of *materia medica* that contains many names for varieties of sandalwood, as well as descriptions of the properties of sandalwood. The text has a complex history and may have been compiled from earlier sources,[26] but Meulenbeld suggests a date of composition in the period between 1000 and 1100 CE.[27] In the text, the various *materia medica* are divided into seven large groups (*varga*). One of these groups consists of fragrant substances and notably this group is called the "Group of Sandalwood and so forth" (*candanādivarga*). *Candana* appears here as an exemplary aromatic substance. Unlike the "canon" of pleasurable and literary aromatics, the "spices" discussed in the previous chapter, this section also lists less exotic aromatics such as vetiver (*uśīra*)—combining both the aromatic spices and herbs, as it were, as well as some animal and mineral products.

Not surprisingly, the first aromatic listed is *candana*. In fact, the *Dhanvatarīyanighaṇṭu* lists five varieties of *candana*, together with their synonyms and properties: *candana*; red *candana* (*raktacandana*); "bad" *candana* (*kucandana*); *kālīyaka*; and "barbarian" *candana* (*barbarika*). In this context, the first type, *candana* might well be the wood of *Santalum album*, as the editor of the text, Priya Vrat Sharma suggests.[28] Sharma also suggests that red sandalwood (*raktacandana*) is *Pterocarpus santalinus* and that bad sandalwood (*kucandana*) is a red wood called sappan wood (*Caesalpinia sappan* L).[29] Assuming these identifications are correct, this further supports my hypothesis that *candana* embraces a wide variety of woods. But in that case what makes all these materials types of *candana*? "Plain" *candana* is described thus, starting with a list of synonyms (I translated these very literally because they are not without interest), and then with a description of its medicinal properties:

> *Candana*, "perfume-heartwood," "very-valuable," "white *candana*," "blessed-fortune," "produced on Malaya" (i.e., the southern mountain), ox-head, and "sesame-seed leaved."
>
> "A-piece-of-fortune" (*śrīkhaṇḍa*, another common synonym of *candana*) is cold, sweet (*svādu*), bitter (*tikta*), destroying bile, clearing the blood, sexually invigorating, removing internal heat,
>
> It destroys bile, blood, poison, thirst, fever and worms, it is heavy, and makes the body thin. All *candana* is bitter and sweet and most cold.[30]

It is notable that what appear to have been quite different varieties of *candana* or altogether different aromatics in the *Arthaśāstra* (*gośīrṣa, bhadraśrī*) with different colors, odors, and origins are presented simply as synonyms of *candana*, although the final statement—"All *candana* is . . ."—hints that there is some variety even within this category. The other varieties of *candana* in the text have various qualities, for example red *candana* and bad *candana* are apparently red (from their names and synonyms), whereas *kālīyaka* would appear to be yellow (from one of its synonyms, *pītam*), and barbarian *candana* (*barbarika*) is evidently white and odorless. Again, what then do all these apparently different woods have in common that allows them to be grouped as *candanas*? At the conclusion of the discussion of the five sandalwoods we are told:

> All these are equal with respect to taste and potency, and the distinction is in terms of odor; the first one (i.e., *candana*) is the very best in terms of qualities.[31]

The tastes in question are sweet and bitter, and the potency cold. This cold potency is, perhaps, the most notable quality of *candana* in the passage from the *Arthaśāstra* and is a quality we will see emphasized in other sources. As the passage suggests, the odor varies from one type of *candana* to another, but the best type of *candana* is evidently fragrant, as are some other varieties. The colors of *candanas* vary but are often notable. All considered, it appears that *candana* is a term that has both broad and restricted meanings. The restricted meaning, at least in this text, is a type of *candana* that is perfumed—an exemplary fragrant material—cold, light in color, produced on Mount Malaya—quite possibly the wood of *Santalum album*.[32] In the broader sense, *candana* is a special type of wood, often used ground to a paste (as in the references to red *candana* in the epics), with varying color and smell. This *candana* in the looser sense is also above all cold and/or cooling—a property that we will see attributed to *candana* in almost all the sources in this chapter and the next, in very diverse genres from different periods. Indeed, the semantic range of Sanskrit *candana* is similar to English "sandalwood," and thus, although I have so far been careful to leave *candana* untranslated, it seems now that to translate this word by the similarly complex and possibly ambiguous English word "sandalwood" is appropriate.

But in reading texts that mention sandalwood, how are we to understand it, and how are we to imagine the reception of this term in early and medieval South Asia? If certain attributes of sandalwood are highlighted in a text—it is white, fragrant, from Mount Malaya, and so forth—it might be reasonable to assume this refers to *Santalum album* of some variety, or at least to a very similar wood; and the term might well have been understood as such by readers or hearers of the text who were familiar with that particular wood (at least in areas where that wood was available and valued). If the plain term *candana* is used, and we are told little else about the wood apart from its coldness, the response to this term was probably diverse. This ambiguous term might have had an ambiguous reception, and not uncommonly people might have been uncertain as to precisely what it implied beyond a precious and cold wood that was often used as a paste. Also, the response might well have varied according to time, place, and context. If you imagine a community that, for some reason, was well supplied with what we now call red sandalwood, and who also very much valued this wood, members of such a community might well understand *candana* as implying red sandalwood. Indeed, for the community of recent Western scholars reading Sanskrit texts, sandalwood tends to mean *Santalum album*, and this particular wood is most culturally valued in the contemporary West as a source of fragrance. Thus, for a long time when reading Sanskrit texts, I tended to assume *candana* meant *Santalum album*, and that sandalwood in Sanskrit texts was therefore always highly fragrant. I believe that we should be careful of making such assumptions—when, in a narrative, a king has the streets sprinkled with sandalwood water, this could equally be imagined as the intense-red, relatively scentless variety, so a visual image is thereby evoked.

The Examination of Aromatics

Let us now consider the textual culture of commodity evaluation more broadly. Our earliest source on the evaluation of aromatics is the section on aromatics in the *Arthaśāstra*. In addition to the *Arthaśāstra*, there are many passages on the examination of aromatics in other texts, such as in the final section of the perfumery text we examined previously, the *Essence of Perfume*, *Gandhasāra*, following the glossary of terms for aromatics.[33] Some verses mentioning the characteristics of good sandalwood and musk are found in the *Mānasollāsa*, in the section on unguents (*vilepana*), which we also examined. The verses are interspersed with formulae for unguents.[34] There exists at least one short manuscript devoted entirely to the examination of musk.[35]

A Case Study: Ṭhakkura Pherū

Perhaps the richest source for understanding the broader context of the sources on the examination and evaluation of perfumes is a section on evaluating aromatics in a text called *The Origin of Minerals* (*Dhātūpatti*) by Ṭhakkura Pherū (mentioned in the previous chapter when discussing the lowly origins of some luxury materials).

Pherū, a Jain of the Śrīdandha *gotra* of the Śrīmālakula, belonged to the Kharatara Gaccha of Śvetāmbara Jains.[36] He was probably born in the second half of the thirteenth century and was a native of Kannāṇā in present-day Haryana. He worked at court in Delhi during the reigns of sultans 'Ala' al-Dīn Khaljī (1296–1316); Shihāb al-Dīn 'Umar (1316); Quṭb al-Dīn Mubārak Shāh (1316–1320); and perhaps Ghiyāth al-Dīn Tughluq (1320–1325); and he began his work at the court of Sultan 'Ala' al-Dīn Khaljī most likely some time before 1315.

These were very bloody and unstable times at court; the sultans were repeatedly overthrown.[37] Life could also be insecure within the Jain community during this period. We know that in 1318, Pherū joined a pilgrimage group led by the then leader of the Jain Kharatara Gaccha, Jinacandra Sūri.[38] During their travels, a rival leader from the Jain Drammakapurīya sect informed the sultan that Jinacandra Sūri was using a golden parasol and royal throne permitted only to the sultan. When the sultan asked to see Jinacandra Sūrī, he found the accusation baseless and imprisoned instead the rival leader. Yet clearly the Jain community felt it should look after its own, or at the very least they wished to represent themselves as so doing in their own histories. When the rival leader was punished:

> Right in front of his Holiness, at the King's gate, in direct sight of a hundred-thousand count of Muslims (*mleccha*)[39] and Hindus (*hinduka*),[40] having pounded him with blows from sticks, fists, clubs, and so forth, and having exposed him, he was made a prisoner.[41]

Jinacandra Sūri successfully asked for his release, helped in part by Pherū, who was presumably relatively well-known at court.

Pherū composed a variety of works in Apabhraṃśa, of which seven have survived: the earliest, dated 1291, is a work in praise of the pontiff of the Kharatara Gaccha of the Śvetāmbaras: the *Kharataragacchālaṃkāra-yugapradhānacatuḥpa dikā*.[42] In 1315, working, no doubt, at the court of Sultan 'Ala' al-Dīn, he composed the *Rayaṇaparikkhā* dealing with gemology,[43] the *Jyotiṣasāra* on astronomy and astrology,[44] and the *Vāstusāra* on architecture and iconography.[45] In 1318, during the relatively brief reign of Quṭb al-Dīn Mubārak Shāh, he composed the *Dravyaparīkṣā*, a detailed discussion on coinage and exchange, which he claimed was based on his experience working in the Delhi mint, probably as an assay-master.[46] He also composed the arithmetical *Gaṇitasārakaumudī* sometime before 1318, which describes many practical forms of calculation, such as the volumes of domes, the area of cloth required to make various tents, and the yield of ghee from buffalo milk.[47] Finally, we possess the *Dhātūtpatti* (of uncertain date), which deals with metallurgy and also contains the material on aromatics that we consider later.[48]

Though writing later than some of the texts we examined in this book, Ṭhakkura Pherū is a particularly interesting figure, and we know far more about his life than we do about many of the other authors. An educated and pious Jain, he worked at the court of the Delhi sultans, probably holding an important position as an assay-master in the mint. It would appear that this trade ran in the family, because he states that he composed the treatise on coins and exchange, the *Dravyaparīkṣā*, for his son and brother.[49] In addition to his expertise in coins and metals, he was an expert in gemology, and he knew about the examination and evaluation of aromatics. He was accomplished in applied mathematics; and, thus, was able to write on astrology, architecture, and the sort of arithmetic indispensable for many trades and professions.

It seems that the treasury (and probably the market and warehouse) was a site where mathematical and material expertise combined.[50] This might supplement what I said about the enduring and complex mathematical character of many perfume formulae (and it underlines the strong connection between gemology and astrology). Arguably, this mathematical "mental habit" of parts of the Jain community is not only seen in the life and works of Ṭhakkura Pherū, but it is also reflected in the highly developed Jain cosmography.

The Culture of Commerce

As noted, the materials in this chapter lend themselves particularly well to the methods used by Michael Baxandall in examining fifteenth-century Italy. In particular, it may prove very fruitful to examine the life and works of Ṭhakkura Pherū in the light of Baxandall's work.

There are interesting parallels we can draw between the appreciation of the economic value of the materials of painting, such as the gold leaf and ultramarine pigment (based on lapis lazuli), required in certain Renaissance paintings and the use of certain costly aromatics in perfumes. Baxandall notes the careful specification of certain qualities of pigments in the contract between patron and painter, as well as the use of costly ultramarine to highlight certain items in paintings—such as the cloak that St. Francis of Assisi relinquishes in one particular painting.[51] The educated viewer of the period would be able to discriminate this pigment and be aware of its cost, thus reinforcing the meaning of the gesture. Similarly, the great cost and rarity of the various aromatics we discuss would have been known to many of those who saw (or heard or read) about them, especially those from a mercantile background. Like the use of these pigments and gold leaf in Italy, descriptions of the use of sandalwood, or of certain special varieties of sandalwood, would have had enriched the meaning of texts and practices in South Asia.

Baxandall also examines educational practices in fifteenth-century Italy, stating that geometry and arithmetic were prominent features of the "intellectual formation and equipment" of most middle-class people.[52] The contents of an education in geometry and arithmetic bear extremely close similarities to the contents of Pherū's treatise on arithmetic, the *Gaṇitasārakaumudī*: the calculation of the amount of cloth required to make a pavilion, the rule of three, and so forth. Indeed, Baxandall states that Italian treatises on arithmetic derived their problems from Arab ones, which in turn derived them from the traditions of India. In some respects, the education of the fifteenth-century Florentine merchant had a lot in common with that of the Indian of the mercantile class; just as both the production and reception of Renaissance art was, according to Baxandall, conditioned by such a process, so the aesthetic practices and discourses of mercantile South Asians might have been shaped by their great familiarity with the evaluation of gemstones, precious woods, and the calculation of proportions and volumes. I noted that the mathematical-material expertise found in certain circles over a long period might partly explain the use of the complex combinatoric perfumery grids. Understanding the training of the mercantile classes might help explain the production of such grids and one aspect of their reception in certain circles: not only were some perfumers and wealthy mercantile men-about-town inclined to analyze the world in a complex and numerical manner, but they could plausibly have enjoyed doing so, relishing the exercise of the skills they valued.[53]

The Evaluation of Sandalwood

We should now look at what Pherū, the Jain arithmetician, astrologer, gemologist, and royal assay-master, had to say about sandalwood. Following the introductory verses on the strange origins of many materials, Pherū discusses metals, minerals, and precious sacred objects such as right-handed conches, *rudrākṣa* seeds, and *śālagrāma* stones, in the discussion of which he also includes directions for *pūjā* worship using these items. Finally, at the end of this short text, he describes some important aromatics, and we see many of the "spices" discussed above: camphor (verses 42–44); aloeswood (verses 45–46); sandalwood (verses 47–50); musk (verse 55); and he concludes by providing formulae for an incense, the *daśāṅga* incense, as well as a perfume (*vāsa*).[54]

The passage on sandalwood is particularly interesting because, for the first time, we are told the actual price of sandalwood. As we have seen, such numerical economic data are quite thin on the ground in the sources, and although this text is somewhat later than many of the other sources in this book, it is probably not enormously far removed in time from the perfumery texts, the *Gandhasāra* and *Gandhavāda*, and it only postdates the *Mānasollāsa* by around two hundred years. At the very least, we gain an insight into the relative value of this commodity in the early fourteenth century.

Pherū first describes this commodity as cool and fragrant and also repeats the well-known poetic convention that the tree grows on the Malaya mountain, where it is infested with snakes. Following these typical praises of sandalwood, Pherū lists the varieties of this wood. The presence of such a list of varieties is reminiscent of the passages on sandalwood mentioned previously, except Pherū lists the names of the varieties without giving any individual characteristics. Also, the list of sources has changed since the time of the *Arthaśāstra* and the *Dhanvatarīyanighaṇṭu*. Pherū appears to mention as one source a particular port (Malindi) on the East African coast, in addition to a new variety called *sūkaḍissa*. This latter variety is also mentioned (called *sukvaḍi*) in the *Rājanighaṇṭu* of Narahari/Narasiṃha,[55] composed in the fifteenth or sixteenth century CE.[56] In the next verse, Pherū lists the prices of various weights of sandalwood. Finally, he lists the characteristics of the best variety of sandalwood: *śrīcandana*. Here he describes the color, taste, and shape of this type of sandalwood, in addition to remarking on its effect on heat. We should note that the examination of sandalwood involves all the senses apart from hearing: it looks yellow, is red when ground; it tastes pungent; feels cool; and the smell is mentioned in the first verse. Though composed possibly over a thousand years after the *Arthaśāstra*, this passage is nevertheless quite similar to the passage we saw describing the sensory qualities of sandalwood, which I shall quote again here for convenience:

> *Arthaśāstra*:
>
> Light, unctuous, not dry, smearing oil like ghee, of pleasant smell, suitable for the skin, mild, not fading, tolerant of warmth, absorbs great heat, and pleasant to touch—these are the qualities of sandalwood.[57]

And here is Pherū's description of sandalwood as mostly provided to me by S. R. Sarma:

> On the Malaya mountain [there are] the best *Śrīcandana* trees, which are the abodes of snakes. [These trees are] extremely cool and fragrant; by their fragrance the [whole] forest [becomes] fragrant.
>
> *Śrīcandana, Nīlavaī,*[58] *Sūkaḍissa*[59]—three varieties of sandalwood. Likewise *Malindī,*[60] *Kaühī,*[61] *and Vavvaru.*[62] [Thus] this sandalwood is of six varieties.
>
> [These six varieties of] sandalwood [have respectively the grades of] 20, 12, 8, 1, 1/3, 1/4 *visuvas*. [Their] price per 1 *ser* is 5, 3, 2, 1/4 *ṭaṅkas*, 4, 3 *jaithalas* [respectively].

> The characteristic of fair sandalwood (*śrīcandana*): yellow in color, with a red appearance when ground, pungent in taste, knotty, destroying heat.[63]

A quality grading out of twenty is used for sandalwood, and the best variety is *Śrīcandana*, which has a quality of twenty and costs five *ṭaṅkas* per *ser*.[64] We are fortunate in this case to know a lot about the ideal measures, exchange rates, prices, and wages during this period, in part owing to the efforts of Pherū himself.[65] Although this text may have been composed after the reign of 'Ala' al-Dīn Khaljī, comparing these prices with what we know of the economy during his reign, we can ascertain that whereas 1 *ser* (approximately 2/3 to 3/4 of a pound av.) of the best quality *Śrīcandana* sandalwood cost 5 *ṭaṅkas*;[66] 20 yards of fine cloth cost 1 *ṭaṅka*; a good beast of burden cost 4 to 7 *ṭaṅkas*; and a soldier would earn 234 *ṭaṅkas* annually, 19.5 *ṭaṅkas* per month. Thus about 2/3 to 3/4 lbs. of the best sandalwood cost about the same as a good beast of burden, or about a quarter of a soldier's monthly wages.

Learning to Be a Merchant

Pherū, and those like him who wrote texts on the evaluation of commodities, valued their professional knowledge. Indeed, for those involved in this way of life, their expertise was the commodity that they traded, and the same expertise was also invaluable to actual traders. The expertise of the evaluator was a crucial element of trade, assuring the livelihood of certain communities, and this expertise was believed to have the potential to make someone very rich. The production of texts containing poetic and ethical lore that describe this expertise puts it on a par with other branches of learning possessed of traditional textual authority. But, as with writing about wine, it is clear that these texts alone are not enough to make a good evaluator—hands-on training would be needed to supplement these authorities. Indeed, when I was searching for good aloeswood in Mumbai, I was well aware of the contents of many of these (and more recent) texts, and they were of little help. Possibly, these texts functioned in part as mnemonics for the standard processes of evaluation, containing important definitions and terminology that were required for someone to appear qualified in this area, but above all they constituted a *śāstric* authority for the profession of the evaluator.

Śāstras, "cultural grammars" as Sheldon Pollock called them, are thus doing two things in this context, as they were in the previous chapters on perfumery texts.[67] First, they standardize and guide the training of one's attention to be aware of, and affected by, certain features of the world: it sometimes requires considerable sophistication to attend to these features, and it is also important to know how to pick out the pertinent features in a particular context. Second, *śāstras* provide one with the linguistic materials most appropriate to the culturally and professionally approved articulations of these artfully perceived, and in some cases affective, features of the world. Indeed, akin to the trainee perfumers Bruno Latour has discussed, both these aspects of *śāstra*—the words and the perceptions—are one "articulation": "Once we have gone through the [perfumery] training session, the word 'violet' carries at last the fragrance of the violet and all of its chemical undertones. Through the materiality of language tools, words finally carry worlds. What we say, feel and act, is geared on differences registered in the world . . . Contrary to Wittgenstein's famous saying . . . what cannot be said can be articulated."[68] And *śāstra* is a key component in constructing these worlds.

Nor is there a question in this case of tension between theory and practice. These texts codify and standardize the training that regulates the perceptions and articulations of professional examiners—the nature of their bodies and world—and it is these sensory-verbal perceptions and articulations ("theory") that are the defining practices of those who live in part or wholly by the commodity of mercantile knowledge.

It is when we realize that knowledge of the texts needed to be joined to practical training that we can see the significance of the evaluator's senses: this valuable knowledge is knowledge about matter, the link between the knowledge and the matter being the body and in particular the senses. As we saw in the accounts of sandalwood, all the senses except hearing were put to use in the evaluation of the wood, yet whereas in the previous chapter, the cultivated connoisseur used his knowledge and senses to *enjoy* the perfumes, here the evaluator applies his senses to the aromatics to ascertain—to *articulate*—the true nature of the goods according to a set of internalized professional conventions and ultimately to decide how they relate to the goal of profit (*artha*).

Having reflected on the nature of the examination of aromatics, we now move on to examine the artifice of aromatics—a practice that must have constantly troubled the evaluator of aromatics, yet which also kept him in business.

The Artifice of Aromatics

The professional examiner of commodities not only had to identify the varieties and quality of aromatics, but he also needed to spot fake and artificial aromatics. As we saw in the last chapter, it would appear that one part of the science of perfumery was the artifice of fakes/substitutes. There are instructions on making artificial aromatics in the large compendium of formulae, the *Haramekhalā* or *Girdle of Hara*, as well as in the perfumery texts, the BORI *Gandhasāra* and the *Gandhavāda*. In the *Haramekhalā* and the *Gandhasāra*, the materials on the artifice of aromatics are placed toward the end of the numerous formulae, preceding the glossaries of ingredients—thus conceptually located between formula and ingredient. The *Gandhavāda* does not follow this pattern, and in that text formulae for artificial musks are found toward the beginning, possibly indicating the increased prominence of this aromatic in a world where the preferences and vocabulary of Islamic and Persianate traditions of perfumery were starting to transform medieval "Sanskritic" perfumery.

The *Haramekhalā* and the *Gandhasāra* describe a wide range of artificial preparations, and we might usefully repeat the commentarial verses giving these particular contents of the *Haramekhalā*:

> The artificial manufacture of musk and the method of the extraction of various perfumes,
> And [artificial] camphor, saffron, *nakha*, aloeswood, and Indian olibanum[69]
> And the manufacture of mango [oil], as well as the manufacture of camphor oil,
> The [artificial] manufacture of cloves, cardamoms, and costus root respectively.[70]

The term used here for making these substances is the "artifice" (*kṛti*) of (that is, the genitive case) the aromatics. The first aromatic on this list, musk, was presumably an especially successful and profitable substance to fake, which is not surprising given that musk grains look very similar to dried blood and other common materials, and a little real musk mixed with such materials would go a long way.

The *Gandhasāra* discusses artificial substances (*kṛtrimadravyāṇi*), in a somewhat challenging passage. Nevertheless, amongst other formulae, the text provides instructions on the manufacture of artificial camphor and camphor water;[71] the preparation of civet (called *javādi*);[72] a fragrant mango (*sahakāra*) preparation;[73] saffron;[74] complex procedures for making aloeswood;[75] a method of making wood (like aloeswood?) for incense;[76] artificial costus root;[77] and a substance called *sthauneyaka*.[78] This list, though somewhat different from those described above and below, nevertheless contains many of the principal "spice" aromatics: camphor, saffron, musk, and aloeswood.

Directions on the preparation of artificial aromatics are also given in an alchemical text, the *Rasaratnākara* of Nityanātha,[79] dating from the first half of the fifteenth century CE.[80] It is this source that we will now examine in detail, because it contains some interesting material on the artifice of aromatics, and it also places this phenomenon in another context that we have not as yet seen: alchemy. Like some of the texts discussed, this text is concerned with increasing wealth, which is achieved by the application of knowledge. Yet, unlike the case of the texts on examination that demonstrate how to evaluate (by informed perception and description) the real nature of materials with a view to making a profit, in these texts we learn how to manipulate matter (by informed action) to make substitutes for the real aromatics—artificial versions that hopefully appear to the senses like the real thing, and thus trick perception, at least untrained perception—which presumably may be traded for even more profit.

In the *Rasaratnākara*, in the "Section on Theory" (*Vādikhaṇḍa*), dealing mainly with alchemy, chapter 19, "On Increasing Wealth" (*dhanavardhanam*), provides instructions for making artificial gemstones and minerals, the manufacture of ink, the adulteration of ghee, the preparation of artificial aromatics, the manufacture of divine incense (*divyadhūpa*),[81] liquid extracts of flowers, and methods to increase crop yields.[82] The artificial aromatic raw materials described in this section of the *Rasaratnākara* are (with the exception of the absent aloeswood) the major aromatics discussed previously, that is to say, in the following order: sandalwood, camphor, musk, and saffron.[83] Not only are the methods for the artifice of aromatics interesting, but so too are the introductory verses to the chapter on increasing wealth, where the connection between the manufacture of these substances and wealth is made explicit:

> In the world of rebirth, very abundant wealth is indeed the most excellent thing, producing all pleasures; that is to be attained by lords of *sādhakas*. According to the method from the mouth of the teacher, specifically the manufacture of jewels, etc., and the auspicious lore of perfumery is related here for the purpose of attaining it.
>
> For, having understood everything, those various things are easily attained, being in the direct experience [and] purifying for wise ones.[84]

This passage contains much of interest to us. First of all, we are told that in the world of rebirth (*saṃsāra*), the best thing is great wealth (*dhanam*). In this context, great wealth is the most excellent thing because it produces all pleasures (*sakalasukhakara*) to be had in the realm of rebirth. One way in which *sādhakas*, adepts in "magic," can attain this great wealth, is not by tantric practices or the use of magic, but by the physical manufacture of artificial jewels, perfumes, and so forth. Clearly, the procedures in this chapter are intended to produce wealth, a proper and good aim in the world of rebirth, associated with the goal of profit (*artha*). This wealth is also qualified as the producer of pleasures and is therefore foundational to the goal of sensuous pleasure (*kāma*).

We examine only one method for making an artificial aromatic: sandalwood. The method requires some work and also uses materials (*guggulu*, salt) that presumably, by this period, were far cheaper than the potential price of the artificial sandalwood produced—one assumes the neem tree did not cost anything:[85]

> Having fully cut down a neem tree, you should retain a cubit at the base. You should make a hole in the top of that and fill it with fresh *guggulu* resin. Having closed it with that wood, you should smear the joint with mud and salt, and you should cook it (once it has) dried, in a small fire on

> the ground. The root of that (or "That root"), cool by nature, is to be collected and should become sandalwood (*candana*).[86]

It would seem that this method is quite practical, since wood baked and soaked with the dark brown fragrant resin of *guggulu* would darken a little and have a rich smell. We are told little about the final product: only that it is by nature cool (*svabhāvaśītala*), perhaps the most important sensory and medicinal quality of sandalwood. Indeed, if we understand *candana* in the broadest sense as a wood with a cooling potency, then this is not necessarily a method to fake *candana*, but rather the artificial manufacture of what is actually a *candana* of sorts.

This text and others like it raise the issue of the place of authenticity in medieval Indian culture. This text does not in any way present these methods as a shameful necessity, and, indeed, it praises them as allowing one to attain the most important goal in the realm of rebirth. Similarly, the perfumery texts that provide instructions on the manufacture of artificial aromatics do so with no mention of practicing this art in secrecy. Although it was important to be able to evaluate the quality and origin of aromatics and gemstones, nevertheless, we should not assume that all artifice was seen as a bad thing in this culture. I suggested that the cooling wood produced by this method might arguably be counted as a type of *candana* in the broadest sense of the word. I should note that today we draw a distinction between synthetic versus natural, authentic versus fake, as well as fake versus artificial. Synthetic rubies and synthetic camphor are chemically identical to natural ones—they are real (rubies and camphor) but not natural. If we understand the *candana* manufactured by the method given was considered to be a type of *candana* by virtue of its cooling nature, then perhaps the best term for this is "synthetic *candana*." In certain contexts, it may be useful to have a cheap artificial/synthetic or heavily adulterated version of the "real" thing that shared some of the same essential qualities—just as we saw in the case of the aloeswood I was offered "that is only good to give as a gift," or as we see in the case of the cheap pressed pellets of "sandalwood" that are sold for use in *pūjā* rites in India today. Indeed, in our society a fake is not necessarily undesirable: tourists flock to certain markets in Bangkok to buy fake versions of prestigious luxuries: Rolex watches, Louis Vuitton purses, and so forth. Some of these products may be illegal, but that does not mean they are undesirable, and in the case of the cheap sandalwood pellets they are fully legal and useful substitutes, if not particularly prestigious. Artifice and adulteration of raw materials also allows for certain types of innovation, as in the case of the rose or vetiver-scented *lobān* (frankincense) that I have seen sold in abundance in the streets of Ajmer. Although the sophisticated *vidagdha* might not want to wear artificial aromatics, and the medieval king might not want to fill his treasury with fake sandalwood, there is no reason why there could not have been markets for artificial versions of rare and costly aromatics in medieval India, just as there are today.

What Is Sandalwood?

On the basis my examination, one might think of "sandalwood" or *candana*, both the word and the thing, less as a stable substance moving through time and space but rather as an *institution*. As Bruno Latour notes when stating that he would prefer to designate substances as institutions: "The word 'substance' does not designate what 'remains beneath,' impervious to history, but what gathers together a multiplicity of agents into a stable and coherent whole . . . substance is a name that designates the *stability* of an assemblage."[87] Latour's language breaks down the boundaries between materials and societies such that the category of material culture itself is called into question. Zimmermann makes a related point in discussing early Indian theories of food and medicine where substances likewise were understood to exhibit a certain changeability: "what it comes down to is that there really are no substances, only relations, transitions, sacrifices, stages which must be passed though."[88] Nevertheless, it is vital to state that there are undoubtedly limits to the instability of sandalwood-as-institution. Just because a certain category is fuzzy does not mean it extends indefinitely in all directions. As we saw, only certain materials could pass for sandalwood at any given time and place (hence the literature on artifice and evaluation), and sandalwood was deemed to have certain core properties such as coolness. Also, certain woods, such as that of *Santalum album*, were, and still are, prototypical and especially valued manifestations of sandalwood, possessed of ideal sandalwood properties to the highest degree. Sandalwood and *candana* are complex, changing, and imperfectly defined categories of material; but that does not mean that we are faced with a wood free-for-all, at least not in South Asia, though when the category and the wood traveled elsewhere (for example, to Japan) this might have changed.

This brief survey of the raw materials of perfumery and their role in the mercantile intellectual culture of early and medieval India is now complete. We are now in a position to attempt a close reading of a religious text in the next chapter. In that Buddhist text, sandalwood and themes such as mercantile knowledge, trade, and the distant origins of aromatics play an important role. As with the narrative we read at the end of chapter 6, we will also see to what extent the knowledge we gained in this chapter may be usefully applied elsewhere.

PART FIVE

SMELL AND RELIGION

9

Bois des Îles

A Buddhist Sandalwood Merchant: The Story of Pūrṇa

Among the aromatics of South Asia, exotic, expensive, cool, and perfumed sandalwood plays the most important role in many religious traditions. I now examine one narrative in which sandalwood plays a significant role. *The Story of Pūrṇa*, or *Pūrṇāvadāna*, describes the trade in sandalwood from a Buddhist perspective, and this tale also provides a good example of a distinctively Buddhist use of the wood from this early period.

The text is a type of Buddhist story called an *avadāna*; an ethical and didactic story, illustrating the nature of *karma* and its results, as applied to the lives of people other than the Buddha.[1] This *avadāna* story, the *avadāna* of Pūrṇa (*Pūrṇāvadāna*),[2] belongs to a larger and variable collection of thirty-eight stories, called the *Divyāvadāna* produced "within the context of early Indian Buddhist monastic culture—probably during the period of Sarvāstivādin Buddhism in Northwest India during the first half of the first millennium [CE]."[3] These stories contain numerous references to mercantile culture, such as accounts of sea voyages and trading in precious goods. This possibly reflects the close relationship between Buddhism and mercantile groups in the early centuries CE.[4]

Summary of the *Pūrṇāvadāna*

First, it is useful to provide a very brief account of the plot of the *Pūrṇāvadāna*.[5] Much of the story takes place in the trading port town of Sūrpāraka,[6] during the lifetime of Śākyamuni Buddha, who is at that time staying in the Jeta forest at Śrāvastī. In Sūrpāraka lives a wealthy householder called Bhava, who has three sons by his wife and also one son, Pūrṇa, our protagonist, by a servant girl. The son of the servant girl, Pūrṇa, receives a commercial education, but when the three sons by Bhava's wife leave to trade overseas and make their fortune, Pūrṇa

*Bois des Îles was created by Ernest Beaux for Chanel in 1926.

has to remain at home and manage the family business. When the three sons return and tally up the profits, it turns out that Pūrṇa, though he never left the town, has made the most, and his father concludes that this is because of the great merit he must have accrued in former lives.

The father dies, having previously begged his family to avoid a rift after he had passed away. Then the three sons go on trading voyages again, leaving Pūrṇa behind as before. While the brothers are away, their wives become resentful of such issues as the fact that Pūrṇa controls the family housekeeping money. When the brothers return, the discontent forces them to split the family's fortune, just as their father had feared. It is decided that Pūrṇa is merely a property to be divided, and the eldest son takes Pūrṇa as his share of the fortune, having been instructed to care for him by their late father.

Then, Pūrṇa and the eldest brother's wife are thrown out of their joint family home and removed from the family business. After this, Pūrṇa and the eldest brother's wife wander about and her children become hungry. To find food for them, Pūrṇa brings some coins and leaves to search for food. On his way, he sees a man carrying some wood and shivering with cold. Pūrṇa recognizes that this is ox-head (*gośīrṣa*) sandalwood and buys it off the man at a very cheap price. He then sells a little of the wood, which makes a small amount of money to keep his brother's family going.

Later, the king of the town of Sūrpāraka is ill with a fever and is told by his doctors that he needs ox-head sandalwood. The ministers go to buy some and after some inquiries, they come to Pūrṇa from whom they purchase some sandalwood for twice the price that Pūrṇa paid for the whole load of wood. They apply a paste to the king and he recovers. Once recovered, the king decides it is appropriate for him to have some sandalwood at home, so he summons Pūrṇa and buys some more sandalwood, to which Pūrṇa adds an extra piece as a gift. The king, pleased, offers him a boon, and Pūrṇa asks that he may live in the town undisturbed.

Around this time, many merchants sail into town. The local guild announces that no independent trade, outside the guild, is allowed, but Pūrṇa, unaware of this, goes to the merchants and places a deposit on their goods. The guild is angered and tries to punish Pūrṇa, but they are stopped by the king. The king needs some of the new goods, but rather than ask Pūrṇa himself, he asks the guild to first buy the goods from Pūrṇa so that the king may then in turn buy them from the guild. Despite the tensions, Pūrṇa treats the guild well. Very wealthy as a result of this trade, he decides to embark on a sea voyage himself, so he collects merchants and goes on six successful sea voyages.

At this time, some merchants arrive from Śrāvastī wishing to go on a sea voyage with Pūrṇa, given his record of success. Whilst on the voyage, they recite some Buddhist texts, and when Pūrṇa asks what the texts are he is told they are the words of the Buddha. When he returns home, Pūrṇa rejects the opportunity to find a wife and renounces the worldly life, telling the oldest brother not to go on sea voyages with the other brothers. Pūrṇa then travels to Śrāvastī to see the Buddha and becomes a monk. After the Buddha preaches to him, Pūrṇa expresses a wish to go to a place called Śroṇāparāntaka, where he eventually gathers followers and becomes enlightened.

Back in the port of Sūrpāraka, the two younger brothers have run out of money and persuade the eldest brother to embark on another sea journey. They set sail together with some merchants and arrive at a place called Ox-head Sandalwood Forest (*Gośīrṣacandanavana*) where the merchants proceed to cut down the trees. It turns out that this place is under the protection of a *yakṣa*, who, when he hears that the trees are being felled, creates a windstorm. The merchants pray to the gods to no avail, and then the eldest brother mentions that he was warned by Pūrṇa not to go on another voyage. They decide to call on Pūrṇa who, by means of special powers, comes to their aid and repels the storm. The *yakṣa* explains to Pūrṇa that the forest is maintained for a universal monarch (*cakravartin*), and Pūrṇa asks whether an enlightened being is not better than a universal monarch. When the *yakṣa* learns such a person has arisen, he allows them to take the sandalwood.

On their return home, Pūrṇa keeps the wood, gives the merchants jewels instead, and uses the sandalwood to construct a sandalwood pavilion for the Buddha. He instructs the brothers to invite the Buddha and his disciples to that place in order to offer them a meal, and then performs a ritual on the roof of the palace with flowers, incense, and water that become a magical flower pavilion that flies to Jeta forest. The Buddha realizes the nature of the invitation and travels to Sūrpāraka converting people on the way. On entering the sandalwood palace and being seated, many other people try to get in but there is not enough room, so the Buddha transforms it into a (transparent) rock crystal palace and then delivers a sermon. The Buddha's monks ask the Buddha about Pūrṇa's past life, and he explains that Pūrṇa was a disciple of a previous Buddha, Kāśyapa, and that one time he chastised another monk, calling him the son of a slave girl. He confessed this sin and thus avoided hell, but he was reborn many times as the son of a slave girl, including in this life, yet, because of his service to the *saṅgha*, he was born in a good situation in this life.

Commercial Education

The first thing that strikes us on reading this narrative is the nature of Pūrṇa's education. We are told:

> When he was an adult, he was taught in writing, calculation, accounting, coinage,[7] debts, deposits, open-deposits, in the examination of goods, in the examination of gems, in the examination of elephants, in the examination of horses, in the examination of boys, in the examination of girls—in the eight (types of) examination—he became an expounder, a reader, learned, of sharp conduct.[8]

This ideal mercantile education shares much content with the textual production of Pherū, seen in the previous chapter. Here, commercial arithmetic belongs with the inspection of commercial goods, such as gemstones and so forth (as seen in both Pherū and Varāhamihira), as well as with the examination of boys and girls (presumably on the lines of the prognosticatory examination of the body described by Varāhamihira). Also, writing is mentioned in this list, enabling the trader to create and check his all-important records. Mercantile communities had a higher literacy rate (in both reading and writing) than many other groups; this was true not just in discourse but also in reality.

If we look closely at the list, we see that the set of "eight types of examination" is not complete—there are only six on the list. This matter is discussed by Sastri, who notes that this stock passage occurs in several places in slightly different forms, and thus we are able to attempt to reconstruct the full set of eight types of examination.[9] In another *avadāna*, the *Supriyāvadāna*, we find the following types of examination:

> [I]n the examination of elephants, in the examination of horses, in the examination of gems, in the examination of wood, in the examination of cloth, in the examination of men, in the examination of women, in the examination of various articles of trade.[10]

The examination of elephants, horses, gems, men, and women remains the same. The examination of cloth (*vastra*) replaces that of goods (*vastu*) seen in the previous list and also in others;[11] and, indeed, Sastri prefers the reading of cloth (*vastra*), perhaps because it is more specific than goods (*vastu*). In addition to these types of examinations, the second list adds the examination of wood (*dāru*) and the examination of various articles of trade (*paṇya*), a broad category to cover all other items. The examination of wood is clearly of interest to us in considering commercial learning about sandalwood, though it is notable that this type of examination is not actually mentioned in the Sanskrit *Pūrṇāvadāna*. Nevertheless, the Tibetan version of the *Pūrṇāvadāna* lists the examination of goods and cloth, as well as of wood, giving a different group of eight types of examination than that in the earlier quotation.[12] What did this education in wood consist of? As we have seen, the contents of a text on the examination of sandalwood, whether this be the *Arthaśāstra* or the much later text of Pherū, remained relatively consistent over time, containing a list of varieties of sandalwood, as well as a statement of the qualities of sandalwood, both the general qualities of sandalwood and, in the case of the *Arthaśāstra*, of the individual varieties.

Pūrṇa's training in commercial matters proves to be of immense use, and the placing of this stock passage toward the beginning of the narrative sets the scene for his future commercial successes. He is able to run the family business to produce great profit and, most important, when he is thrown out of the house and the business, it is his mercantile knowledge that enables him to identify the sandalwood the man is carrying, and it is his commercial sharpness that allows him to profit from this lucky encounter.

Pūrṇa's Knowledge of Sandalwood

We now examine exactly how the fortuitous find of sandalwood is described:

> And a certain man comes along who, having taken a load of wood that had been driven onto the shore of the ocean, was shivering, overcome with cold. He saw him and asked him "Hey man! Why are you shivering like that?" He explains "*I* don't know. I lifted up this load and I found myself in such a state." He is very skilled in the examination of wood. He started to look at that wood [and] sees there is ox-head sandalwood. He addresses him "Hey man! What price will you take?" "Five-hundred *kārṣāpanas*." He accepted that load of wood, removed the ox-head sandalwood, went to the market [and] made four pieces with a saw. That gets sold for powder for a thousand *kārṣāpanas*. Then he gave five hundred *kārṣāpanas* to the man and said, "Take this load of wood to where, in a certain house, there stays the wife of Bhavila, and tell her Pūrṇa sent it."[13]

Quite by chance Pūrṇa encounters this man, yet it does not take Pūrṇa long to notice something strange is going on, when the man, who is overcome with cold, tells him he has been shivering since he lifted up the load of wood. As we already know, one of the most important conventional sensory and medicinal qualities of sandalwood is that it is cooling. In this narrative, close proximity to a large quantity of sandalwood is also presented as cooling; so much so, that the man is "overcome by cold" and "shivering." Although the cooling nature of sandalwood is mentioned in the texts on the examination of sandalwood, nevertheless, this is not a specialist piece of knowledge, and no doubt anyone hearing or reading this text in early or medieval India would have picked up on this cue. Indeed, these two points—that the most immediately noticeable aspect of sandalwood in this narrative is its cooling (tactile) nature and that this was a widely known quality of sandalwood—are things we should remember in considering the remainder of this narrative, as well as in considering the significance of sandalwood in other contexts discussed later.

In chapter 6, we examined the narrative concerning the perfume-addicted prince, and noted that the highly technical science of perfumery was presented in a rather simplified manner, and that the perfume they mention—*Yakṣa* Mud—was a perfume whose name was probably widely known. Here, the examination of sandalwood is likewise simplified. Although what we are told about Pūrṇa's examination of the wood is accurate according to the technical sources discussed, nevertheless, the sandalwood in question just happens to be a very famous variety, very prominent in Buddhist sources.[14] We are told nothing about the technical manner in which Pūrṇa identified that it was this particular variety of wood. Instead, like the narrative of the perfume-addicted prince, this passage flatters the hearer or reader that they too might aspire to this (simplified) skill in examination: you do not need to be an experienced wood evaluator to follow, and maybe even to predict, Pūrṇa's train of thought. Narrative versions of technical knowledge are simplified to give the audience an opportunity to imagine being possessed of this sophisticated expertise. In this case, the aspirations assumed of the audience relate to the possession of mercantile knowledge that would allow them to become wealthy with great ease. In the case of the perfume-addicted prince, the audience can briefly allow themselves the fantasy of being expert in all the sensual arts associated with the intimate lifestyles of the rich and famous.

Having noticed that something strange is going on, Pūrṇa takes a closer look, and because he is "skilled in the examination of wood" (*dāruparīkṣāyāṃ kṛtāvi*), which he presumably learned during his mercantile education,[15] he ascertains not just that it is sandalwood but also a particular variety of sandalwood: ox-head (*gośīrṣa*)—a variety we have seen several times. Pūrṇa realizes the enormous value of the wood and that the man who found it seems ignorant of its true nature. It appears that Pūrṇa takes a small amount to the market, which he then sells for double the price the man wanted for the whole load of wood. He then takes the whole load and sells parts of it to make further profit. Here we see exactly how the knowledge he gained from his mercantile education (plus, of course, some karmic good fortune) allowed Pūrṇa to become wealthy and successful. We also see the importance of the multisensory examination of commodities, including ones that we might think of as primarily aromatic substances.

Cool and Royal

As outlined in the summary of the story, Pūrṇa's selling of the sandalwood enables him to rebuild the business of his brother, lead trading voyages, and become a famously successful merchant. The most important customer of Pūrṇa is the king, who buys the sandalwood on two occasions. On the first occasion, he buys the sandalwood to cure a fever, and here the cooling nature of sandalwood is again emphasized, and notably this sandalwood is made into an ointment (*pralepa*):

> At this point, the king of Sūrpāraka was distressed by a burning fever.
> His doctors prescribed ox-head sandalwood.[16]

The king's ministers then locate Pūrṇa to buy some of his sandalwood, and when the king has recovered, he reflects as follows: "What sort of a king is he who has no ox-head sandalwood in his house?"[17]

It seems that, in this narrative, this particular costly, cooling wood is something that a king thinks he ought to possess, presumably in his treasury, as we saw in the *Arthaśāstra*. We also see this connection between royalty and the possession of the finest sandalwood when Pūrṇa's brothers go on the voyage to the Ox-head Sandalwood Forest. Furthermore, during that voyage, we find two other aspects of some aromatics we emphasized, namely, their exotic overseas origins and the danger associated with their production. The forest of valuable sandalwood is only reached by a risky sea voyage; and the place is inhabited by *yakṣas*, who are angered when the sandalwood is looted, and they try to prevent it being taken. Although the sandalwood is obtained at the place of production in the form of booty from (a failed) raid, and not through trade, nevertheless, the long-distance travel involved in the production of precious commodities is emphasized in this narrative. We saw the immense value of sandalwood from the way Pūrṇa was able to trade pieces of a single load for great profit, and we can therefore imagine the enormous value of a whole forest. This abundant source of the costly cooling wood has been reserved for one type of person: a universal monarch (*cakravartin*).

Like white elephants in Thailand and sturgeon caught off the coast of England, this sandalwood is reserved for a monarch,[18] being what Kopytoff calls a "singular" commodity: "What these monopolies clearly do, however, is to expand the visible reach of sacred power by projecting it onto additional sacralized objects."[19] In this case, Pūrṇa argues that an enlightened being is superior to such a monarch, and thus the Buddha is also entitled to the vast wealth of sandalwood in the forest. On returning to Sūrpāraka, Pūrṇa offers the ox-head sandalwood to the Buddha in the form of a palace/pavilion/temple,[20] possibly with sandalwood stories (*candanamālaḥ prāsādaḥ*)[21] constructed from the wood, to which he invites the Buddha. This building is constructed with a large quantity of a very valuable exotic commodity, indeed, in this case it is a singular royal commodity, and, above all, we are aware that it has the aesthetic quality of cooling—if carrying a bundle of the wood can overcome a man with cold and make him shiver, how cooling would entering an entire building made of sandalwood be? Indeed, throughout this entire version of the story of Pūrṇa, the fragrance of the sandalwood is not once mentioned. It seems what is most remarkable about the sandalwood pavilion is the sheer presence of such a large amount of a material that is so exclusive and expensive, and so powerfully cooling. The value, rarity, and desirability of the sandalwood are again emphasized when the craftsmen constructing the palace prefer to accept a measure of sandalwood powder the size of a cat's paw rather than their daily wages.[22] But in the end, the sandalwood is ultimately replaced by rock crystal, a transparent material that, amongst other things, allows people to see the Buddha.[23]

Sandalwood Artifacts in Early South Asian Buddhism

References to structures and objects made of sandalwood, such as that in the *Pūrṇāvadāna* are obviously quite impressive—such a thing as a sandalwood pavilion or a sandalwood Buddha image must have sounded expensive and fragrant to anyone hearing the tale. Anyone who has visited India will, no doubt, have come across many sandalwood artifacts for sale, and thus the idea of a sandalwood artifact seems quite normal. The sandalwood pavilion built by Pūrṇa for the Buddha therefore appears to be an impressive statement of the transformation of mercantile expertise into a precious structure that, by means of its fragrance, possibly hints at that other residence of the Buddha, his Perfumed Chamber: the *Gandhakuṭī*.[24]

But things are perhaps not quite as simple as they seem. First, as noted, sandalwood artifacts are somewhat unusual in the context of very early South Asian texts. Despite the numerous references to *candana* in the *Mahābhārata* and the *Rāmāyaṇa*, there is not one single reference to an object made of the wood. The tree is mentioned, as is the wood (as a raw material), but when sandalwood is consumed, it is ground up and used as an adornment or burned in a funeral pyre—it is destroyed in being consumed. The notion that this sandalwood could be made into something relatively permanent—and something quite large at that—appears to be a distinctive feature of Buddhist sources in early India.

In Buddhist sources from the early to mid centuries of the Common Era, there are references to several sandalwood objects, though I will not present an exhaustive survey here. There is Pūrṇa's ox-head sandalwood palace, to which the Buddha comes to preach. Another story in the *Divyāvadāna* refers to a sandalwood pole.[25] A certain rather vain Brahmin named Indra desires to see the top of the Buddha's head but cannot see it. The Buddha tells him that there is, however, an ox-head sandalwood pole buried underneath his fire-altar, which is the same height as the Buddha. The Brahmin discovers this is true and establishes the use of this Buddha-height sandalwood pole in a virtuous festival called the Indramaha.[26] In another story from the *Divyāvadāna*, the *Jyotiṣka-avadāna*, a bowl made of ox-head sandalwood is mentioned in a short episode describing the origins of a rule concerning the types of bowls that monks are permitted to use.[27] A similar episode occurs in the Pali Vinaya where we read the story of a sandalwood bowl commissioned by a merchant of Rājagaha out of a block of sandalwood (*candanagaṇṭhi*) he came to possess. The merchant then places the bowl on a very high structure and offers it to any ascetic who can get it by means of his supernatural powers. A Buddhist monk takes the bowl by a feat of supernatural levitation. However, at least in the Pali version, the Buddha disapproves of this overt display of powers and orders the bowl broken down to be used as ointment.[28]

In another early Buddhist text, a biography of the Buddha called the *Lalitavistara*, which possibly dates from around the second century CE, we find more references to sandalwood artifacts. According to this text, in his mother's womb the Buddha-to-be resides in a beautiful luxurious structure, the *ratnavyūha*, a sort of embryo-palace somewhat analogous to a placenta or caul, which is later enshrined in the heaven of Brahmā.[29] The upper room (*kūṭāgāra*) of this structure is made of sandalwood, and there are two other rooms nested within that sandalwood room, the innermost one being made of perfume (*gandha*), where the unborn Buddha-to-be resided.[30] The variety of sandalwood mentioned is one we have not seen before, called *uragasāracandana*, possibly implying "snake-heartwood sandalwood" (or "snake essence"), which most probably reflects the conventional association of snakes with the place of origin of sandalwood.[31] This wood is said to be very valuable and the color of a precious stone called noble blue *vaiḍūrya*, thus probably a rich dark blue.[32] In the same text, another sandalwood artifact is attributed to the Buddha, namely, his schoolboy writing tablet, which is made of the same variety (*uragasāra-*) of sandalwood.[33]

Last but not least, amongst these Buddhist references to sandalwood artifacts, is the famous sandalwood Buddha image, mentioned in numerous sources with the earliest ones again dated to the early to mid centuries of the first millennium CE. I will not discuss this famous image and the various accounts of it in detail here.[34] Briefly, this image is said to be the first image of the Buddha, created during the lifetime of the Buddha. In the Pali version, this is commissioned by King Pasenadi of Kosala during the absence of the Buddha, and in the Mahāyāna version by King Udayana of Kosambī, again during a temporary absence of the Buddha. What is important is that this is a relatively early account of a sandalwood artifact in a South Asian context, and that artifact is said to be an image of the Buddha.

It would appear that the notion of a sizable object made out of sandalwood is peculiarly Buddhist, at least in earlier South Asian texts. There are references to sandalwood objects in other traditions: in the mid-sixth century CE Varāhamihira mentions sandalwood as one of the woods out of which one can make sacred images, as well as beds and seats.[35] There is also a medieval Jain account of an ox-head sandalwood image of the Jina Mahāvīra that is associated with another king called Udayana, though John Cort suggests this particular story seems to have been borrowed from the narrative of the sandalwood Buddha.[36] Nevertheless, I would cautiously suggest that in sources dating from the early to mid centuries of the first millennium CE, large sandalwood artifacts are things that one tends to find described in Buddhist texts, in narrative contexts.[37]

This really is quite a remarkable innovation. If we accept that previously sandalwood was used in a ground-up form, either as an adornment or a medicine, when we suddenly find substantial objects—bowls, statues, buildings—made out sandalwood, it represents a strikingly original use of the material. So what exactly happened here? What does it mean to make an image or a building out of sandalwood, and how might people have responded to the notion of such objects? (Or to the reality of such objects?)[38]

First, as noted, there is more than one type of sandalwood, as South Asians were well aware. The version of the Pūrṇa story specifies the variety of sandalwood as ox-head sandalwood (*gośirṣacandana*). Two other versions of the story of Pūrṇa (Puṇṇa) in Pali[39] specify that he finds red sandalwood (*lohitacandana*,[40] *rattacandana*[41]), suggesting that those sources were produced in or somehow derived through a context in which that particular type of sandalwood was more valued; or where red sandalwood was more prominent in discourse; where this type of wood was suggested by a vernacular cognate of *candana*; or where it was even used in the construction of a building. Possibly the context in question was the fourth to fifth and late sixth or early seventh centuries CE in South India or Sri Lanka.[42]

In Europe and North America today, sandalwood is, above all, valued as a perfume; indeed, sandalwood was a prototypical aromatic material in South Asian texts from very early times. However, as we saw in the traditional accounts of this material, the smell of sandalwood varies, and some sandalwood is odorless. What all sandalwood seems to have in common, in the early South Asian understanding, is its quality of coldness, which can be used as a medicine or make a man carrying washed-up sandalwood shiver. Even artificial sandalwood is apparently understood to be sandalwood because it is cool. And in the story of Pūrṇa from the *Divyāvadāna*, there are absolutely no references to the fragrance of sandalwood. One might argue that this was simply assumed, but then again, the coldness could likewise be assumed, yet this quality, actual or conventional, is directly implied on at least two occasions: when the man carrying the wood is shivering, and when the king needs sandalwood to cure his fever. Even when sandalwood is used in an aphorism in the *Divyāvadāna*, the application of sandalwood paste is contrasted with the *tactile* pain of being cut with a knife, as it is in other contexts.[43] Thus, at least in this text, it is sandalwood's tactile quality of coldness that is emphasized, and for this reason we should be quite cautious in aligning the sandalwood pavilion with the perfumed-chamber motif.

The properties of sandalwood are not only sensory, and sandalwood was often understood to be both exotic and expensive. The Pūrṇa story makes quite clear that the sandalwood is exotic—it is washed onto the shore in the first instance and found on a dangerous island overseas in the second. As for the cost of sandalwood, this would appear to be especially important in the narrative of Pūrṇa, where it is the impressive exchange value of the sandalwood that is repeatedly emphasized. From the incredible deal he strikes with the man who found the wood washed up on the shore, to the sandalwood he sells to the king for a great price, this sandalwood is extremely expensive, which only contributes to the imagined value of the whole forest of ox-head sandalwood that he ultimately transforms into an abode for the Buddha. Sandalwood, along with aloeswood, is remarkable in being an aromatic that retains its fragrance and other properties for a very long time if stored well, and this explains how it can be kept in a royal treasury in the same manner as gemstones. Sandalwood is not as enduring as gems or precious metals, but over a relatively long period it can be treated as a valuable commodity in the same manner as those materials, and it certainly lasts long enough to be made into a statue—perhaps we might think of it as a precious organic material akin to ivory in durability, especially because, unlike gold but like ivory, sandalwood cannot be melted down and reused. In the Jain *Aṅgavijjā*, a large, possibly fourth-century CE Prakrit text on signs and omens, there is a list of various types of precious material and this includes gold, silver, sandalwood, aloeswood, as well as various types of cloth.[44] Furthermore, in the same text, there is a long list of various professions, and here it is said that "the rich merchants were those dealing in wrought gold, unwrought gold (*heraṇṇika*, *sauvaṇṇika*), sandalwood, cloth and were called devaḍa."[45] Sandalwood would thus appear to be somewhat on a par with precious metals in terms of its value as a bulk commodity. Or, again, we can usefully make a comparison with ivory, which was also stockpiled in treasuries in the ancient Mediterranean world.[46]

Two other materials that we might usefully compare with sandalwood are the purple stone called porphyry and blue lapis lazuli. As Nicholas Penny explains, precious purple porphyry, also called "imperial porphyry," was in the late Roman Empire "associated with the sacred aura of the emperor, whose tomb was made of porphyry and whose heirs were born in a chamber of the same material."[47] Malgouryes notes that "by means of its color, associated with aristocratic prestige, and then with imperial propaganda, it [porphyry] was the most emblematic stone of late antiquity. From then on, anyone who claimed the heritage of the vanished Roman Empire saw in it one of the symbolic means to affirm their affiliation and legitimacy."[48] As I shall argue shortly, sandalwood was represented in texts as a sculpture material that was used almost exclusively to "frame" the bodies of special persons in early South Asia. Indeed, in the Sanskrit language when placed at the end of a compound the word *candana* could imply that a certain thing was "most excellent of its kind."[49] It was, above all, the purple color of porphyry that allowed it to stand for imperial power (supplemented by its rarity and the enormous difficulties involved in carving it). Likewise, certain qualities of sandalwood—its color, fragrance, and coolness—made it an ideal precious material to associate with the bodies of enlightened persons. As with sandalwood, it was sometimes necessary or desirable to use porphyry substitutes, and these were chosen on the basis of their sharing its most important *quality*, the color purple: the sarcophagus of Napoleon is not made of porphyry at all, but of Russian quartzite of a very similar color.[50] We can also compare precious lapis lazuli with sandalwood here because, like sandalwood, this blue stone may be used in two very different forms: as a material of sculpture and ground up as a pigment.

Given the preciousness of sandalwood, I argue that a sandalwood artifact of any substantial size is monumental. Monumentality is arguably a relative notion: for us to call an object made of limestone or sandstone monumental it has to be rather big, like a pyramid or a large national monument. But, I would argue that a diamond the size of a fist is also monumental, at least as diamonds go. Thus, an object made from a large quantity of this precious material—a life-sized sandalwood statue of the Buddha or a pavilion made of sandalwood—is so impressive and rare that it effectively becomes a monumental object. These sandalwood artifacts are not just fragrant, cooling, and precious, but they are also (relatively) monumental.

But we have still not fully addressed the question of this apparently novel use of the material. Unlike ivory, which was typically used in the form of artifacts, sandalwood seems to have been initially used ground to a paste or powder: used in medicine to cool and heal the body; or applied to the skin as a beautiful, cool, and fragrant adornment. A piece of sandalwood used in this manner goes quite a long way and can last many years before it is worn away. At least in the context of early sources that describe this sort of sandalwood use, to talk of making large objects out of the wood is quite remarkable. Sandalwood is only represented as a raw material in the forest or treasury, and, arguably, this radical shift in the use of sandalwood might have been almost as striking as the use of chocolate in sculpture today. If bulk sandalwood did indeed evoke the treasury and the market, then the mercantile culture associated with early South Asian Buddhism might well have appreciated this particular "bulk-commodity" expression of the material, just as Baxandall's wealthy fifteenth-century Italian patrons of the arts might have been impressed by certain prestigious materials used in quantity. In considering this change in the use of sandalwood, I should also point out that Cutler has suggested significant correlations between the availability and the uses of ivory in late antiquity. To my knowledge, we do not have these data for early South Asia, but we should not discount that similar fluctuations in availability might have played a role in the uses and representations of sandalwood in early and medieval South Asia.[51]

These economic considerations are not all that is suggested by this new way of using sandalwood. As noted already, sandalwood in the epics and other texts, including the story of Pūrṇa, is applied to both people and objects, such as weapons, as an adornment. In those cases, sandalwood is applied to someone or something to make it somehow better—cooler, more fragrant, and more visually beautiful. As the art historian Coomaraswamy famously noted, in South Asia ornament is not excess but is "the furnishing of anything essential to the validity of whatever is adorned"; and, indeed, adornment and ornament are key concepts in South Asian aesthetics, both literary and visual.[52] Here, however, in making sandalwood into an artifact, a material normally used to ornament bodies and things instead becomes the very matter that constitutes the body of an object, the substance of the artifact. Sandalwood-as-ornament (of the body) becomes sandalwood-as-body. Such an object, though it might in turn be venerated and ornamented, would nevertheless have no real need of ornament, presumably perfect in itself: intrinsically cool, fragrant, and visually beautiful, just like the "virtuous body" of a real Buddha.[53] Indeed, were such a body adorned with other materials, then, like Viṣṇu in the poems of Vedāntadeśika as translated by Steven Hopkins, such a precious sandalwood body would function as "an ornament for jewels."[54]

But before going further, it is important that we consider exactly what sorts of objects are made out of sandalwood in these texts, and what other uses people put sandalwood to in these texts, besides making artifacts. With one exception—the sandalwood bowl—these sandalwood objects are all very closely associated with the Buddha, and in two cases they are counterparts of his actual body. The sandalwood Buddha is the very image of the Buddha, and the sandalwood pole discovered by the Brahmin Indra is, like a Vedic sacrificial post (*yūpa*), the very measure of the Buddha's body. As for the sandalwood palace built by Pūrṇa, it is created to contain the Buddha's body.

In the story of Pūrṇa, there are, nevertheless, references to other, more traditional uses of sandalwood. When Pūrṇa first discovers the sandalwood carried by the man, he sells it at the market to be made into powder. The king is prescribed sandalwood as a medicine for his fever, in the form of an ointment/paste. The pieces of sandalwood that Pūrṇa subsequently sells to the king are small enough that he can put three in his robe and carry one, so these were presumably not to be made into artifacts but to be ground as medicine or cosmetics. The workmen who are paid in sandalwood also receive it in the form of powder. It would appear that when people—even kings—use sandalwood in this narrative it is in its "traditional" form as a powder or paste, as a medicine, and presumably also as an adornment. That is not to say that sandalwood paste or powder is never used in contexts related to the Buddha's body: when the king decorates the city for the arrival of the Buddha, he sprinkles it with sandalwood water (*candanavāri*).[55]

Yet, it appears that sandalwood artifacts are in some way reserved for the Buddha—either as counterparts to the Buddha or as structures that are intended for the Buddha.[56] Sandalwood is extremely precious, healing, innately cool and fragrant, both a medicine and diffusive of perfume, and a valued ornament in normal human life. It is the ideal material to "frame" the body of enlightened being, to adopt John Cort's turn of phrase.[57] Discussing the iconology of materials in European medieval art, Günter Bandmann observed, with regard to an elaborate book cover:

> The differentiation of materials on the surface of the book cover can illustrate the opposition of history and eternity, earth and heaven, but it can also simply recall a hierarchy in such a way that the lesser figures are realized in two dimensions as drawings and engravings, and the principal figures, on the other hand, are realized in three dimensions in ivory or gold. In this way, through differentiation between form and material, a unified composition can be presented in different spheres of reality.[58]

Of course, Bandmann is discussing an actual book cover, and, in the present case, we are dealing with textual representations of material objects. Nevertheless, Bandmann's comments are insightful, and I suggest the hypothesis that in early Indian Buddhist texts sandalwood is being used in an analogous manner to represent a different sphere of reality, the physicality of the enlightened Buddha, a perfected human. Of course, this might also have been the case in reality, if there actually were sandalwood images of the Buddha, sandalwood temples for the Buddha, and so on. But I only have access to representations of such objects in texts—I am dealing with material culture that comes already represented and therefore to some extent already theorized.

Not all audiences of these texts would have had the same responses to them. For example, in later periods, sandalwood artifacts might have been more commonplace, but I still argue that at a very early period the notion of a large object made of sandalwood—bulk sandalwood—would have seemed particularly striking to a South Asian audience: unimaginably precious, cooling by proximity, fragrant, and generally impressive; perhaps as novel as a chocolate sculpture today and as awe-inspiring as a gigantic diamond.

There are a vast number of early sources available in Indic languages. Here, I have examined a very small sample, so I stress the tentative nature of this theory and express the sincere hope that further research will complicate (or even disprove) this theory by taking seriously the role of sandalwood in other sources. Indeed, there is already one problem: the sandalwood bowl I mentioned.

The sandalwood bowl is not given to the Buddha nor used by him. Nevertheless, it is possible to attempt to reconcile this story with the theory. The merchant who found himself in possession of a large piece of sandalwood did not make an object for himself with it; instead, he offered the bowl to any perfected ascetic who could obtain it by supernatural powers, suggesting that this sandalwood artifact was intended for a highly spiritually accomplished being. When a Buddhist monk obtains the bowl by a supernatural feat of levitation, he is rebuked for his conspicuous show of powers by the Buddha, who, in the Pali version at least, orders the bowl to be broken down to be used for ointment—a return to the regular human use-value of sandalwood. This sandalwood artifact was intended for a being of advanced spiritual accomplishments, but because the Buddha deemed that the demonstration of powers was not, in fact, befitting a monk and that the monk had committed an offense (and was not worthy of the bowl, according to my theory), it is broken down to be used in the regular, more traditional, laypersons' manner. Sandalwood artifacts are thus reserved only for perfect Buddhas and such (sandal)wood bowls are henceforth unsuited for normal monastic use.

Conclusion

In the story of Pūrṇa, his commercial knowledge, the commodity of knowledge, has been transformed into wealth, but he himself does not enjoy the material wealth he accrues—he does not himself consume the sandalwood, even when still living the life of a merchant—rather he offers this to the Buddha, who then consumes it in the form of the expensive, cooling sandalwood palace. Ultimately, Pūrṇa transforms commercial knowledge into religious merit (via sandalwood), and thereby this early Buddhist narrative provides a religious validation for mercantile learning and for the mercantile way of life. Although Pūrṇa became successful through mercantile expertise, it is important to note that the final shipment of sandalwood was never traded as a commodity, nor was the offering to the Buddha attained through skill in navigation or trade. The sandalwood used to frame the body of the Buddha starts out as a material removed from trade and reserved only for universal emperors, and the safety of this particular voyage is established through the powers of the Buddhist Pūrṇa, as well as by invoking the Buddha as the recipient of the wood.[59]

Earlier I suggested that sandalwood is the most important aromatic in early and medieval India. Yet I finished by arguing that sandalwood is far more than simply fragrant in the narrative of the sandalwood trader Pūrṇa, and, indeed, in that story odor was never mentioned. In that case, is it correct to call sandalwood an "aromatic"? Does the smell of sandalwood matter? The smell of sandalwood and other aromatics does matter, but there is more to these substances than their smell alone, and, in particular, there is far more to sandalwood than its aromatic properties. Sandalwood is simply not one type of wood, and, in many instances, texts are ambiguous about the exact identity of the wood. Nevertheless, this does not mean we should abandon all attempts to outline in detail the significance of various references to sandalwood in different contexts. The sandalwood here is a representation of sandalwood, and as such it comes loaded with a variety of meanings that we can try to infer from this and other texts. These meanings are not the same in every genre, and we have seen how the representation of sandalwood changes over time, so we need to take care not to heap all the possible associations of sandalwood onto every incidence of sandalwood. This is perhaps why I have been at pains to emphasize that sandalwood is not just a perfume. Such an association is particularly easy to make for contemporary Europeans and Americans; in our culture sandalwood is primarily valued as a perfume,[60] but I hope it is clear that to emphasize this too strongly in the interpretation (or translation) of early South Asian references to sandalwood might at times be a little anachronistic and at all times simplistic.[61]

In these South Asian discourses, where there is an odor, there is also a source of that odor: an odorant. And that odorant will inevitably be an object, person, or substance that is endowed with a variety of other values and associations. The odorant may be beautiful, evil, impure, expensive, transient, or exotic. In this and the previous chapters, we focused on a particularly important category of odorant: the principal raw materials by means of which people actively constructed and manipulated their olfactory worlds. We highlighted two aspects of these aromatics: their exotic origins and their economic value. We also looked at the textual culture of the people who earned their livelihood from their knowledge of these substances, and we saw that over a long period of time mercantile communities produced texts to substantiate, codify, articulate, and even to adorn their commercial learning. In certain cases, these mercantile communities, and, perhaps more importantly, Buddhist communities who *aspired* to possess such mercantile prowess, appear to have enjoyed hearing that commercial learning could be transformed into religious merit (and vice versa). They produced stories that contain simplified versions of the science of examination; stories that allow the audience to imagine being the sort of person who could obtain the riches and religious merit that result from learning to be a good merchant.

10

The Toilette of the Gods

Aromatic preparations such as scented bathing waters, pastes, and incenses are vital material components of many types of worship in South Asian religions. We have seen references to these religious uses of aromatics; in the introduction to the *Essence of Perfume* (*Gandhasāra*) it is stated that the art of blending perfumes is useful for the three aims of life according to the *trivarga* (set of three) scheme of *dharma* (righteousness), *artha* (power and profit), and *kāma* (pleasure). By now, we should be well aware of the complexities of perfumes in early and medieval South Asia. We have discussed the diverse, sometimes uncertain, and context-dependent nature of the raw materials; the many ways of combining those raw materials; the varied styles of representing perfume formulae in textual form; the different uses of perfumes, from incenses to pastes, from mouth perfume to bathing water; the attention to the correct combination of all the perfumed materials in a given context; and, finally, the importance of correctly matching the constitution and condition of the perfume-user with the perfume.

Not surprisingly, many sources suggest that people need to address these factors when offering perfumes, incenses, and flowers to the gods. Texts on perfumes for worship mention desirable varieties of raw materials. They describe various types of perfumed preparations, and they also explain that some perfumes are to be used for certain types of divine beings, whilst other ones are to be avoided. The latter observations concerning what is good to offer and to avoid, as well as the implied theory of ritual efficacy, can tell us much about perfumes and the people offering them. Also, these passages, and the practices described in them, arguably reveal—explicitly or implicitly—aspects of the imagined aesthetic sensibilities and constitutions of the beings that receive the offerings: the senses, tastes, and natures of the gods and other venerated beings.

When thinking about perfumes in religious rituals, we need to consider why aromatics are used in the first place, and what they are expected to achieve. Also, we need to consider why some aromatics are used for certain gods and situations, and different aromatics are used for others. Finally, we need to consider whether the perfumes of the gods differ from those used by humans. The adorning of the body with aromatics was practiced in, what some scholars might call, both the "sacred" and "profane" realms of life in premodern South Asia. Were the actual perfumes and formulae used, in fact, the same for both contexts? Or, did some premodern South Asians describe a realm of religious perfumery, and thereby of olfactory aesthetics in general?

In Sanskrit texts, the sense of smell often literally connects a smeller to odorous objects or odorous people who are located beyond them in space. Smells are also often commonly presented as affective—pleasing or repelling—and powerfully so. In philosophical and other discourses, the affective nature of odors was presented as a quality of the odors and not a function of the subjective judgment of the person smelling. Perfumes and aromatics also have many other types of significance. For example, sandalwood is cooling, as well as exotic and expensive. Sandalwood, like many other aromatics, is also valued for its visual qualities, be it white, yellow, or red. Cool and colored, sandalwood is both visual and tactile, as are many other aromatic preparations. For example, in the case of incense, the smoke is visible. Perfumes and aromatics, as well as flowers, are therefore multisensory materials—a phenomena the *Mahabhārata* (discussed later in this chapter) explicitly addresses.

Applying a conspicuous and affective material to a religious image may have consequences. First, the image appears perfumed to people perceiving it and, possibly, is made more attractive and pleasing to those people. But, what of the god (or enlightened being) who is sometimes understood to be somehow present in or represented by this image? Comprehensive and nuanced studies of the sensory capacities of gods and other beings worshipped (both as embodied-in-an-image and not) would be of enormous use in understanding the finer details of materials of worship such as perfumes, as would studies of the aesthetic preferences of beings who are the object of worship.[1] An analysis of the *imagined* or *represented* sensibilities of gods and other beings can also connect considerations of beliefs to the study of religious action and materiality.

Why Do We Give Flowers to the Gods?

We now turn to a passage from the *Mahābhārata* that concerns the topic of smell and aromatics in ritual. As we shall see, the passage in question is particularly relevant because it addresses the use of aromatics in religious worship. As such, this text is an ideal test case to read in the light of previous discussions; that is, to discern to what extent this primer in premodern Indian olfactory style might be a constructive tool for reading similar texts in future. Not only does the passage serve the purpose of being a test case in reading South Asian texts in a smell-informed manner, but the passage itself, modest though it appears, addresses a crucial matter for indigenous Hindu theorists of ritual, and it does so in a relatively frank and nontechnical manner.

The text is not only interesting in terms of the intentions of an original author or community who created it, but this account of the use of aromatics in ritual was, no doubt, widely circulated for many centuries, and it was probably recited and heard numerous times in diverse places, placing this text in many varied interpretative contexts over the years. Unlike specialist ritual texts, this passage might have been read and heard by people who were not ritual specialists. This is not to say that the more technical understandings of ritual are of no importance—this is, after all, just one amongst many texts that discusses rituals in different ways, and it was probably not a universal and definitive text on ritual for anyone in South Asia. In this chapter, I could have chosen to read any one of the numerous texts that give some instructions on the use of aromatics in ritual, but I chose this passage mainly for the reason stated earlier—it contains a frank explanation of the purpose of using aromatics in offerings to the gods. Also, this text is quite early in date, and, therefore, it appears to reflect certain olfactory sensibilities and practices previously noted to have been more prominent around the turn of the Common Era. Perhaps, at last, we can start to move beyond the broad strokes of the history of smell over very long periods and begin to piece together a more nuanced chronology of olfactory sensibilities and aromatic practices in South Asia.

The Nature of the Text

The passage consists of a dialogue related in the *Anuśāsanaparvan* of the *Mahābhārata*, where Bhīṣma continues his instruction to Yudhiṣṭhira after the great battle is over. This *parvan* deals with an enormous number of separate topics, often related in the form of embedded narratives or dialogues. Among the topics, giving (*dāna*) is addressed at great length. Although the exact date of composition or inclusion of the passage is difficult to ascertain, the recent scholarship of Hiltebeitel and Fitzgerald suggests that the text was composed and became part of the *Mahābhārata* at some time between the last two centuries BCE and the early few centuries CE. Where Hiltebeitel suggests the text was composed over a relatively short time, Fitzgerald believes the composition took place over a longer period, and he suggests that several important parts of the text, including possibly the passage we examine here, were added later.[2] Fitzgerald also suggests that the section of the *Mahābhārata* on gifts was added to the epic as part of "complex process of negotiation between some members of the brahmin elite of northern India and the putative new *brāhmaṇya kṣatra* [brahmin-friendly ruling class] whom those Brahmins wished to coax into a mutually beneficial existence through invoking the '*Great Bhārata*.'" The section on gifts, in particular, "closes the arrangement with a set of texts that are concerned to specify the flow of wealth to brahmins in return for these blessings and their attendant services."[3] I will argue that we might interpret this passage as an early text that not only promotes donations to Brahmins but also to the gods—not through sacrifices, but through gifts of flowers, incense and lamps, thus legitimating worship practices associated with a form of religion based on temples and images, whilst still remaining orthodox and redolent of the Vedas.

Not only is this *parvan* (as presented in the critical edition) an especially varied book of the *Mahābhārata*, but the available manuscripts apparently display a large number of textual variants. The editor of the critical edition, R. N. Dandekar, a scholar who must have known this text especially well, states in the introduction to this book:

> The scope and nature of the contents of this *parvan* were such that literally any topic under the sun could be broached and discussed in it. Indeed the redactors of the Epic, through the ages, seem to have seen in the *Anuśāsana* almost the last opportunity for a free play of their propensities. And they must be said to have availed themselves of this opportunity to the fullest extent.[4]

In other words, highly varied from the outset, the book's complexity increased over time. While this state of affairs may have created quite a headache for those engaged in producing a critical edition of the text, for our purposes it is especially interesting, because we wish to bear in mind the reception of the text over the centuries following its composition. The continual textual development of this whole *parvan* suggests that this book of the *Mahābhārata* was very much in use over the centuries in India. Whether our passage is an early or late section of the whole text, the fact that people chose to insert materials in *Anuśāsana parvan* to the extent Dandekar states, suggests that it was often viewed as a respectable and authoritative site of knowledge.

Although this *parvan* is extremely varied in subject matter, the discussion turns to the topic of giving in *Adhyāya* 57, in which Yudhiṣṭhira states that he fears he will descend to hell after all the killing in the battle. Bhīṣma embarks on a discussion of the various karmic results of penances and gifts, including some interesting references to gifts of aromatics to Brahmins.[5] After this introduction to the topic of giving, Bhīṣma discusses the variety of types of gifts (*dāna*), as well as the procedures for *śrāddha* rituals, until we arrive at the passage quoted, regarding the gifts of flowers, incense, and lamps.

Why Do We Offer Flowers and Incense to the Gods?

Now, having introduced the passage, it is best if we actually read it before going any further—we will return to many of the points previously raised during the close reading of the passage. I will first present an extremely literal translation:

> Yudhiṣṭhira said:
> Then what is the nature of this giving of light, oh bull of the Bharatas?

Tell me, how did it arise, and the result (of that giving) in this case.
Bhīṣma said:
On this subject, they relate this ancient traditional account—
The discussion of Manu, lord of creatures, and of Suvarṇa, oh Bhārata.
There was an ascetic called Suvarṇa,
[As] he was of a gold-colored complexion, he was celebrated as Suvarṇa (Gold),
He was endowed with the qualities of character of a good family, and had excelled in the recitation of the Veda. By means of his own good qualities he had very much surpassed many of those born in his own lineage.
One time, that Brahmin saw Manu and approached him,
And they then both asked each other about their welfare.
Then, both of them, their wishes satisfied, sat down together on a pleasant spot on top of a stone on Mount Meru, the golden mountain.
There they both related stories about subjects of various kinds, of Brahmins, seers, gods and *daityas*.
And Suvarṇa spoke a speech to Manu, the self-arisen one, the lord: "For the sake of the welfare of all beings you ought to answer my question:
Since deities are worshipped with flowers, oh Lord of Creatures,
Tell me, what is this? How did it arise, and the connection with the results."
Manu said:
On this subject they relate this ancient traditional account
The discussion of Śukra and Bali when they met:
Śukra, the offspring of the family of Bhṛgu, swiftly came up to Bali, the son of Virocana, who ruled the threefold world.
The King of the *asuras*, liberal in giving to Brahmins, having worshiped the son of Bhṛgu with offering water and so on, sat down on a seat afterwards in accordance with the injunction.
At that time there occurred this story that you [i.e., Suvarṇa] related, concerning the result of flowers, incense and lamps when they are given.
Then the lord of *daityas* asked the lord of poets an excellent question:
"What, oh one most knowledgeable of Brahman, is the result of the offering of flowers, incense and lamps? Oh best of twice-born! You ought to relate that."
Śukra said:
Tapas arose first, then dharma immediately after that.
And, during this interval, plants and herbs [arose].
Having the nature of Soma, they became manifold on the surface of the earth:
nectar of immortality and also poison, and also whatever things there are of the same nature.
Nectar of immortality instantly imparts mental joy and prosperity;

Sharp poison universally makes the mind despondent by its smell.
Know nectar of immortality to be an auspicious thing and poison to be a great inauspicious thing.
All of the nectar of immortality is herbs:[6] poison is energy (*tejas*), arisen from fire.
Since it gladdens the mind and also imparts fortune,
Therefore they [i.e., flowers] are called *sumanas* (good-minded) by those who have performed their deeds well.
The pure man who gives flowers (*sumanas*) to the gods—
Since the gods are satisfied, therefore they are called *sumanas* (good-minded)[7]
For the sake of whichever god, oh lord, flowers happen to be given for the sake of auspiciousness, that [god] is pleased with him by means of that.
Those herbs are to be understood severally as fierce and mild and energetic,
And with many potencies, and also of many forms.
Amongst those trees fit for sacrifice, listen to me [regarding] those that are not to be sacrificed, and also the flowers[8] that are suited to the *asuras*, and those that are good for the gods,
And likewise the ones loved by *rākṣasas*, gods, and *yakṣas*,
And those which are dear to the ancestors and to humans respectively.
[Flowers?] are of the forest, of the village; [some] are sowed after ploughing, [some] are found on mountains;
They are without thorns and with thorns, endowed with odor, visible form, and flavor.
For the odor produced from flowers is taught to be twofold: desirable and undesirable.
One should understand the flowers with pleasant odor to be for the gods.
The majority of thornless trees are white in color,
The flowers of those ones are constantly desired by the gods, oh lord.
And those flowers that are produced in the water, and lotuses, and so forth,
The clever one should give them to *gandharvas*, *nāgas* and *yakṣas*.
And the herbs that have red flowers, that are pungent and endowed with thorns
are indicated in the *Atharvas* for the purpose of incantations against enemies.
and those with sharp-potency, unpleasant to hold, thorny,
and predominantly of red color, and also black, one should offer to *bhūtas*.
Those flowers that delight the mind and heart, that are sweet on being crushed,
with pleasant appearance, are taught as for humans, oh lord.

But, one should not procure those produced in the cremation ground nor those arisen in the temple (*devāyatana*),
in [rites] connected with prosperity, in weddings and in privacy.[9]
One should present to the gods those that grow on a mountain ridge and that are mild; they are mild that have been consecrated by being sprinkled according to what is fitting, according to *smṛti*.
By means of the perfume the gods are satisfied; from seeing [them] *yakṣas* and *rākṣasas* [are satisfied];
nāgas [are satisfied] by eating [them], and humans [are satisfied] by these three things.
It instantly pleases the gods, and they, pleased, all their desired objects fulfilled, make [humans?] thrive by means of mortals' desired objects.[10]
The gods are constantly pleased, and honored they honor.
Disrespected and rejected they burn up the most lowly of men.
Now, below I will relate the results of the rite of giving incense,
and various incenses, good and not-good, listen to me!
They are three: resin, heartwood-possessing woods,[11] and also artificial;
the smell is desirable and undesirable, so listen to me in detail.
The resins, except for *sallakī*[12] are dear to the gods;
Guggulu is the very best resin of all of them.
Aloeswood is the best of heartwoods for *yakṣas*, *rākṣasas* and *nāgas*;
sallakī [resin] and that of the same type is longed for by *daityas*.
Now, for humans [incense] is made with the perfumes of earthly trees: of *sal* tree resin[13] and so on, mixed with thickened cane syrup.
It [i.e., incense] is taught as instantly satisfying to gods, *dānavas* and *bhūtas*,
But those other ones that are for pleasure (*vaihārika*) are taught to be for humans.
Those causes [derived] from the qualities that were said about the giving of flowers
Are also to be understood [to apply] for incenses—they indeed increase joy.[14]

The Orthodox Nature of Giving Flowers and Incense

The first thing one notes on reading the passage is the somewhat confusing multiple layers of narrative recounted at the beginning—which is common in the *Mahābhārata*. The main passage about the use of flowers in rituals has apparently been related at least three times, every time by a notable authority to a respectable questioner. Not only is this passage found in the *Mahābhārata*, but it is also associated with the teachings of Manu, as well as with the teachings of the preceptor of a group of divine beings, the *asuras*. One might say that the threefold narrating of the passage constitutes somewhat of a belt-and-braces approach to both validating the passage as orthodox and locating these ideas in authoritative experts. Not only is the passage triply validated by authoritative figures, but, having been related on three occasions, it is also an extremely *ancient* piece of knowledge. And of, course, every time the passage is read or performed, it is related yet another time. The passage is not just about the nature of flowers and incense, but it is also about the nature of an exchange between humans and gods involving these materials. When, at the end of the passage, it is noted that humans also use various incenses for their own pleasure, the nature of these is passed over quite briefly. How, then, is the exchange with the gods and other beings characterized?

Several terms are employed to describe the exchange. When Yudhiṣṭhira asks his question, he uses the term "gift of light" (*ālokadānaṃ*), referring to the transaction as a *gift*—this is the outermost layer of discourse. The ascetic Suvarṇa asks about the fact that deities are "worshiped/sacrificed to" with flowers (*ijyante*), using a passive form derived from the root √*yaj*, which is the common verbal root meaning "to sacrifice." When Bali formulates his question, he talks of the giving/offering (*pradānasya*) of these materials. Again, this is a form derived from the root √*dā* "to *give*" and it is in response to the question formulated in this manner that the passage is finally related.

In the outermost dialogue of Yudhiṣṭhira, a term is used that suggests this transaction is a gift, and this is also the case in the innermost layer. Yet the question of the ascetic Suvarṇa, a man said to be well versed in the Vedas, uses a verb associated also with the sacrifice, and thus it appears there is some ambiguity about how exactly this transaction is to be characterized in the passage. Indeed, elsewhere in this book of the *Mahābhārata*, the relation between these two transactions is explicitly addressed. At the beginning of the discussion of giving in this book of the *Mahābhārata*, when Bhīṣma introduces the topic, he discusses the relationship between ritual giving and sacrificing at length with King Yudhiṣṭhira.[15] We cannot linger on this material here, but to give a brief example, Bhīṣma relates:

> Like the fire sacrifice that is well oblated, evening and morning by the twice born,
> So indeed is that thing given to the twice-born by one whose self is disciplined.[16]

Thus giving and the sacrifice are explicitly compared from the outset of this section. Although many diverse topics are discussed in this *parvan*, such is the prominence of giving, that in some manuscripts the *Anuśāsanaparvan* is referred to as the *Dānadharma* ("Law of Giving") section of the *Śāntiparvan* or, indeed, as a separate *Dānadharma parvan*, available in at least one case as a separate manuscript. Moreover the editors of the critical edition believed it appropriate to give the name *Dānadharma* to the first sub-*parvan* of the whole *Anuśāsanaparvan*.[17]

Therefore, not only does the passage itself sometimes use the language of giving in describing this transaction of flowers and incense between humans and gods, but also the context, in what was often understood to be the section on the "Law of Giving," strongly suggests that this exchange should be perceived as an act of orthodox giving. The passage locates this type of worship with aromatics within a nonsacrificial, yet equally orthodox,[18] paradigm for sacred transactions: religious giving. Offering flowers and incense to the gods in this manner is not an action enjoined by the Vedas, and thus this practice cannot be categorized as an orthodox sacrifice (*yajña*). Nevertheless, by embracing this type of worship within the discourse of giving, it is seamlessly aligned with another respectable and orthodox type of transaction, which does involve gifts of flowers and incense.

The Origin, Nature, and Action of Flowers

Śukra, the preceptor of the *asuras*, begins his discourse on the nature of offering flowers, incense and lamps by explaining the ultimate origin of the fragrant flowers that people give. Although the passage is confusing at times, Śukra first connects the fragrant flowers to an account of cosmogony, in a veritable olfactory theodicy: *tapas* (heat/austerity) first came into being, then *dharma* (righteousness). After them,[19] plants and herbs, whose nature/self (*ātman*) is Soma, arose in a manifold manner on the surface of the earth. These took the form of nectar of immortality (*amṛta*), as well as poison (*viṣa*), and also things of the "same nature."[20] This dual creation of substances that preserve or destroy life is then defined with reference to their affect on the mind. Nectar imparts mental joy, and poison makes the mind despondent by means of its smell. The manner in which these substances reach the mind is by smell. Not only does Śukra explain how these substances affect the mind, creating joy and despondency, but he also relates them to another set of important categories—auspicious and inauspicious (*maṅgala* and *amaṅgala*); the nature of nectar and poison respectively. Moving to a somewhat less abstract level, Śukra now explains in what form nectar is found in the world—herbs.[21] Poison is said to be energy/brightness (*tejas*) arisen from fire.

This dualistic classification of plants as nourishing and poisonous is reminiscent of another classification system of everything in the world as Agni (fire, or the Vedic fire god) or as Soma (the divine plant and the drink prepared from it offered in Vedic rituals, also identified with the moon). Here, plants are first said to be of the nature of Soma, and poison of the nature of brightness (*tejas*). Although it seems that all plants are of the nature of Soma, the passage is a little unclear at times and possibly there is an implied dualism of Soma-plants that are nourishing as opposed to *tejas*-materials (also plants?) that are poisonous. Dominik Wujastyk discussed this particular classification of the world,[22] noting that for classical Indian medicine: "the category of Agni-related items includes everything of a hot, fiery, dry, or parching type, while Soma-related items are moist, nourishing, soothing, and cooling . . . 'The whole world,' says one author, 'is of the nature of Agni and Soma.'" He concludes by emphasizing "the fundamental importance of the *agni/soma* polarity as a conscious organizing principle for understanding the relationships of many categories of the world."[23] Here, in the passage from the *Mahābhārata*, this principle appears possibly related to the dual classification of odors as good and bad, in addition to being connected with primordial nectar and poison. Beyond this passage, yet within the realm of smell, I suggest that the ubiquitous pairing of white, cool, moist, smeared sandalwood with black, warming, burned aloeswood evokes this general classificatory tendency.

The creation of nectar and poison here is also very reminiscent of the well-known myth of the churning of the milk ocean, in which these substances are also produced. In the account of the churning of the milk ocean in the *Ādiparvan* of the *Mahābhārata* it appears that the creation of nectar (*amṛta*) depends on reversing this very movement of nectar into plants, in part through the release into the ocean of their resins/exudations.[24] To illustrate this reverse movement of nectar, here is a short extract from the account of the churning of the milk ocean as narrated in the critical edition of the *Mahābhārata*:

> Then various kinds of resins of great trees, and many herb-juices streamed into the water of the ocean there. And by means of the fluid of those juices, which had the potency of nectar (*amṛta*), and because of the surplus of gold, the gods attained immortality.[25]

The presence of nectar in plants is not just to be exploited in such a cosmic event but can also be of use on a lesser scale, such as the offering of flowers to the gods.

Having established the ultimate origin and fundamental nature of plants and herbs, Śukra turns to the question of flowers in particular. He provides a traditional etymology of a common Sanskrit word for "flower" (*sumanas*), and in doing so he implicitly links flowers with the preceding discussion. He explains that as flowers gladden the mind (which suggests they are related to nectar, as discussed) and impart good fortune (which is presumably connected with the auspicious nature of *amṛta*) they are called *sumanas* ("good-minded"). This is all a rather complex way to explain why we offer flowers to the gods; but now we understand that, owing to the origins, the fundamental nature, and the innate affective powers of flowers, when someone gives flowers to the gods they are pleased. And, according to the account of several manuscripts, once satisfied, they in turn impart prosperity.

Śukra now complicates matters by hinting that this process is in turn organized according to another fundamental classificatory system of early Indian thought: the three *guṇas* or "strands" or "qualities": *sattva* (clarity), *rajas* (activity), and *tamas* (inertia). As Zimmermann notes, early Indic texts can refer "to multiple schemas of thought between which there is a measure of interference yet each of which is perfectly coherent at its own particular level."[26] And that is exactly what we see here. But first, Śukra relates that there are several beings to whom one can offer flowers, and he also notes that herbs themselves are of three varieties: fierce (*ugra*), mild (*saumya*), and energetic (*tejasvin*). They also have various potencies (*vīrya*)[27] and forms (*rūpa*). Given this diversity of both divine beings and plants, Śukra now must relate the flowers that are fit to be sacrificed/offered to gods, *asuras* (the enemies of the gods), and so on, down to humans. He classifies the flowers according to their source—the forest, the village, those produced by agriculture, and those from the mountains. He then notes the sensible qualities of the flowers: some are thorny, some are not thorny (touch); they possess odor (smell); visible form (sight); and flavor (taste).[28] It would appear that the only sensible quality flowers lack is a sound. Amongst these sensible qualities, Śukra first discusses the nature of their odor, and he provides a definition of the nature of the smell of flowers that echoes many of the classifications of odor we have seen already: "the odor produced from flowers is taught to be twofold: desirable and undesirable."[29]

Next Śukra relates which types of flowers are to be offered to which type of being. He starts at the top of the hierarchy of beings, with the gods. They are to be offered flowers with pleasant odor and no thorns (therefore pleasant to touch). He also notes that the majority of these flowers are white in color; a color associated with the clarity (*sattva*) *guṇa*.

Next Śukra relates the other classes of flowers to be offered to different classes of being. Flowers produced in the water, such as lotuses, are to be given to a variety of beings: *gandharvas*, *nāgas*, and *yakṣas*. Although *nāgas* are associated with water, the association of *gandharvas* with water is less clear, and that of *yakṣas* is also somewhat less obvious.[30] Only the element of origin of these flowers is specified and not their sensible qualities. Moving on, Śukra discusses flowers with less pleasant sensory qualities—thorny flowers with pungent fragrance (*kaṭuka*) that also happen to be red in color (just like the *guṇa*/quality called *tejas*) are said to be indicated in the *Atharvaveda* for incantations against enemies. Other flowers, that appear relatively similar to those just mentioned, are to be offered to *bhūtas*. These latter flowers are additionally said to have a sharp potency (*tīkṣnavīrya*); they are thorny and unpleasant to grasp (*durālambha*); and mostly red in color, but also sometimes black (the color of the *guṇa tamas*). These pungent, red, black, and painfully thorny flowers appear, therefore, to be somewhat the floral inverse of the fragrant, white, and thornless flowers offered to the gods.[31] Finally, we are told of the flowers that are for humans. We are given fewer details on the nature of these latter flowers: they delight the mind and heart, have a pleasant appearance, and, perhaps, most important, they are sweet (presumably to taste) on being crushed. As noted, these colored flowers appear to be classed according to the system of the three *guṇas* or strands/qualities, and, indeed, flowers lend themselves particularly well to this sort of organization because they are colored: white, red, and black, just as the three strands are associated with these same colors. This classification of flowers by color according to the three *guṇas*, only hinted at here, is stated quite explicitly in the much later text on worship called the *Īśānaśivagurudevapaddhati* that I shall discuss below.[32]

But that is not the end of the matter, because, as we saw, flowers are produced in different places, and Śukra now explains the manner in which the place of origin of flowers is related to their ideal use. He explains that flowers from the cremation ground and the temple (the abode of the god, *devāyatana*) are not to be used in rites of prosperity, weddings, and in privacy (or "in secret rites"). Those that grow on a mountain ridge, and that have been purified by being sprinkled are the most appropriate. Thus, not only must the flowers offered be of the correct type and place of origin, but they should also be ritually sprinkled to consecrate them.

The Appreciation of Flowers

Having thoroughly discussed the flowers, their nature, origins, and uses, Śukra now turns to the recipients of the flowers. It appears that on receiving flowers, different types of being appreciate them via different senses. Smell is the sense by which the gods—at the top of the hierarchy of beings—appreciate flowers. *Yakṣas* and *rākṣasas* appreciate them by sight; *nāgas* appreciate them by eating them; and humans appreciate flowers through smell, sight and taste.

Why are the gods pleased by the smell of flowers and not by the other sensible properties? Perhaps it might help to consider the question in the light of the three quite sophisticated classifications of the senses we examined earlier because this might provide some insights into Indic theories of the senses. For the Nyāya-Vaiśeṣikas and Sāṃkhyas, smelling and odors are placed at one extreme of the order of the senses: odor is the special characteristic of earth, an element that possesses all other sense qualities, and where odors are present in an object, inevitably, all the other sense-objects will be also present. Thus odors are associated with objects that are the most sensuously rich or coarse. Yet here the gods seem to appreciate *only* the smell of the flowers, and indeed it is humans who appreciate them via the most senses. Thus it is humans who, according to the Nyāya-Vaiśeṣika understanding of the nature of odorous materials, take most advantage of the qualities of flowers and gain most pleasure from them. Reflecting on the Nyāya-Vaiśeṣika classification of senses would not seem to be of enormous help in understanding why the gods are *only* interested in the smell of flowers.

Nor is the Jain understanding of the senses much help here: for the Jains, smell is a sense possessed by some creatures but not all. The most sensually limited beings possess only touch, and those beings with the most complete set of senses are defined by the possession of hearing. Smell falls in between these extremes for the Jains—beings that can smell are not the most simple nor the most complex, and possessing a sense of smell in this context would not seem to be a mark of anything remarkable in a particular type of being. This would not appear to help us understand the gods' singular use of their sense of smell in this context.

Finally, the Buddhist understanding of smell might be of some use here. For the Buddhists, as for the Jains, the place of the sense of smell in the order of the senses was at neither extreme: smell falls in the center of the typical Buddhist order of the senses. In chapter 2, we saw that one explanation of the place of smell in the Buddhist order of the senses is that the senses are ordered according to the spatio-temporal relation between the perceiving subject and perceived object: thus, one can (supposedly) see farther than one can hear. One can smell an object, such as a flower, at a distance, but not to the same extent that one can see and hear it; in order to taste an object it has to be placed in the mouth; and, finally, one is capable of feeling sensations throughout one's whole body. As I also noted, in smelling an object one actually has contact with particles of it; a fact that early South Asian philosophies and contemporary smell science agree on: the odor of a flower, consisting of particles of the flower that possess odorous qualities may travel away from the flower to another place and be experienced remotely.

Considered along with the spatial aspects of smell emphasized by the Buddhists in their classification system, the latter point may help us understand why the gods appreciate flowers only by smell. Smell is the only sense that allows one to partake of an object's particles at a distance. In the Vedic sacrifice—an important early South Asian model for divine consumption—food is cooked, burned, and transformed into smoke—the fragrant smoke of the sacrifice, which the gods seem to consume via the sense of smell, in some accounts, whilst the odor of the sacrifice feeds other beings, in at least one other account.[33] Yet, in the Ṛg Veda it appears that the model of how the sacrifice works is somewhat ambiguous. The gods are beseeched to come to the place of sacrifice, yet Agni (Fire) is also asked to carry the sacrificed materials to heaven,[34] and these two models are implied in the same hymn:

> Oh Agni! bring the gods to eat the burnt offering. With Indra foremost, may they be satisfied here! Place this sacrifice amongst the gods in heaven![35]

In the *Mahābhārata*, there is a more extensive description of the model according to which the smoke of the sacrifice rises to heaven. This occurs in the story of King Yayāti, who, while in heaven, lost his prestige owing to his pride and attitude of disrespect toward the gods and seers. On losing his prestige, he became unworthy and literally fell from heaven. Before he fell, he asked to fall among good men. He saw a sacrifice taking place in the forest, he smelled the smoke from the sacrifice, followed the smoke trail to the place of sacrifice, and descended to earth (before ultimately being returned to heaven). The passage describing his manner of descent is of particular interest because it is a vivid representation of the "view from heaven" of the Vedic sacrifice as represented in the *Mahābhārata*:

> And at that very time, the king saw four bulls of kings in the Naimiṣa forest, [and] he fell amidst them.
>
> Pratardana, Vasumanas, Śibi Auśīnara, and Aṣṭaka were satisfying the lord of gods with the *vājapeya*[36] sacrifice.
>
> Yayāti, smelling at the smoke produced from their sacrifice that had approached heaven's gate, fell toward the earth.
>
> That king, the lord of the earth, clinging to the river made of smoke connected to earth and heaven, like the moving Ganges,
>
> That king descended amongst the four glorious best of ones who are well-bathed for purification after sacrifice, who were like his own relatives, like the world protectors.[37]

In this later, yet more descriptive account of the sacrifice—in which smoke from the sacrifice flows to heaven to satisfy the gods—there are several items worthy of note. First, it is suggested that from heaven one can see the sacrifice on earth, and one can also see who is performing the sacrifice. The smoke from that sacrifice connects earth to heaven, like a river, and when arriving at the gate of heaven, it may be smelled by those in heaven. We are not told whether the gods can smell the sacrifice, but at least Yayāti can smell it. This appears to reflect the model we saw in the much earlier *Ṛg Veda,* where Agni takes the sacrifice to the gods in heaven in the form of the smoke of the sacrifice.

As a final example, I mention a description of a sacrifice found in part of the *Mahābhārata* called the *Nārāyaṇīya*. The exact date of this part of the epic is controversial but that need not concern us here—whatever the date of this passage, it is still a quite early representation of a Vedic sacrifice.[38] Here we read how when King Vasu (Uparicara) offered a sacrifice the god Narāyaṇa accepted it, having first smelled it: "Having smelled his own portion he accepted the sacrificial cake" (*svayaṃ bhāgam upāghrāya puroḍaśaṃ gṛhītavān*).[39]

On the basis of the previous, I would like to suggest why the gods appreciate the flowers by smell. According to the passages, the sacrificial smoke conveys the sacrifice to the gods in heaven where they can (presumably) smell it. This is also reflected in the story of Yayāti in the *Mahābhārata*, and this model might explain why the gods are said to appreciate flowers by smell. Although burning flowers was not a feature of the Vedic sacrifice (yet *guggulu* incense was), nevertheless, it is possible that people may at times have understood the gods to partake not so much of solid food but of smoke, which was presumably smelled. If someone who understood the model of the Vedic sacrifice in this manner attempted to explain the mechanism of giving flowers to the gods, he might assume that the gods appreciate flowers in the same way they appreciate the Vedic sacrifice. Not only is this a consistent understanding of the manner in which gods partake of offerings, but also by retaining this instrumental model of the Vedic sacrifice, and by explaining the offering of flowers to the gods in a manner that echoes this same model, the use of flowers in ritual is possibly furnished with yet more orthodox Vedic resonances. And offering flowers (though not incense) to the gods is particularly in need of explanation because unlike all the materials used in the Vedic sacrifice they are not cooked.[40] We have seen this strategy of associating these practices with various orthodox notions before, and we shall see it again.

Yet, it is not only the gods (*devas*) who are satisfied by means of a characteristic sense modality. We are also told that the beings called *yakṣa*s and *rākṣasa*s are satisfied by seeing flowers; *nāga*s by eating them; and humans by three methods: smelling, eating, and seeing them. Though the tactile qualities of flowers (e.g., thorny) were previously mentioned in the passage, they are not noted here as a mode of enjoyment. Earlier in the passage, it is stated that humans appreciate flowers that delight the mind *and* are sweet on being crushed, and this presumably correlates to what we are told about humans appreciating flowers via the three sensory modes. That earlier passage, referring to the sweetness of certain flowers when crushed, also provided a clue as to what exactly is implied by eating flowers. *Madhūka* flowers,[41] heavy with nectar, have long been eaten in South Asia, as well as fermented into an alcoholic drink. This also implies that flowers are potentially edible: a raw food. As for the other manners in which beings appreciate flowers, I confess I am unable to offer any good suggestions why they do so. Perhaps the *nāga*s, associated with water, eat the flowers as water is the element associated with taste?

On receiving these flowers and appreciating them via smell, the gods are said to be instantly pleased. Thus they "constantly please, and honored they honor." Here we are told the final part of the process. Conversely, when disrespected, they "burn up" the lowly men who displease them.

The Nature of Incense

Śukra now turns to the nature of incense. He explains that he will relate the result with respect to the rite of giving incense. As with flowers, Śukra says incenses are of various kinds, and he will explain these, including those incenses that are good (*sādhu*) and not-good (*asādhu*)—categories that we have not so far seen applied to aromatics in this book, which seems to imply that the incenses are either proper and effective (or "right" as in "the right tool for the job") or improper and ineffective.

Beyond this initial categorization, Śukra explains that there are three types of incense: resin/exudation (*niryāsa*); heartwood-possessing (woods, *sārin*); and, finally, a term that seems to imply manufactured or compounded incenses (*kṛtrima*). As earlier, we see the typical classification of the smells of incenses as pleasant and unpleasant, and again the materials are described in detail, though Śukra tells us far less about incenses than about flowers. Unlike in the case of flowers, there is no cosmogonic explanation of how incenses came to smell the way they do, though, quite possibly as materials derived from plants they are included in the account given at the start. Śukra states the sorts of incenses appropriate for various types of beings. As with flowers, he starts by stating which type of offering is most suitable for the gods (*devas*). Resins/exudations (*niryāsa*) are said to be dear to the gods,[42] with the exception of *sallakī* resin. Amongst all these resins for the gods, *guggulu* is said to be the very best. Next we are told that aloeswood/agarwood is the very best heartwood (*sāra*) appropriate for *yakṣas*, *rākṣasas*, and also *nāgas*. Finally, *sallakī* resin, which is to be avoided in offerings to the gods, is desired by the *daityas* (the enemies of the gods or *asuras*). Substances mentioned in relation to human incense are *sal* tree resin and cane syrup, and, presumably, these are the compounded (*kṛtrima*) variety. The incenses for humans are, furthermore, said to be for pleasure (*vaihārika*). As with flowers, the incenses are said to be instantly gratifying to gods, and it appears that in the last lines I translated, Śukra says that the process by which these offerings work, which involves the qualities (fragrant and auspicious or otherwise) of the incenses, is the same for incense as for flowers. Namely, perceiving these substances increases joy, and, presumably, the joyful gods and other beings reciprocally please the people who made the offerings.

Although Śukra provides a sparse account of the nature of incenses, nevertheless, the text is very intriguing. Why are these substances suitable for certain beings? The substances are classified according to their use in table 10.1.

Thus resins are for the gods and for *daityas/asuras*. Yet, although gods and *asuras* are pleased by the same category of incense (resin), they differ in terms of the exact variety. Presumably, the fact that *sallakī* is said to be a typical incense for the *daityas* explains why Śukra states that it is to be avoided for the gods. The other beings, *yakṣas*, *rākṣasas*, and *nāgas*, desire heartwoods; and the best of these is said to be aloeswood, the precious, warming, black, exotic burning-wood par excellence we have encountered many times. It appears that these latter three types of being are by no means being passed off with ordinary and cheap aromatics. Finally, humans would appear to accept what may be compounded incenses of resins and also cane syrup—again we see the resin mentioned here is not the same as that used for the gods and *daityas*.

As with the different sense modalities by which the different beings appreciate flowers, it is interesting to consider the significance of this "hierarchy" of incenses. I am again only able to suggest an explanation of the relation between the gods and their special type of incense.

In the case of the gods, the best incense is *guggulu*. This dark brown resin, also sometimes called *gulgulu* in Sanskrit, is a type of myrrh sometimes translated as

Table 10.1 **Incense Ingredients and Suitable Recipients According to *Mahābhārata* 13.101**

Incense Recipient	*Type of Incense*
gods (*devas*)	**resins** (*niryāsa*) *guggulu* = the best *sallakī* = to be avoided
yakṣas, rākṣasas, nāgas	**heartwoods** (*sāra*) aloeswood (*aguru*) = the best
daityas (enemies of the gods, or *asuras*)	**resins** (term only implied) *sallakī* (resin) = typical
humans	**manufactured** (*kṛtrima*) *sal* resin etc., cane syrup

"bdellium" or "Indian bdellium" and is well-known as an incense and medicine in India today. It is identified as the resin of the tree *Commiphora mukul*, found in South Asia, and we have seen references to this product several times. As noted in the case of costus root, *kuṣṭha*, this substance, by the name *gulgulu* is also mentioned in the *Atharvaveda* where its burning fragrance is said to disperse *yakṣmas*, consumption-causing disease-demons. In the *Atharvaveda*, it is said to be brought from overseas, and it was considered very valuable.[43] In the *Anuśāsanaparvan* of the *Mahābharata*, Bhīṣma, discussing the merits of cows, relates a previous discourse in which the very first comment is, "Cows have a fragrant smell, and also smell of *guggulu*." We also saw in chapter 3 that the *kṣatriya* variety of elephant smells of *guggulu*. Associated with cows and *kṣatriyas*, it would appear that this resin has culturally prestigious associations in the South Asian context, but that is a rather vague conclusion at best.

Fortunately, that is not all: *guggulu* is not only mentioned in the *Atharvaveda* but also in other Vedic texts, both *śruti* and *smṛti*.[44] *Guggulu/gulgulu* is mentioned in the *Taittirīya Saṃhitā* of the *Black Yajurveda*,[45] in the *Śatapatha Brāhmaṇa* of the *White Yajurveda*,[46] and also in the *Aitareya Brāhmaṇa* of the *Ṛg Veda*.[47] For example, in the *Aitareya Brāhmaṇa*, translated by Keith, during the "bringing forward of the Soma and the fire":

> [A] nest as it were is made in the sacrifice by the enclosing sticks of Pītudāru wood, bdellium [*gulgulu*], the wool tufts, and the fragrant grasses.[48]

Moreover, in the *Black Yajurveda*, *guggulu* is said to be the very flesh of the fire god and sacred fire, Agni. In a section of the *Taittirīya Saṃhitā* recension of the *Black Yajurveda* dealing with the myth of the demise of Agni's three brothers, we are told that Agni's three brothers died, so Agni fled, and on being persuaded to return to the sacrifice by the gods it is related:

> He reflected, "My brothers of old perished because they had bones. I will shatter bones." The bones he shattered became the *Butea frondosa*, the flesh that died (*upamṛtaṃ*) on them bdellium (*gulgulu*). In that he brings together these paraphernalia, verily thus he brings Agni together.[49]

Thus, making a fire with the wood of *Butea frondosa* and *guggulu* unites the body parts of Agni, and this incense is not so much an addition to the fire as the making whole of Agni, the fire god. Similarly in the *Śatapatha Brāhmaṇa* of the *White Yajurveda*, in the section on the leading forward of the fire to the high altar (*uttaravedi*), we are told:

> And the bdellium [*gulgulu*], forsooth, is his [Agni's] flesh: hence in that there is bdellium, thereby he supplies him with flesh, makes him whole.[50]

This same theme is also taken up in the *Bṛhaddevatā*,[51] where it is said of Agni that:

> His bone became the Devadāru tree; his fat and flesh bdellium [*guggulu*]; his sinew, fragrant tejana grass; his semen, silver and gold.[52]

A more detailed account of the origins of certain aromatics also appears in a text called the *Pañcaviṃśa Brāhmaṇa* or *Tāṇḍyamahā Brāhmaṇa*, to which we might assign an approximate date of around the fifth century BCE.[53] This account is perhaps the most interesting to us because it describes the use of these materials as cosmetic, as opposed to simply being placed in the fire. The passage even provides a mythical explanation of how the practice of anointing the eyes and body began. In a discussion of the forty-nine day sacrificial session (*sattra*) we are told:

> Prajāpati created the creatures; he got parched up [*rūkṣa*]; they did not know him as he was parched up; he anointed his eyes and his limbs.
>
> They who do not notice themselves (i.e., each other) should undertake these (days: should undertake this forty-nine-rite). When they anoint their eyes and their limbs, they bring handsomeness on themselves; they (the others) notice them.
>
> With (salve) mixed with bdellion (they should anoint themselves) at the morning service; with (salve) mixed with the (extract) from fragrant reed-grass, at the midday service; with salve (mixed) with (resin) of the pine tree, at the afternoon service.
>
> As Agni was about to enter on the office of Hotṛ for the Gods, he shook himself: what was his flesh [*māṃsa*] became the (bdellion) [*guggulu*]; what were his muscles [*snāva*], became the fragrant reed grass [*sugandhitejana*];

> what were his bones [*asthi*], became the pine-wood [*pītudāru*]. These forsooth are the perfumes of the Gods [*devasurabhīṇi*]; they, thereby, anoint themselves with the perfumes of the Gods.[54]

In addition to reiterating the idea that certain aromatics, and especially *guggulu*, originate from the body of the fire god Agni, this myth highlights some of the main features of perfumes as represented in premodern Sanskrit sources that I have mentioned previously—it is quite notable that these aspects of perfumes are prominent at such an early date. First, the aromatics described are presumably visible, and this is what helps make those anointed noticeable to others. Second, aromatics are understood to have a social role, rendering the person anointed striking to others, highlighting them as an object of perception. People anointed with kohl and perfumes get noticed, and those who are not anointed are somewhat effaced as far as other people are concerned.

Given that this myth about *guggulu* is widespread, it appears that this resin, of all aromatics, has the closest associations with the Vedic sacrifice—mentioned in the Vedas and early texts related to the Vedas. It is repeatedly said to be the very flesh of Agni and would appear to be burnt in some Vedic rites. Thus, the burning of fragrant resin *is* mentioned in the Vedas, though it seems to be less an offering and more a part of the sacrificial fire itself—in those contexts the action of burning *guggulu* is not a gift, or a sacrifice, or a type of cooking but actually seems to reconstitute the body of Fire (Agni) or create a unguent sanctioned by ritual.

This may go some way in explaining why this resin is singled out as that most appropriate for the gods. Just as the Vedic model of the sacrificial smoke going to heaven might account for the model here of the *devas* appreciating flowers by smell, so it would appear *guggulu* was a substance mentioned in the Vedas, used in Vedic rites, and moreover in some contexts this resin was said to be the actual flesh of a god, namely of Agni the sacrificial fire—a particularly appropriate origin for a type of incense. Again, the use of aromatics is given the appearance of continuity with Vedic practices. This is consistent with a claim made about the *Mahābhārata* as a whole. For example, Hiltebeitel says of the *Mahābhārata*: "The frame stories link with other conventions and allusions to make the *whole appear Vedic*."[55] In this passage, aspects of the *sacrificial* model of human-divine transaction are evoked by the description of the gods smelling flowers and by the preference given to *guggulu*. This is in contrast with the emphasis on this transaction as a form of *giving*, also an orthodox practice, which is used to frame this passage more generally.

The other major aromatics we have seen in this book were not attributed a divine origin, with the exception of costus root (*kuṣṭha*) that we saw to be personified and semidivine in the *Atharvaveda* in chapter 3. It is notable that the two aromatics given such a mythical origin—personified or said to be part of the body of a god—are what one might tentatively call the "Vedic aromatics": costus root and *guggulu*. Although the references to *guggulu* as the flesh of the fire god Agni are unique among aromatics, such mythical accounts of the origins of other special substances (gemstones, shells) are typical of many Hindu discourses. As Phyllis Granoff convincingly argued, "The objects used in ritual or pūjā, like the conch or the tulasī grass in Vaiṣṇavism, or the rudrākṣa or rosary beads in Śaivism, can be understood as bodily relics, in some cases of the god himself, in others of demons or even mortals." Moreover, "the Buddhist 'relic cult' . . . could well be an example of a striking continuity in practice between Buddhism and earlier Indian religions and need not be seen as a foreign import."[56] The data shown here on *guggulu* in Vedic sources seems to support this argument, supplementing the other early materials that Granoff cites. In contrast with texts on gemology, however, in the case of aromatics, it is only these very early sources that attribute a divine-bodily origin to such materials; later texts replace these divine origins with stories of the exotic, strange, and dangerous origins of aromatics.

With regard to the other aromatics, I am not yet able to offer an explanation for the distribution amongst various beings, though it should be noted that all the substances mentioned are found in parts of South Asia (for example "turkey-gum" *turuṣka* is not mentioned). Also, there is no mention of musk, sandalwood,[57] camphor, cubebs, saffron, and the other "principal" aromatics we discussed. To the ears and olfactory imaginations of people reading and hearing this text in later periods, such as at the ideal twelfth-century court described by King Someśvara III, these incenses—both those for the gods and those described for the pleasure of humans—must have seemed very simple and possibly even archaic: the archaic smell of Vedic orthodoxy.

Excursus: Coomaraswamy, *Yakṣas*, and *Pūjā*

At this point, I wish to digress for a moment to consider the impact of our reading of this passage on a famous theory of the origin of the form of worship known as *pūjā*. In his famous and influential work on the beings called *yakṣas*, Coomaraswamy implies that the sorts of practices now known as *pūjā* have their origin in the worship of an important class of beings called *yakṣas*:

> [I]t will be evident that the facts of *yakṣa* worship correspond almost exactly with those of other *bhakti* traditions. In fact, the use of images in temples, the practice of prostration, circumambulation, the offering of flowers (the typical gift, constantly mentioned), incense, food and cloths . . . all these are characteristic of Hindu worship even at the present day . . . Nothing of this cult type is to be found in the Vedas.[58]

In the essay where he famously suggests this connection, Coomaraswamy discusses the very passage we have been examining, noting:

> The *Mahābhārata* mentions that the flowers offered to *yakṣas, gandharvas*, and *nāgas* make glad the heart, hence they are called *sumanasas*, eumenides; such flowers being other than the sharp-scented, thorny and red flowers used in magical rites (Hopkins, *Epic Mythology*, 68f.). The incense made from deodar and *Vatica robusta* is liked by all deities; but *sallakīya* incense is disliked by the gods and suitable only for the *daityas*.[59]

Coomaraswamy's account differs from what we just read; his account is based on the discussion of these matters by Hopkins.[60] Both accounts of this passage, unfortunately, fail to state sufficiently clearly that the flowers are said to "make glad the heart" in a context more closely associated with their effect on the gods (*devas*). Also, as we saw, the white, thornless flowers are reserved for the gods alone, and the *yakṣas* and so forth are to receive flowers grown in the water.[61] It would appear that this part of Coomaraswamy's account, through no fault of his own, is not entirely accurate, and this would perhaps undermine the inference that the *pūjā* style of worship originates in the worship of *yakṣas*.

Indeed, the text we examined, and which Coomaraswamy uses as a piece of primary evidence for his thesis, is preoccupied with the gods above all other types of beings. In this early discussion of what we might call *pūjā*-style worship, in a passage from the *Mahābhārata*, the worship of the gods/*devas*, and not the worship of the *yakṣas*, features most prominently. In this passage, worship with flowers and incense would seem to apply to gods just as much to *yakṣas*, and to suggest on the basis of this passage alone that *pūjā* has its origin in *yakṣa* worship is unconvincing. This one passage is simply not enough evidence.

The passage tells us very little about the ultimate origins of the use of these materials in worship and about the origins of *pūjā* more generally, though it does constitute an early description and discussion of this form of worship with flowers, and the reference to the abode of the god (*devāyatana*) is interesting. I should, however, emphasize that the word *pūjā* is not once used in the passage. Nevertheless, the passage reveals that certain aromatic materials were thought suitable for the worship of gods, *yakṣas*, and other beings, and that certain materials were deemed more suited to some beings than to others. It seems reasonable to conclude that this type of worship was familiar when this passage was first composed: a contentious, but probably early date. Most important, it appears that the nature and validity of this sort of worship was deemed worthy of inquiry, and that in the context of the *Mahābhārata*, it was seen as desirable to align this type of worship with all things Vedic. However, it would be wrong to conclude that because the passage explains flower and incense offerings in a manner that uses Vedicizing terminology to legitimize them, the passage implies that the use of these materials in worship is derived from outside the world of Vedic ritual. Burning *guggulu*—that is to say, burning incense—was clearly a well-established Vedic practice in no need of an apology. Although this representation of ritual offerings as a type of giving (*dāna*) is an entirely emic discourse, we are in no way prevented from considering that the offering of flowers and incense to both gods and *yakṣas* may indeed have originated in the practice of offering gifts of these sorts of materials to *people*, as has been noted by Thieme and more recently Willis.[62] Nevertheless, as I have observed several times already, this passage does argue for offering incense, flowers, and lamps in terms that evoke the language and theories of Vedic orthodoxy; and thus it is an important window into early (around the turn of the Common Era and/or the first few centuries CE) perceptions and debates on the validity and nature of a form of worship that subsequently became so common in medieval temple Hinduism.

Hindu Aromatics According to Later Sources

The quoted text from the *Mahābhārata* is very early, and the aromatics mentioned in that text (*guggulu*, aloeswood) reflect that. As we have seen, by the early-to-mid first millennium CE, there was an increase in the range of aromatics commonly mentioned in South Asian texts. Perfumes were more complex, and certainly by the early second millennium CE, texts on perfumes had in some cases become extremely complex and quite literary.

The perfumes of the gods appear to have changed in accordance with the trends, and later texts on religious perfumes refer to far more ingredients, including the typical lists of aromatics. There are also some formulae for aromatic preparations for the gods in the *Essence of Perfume*, *Gandhasāra*, and these are composed in the typical more literary and oblique style of many of the formulae found there. I shall now very briefly review two later texts that deal with aromatics for worship.

The *Īśānaśivagurudevapaddhati* is a manual of temple worship that is Śaiva in sectarian affiliation, dating from the eleventh or twelfth century of the Common Era.[63] Here, we find a discussion of the merits of aromatics to be used in incenses that suggests a new and different hierarchy of aromatics for use in religious rites:

> Amongst all materials for incense the best is black aloeswood.
> And camphor is extra-best, preceded by[64] aloeswood
> The *guggulu* called *mahiṣākṣa* is alone the best, beloved of Śiva.
> And sandalwood and vetiver are declared to be middling.
> Pine resin and *sal* tree resin are the lowest; then lac, ghee, honey.
> All the above with white sugar is the incense called Ten-part (*daśāṅgaka*).[65]

Although this differs substantially from the discussion of incense ingredients in the *Mahābhārata*, nevertheless, these materials are familiar. Only a certain variety of *guggulu* is acceptable, and this is not mentioned first as an offering for Śiva. *Guggulu* is now joined by other aromatics, and in particular camphor takes pride of place, along with aloeswood, reflecting the more typical aromatic priorities of this later period. The list of incense ingredients: aloeswood, camphor, *guggulu*, sandalwood, vetiver and other resins is far more reminiscent of the typical lists of aromatics we have seen in this book: the perfumes of the gods have stayed up-to-date and become more cosmopolitan over time.

Although the ancient aromatics *guggulu* and agarwood were, no doubt, items of long-distance trade for most people living in early South Asia, the addition of the full canon of aromatics to the lists of perfumes preferred by the gods must have had an effect on medieval economies of temples, donations, and trade. For example, a donation of land or of a village to a temple would not be sufficient in itself to produce many of the materials (for instance, camphor) required to maintain a temple.[66] An income (albeit possibly derived from donated land) was also required to keep the god supplied with camphor and other aromatic items of long-distance trade. Perpetual temple endowments that guarantee a supply of exotic aromatics to the gods thus channel part of an economic surplus into the profits of long-distance traders and merchant guilds, people who were, in many cases, the sorts of people who endow such institutions in the first place. But I do not wish to paint too cynical a picture of merchants endowing a perpetual market for their goods. Rather, I wish to point out that the changing tastes of the gods, particularly with regard to exotic aromatics, had a major, complex impact on medieval South Asian economies, not to mention the economies of areas, such as parts of Southeast Asia, that supplied these materials. And texts that prescribe the perfumes for the gods would have both reflected and helped further these changes.

In the perfumery text we examined at length previously, the *Essence of Perfume* (BORI *Gandhasāra*), there are some formulae for incenses that seem more closely associated with divine worship. In the case of the incense formulae, the ones intended for the gods are grouped together. There are formulae for incenses for Śiva, as well as for Pārvatī, for the Sun, for the goddess Speech, for Ganeśa, for Śrī, for Lakṣmī, and for Durgā.[67] Following is the formula for the incense apparently liked by Śiva, who is called here by the epithet *Tripurahara* (Capturer of the Three Cities):

> Incense pounded with bee, together with beloved, filament, rain-cloud, snake, heavy, fingernail, unsteady, lac, and *sal* tree resin is the [incense called] Delighter of Śiva Capturer of the Three Cities (*Tripuraharānand aka*).[68]

I will not attempt to translate all the ingredients of this formula—we saw just how challenging such verses can be. However some terms are not so difficult to read in the context of the poetically cryptic *Essence of Perfume*: "filament" is possibly saffron;[69] "cloud" is undoubtedly camphor; "heavy" is probably aloeswood; "nail" is no doubt fragrant shell operculum; lac is simply lac; and "bee" is probably honey, because it is evidently the binding agent in this pounded incense.

Like the incense from the later medieval temple manual, this formula is both more complex than those suggested by the discussion in the *Mahābhārata*, and it also contains more "exotica": camphor and saffron. Perhaps more striking than the material contents of the incense is the style of the text providing this formula. Like many of the other preparations in the *Essence of Perfume*, this formula is written in a style that is suggestive in its double meanings of words and difficult to decipher for someone not familiar with the conventions of the *Essence of Perfume*. The previous incense formula we examined, from the *Īśānaśivagurudevapaddhati*, was composed in a very straightforward style and was, no doubt, understood by most readers. Yet, this clever and cryptic formula challenges and excludes readers. By the later medieval period, the incenses of the gods had developed parallel to those of the people: the palette of aromatics had developed and become more cosmopolitan. Indigenous materials such as *guggulu* are still present, though perhaps less prestigious. In the case of the perfumes for the gods in the *Essence of Perfume*, the style of the text that provides the formulae has become increasingly literary.

Sacred and Profane Perfumes?

In early and later medieval South Asia, adornment with perfumes and the use of incense was common practice both for affluent people and for gods enshrined in temples, and, as we have seen, the contents of these preparations, as well as the manner they were described appears to have developed in parallel. In a recent, excellent study of the role of adornment in South Asian art and literature, Vidya Dehejia rightly noted that, where ornament is concerned, a binary distinction in the realms of the sacred and profane "has a limited resonance on the Indian scene."[70]

With perfumes of various sorts this is the case, and adornment with aromatics is not in any way limited to some sort of secular, materialistic realm of sensuality. Enjoying olfactory pleasures and adorning the body with perfumes were practices common to gods and people. However, there are some interesting distinctions between the two areas that suggest that the olfactory material culture of the gods was somewhat set apart from that of the "profane" world. First, in the early discussion of flowers and incense in the *Mahābhārata*, we saw that only certain materials were appropriate to offer to the gods, and the same applies to other supernatural beings. Humans seem to have more promiscuous tastes in these materials. Also, the sensory modes by which gods, other supernatural beings, and humans enjoy these materials vary. Last, but not least, according to the passage from the *Mahābhārata*, it seems that only the offering of such materials to gods needs explanation, and the human use-value of these materials more or less goes without saying. In the *Essence of Perfume*, the incenses for gods are very similar to those for people, and the style of the formulae is also the same. Yet, the incenses for the gods are listed together in one part of the text, somewhat separate from those intended for more worldly uses. Material adornment and sensual pleasure are indeed common to the "sacred" and "profane" realms, but, at the same time, perfumes for the gods are clearly treated differently in these texts. When it comes to perfumes, there is something like a realm of the sacred, or if "sacred" is too loaded a word, there are clear hints that at least some people in South Asia understood there to be a god-related, divine realm of both olfactory material culture and olfactory theory, something that we today might call a *religious* olfactory aesthetics. The world of people and that of gods might not be divided along the lines of an acceptance or rejection of sensuality and materiality in these sources, but this does not mean that there are no distinctions between the two areas.

Conclusion

In the passage from the *Mahābhārata*, offering flowers and incense, a non-Vedic mode of interaction with the gods, and a mode of interaction shared with other types of divine beings, such as *yakṣas*, is presented in a manner that implies its consistency with two major orthodox Vedic paradigms for interaction with others: the gift and the sacrifice. The fragrant flowers are also assigned a place in a cosmogony that links them to other fundamental categories, and then a traditional etymology of a common Sanskrit word for "flower" is invoked to explain the offering—all these are typical strategies for explanation of tradition in early South Asia.

The sorts of aromatic materials mentioned in this passage from the *Mahābhārata* are exactly what we would expect from that somewhat early period. In later texts, the perfumes of the gods contain a greater number of aromatics, more representative of the typical list of aromatics that dominates discourses and probably practices in the first and early second millennia of the Common Era in South Asia. In the *Essence of Perfume*, not only have the ingredients followed fashions but so has the very form of the text.

Adornment of the body with materials that please the sense of smell is a practice common in all realms of life, including those that some today might think of, or demarcate, as "sacred" and "profane." Yet, our sources suggest, explicitly and implicitly, that the perfumes of the gods and the aesthetic sensibilities of the gods are not quite the same as such persons as kings and human lovers. In the world of perfumes in South Asia, the lines between the religious and the nonreligious are not always drawn according to the level of engagement with materiality and the senses;[71] rather, the lines are sometimes drawn according to fine and complex differences in the aromatics, perfumes (and of course flowers) allocated for the gods and for people, according to the sensory capacities of the gods and humans, and also in the structure of perfumery texts.

To people in South Asia who were familiar with later perfume culture, the aromatics described in the *Mahābhārata* would have possibly seemed rather limited and archaic, though *guggulu* appears to have been a particularly enduring feature of religious incenses. At a later period, to someone living in South Asia who was exposed to the elite culture of the Mughal court, where such materials as rose water and ambergris were especially valued, even the more complex temple perfumes and incenses might likewise have seemed rather archaic or traditional, as they often do when used in South Asia or amongst diaspora communities today. Thus, the passing of time tends to create an additional division in olfactory aesthetics and material culture in South Asia, in which religion smells of tradition, *guggulu* based *dhūp*, and sandalwood paste, and this comes to differ even more from the perfumes of "profane" life.

Epilogue

Hey! Hey! Son of Dharma! Royal sage! Oh one of virtuous descent!
Oh Pāṇḍava! Just stay a little while for our benefit:
On your coming, Oh unconquerable one, there blows a pleasant wind
in the wake of your fragrance, brother, that has brought us joy.
—*Mahābhārata*

At the very end of the *Mahābhārata*, Yudhiṣṭhira finds his brothers and family trapped in a foul hell-like realm. A particularly noticeable and unpleasant aspect is the bad smell. This place has the smell of evildoers[1], it is inauspicious and has the stink of corpses.[2] For the Pāṇḍavas trapped there, the arrival of Yudhiṣṭhira brings joy as they catch the fragrance of his body carried by the wind. The fragrance of the son of Dharma displaces the stink of evildoers and death.

Once again, smells are carried on the wind and are polarized—foul, inauspicious stinks and pleasant fragrances bring suffering and joy respectively to those who smell them. In some ways, this passage reflects one of the more important themes seen in many of the materials in this book, namely that smell is twofold: good smell and bad smell. Although such a binary aesthetics of odor is a key feature of many early South Asian theoretical discourses, nevertheless the full picture is far more complex. As we have also seen, in South Asian culture and religion, smell is an affective sense: the sense of smell brings pleasure or disgust; and, above all, this sense reveals the values of material odorants, be they people, places, or things. This is not to say that other senses do not play important roles in the epistemology of value, but rather that smell was understood to be especially suited to this function where matter was concerned. Where smell takes on other roles and provides cognitive information similar to that provided by sight, for example, this is presented as an exception and can be used in a literary conceit, as we saw when smell replaced sight in navigating the garden in the play *Ratnāvalī*. When smell is diverted from its most common human role, this is not only strange and charming, but it may also be associated with the ways of animals as we see in the following aphorism:

Cows see with odor,
Brahmins see with the Vedas,
Kings see with spies
Ordinary people see with their eyes.[3]

This by no means implies that South Asian discourses, like some Euro-American ones, hold that smell is bestial and primitive; rather it implies that for humans smell is mainly used for certain functions, and that to rely on this sense alone to investigate the world, in the manner one does with some other senses, would be quaint to say the least: it is only *smell out of place* that is bestial or amusing, to echo Mary Douglas's famous formulation of the nature of dirt. Although the affective side of smell takes the lead in many South Asian discourses, and smell does not, in general, provide the same sort of cognitive information as a sense such as sight, nevertheless, the sense of smell was understood to do more than just detect fragrance and stinks. This unique sense and its objects played an important role in both South Asian discourses and practices; a role difficult for us to imagine in our relatively deodorized world, where the bodily adornment of the typical male graduate student is not dissimilar to that of "ascetic" Buddhist monks; where for many people, religious practices are devoid of smell, and where smell plays only a relatively minor role in literary discourses.[4]

South Asian texts present a rich smellscape of spring mango blossom, cool lotus breezes, fragrant damp earth, milk, honey, and smoking sacrifices. The odors of cows and goats are other prominent olfactory benchmarks in technical texts, as are the stinks of fish, raw meat, and foul corpses. Intestinal gas is notably barely ever mentioned, probably for reasons of literary propriety.[5] The greatest range of smells is found in the world of plants—this includes most fragrances—and stinks are, above all, associated with impure secretions, and with diseased and dead flesh. The vast numbers of odors, both good and bad, in the texts we surveyed, not only attract and repulse, but these odors also permit the smeller to locate odorants in more complex schemes for classifying the world: divine and social hierarchies, cooling and heating, pure and impure, and so on. Both literally and metaphorically evil stinks and virtue tends to be fragrant, as we saw with the hell realm described in the epigraph to this chapter.

In South Asia, it was believed that on smelling a remarkable and pure fragrance, one could not help but be delighted and possibly erotically excited. The wise thing to do with a sense that is so dominated by its affective ability is to manipulate and control its enormous power, both in practice and in discourse, and this may explain the remarkable productivity of South Asian culture and religion in these areas. From all periods, there are accounts of the use of perfumes to adorn the body and environment, as well as to please divine beings. Placing perfume on an object or person has both the ability to please that object/person (so long as it is appropriately sentient) as well as to render it more attractive and pleasing to those who experience it. Yet within the category of "good smell" alone, there is much complexity: perfumes are seasonal, cooling, arousing, and so on. A preoccupation, even an obsession, with *combinations* is a notable characteristic of Indian perfumery. Many perfumes, such as a paste of sandalwood, musk, and saffron were also known to be visually beautiful, and this permitted a more conspicuous use of aromatics, not necessarily associated with physical intimacy.

The elite affective art of perfumery was codified in many Sanskrit and Prakrit texts. In some cases, these instructions on manipulating aromatics and the sense of smell were included in texts dealing with temple worship, medicine, or erotics; but at a later period, manuals solely devoted to perfumery were produced. In these manuals, the textual expression of perfumery reached a level of sophistication that has not, to my knowledge, been equaled in any other time or place. Moreover, the material culture of smell was imbued with literary values: perfume names reflected textual culture, perfume formulae exploited the technologies of puns and metrics, and literary texts themselves were redolent with descriptions of sophisticated aromatics. The educated and wealthy consumer of poetry and fine perfume was immersed in a textual and olfactory discourse that we have just begun to understand. South Asian perfumery took advantage of a range of formats, including hair oils, mouth perfumes, pastes, garlands, and incenses. The emphasis on pastes correlates with the manner in which sandalwood—the most important and distinctive South Asian aromatic—was used from earliest times, as a cooling paste.

The demand for powerful aromatic substances to use in perfumery led to an extensive trade in such items as camphor, musk, frankincense, sandalwood, nutmegs, and aloeswood. Although, from the point of view of medieval Europeans, these items all came "out of the East," the "East" is, of course, a large and complicated place, such that India, the nebulous source of many aromatics in the medieval European imagination, actually produced its own discourse of the exotic and strange origins of these valuable "spices." The elite demand for these rare materials led to their high exchange value, both in practice and as represented in discourse. Both the high economic value and the aura of their exotic origins contributed to the manner in which the significance of perfumes was constructed: a certain golden, fragrant paste might not only be understood as a powerful cause of pleasure and arousal, it was also a marker of cosmopolitan values, wealth, and cultivation. Yet, discourses associated with mercantile communities that traded and evaluated these commodities, such as some Buddhists in the early first millennium CE, focus, above all, on the relationship between expertise, profit, and religious merit. In the narrative of Pūrṇa, we see that he is well informed about aromatics, but, unlike the cultivated man-about-town, he does not consume these materials in order to enjoy sophisticated, erudite, and sensual pleasures; but rather, he exploits his expertise and his senses to master the world of exchanging aromatics. The most worthy terminal consumer of the material fruits of his exchanges is the Buddha, and the ultimate fruit of his skill with sandalwood is not sophisticated pleasure but religious merit.

The use of perfumes and descriptions of their use are just as important in the world of worship as they are in the palace and the bedroom. A significant feature of many South Asian religious traditions is the use of aromatics in rituals. We can finally begin to explore the nature of divine perfumes now that we have established the basic principles of olfactory culture in early and medieval South Asia and started to consider more closely the chronological development of ideas and practices. In the *Mahābhārata*, there is one rather early discussion of the nature of divine offerings of aromatics, both flowers and incense. In that passage, we see again the belief in the affective powers of fragrances; yet, as with the later materials on perfumery, a good smell is not simply a good smell, and certain materials appear to be hierarchically superior to others. Furthermore, in the light of the medieval materials on perfumery, the aromatic culture reflected in this passage from the *Mahābhārata* seems quite rudimentary, and it is possible that certain uses of aromatics in practice and discourse might have evoked a sense of a revered, even classical, tradition.

That we can see such possibilities suggests that we might now be able to contemplate writing a more diachronic history of smell and aromatics in premodern South Asia, possibly extending into the rose-scented olfactory world of Indo-Muslim culture and beyond. Indeed, this study should be considered a mere prelude to the writing of a larger history of smells and aromatics in South Asia.

Appendix

SANSKRIT AND PRAKRIT TEXTS ON PERFUME BLENDING AND PERFUMERY

It is useful to present in the form of a list some short descriptions of texts in Sanskrit and Prakrit that were entirely devoted to the topic of perfumery, *Gandhaśāstra*. As discussed in chapter 5, as far as I am aware, all but three of these texts are now lost and survive as fragments quoted in other texts on topics, such as medicine, where they were deemed authoritative. As also noted in chapter 5, it is the case that some texts that share the same name are not the same text—this is what we see in the two texts called the *Gandhasāra*, and so we should bear this in mind, especially where texts have such names/designations as *Treatise on Perfumery* (*Gandhaśāstra*). Sources that have been of great use to me in compiling this list are the works of P. K. Gode, Meulenbeld's *History of Indian Medical Literature* (HIML), and also the *New Catalogus Catalogorum* (NCC). It is likely, given the extent of Sanskrit literature, that there are other fragments and references to perfumery texts that I missed, and we can also hope that some of the texts that seem to be lost might show up in manuscript collections.[1] Unfortunately, there is no space here to reproduce the longer fragments of these texts, in particular those found in the extensive *Ratnaprabhā* commentary of Niścalakara on the *Cakradatta* (also called the *Cikitsāsaṃgraha*) of Cakrapāṇidatta. Also, I believe that a detailed comparison of all of these texts on perfumery, along with sections on perfumery found in other sources such as encyclopedic texts might yield interesting results, but this is also something I do not attempt here for reasons of space. Although the dates given here are, for the most part, very tentative, nevertheless, this list form of presentation makes clear that texts devoted entirely to describing the technical art of perfumery, *Gandhaśāstra*, are probably a relatively late genre because they are nowhere attested until around the tenth century CE.

Gandhakalpa

A sulphurous red herring. According to the NCC: "*Gandhakalpa*, 5 folia, Collection Palmyr Cordier 29 (125) at the Bibliothèque Nationale 2 med. As given by J. Filliozat in his 'Etat des Manuscrits etc. De la collection Palmyr Cordier.' *Journal Asiatique*, Paris: Société Asiatique, Jan.–Mar. 1934." Upon examination of this manuscript it turns out that the real title is the *Gandhakakalpa*, and it is a short medical treatise concerning the use of sulfur.

Gandhatantra: anonymous, Sanskrit, attested late twelfth century CE

Lost Sanskrit treatise on perfumery quoted in *Ratnaprabhā* of Niścalakara in (probably) the late twelfth century CE. Niścalakara also refers to *gandhatantraśāstra*, which seems to be the same text.[2] This would appear to be a distinct text from those of Bhavadeva and Pṛthvīsiṃha.

A text by this name is also named and quoted in the late sixteenth-century *Ṭoḍarānanda*.[3]

Gandhadīpikā: anonymous, Sanskrit, attested mid–late fourteenth century

Lost text quoted in the verse compilation called the *Śārṅgadharapaddhati*. See discussion in chapter 5.

Gandhapradīpapatrikā: anonymous, Sanskrit, attested late sixteenth century

Lost text. Formula from this text for perfumed water quoted in the *Ṭoḍarānanda*.[4]

Gandhayukti: by Īśvara, Prakrit, attested late tenth century CE

Lost Prakrit treatise on perfumery by Īśvara and quoted by Bhaṭṭotpala in the mid–late tenth century CE in his commentary on the *Bṛhatsaṃhitā*. See the discussion in chapter 5.

Padmaśrī mentions the works on perfumery of a certain Lokeśvara in the *Nāgarasarvasva*, which possibly dates from 800 to 1300 CE, but I identity these two authors only very tentatively. See discussion in chapter 5.

Gandhavāda: anonymous, Sanskrit and old Hindi with old Marathi commentary, 1330–1550?

Extant text, in the same manuscript as BORI *Gandhasāra*. Shares many formulae with Anup *Gandhasāra* (which also mentions a *Gandhavāda*) and contains references to ambergris and other Indo-Persian aromatics. See discussions in chapter 5.

Anup *Gandhasāra*: anonymous, Sanskrit, 1400–1600?

Extant text, not published. See discussion in chapter 5.

BORI *Gandhasāra*: by Gaṅgādhara, Sanskrit, 1300–1600?

Extant text. See discussion in chapter 5.

Gandhaśāstra by Bhavadeva, Sanskrit, ca. 1100 CE

Lost text by Bhavadeva quoted in *Ratnaprabhā* commentary of Niścalakara (Bengal, late twelfth century).[5] See the discussion in chapter 5. Passages attributed to this text and author by Niścalakara also appear in the *Ṭoḍarānanda* (Benares, late sixteenth century), though these could be from a common source or from another compilation that quotes Bhavadeva—we cannot be absolutely certain that the compilers of the *Ṭoḍarānanda* had access to Bhavadeva's text.

Niścalakara also mentions a "perfumery treatise" (*gandhaśāstra*)[6] and a "Bengali perfumery treatise" (*vaṅgadeśīyagandhaśāstra*),[7] which may or may not be distinct sources.

Another lost *gandhaśāstra* is quoted in the *Adbhutasāgara* of Ballālasena which was compiled in the Bengal region in the late twelfth century CE.[8] The date and location make it possible that this is Bhavadeva's text, but the title *gandhaśāstra* is such a common and generic term that we must be wary of assuming any connections here. In the context of a special bath to be given to appease the ill effects of *sāmudāyikanakṣatra*, i.e., "the eighteenth Nakshatra after that in which the moon was situated at the birth of a child" (MW), Ballālasena quotes a recipe from the *Gandhaśāstra* for *sarvagandha*:

> *agaruṃ kuṅkumaṃ candraṃ candanaṃ ca catuḥsamam /*
> *sarvagandham iti prāhuḥ samastasuravallabhaṃ //*
> [Aloeswood, saffron, camphor, and sandalwood in four equal parts,
> (Is what) they call "every-perfume," \ dear to all the gods.]

Note that the first line here would appear to give a recipe for what is elsewhere called, not *sarvagandha*, but *catuḥsama*, where the quantity of ingredients has become the name of the formula.

Parimalapradīpa: anonymous, Sanskrit, attested late sixteenth century CE

This lost perfumery text is quoted in the *Ṭoḍarānanda* in a passage where the classes of aromatics (woods, etc.) are listed.[9]

The author Pṛthvīsiṃha: composed in Sanskrit, attested late twelfth century CE

Named and quoted in quoted in *Ratnaprabhā* commentary of Niścalakara.[10] Very similar passages to those attributed to Pṛthvīsiṃha by Niścalakara are quoted (but not named) in the *Ṭoḍarānanda*.[11] Again, these passages might be from a common source or from another compilation.

NOTES

Preface

1. In doing so, I have been inspired by the work of Maria Heim on the gift in South Asia, (2004).
2. This is not the place to present a bibliographic survey of such materials. A classic and wide-ranging discussion of these issues is King 1999.
3. Of course, discussions about periodization are very important, but in this book a somewhat looser framework is useful to me as I explore an alternative perspective on history.
4. For a detailed account of civet in South Asia, see McHugh, forthcoming.
5. Gode 1961e, 8.

Chapter 1

1. As discussed in Pollock 2006, 109–110. Noted also in Dehejia 2009, 74.
2. For this discussion, see *Śṛṅgāraprakāśa* of Bhoja, 578. I am grateful to Professor Sheldon Pollock for this exact reference (e-mail to author, May 27, 2010).
3. Miller 2010, ch. 1.
4. Ibid., 14.
5. Banerjee and Miller 2003.
6. My emphasis. Miller 2010, 40.
7. Ibid., 16–17.
8. For a discussion of this contrast see Ali 1998, 159–184.
9. Miller 2005, 25.
10. *Brahmajāla Sutta* 17. The *Dīgha Nikāya*, vol. 1, 7.
11. Dehejia 2009.
12. As seen in the case of a jasmine-scented (*jātīkusumavāsita*) cloak in the Sanskrit play the *Mṛcchakaṭika* of Śūdraka, 22–23.
13. To adapt Latour's term; Latour 1994, ch. 1.
14. Freedman 2008, ch. 3.
15. Abu-Lughod 1989, 261–290. As cited in Freedman 2008, 105.
16. First published Chambersburg, PA: Anima Books, 1981 with several reprints.
17. Rotman 2009; Dehejia 2009.
18. Mrozik 2007.
19. Already in 1998, Lafleur noted that the "'body' has become a critical term for religious studies" (1998, 36).
20. One might include structuralist Marcel Detienne's celebrated book *Les jardins d'Adonis (The Gardens of Adonis)*, which challenges Frazer's interpretation of the myth of Adonis. Detienne 1972.
21. Caseau, 1994; Harvey, 2006.

22. Caseau 1994, preface, i.
23. In which a modified form of chapter 2 of this book appeared.
24. Benavides and Thomassen, 371–373.
25. Ali 2004.
26. For example, Granoff 1998 and Granoff 2004.
27. I shall not provide a complete bibliography here. Perhaps the most complete statement of his theories is found in Pollock 2006.
28. Zimmermann 1987a.
29. Meulenbeld 1999–2000.
30. Schafer 1963.
31. Freedman 2008.
32. Smith 2007.
33. Classen, Howes, and Synnott 1994; Howes 2005; Drobnick 2006.
34. Corbin 1982, 1986.
35. Corbin 1986, 6.
36. Ibid., 7.
37. Ibid., 7–8.
38. Ibid., 229.
39. Ibid., 230.
40. Stamelman 2006.
41. Ch. 10 of *A rebours* discusses perfumery.
42. Hopkins 1907, 120–134.
43. Ibid., 120.
44. Ibid., 121.
45. Ibid., 134.
46. Thomas 1931.
47. Strong 1977.
48. Along with the persistent (and friendly) questioning of Donald Swearer as to the significance of a sandalwood image of the Buddha.
49. Shulman 1987.
50. Hara 2010. I am grateful to Professor S. R. Sarma for alerting me to the publication of this important paper.
51. King 2007, 2008, 2011; Husain 2000, see especially ch. 5; Jung 2010.
52. The comprehensive history of smell and perfumery in China and Chinese religions would be especially interesting. On smell and perfumery in China see Needham and Gwei-Djen 1971, 128–154; Schafer 1963, 155–176; Ter Haar 1999, 1–14. This article by Ter Haar also contains a good, annotated bibliography. Finally, Bedini 1994. I am grateful to Professor James A. Benn for providing me with some of these references.
53. Burke 2004.
54. Ibid., 104–105.
55. Majumdar 1935.
56. Ibid., 662.
57. Chandra 1940.
58. Bandhu 1960, intro., 60.
59. Gode 1947, preface, 6.
60. Tikekar 1964, 50.
61. Hariyappa and Patkar 1960, intro., 19–46.
62. It is interesting to reflect on the context that produced this new kind of Indian history, because Gode turned to the study of history in a unique manner that is intimately tied to the peculiar nature of many textual sources in India. Whilst working in the Bhandarkar Oriental Research Institute he had to deal daily with masses of manuscripts. In 1925, he was charged with the subject classification of about twenty thousand manuscripts of the Government Manuscripts Library and, in organizing these, he apparently became frustrated by the lack of information on the date of many of the authors of Sanskrit texts—a situation familiar to scholars of Sanskrit (Hariyappa and Patkar 1960, intro., 14; also Gode 1947, 1–13).

Thus, he undertook to study how he might establish the chronology of Sanskrit literature, and indeed, his earlier papers, from 1920 until the late 1930s, mainly address questions of certain texts' dates. Around 1941, he turned to studying matters concerning the cultural history of India, and here again he displayed a particular interest in the chronology of the material culture of India (Hariyappa and Patkar 1960, introduction, 14). For a typical example, refer to the table of dates in his paper "History of Ambergris in India Between about A.D. 700 and 1900" (1961, 10).

It appears it is precisely the difficulties of dating many South Asian texts that initially drove his historical investigations, and, as a historian, at a later stage in his career, he became aware of the absence of good data on the material culture of India. At times, he presented his efforts in this direction in a patriotic light—by putting the technical achievements of India on the map. Just over a year after India achieved independence, he noted (regarding P. C. Ray's *History of Hindu Chemistry* and G. Mukhopadhyaya's *History of Indian Medicine*) in a speech to the All India Oriental Conference:

> These are really inspiring examples of the patriotic fervour and scholarly devotion, which need to be followed by our scientists in studying the history of our technical Arts and Sciences to the minutest detail. When hundreds of monographs on the different aspects of this history are published by competent scholars it will be possible for us to produce a monumental survey of what had been achieved by our forefathers of antiquity in the field of technical knowledge (Gode 1952, 181).

The type of studies he called for were comprehensive collections of data and the production of bibliographies, work very much on the lines of his papers. But we should refrain from criticism of his single-minded preoccupation with the creation of catalogues of data, since in writing the history of South Asia a great many texts *are* undated, and the state of catalogues and bibliographies is largely inferior to that available to scholars of medieval Europe, to take one example. The articles of Gode, overflowing with unique data and careful suggestions on the dating of texts, played a crucial role in paving the way to writing the sort of cultural history of India that is abundant in the historical writing on France—a type of historical writing on India that is still in its infancy.

63. Tikekar 1964, 50.
64. Gode 1940; Gode 1961e, 410–417.
65. Apparently Gode turned his attention to the history of perfumery and cosmetics in India at the suggestion of a chemist, Dr. Sadgopal of the Indian Standards Institution (Gode 1961e, preface 4; also see Gode 1952, 130). In the process of his work on this topic he discovered two manuscripts on perfumery, the *Gandhasāra* and *Gandhavāda*; works crucial to this book. It is particularly fortunate that Gode, given his broad interests, was curator of the Bhandarkar Oriental Research Institute, otherwise, these texts may well have languished in obscurity until the present day. In 1945, Gode wrote papers concerning these manuscripts, discussing their contents, possible dates, and relation to other texts on perfumery (1945a, 1945b).
66. This also applies to the recent work of Finbarr Flood on material culture in medieval North India, because Flood also has access to many material artifacts (2009).
67. Though I believe that both reconstructions and contemporary observation can, in fact, be of considerable use in the study of the material culture of the past. See McHugh 2011.
68. Baxandall 1988.
69. Panofsky's term, for which he gives a precise definition: "In contrast to a mere parallelism, the connection which I have in mind is a genuine cause-and-effect relation; but in contrast to an individual influence, this cause-and-effect relation comes about by diffusion rather than by direct impact. It comes about by the spreading of what may be called, for want of a better term, a mental habit—reducing this overworked cliché to its precise Scholastic sense as a 'principle that regulates the act,' *principium importans ordinem ad actum*" (1976, 20–21).
70. It appears the main objector was E. H. Gombrich. See Langdale 1999, 21.
71. Baxandall 1988, 38–40.

72. Ibid., 151–152.
73. Ibid., 152.

Chapter 2

Epigraph is from *Mānasollāsa* of Someśvara, *Adhyāyaḥ* 2, *Viṃśatiḥ* 4, 187 verses 73, 74; 189, verses 2–4.

1. Note G. K. Shrigondekar's discussion of these dates is in the introduction to the *Mānasollāsa* of Someśvara. vol. 1, 6–7.
2. My emphasis. Corbin 2005, 134.
3. On the increase in the use of Sanskrit, see Pollock 2006.
4. Clayton 2006.
5. For example, one order is used repeatedly in the *Saḷāyatanavagga* of the Pali *Saṃyutta Nikāya*. See *Saṃyutta-Nikāya*, part 4 *Saḷāyatana-vagga*, 1.
6. Preisendanz notes a similar situation for the study of optics in South Asia, Preisendanz 1989, 146.
7. For a more detailed treatment of sources see McHugh 2007, 2008.
8. Larson 1987, 9.
9. Ibid., 376.
10. Ibid., 35.
11. Dezsö provides an excellent recent study of the life and times of Jayanta Bhaṭṭa. I have adopted here his translation of the title of the *Nyāyamañjarī*, Dezsö 2004.
12. Here the edition I use has *-parimāṇa-*, which made for a very difficult reading. Larry McCrea pointed out to me that an emendation to *-paramāṇu-* makes for a far better reading in the context (e-mail to author, Sept. 3, 2010).
13. *Nyāyamañjarī* of Jayantabhaṭṭa, vol. 2, 371. I was made aware of this passage by Preisendanz 1989, 164, n. 101. I am also grateful to Rajam Raghunathan for her advice on translating this passage.
14. Olivelle's translation. *Mānavadharmaśāstra*, ed. Olivelle 2005, 218, 849.
15. *Mānavadharmaśāstra* 11.55. *Mānavadharmaśāstra*, ed. Olivelle 2005, 847.
16. Olivelle's translation. *Mānavadharmaśāstra* 11.55. *Mānavadharmaśāstra*, ed. Olivelle 2005, 217–218.
17. Olivelle's note on *Manu* 11.96. *Mānavadharmaśāstra*, ed. Olivelle 2005, 342.
18. *Mānavadharmaśāstra*, ed. Olivelle 2005, 368.
19. The text has the strange form *vikarati* here, which is clearly wrong. Nevertheless, the general sense is clear.
20. This is how Jhā reads the commentary (*Mānavadharmaśāstra*, trans. Jhā 1926, vol. 5, 395). However, I think it might mean the deodar cedar tree, sometimes called *dāru* and also known by the name *pūtikāṣṭha* (stinking wood). If this tree is meant, the point could be that odorous objects called by the term "stinking" but which do not actually stink (deodar wood is used in perfumery) and are not forbidden to eat, are not included.
21. *Mānavadharmaśāstra*, Kalakattā 1967–71, vol. 2, 1047.
22. Namely Sarvajñanārāyaṇa and Rāghavānanda as given in the edition of Mandlik, *Mānavadharmaśāstra*, ed. Mandlik 1886.
23. As Zimmermann notes wind (the humor) also has a central role in Indian medical theory as a vehicle for transmitting qualities, Zimmermann 1987a, 147, 169.
24. Another play on the senses in navigating the darkness, this time humorous, is in the first act of the *Mṛcchakaṭika* of Śūdraka, trans. Kale 1962, 40–41. Here one character notes, in looking for some sign of a woman they are trying to find, that "I hear the scent of her chaplets: but, my nose being choked up with darkness, I do not very clearly see the sound of her ornaments" (Kale's translation).
25. *Ratnāvalī* of Harṣa, 68–69.
26. For a discussion of numerous Western, and, mostly, relatively recent attempts at a solution, see chapter 2 in Harper, Bate Smith, Land 1968. As perfumer Christophe Laudamiel pointed out to me, and has demonstrated in person, trained perfumers are able to discuss precise

ingredients, molecules, and aromatic materials with great fluency, so they are better able to talk about smells than most people.

27. Although a study of the senses in the *Upaniṣads* would no doubt be very valuable, this part of the history of the categorization of the senses unfortunately lies beyond the scope of the present study.
28. Frauwallner 1973, vol. 2, part 7, 3–180.
29. With regard to the dialogue of Bhṛgu and Bharadvāja, there are several similarities with Jainism, as noted in Frauwallner 1973, vol. 1, 104. As in the early Jaina *Sūtrakṛtāṅgasūtra* discussed later, there is in this passage a refutation of materialist philosophies. Clearly, the dialogue of Bhṛgu and Bharadvāja shares some terminology with the early Jains and appears generally to be grappling with similar issues. Yet, the order of the senses and sense data are typically Hindu.
30. *Mahābhārata* 12.177.14.
31. It was discussions on the senses, plants, and vegetarianism in Jainism with Professor Kamal Chand Sogani, director of the Apabhramsa Sahitya Academy in Jaipur in summer 2010 that led me to see the import of this passage from a Jain point of view.
32. As Bhattacharya notes, the same dialogue, including this identical passage, occurs in the *Nārada Purāṇa*, I. 42.81–83 (Bhattacharya 1983, 248). Nambiar estimates that that text was compiled sometime from 700–1000 CE incorporating the passage from the *Śāntiparvan*, Nambiar 1979, 229. A very similar passage also occurs in *Mahābhārata: Āśvamedhikaparvan* 14.49.40–42. There, ten types of odor are listed, the addition being "sour" (*amla*). Including sour makes little difference to the list as a whole; both lists use taste qualities to describe odor qualities, and the difference is more of quantity than quality. A familiarity with the qualities given for taste only a few verses later may have led to the almost habitual inclusion of "sour" in this list. However, this is not like the addition of a word for metrical reasons, because it alters the predominantly binary structure of the list and requires that the final verse giving the number of odor qualities be changed from ninefold to tenfold. Note that the critical edition notes one variant: *madhuraḥ kaṭus tathā*, which is quite similar to the line in the *Śāntiparvan*. Nevertheless, it appears that this same version does not change the "tenfold to "ninefold."
33. *Mahābhārata* 12.177.27–28.
34. *Mahābhārata* 12.177.30.
35. Apte gives "2. diffuse, spreading wide (as fragrance). 3. fragrant," for *nirhārin*, and it would appear that this term is indeed contrasted with *saṃhata*, "compact," in which case this latter quality seems to refer to a smell that does not diffuse so much. Yet, for *saṃhata*, Apte gives "Composite, compound (said of a kind of odour)" and quotes Nīlakaṇṭha's (much later) commentary on this very passage: *saṃhataś citragandho 'nekadravyakalpagataḥ*. Despite this, I believe that, given the binary groupings in the rest of the passage, it is sensible to read this term as paired with the previous which would support my reading of *saṃhata* as "compact" (and not "composite"). For *nirhārin*, Nīlakaṇṭha gives *sarvagandhābhibhāvako hiṅgvādau*, "overpowering all smells, as in asafoetida etc." which interpretation, in emphasizing the pervading power of the smell, is basically in agreement with my own.
36. *Mahābhārata* 12.177.34. In translating this passage I became aware that, far more than for smell, our knowledge of the subtleties of touch-terms in Sanskrit is quite poor.
37. *Mṛcchakaṭika* of Śūdraka, 10.
38. Christophe Laudamiel has suggested the term "fatty rich" as a translation of this term (e-mail to author, August 7, 2007).
39. *śālyannādau*.
40. "All subsequent commentators have accepted Patañjali's liberal interpretation of *bhakṣya* in this *sūtra*, viz. that it stands both for solid (*khara-viśada*) and liquid (*drava*) foods" (Agrawala 1953, 100).
41. In his excellent paper on the classification of smell in India, to which I am indebted, Bhattacharya is quite eager to demonstrate the superiority of the "objective" classification seen here to the purely "subjective" ones found in later Nyāya-Vaiśeṣika. It seems he would prefer

the later Nyāya-Vaiśeṣika classification to be "objective" and not evaluative (and thus apparently also "subjective"), so as to be consistent with the other sense-object qualities (such as colors) given in the system (Bhattacharya 1983, 246–253).

42. With regard to the date of the *Nyāyasūtra*, Potter states, "One may sum up the situation pretty safely by saying that we have not the vaguest idea who wrote the *Nyāyasūtras* or when he lived" (Potter 1977, 221). Potter also notes the opinion of Oberhammer that chapter 3, which concerns us here, is from a later date, after the fourth century CE. In fact, it is principally the commentary of Vātsyāyana that concerns us here, and on the dating of this text Potter is fortunately more confident.
43. Potter "hazards" a date of 425 to 500 CE, though he notes the opinion of Ingalls that the text dates from the third century. An approximate date between the third and the fifth century nevertheless places the *Nyāyabhāṣya* as most probably later than the *Mahābhārata* passage and is sufficient to demonstrate the development of ideas I outline here (Potter 1977, 239).
44. Vātsyāyana's commentary on *Nyāyasūtra* of Gautama 3.1.57: *gandhā iṣṭāniṣṭopekṣaṇīyāḥ*.
45. Potter notes the suggestion of Frauwallner for a date of the last half of the sixth century, Potter 1977, 282.
46. Ibid., 282.
47. *Praśastapādabhāṣyam* of Praśasta Devāchārya, 443.
48. Potter 1977, 523.
49. Note that Tachikawa's (1981) translation, which I use here, uses the terms "good and bad" (smell).
50. Tachikawa 1981, 117.
51. Ibid., 119.
52. In the summer of 2005, when I mentioned I was working on smell to Dr. Bhat of the Maharajah Sanskrit College in Mysore, his first reaction was to recite the quoted classification from the *Bhāṣāpariccheda*.
53. *Bhāṣāpariccheda* of Viśvanātha Nyāyapañcānana Bhaṭṭācārya, 102 ab. *saurabhaś cāsaurabhaś ca dvedhā parikīrttitaḥ*.
54. For more of these sources see McHugh 2007, 2008.
55. Dundas 2002, 23.
56. Malvania notes this also, as well as pointing out that the opposed categories of *jīva* and *ajīva* are not found in the *Ācārāṅgasutra*; rather the terms *cittamanta* and *acittamanta* seem to have been in operation at this stage in Jaina thought (Malvania 1981, 152–153).
57. Jacobi's translation, 1968, 52.
58. Jacobi's translation, 1968, 340.
59. Notably, the Prākrit terms differ: *surabhi-gandhe* and *durabhi-gandhe* in the *Ācārāṅgasūtra*, and *subbhigandhe* and *dubbhigandhe* in the *Sūtrakṛtāṅgasūtra*, though Pischel, noting this variation in Ardhamagadhi, does not mention whether he believes one form older than the other. He also observes that the forms *subbhigandhe* and *dubbhigandhe* are also found in the *Ācārāṅgasūtra* (Pischel 1973, 112).
60. On the nature of the soul see Malvania 2000; and Bronkhorst, 2000; Bronkhorst 2000, 591; Malvania 1981, 152.
61. Sound is omitted. The question of sound in Jaina philosophy is interesting and appears to be a relatively neglected topic. In the order of the senses, it would go first, or last, as the same order is presented in both directions, i.e., ABCDE and EDCBA. It is because of the flexibility in the direction of the order of the senses that I decided not to talk of a "hierarchy" of the senses—it is more the internal relations of the order of the senses that matters.
62. "The range (*visaya*) is largest with vision where is goes beyond 100, 000 *joy*.; with hearing it goes up to 12, and with all the other senses up to *9 joy*" (Schubring 2000, 147).
63. Date is from Dundas 2002, 86.
64. Both Schubring and Tatia interpret the *sūtras* as such, Schubring 2000, 134–135; Tatia 1994, 132–133.
65. Date is from Dundas 2002, 87.

66. *Tattvārthasūtra* 5.23. *Sarvārthasiddhi* of Pūjyapāda, 293–294.
67. The terms numerable, innumerable, and infinite refer to the Jain classification of numbers. For a clear basic treatment of this matter, see Tatia 1994, 265–270.
68. This is, of course, contingent on the dating of the early Jain texts.
69. Bhaṭṭāraka Cārukīrti Swami Jī, the Bhaṭṭāraka of Śravanabelagola, and Dr. Shubhachandra of the Dept. of Jainology and Prakrit, Mysore University. Personal communications, July and August 2005.
70. Potter notes the varied opinions on this matter, which range from 386 BCE to the second century BCE (Potter 1996, 137).
71. *gandhāyatanam*, as opposed to "sphere of smelling" *ghāṇāyatanam*.
72. Note that it is the heartwood of the sandalwood tree that is fragrant.
73. I quote only the beginning of this very repetitive section, *Dhammasaṅgani* 626, 141.
74. I thank Ryan Overbey for drawing my attention to this.
75. *Atthasālinī* of Buddhaghosa, 319–320.
76. This fourfold definition occurs in other Buddhist sources. It is found in the *Dharmasaṃgraha* attributed to a certain Nāgārjuna, second century CE. Here the text explains, "There are four smells. They are as follows: good-odor, bad-odors, even-odor and uneven-odor," verse 37: *catvāro gandhāḥ. tadyathā. Sugandho durgandhaḥ samagandho viṣamagandhaś ceti.* (*Dharmasaṅgraha* of Nāgārjuna, 8). Note that the ninth-century Sanskrit-Tibetan Encyclopedia, the *Mahāvyutpatti*, also gives the same four types of smell.
77. My translation. *Abhidharmakośa*, ed. and trans., Hall 1983, 192.
78. I am grateful to Lawrence McCrea for his help in translating this passage, *Abhidharmakośa*, ed. Śāstrī, 1998, 1.28–29.
79. *Prakaraṇa* fol.13 b 1. Vallée Poussin 1971, tome 1, 18.
80. Potter 1996, 375.
81. Frauwallner 1995, 32.
82. Ibid., 14; ibid., 20.
83. Potter 1996, 179.
84. I thank Ryan Overbey for locating and translating this passage (T1537.500b12–13).
85. See the *Āyatanavibhango. Vibhanga*, 72.
86. The origin of the fourfold classification of smell seen in the *Abhidharmakośa* and the reason why Vasubandhu adopted this as opposed to the threefold one are beyond the scope of this chapter.
87. In discussing the order of the senses I have omitted to discuss the sixth sense described by South Asian philosophy: the mental organ/sensorium (*manas*). This is an enormous topic in its own right, but, more important, it is generally listed and discussed somewhat apart from the other senses.
88. *Abhidharmakośa*, ed. Śāstrī 1998, 1.23.
89. Ibid.
90. Date is from Wijeratne and Gethin 2002, intro. xii. I am grateful to Ven. Piyobhaso Bhatsakorn of Mahachulalongkorn University, Bangkok, for drawing my attention to this passage (e-mail to author, January 23, 2006).
91. Translated by Wijeratne and Gethin 2002, 278.
92. Jütte provides a short clear introduction to the history of the order of the senses in European thought. See Jütte 2005, 54–71.
93. Note that the Jains, who do actually order the senses by the sensory capacities of beings, have hearing as characteristic of beings with the greatest potential to sense the world.
94. See Larson 1987, 3–41 for a review of the various "styles" of Sāṃkhya.
95. *Sāṃkhyakārikā* 57, Larson's translation, 1979, 272–273.
96. Larson 1987, 51.
97. Ibid., 5.
98. Hacker 1961, 75–112; Hacker 1959.
99. Hacker 1959, 89–91. On *Mahābhārata* 12.231–232.
100. Hacker 1959, 90.

101. See Olivelle's note on this somewhat cryptic passage. Possibly these seven are the Creator plus six previously mentioned entities. These in turn might be the mind plus the five subtle elements. *Mānavadharmaśāstra*, ed. Olivelle 2005, 239.
102. Olivelle's translation, ibid., 1.19–20, 88.
103. Olivelle's translation, ibid, 1.74–78, 90.
104. For the details of the various types of being possessed of various senses presented in the order of one-sensed beings onwards, see Tatia's accessible translation of the *Tattvārthasūtra* (Tatia 1994, 41–46).
105. The question of exactly how contact occurs between senses and their objects was considered of great importance, though unfortunately I cannot explore this issue fully in this chapter. In the Buddhist *Abhidharmakośa*, Vasubandhu provides a classification of the senses in terms of whether they contact their objects, and this classification is consistent with the given order of the senses, since sight and hearing are not contact senses (*aprāptaviṣayam* "whose fields of operation are not contacted"), but smell, taste, and touch are senses of contact (*prāptaviṣayam* "whose fields of operation are contacted"). See *Abhidharmakośa* of Vasubandhu 1.43 and commentary for a complex discussion of this issue. With regard to other schools of thought, see Preisendanz 1989.
106. Vogel 1979, 310.
107. I find it interesting to reflect on the tradition of memorization of the *Amarakośa*, which has several Buddhist features and structures. That this Buddhist text was so influential, and together with its somewhat Buddhistic ordering of the universe, was memorized by many scholars of Sanskrit of various sectarian affiliations, is a good example of the many, relatively unconscious and *non*-dialogical, intersectarian intellectual exchanges that must have taken place in classical and medieval South Asia.
108. *rūpaṃ śabdo gandharasasparśāś ca viṣayā amī*, *Amarakośa* 1.5.7 (*Dhīvarga* 7).
109. Larson 1987, 49.
110. Larson's translation. *Sāṃkhyakārikā* 26 ab. *buddhīndriyāṇi cakṣuḥ śrotraghrāṇarasanatvagākh yāni*, Larson 1979, 264.
111. In locating these passages, I am indebted to the useful summaries provided in Larson 1987.
112. Larson 1987, 167–169.
113. See Larson 1987, 167–178 for a summary of this text. I used the French translation of Takakusu 1904.
114. Takakusu 1904, 1014.
115. Larson's translation. *Sāṃkhyakārikā* 27 e. Larson 1979, 264.
116. Larson 1987, 271.
117. *Jayamaṅgalā*, 1. See also Larson's discussion, 1987, 271–272.
118. Commentary on *Sāṃkhyakārikā* 26: *śabdavaśād atrākramaḥ kṛtaḥ. kramas tu śrotratvakcakṣuriti*. *Jayamaṅgalā*, 33–34.
119. Clayton 2006, 73; ibid., 53; ibid., 57.
120. Ibid., 74.
121. Ibid., 29.
122. Ibid., 57.
123. That is to say, among the terms used to name the fundamental qualities of the objects of sense experience in these discourses, those terms for odors, "fragrant" and so forth, are the most consistently evaluative, unlike those for other senses, such as "red," "cold," "salty," and so forth. Of course, we examined a restricted number of sources, and were we to look at others, such as the *Purāṇas*, we might find a different account of the sense objects. Also, we must not forget an important distinction here: although, on this level of fundamental analysis, odors are the sense objects that are most consistently described in evaluative terminology, this is not to say that aesthetic values are not attributed to other sense objects in other types of discourse—that, for example, "cold" could not be said to be good or bad.

Chapter 3

1. Shapin 2009. I am very grateful to Professor Shapin for giving me permission to cite from this talk.
2. Corbin 2005, 129.
3. Thuillier 1977.
4. Corbin 2005, 130.
5. I adapt Shapin's admirably clear and useful turns of phrase (2009).
6. I am not interested here in simple references to the presence of odorants (e.g., "the forest was full of fragrant jasmine").
7. The classification in Pāli sources, discussed in chapter 2, is not really an exception, because that classification refers to the smells "of roots, woods etc." To say that a piece of wood has a "woody smell" is not the same as to say that a *wine* has a "*floral* smell." It is not clear that the terms in the classification, e.g., "root-smell," are applicable to anything other than roots, etc., and their products.
8. Spanish leather was a costly perfumed leather, popular in making scented gloves in the sixteenth century. By the nineteenth century, it was only used in the form of small squares of the leather used to perfume note-paper. To my knowledge, this perfumed Spanish leather is no longer manufactured, though a small number of perfumers still make perfumes called Spanish Leather. Nevertheless, for a long period, it must have been a quite well-known generic smell-family among wealthy Europeans.
9. The sort of smell descriptions I examine correspond to the exact and technical descriptions of colors that occur in gemological texts, where specific hues of sapphire, for example, are denoted in terms of certain types of flower, feather, and so forth.
10. Scharfe 1993, 292. Unfortunately, Scharfe does not analyze this passage, which contains so much unusual terminology relevant to the study of trade. See also Witzel 2006, 488. I am grateful to Michael Witzel and Mark McClish for their advice on the tricky question of the date of this text.
11. *Nelumbium speciosum* Willd.
12. *Vetiveria zizanioides* L. The roots of a variety of grass, with a musty, earthy smell, traditionally believed to be cooling. These roots were/are woven into mats (*khus tatties*) and fans that, when dampened, acted as an air coolant. Vetiver is a very important ingredient in traditional South Asian perfumes as well as in modern Euro-American perfumes.
13. Also known as *navamallikā*, a type of jasmine. The numerous varieties of jasmine in India can cause confusion in reading Sanskrit texts.
14. These are aromatics other than sandalwood and aloeswood, and this section is followed by *iti sārāḥ* which Kangle translates as "thus the objects of high value" (*Arthaśāstra*, part 2, 117). Although, as we shall see in chapter 10, *sāra* can often refer to a heartwood, Patrick Olivelle informed me (personal communication March 19, 2012) that in this text the contrast is clearly between *sāra* meaning "precious substance" and *phalgu* meaning "worthless/ordinary substance."
15. A synonym of *haricandana* according to *Amarakośa* 2.6.131.
16. *Arthaśāstra, Adhyakṣapracāraḥ*—"The Activities of the Heads of Departments," on the Evaluation of Sandalwood, 2.11.43–68.
17. Of course, we should not forget the difficulties with ancient color words. A midbrown sandalwood might plausibly have been called "red."
18. For example in *pañcagavyam* consisting of milk, curds, ghee, urine, and cow dung.
19. Pliny, trans. Rackham, vol. 4. XII.41.
20. Zysk 1993, 39–40.
21. I pause briefly to consider the cultural importance of this often forgotten fruit in the West. As the etrog used in the Jewish festival of Sukkot was not grown in northern Europe, a complex trade developed in this ritual item that was indispensable for Northern European Jews. In a wonderful article representative of the subdiscipline of "religious geography," Erich Isaac asserts that by the fourteenth century: "So important had citron become that in

1329 victorious Guelph Florence prohibited the Republic of Pisa from engaging in the trade of citron and allocated to itself this lucrative export" (1959, 71–78).

22. *Kāmasūtra* 1.4.4: *Kāmasūtra*, ed. Śāstrī, 101.
23. I should also emphasize that the term *tvac* here means citron "peel," not "bark": the term *tvac* as applied to plants has a similar semantic field (both "bark" and "peel") as the word *écorce* in French. Citron peel is still an important component of some perfumes.
24. See for example Gupta 1996, 176. On the *mātuluṅga* in art (though not making the "maize argument") see also Atre 1987.
25. See Hara 2010, 65.
26. *Raghuvaṃśa* of Kālidāsa, 50.
27. Gode cites and discusses Buchanan's account of this type of perfume (Gode 1945b, 49).
28. Eichinger Ferro-Luzzi 1996, 81–82.
29. The famous perfume called *Dirt* by Demeter Fragrance Library was above all celebrated as an eccentric and anomalous fragrance.
30. *padma* = *Nelumbium speciosum*=*Nelumbium nuciferum*.
31. According to Amarakośa, *aravinda* is a synonym of *padma*. *Amarakośa* 1, *Vārivarga* 39.
32. *Raghuvaṃśa* of Kālidāsa, 15.
33. *Sthavirāvalīcaritra* of Hemacandra, fasc.II, 130. Thanks to Fynes's translation of this text, I noticed this passage (Fynes 1998, 93).
34. In *Sarga* III of the *Ṛtusaṃhāra* attributed to *Kālidāsa*, the season *śarad* is described, and here we see the *padma*-lotus. *Śarad* is said to "have a pleasant face that is the opened lotus." (*vikacapadmamanojñavaktrā*, *Ṛtusaṃhāra* III.1). The autumn lakes are also said to be "made white by *kumuda* lotuses" (*kumudaiḥ sarāṃsi . . . śuklīkṛtāny . . . Ṛtusaṃhāra* III.2). *Padma*-lotuses also appear in spring (*vasanta*) when the "waters contain *padma*-lotuses" (*salilaṃ sapadmaṃ*, *Ṛtusaṃhāra* 6. 2). The cold season (*hemanta*) on the other hand, is characterized by the *padma*-lotuses vanishing (*vilīnapadmaḥ*, *Ṛtusaṃhāra* IV.1), and this time of year is "beautified by bloomed blue *utpala* lotuses" (*praphullanīlotpalaśobhitāni*, *Ṛtusaṃhāra* IV.9).
35. Borges 1964, 124.
36. Wujastyk provides a good discussion of the complexities surrounding the date of this text, the earliest version of which possibly dates from the third or second centuries BCE, and was last revised by Dṛḍhabala in the fourth or fifth century CE (Wujastyk 2003, 4). I am grateful to Dr. Karin Preisendanz for kindly making me aware of this passage (e-mail to author, December 28, 2005).
37. As astutely observed in Scharfe 2002. *Carakasaṃhitā, Indriyasthānam*, 5.2.3.
38. *Carakasaṃhitā, Indriyasthānam* 2.8–16, vol. 1, 496.
39. Similarly Zimmermann notes certain formulae as common to the genres of *āyurveda* and *dharmaśāstra* (1987a, 39).
40. For a discussion of this issue see McHugh 2008, appendix 1.
41. MW and Apte both give *Tabernaemontana coronaria* Willd. basionym of *Ervatamia divaricata*. UPI, for Sanskrit, *tagara*, gives *Ervatamia divaricata*, and notes that the wood is used as an incense in perfumery. Yet in UPI a variety of terms that would appear to be cognates of *tagara* in modern vernaculars are also given for *Valeriana hardwickii* and *V. jatamansi*. Meulenbeld confirms this confused state of affairs, suggesting additionally *Valeriana wallichii* (= *Valeriana jatamansi*, i.e., *jaṭāmāṃsī*). I have not had an opportunity to discuss this question with traditional perfumers in India.
42. Deleu 1970, 228. The text I use here appears to be abridged here with *tagara* mentioned in the commentary as the completion of the passage: *koṭṭhapuḍāṇa vā jāva keyaïpuḍāṇa . . .*, *Bhagavatīsūtram* vol. 12, 249.
43. Deleu understands *koṭṭha* in this passage as Sanskrit *kuṣṭha*, so "costus," noting, however, that Abhayadeva takes this to mean *koṣṭha* (in the sense of a "pot") in his commentary (Deleu 1970, 228). In the light of the commoner aromatics mentioned in such earlier texts as this I think Deleu's interpretation may well be correct.
44. *Jasminum sambac*, Arabian jasmine.
45. PTS dictionary also gives this as *Jasminum sambac*.

46. *Dhammapada, Pupphavagga* 54–56, 15–16.
47. Schopen 1997a, 126–128. One of the sources Schopen mentions (*Milindapañha* 361.23) talks of people who are "saturated with the lovely and excellent unparalleled sweet perfume of morality" (*sīlavarapravara-asamsucigandha-paribhāvito hoti*). In that source, at least, the perfumery associations of this terminology are clear. In later texts on perfumery, it is clear that the technical process of "steeping" *bhāvanam* involves steeping a ground-up substance (that is to be infused with fragrance) in perfumed water, followed by drying that substance, and then repeating the process several times until the powder is infused with the fragrance of the perfumed water. For a fuller description of the processes of perfumery see chapter 6.
48. Brown 2006, 200–201.
49. *kīrtyā 'bhitaḥ surabhitaḥ*. *Daśakumāracarita* of Daṇḍin, 2. See also the examples in Hara 2010, 82.
50. This list of aromatics could also be regional, or somewhat sectarian, Buddhist and Jain, for example.
51. Honey is indirectly derived from plants and more closely associated with bees.
52. Wujastyk notes that, as with the *Carakasaṃhitā*, this is a complex work, difficult to date. It seems that the final section, in which this passage occurs, is an addition by a certain Nāgārjuna who edited the work in the centuries before 500 CE (Wujastyk 2003, 64).
53. For a detailed discussion of these beings and texts see Smith 2006, 272–275, 471–578. See also Wujastyk 1999, 256–275.
54. As Dalhaṇa points out in his commentary on this verse, this is the same as Mukhamaṇḍikā. If we interpret this term as meaning something on the lines of "Face-Ornament," then along with Revatī, "Lady Opulence" (as discussed by Wujastyk 1999, 261–2, 266), we see perhaps a sense of the uncanny in the nomenclature of Indian medicine. *Suśruta Saṃhitā*, ed. Vaidya Jādavjī, 660.
55. *Suśrutasaṃhitā* ed. Sharma. *Uttaratantra Adhyāya* 27.8, 10, 12–16, vol. 3, 279–283.
56. Douglas 1966.
57. For some discussion of these, see Smith 2006, 531–535.
58. *Uttaratantra Adhyāya* 29.6. *Suśrutasaṃhitā* ed. Sharma, vol. 3, 287–88.
59. Smith 2006, 541.
60. *Kāśyapa-saṃhitā* 319–325. For a discussion of the date of this text see HIML 2a, 39–41.
61. *Kāśyapa-saṃhitā*, 321–323.
62. Ibid., 323.
63. Smith 2006, 274, 481–482.
64. I refer here to Smith's quotations of these passages indicating the verses *as given* in these translations. Smith 2006, 488–497, 510–513. For *devas* see *Carakasaṃhitā* 6.9.20.1. *Suśrutasaṃhitā* 6.60.8. *Aṣṭāṅgahṛdayasaṃhitā* 6.4.13–15.
65. *Carakasaṃhitā* 6.4.20.4. *Aṣṭāṅgahṛdayasaṃhitā* 6.4.18–19b.
66. *Suśrutasaṃhitā* 6.60.15. *Īśānaśivagurudevapaddhati paṭala* 42.22ab.
67. *Carakasaṃhitā* 6.4.20.4. *Suśrutasaṃhitā* 6.60.10. *Īśānaśivagurudevapaddhati paṭala* 42.13cd.
68. *Carakasaṃhitā* 6.4.20.5. *Aṣṭāṅgahṛdayasaṃhitā* 6.4.21c–24b. *Īśānaśivagurudevapaddhati paṭala* 42. 12c–13b.
69. *Aṣṭāṅgahṛdayasaṃhitā* 6.4.13–15.
70. *Aṣṭāṅgahṛdayasaṃhitā* 6.4.40.
71. See Smith 2006, 281, n. 52 where he also notes David Gordon White's interesting suggestions of such a relation between the names of the *graha*s and the symptoms of the diseases.
72. Skanda is also listed here as a *graha*, and of course Kārttikeya has a certain influence with the *mātṛkā*s. There is a similar "alliance" between the Buddha and the child-seizing *yakṣiṇī* Hārītī, though this is not connected with the birth of the Buddha. See Kinsley 1986,151–155. Also Getty 1962, 84–87.
73. *Bhāgavata Purāṇa* 10.6.2, Bryant 2003, 32.
74. *Bhāgavata Purāṇa* 10.6.10, Bryant 2003, 33.
75. *Bhāgavata Purāṇa* 10.6.34, Bryant 2003, 35.
76. *Bhāgavata Purāṇa* 10.6.41–42, Bryant, 2003, 35.

77. See the number of plant names Monier Williams lists as compounds of the stem *pūti* (stinking).
78. According to Pingree, Varāhamihira, active ca. 550 CE, "The son of Ādityadāsa, a Maga Brāhmaṇa . . . was born in Avantī, lived in Kāpatthaka, and referred to Ujjayinī as lying on the prime meridian" (Pingree 1970, series A, vol. 5, 563).
79. *Bṛhatsaṃhitā*—On the Signs on Men 68, 14–16. *Bṛhatsaṃhitā* (Bhat), part 2, 606.
80. *Pālakāpyaṃ* quoted by Apte under *gandhahasti*.
81. *Mātaṅgalīlā* 1.40. *Mātaṅgalīlā* of Nīlakaṇṭha, 7.
82. See, for example Greenwood, Comeskey, Hunt, and Rasmussen 2005; Rasmussen, Riddle, and Krishnamurthy 2002; Slotow, van Dyk, Poole, Page, and Klocke 2000.
83. *Mātaṅgalīlā* of Nīlakaṇṭha, 18–20.
84. HIML vol. 2a, 570. *Mātaṅgalīlā* of Nīlakaṇṭha, preface.
85. Like Frederick Smith, I use Meulenbeld's translation of this terminology (HIML vol. 1a, 42, and notes).
86. Smith 2006, 480–481, 498–499.
87. For a clear summary of the account of *sattvas* in the *Carakasaṃhitā*, see Smith 2006, 498–499.
88. Smith 2006, 493 referring to *Suśrutasaṃhitā* 6.9.25.
89. I have adopted some of Frederick Smith's thoughtful translations for these types of beings.
90. *Alstonia scholaris* R. Br.
91. *Cassia fistula* L (= *Cathartocarpus fistula* Pers.)
92. *Vitex negundo* L. Amarasiṃha notes this is a synonym of *nirguṇḍī* (Amara II.4.68).
93. *Hiptage benghalensis* Kurz. Also known as *mādhavī*.
94. Again, a variety of jasmine. MW gives *Jasminum auriculatum* Vahl.
95. Most likely *Calophyllum inophyllum* L., which MW gives as one possibility. *Maheśvara*'s commentary on Amarasiṃha II.4. 25 gives also *uṇḍī*, as a synonym. This is given as the Marathi for *C. inophyllum* in UPI.
96. Possibly *nāgakesara*, *Mesua ferrea* L. or also *Rottlera tinctoria* Roxb. (= *Mallotus philipinensis*.)
97. It is not clear whether this elephant smells of the urine and excrement *of* the animals, or whether this list is just a long *dvandva* compound.
98. MW gives *Blyxa octandra* (Roxb.) Thwaites (=*Vallisneria octandra* Roxb.)
99. A difficult term; possibly a type of basil.
100. Apte notes the distinction between *sarpis* and *ghṛtam* as molten and solid forms of the more generic *ājyam* respectively. Clearly the smell of molten ghee is something the reader would associate with sacrifices and Brahmins.
101. *ājyam*, which according to Apte appears to be a more generic term for ghee.
102. *haritāla* is orpiment and *manaḥśilā* is realgar. Both are sulfides of arsenic. Orpiment (As_2S_3) a term derived from the Latin *auripigmentum*, "gold-paint," is a particularly beautiful yellow pigment, unpleasant to use because it is poisonous with a foul smell. Realgar (As_2S_2) a term derived from Arabic *rahj-al-ghar*, "powder of the mine," is orange-red in color, also poisonous. The Greek sea trader's manual, the *Periplus maris Eryrthaei*, notes trade in orpiment to the Indian posts of Barygaza and Bacare. Realgar is also prepared by heating orpiment (Eastaugh 2004, 285–286, 318–319).

    I am unable to say quite what they smell like, despite my best efforts, the kind staff of the Straus Center for Conservation at Harvard University Art Museums was unwilling to allow me to sniff the samples of these toxic pigments in their collection. Nevertheless, Hurlbut and Sharp note that both these minerals have a "characteristic garlic odor" (1998, 162).

    Manaḥśilā, "mind-stone," is a notable term. Amara (*Vaiśyavarga* 2.9.108) gives the terms *manoguptā*, *manojñā* and *manohvā* as well as *nāgajihvikā* as synonyms for red arsenic.
103. See chapter 10 for a discussion of this resin.
104. *Pentepetes phoeniea* L. Plant with scarlet flowers, also known as *raktaka*. I have not discovered anything about its smell.
105. *Pandanus odoratissimus*, a fragrant screw pine, with large extremely fragrant spikes of flowers, important in numerous contexts in Indian culture.
106. *Jasminum grandiflorum* L. synonym of *Jasminum officinale* f. *grandiflorum* L.

107. *Mātaṅgalīlā* of Nīlakaṇṭha, 18–20.
108. Sarma 2003, 77.
109. As noted by Sarma 2003, 72. Of course, technically all the flowers we mentioned may give rise to a fruit in botanical terms, but as far as Sanskrit literature is concerned these fruits (of a jasmine flower for example) would probably not be classed as *phalas* in the same manner as a mango.
110. Ibid., 72.
111. Ibid., 74. Quoting *Śārṅgadharapaddhati*, 1016.
112. I adopt Blackburn's useful terminology to distinguish between the idealized lists of aromatics given in certain texts and the no doubt messier reality of perfumery (1999).
113. The classification of plant-parts here appears to be from the bottom up; from the inside out; and from earlier to later. Thus: from root to trunk; from heartwood, via bark, to leaf; and from flower to fruit.
114. Plants are for the most part referred to as fragrant, yet as we will see, flowers too, as odorous objects, fell under the twofold classification as fragrant and bad smelling. Also, for higher castes garlic and onions were classed as foul smelling.
115. Indeed, all the animal smells would appear to be smells of civilization: village and urban animals, animal products such as ghee, and so forth. There are no smells of deer, jackal, or tiger here. Indeed, there is a close correspondence with the *grāmya* category of animals found in medical texts. See Zimmermann 1987a, ch. 2.
116. E-mail to author, August 14, 2007.
117. An exception would be something like a colorless, odorous gas isolated in a jar.

Chapter 4

1. Like food, toilet paper, and coffins. As discussed in Kopytoff 2003, 75.
2. This is not to mention the importance of flowers in Tamil Caṅkam poetics. I am grateful to Professor Anne Monius for reminding me of this aspect of flowers. Unfortunately, I do not work with Tamil sources, and therefore I focus on Sanskrit sources in this book.
3. *Āpastambha Dharmasūtra* (ADh) 2.28.10 in *Dharmasūtras*; *Mānavadharmaśāstra* 8.330 in *Mānavadharmaśāstra*, ed. Olivelle 2005, 184.
4. *Gautama Dharmasūtra* 10.51 in *Dharmasūtras*. *Mānavadharmaśāstra* 7.131 in *Mānavadharmaśāstra*, ed. Olivelle 2005, 161.
5. *Gautama Dharmasūtra* 12.28.
6. Ibid., 7.12.
7. *Baudhāyana Dharmasūtra* 1.9.4 in *Dharmasūtras*. This appears to disagree with the sentiments regarding the origin of flowers as we will see later in the book.
8. *Mānavadharmaśāstra* 4.66 in *Mānavadharmaśāstra*, ed. Olivelle 2005, 127.
9. *Mānavadharmaśāstra* 2.177 in *Mānavadharmaśāstra*, ed. Olivelle 2005, 104.
10. *Mānavadharmaśāstra* 2.175 in *Mānavadharmaśāstra*, ed. Olivelle 2005, 104.
11. Amarasiṃha has *saugandhika* as a sort of lily (*Vārivarga* 1.10.36) as well as a sort of grass, also known as *kattṛṇa* (*Vanauṣadhivarga* 2.4.166) and also sulphur (*Vaiśyavarga* 2.9.102). Bhānuji Dīkṣita's commentary on Amarasiṃha 1.10.36 gives a Hindi synonym of the lily as *muṇḍa*, which, according to UPI, is the white water lily, *Nymphaea lotus* L. Of course, in reading this text the "real" identity of the flower is not relevant, since here it is a divine and imaginary sort of flower. Among the other meanings of this word, one in particular stands out. This occurs in the *Suśrutasaṃhitā* during a discussion on embryology, in a fascinating passage on the origin of various abnormalities in sexual function, as caused by abnormalities in sexual organs, fluids, or practices. This stanza and others in the same passage, at the very least bear witness to a variety of sexual practices in the traditional Indian imaginary that are not to my knowledge mentioned in *kāma* literature. The whole passage is discussed in detail in Meulenbeld 1997, 216–217.

    > He who is born in a stinking vagina, is called a "fragrant" (*saugandhika*) Having smelled the smell of a vagina and a penis, he gains vigor.

It seems the logic of this passage is that some sort of deficiency in conception will need to be supplemented in adult sexual practice, for the previous line describes how a man whose parents have scant seed must first consume semen in order to achieve an erection:

> Because of excessive shortage of the seed of the parents arises an *Āsekya* (to be sprinkled) man, who, having consumed semen, without a doubt achieves an erect penis.

My translations. *Suśrutasaṃhitā*, ed. Sharma, 1991–2001, vol. 2, 135–136.

12. The *Kalyāṇasaugandhikavyāyoga* ascribed to certain Nīlakaṇṭha, of uncertain date, between the tenth and fifteenth centuries CE. Also, the *Saugandhikāharaṇa* of Viśvanāthakavi, probably from the early fourteenth century. Also, Krishnamachariar mentions references to the performance of a Buddhist dramatic version of this story. See Krishnamachariar, 1970, para. 553 and footnote, p. 535.
13. *Mahābhārata, Āraṇyakaparvan* 3.146, 5–11, 14, 21–22.
14. As Lawrence McCrea pointed out to me, Draupadī is de-eroticized throughout this whole part of the epic, and the flower may be a substitute for physical desire. We will examine the offering of flowers in chapter 10.
15. I omitted analyzing the whole episode here—the first part is sufficient for our purposes.
16. HDS, vol. 2, pt. 2, 782.
17. Ibid., 782.
18. Also because she was born of a fish, as we will see later.
19. *Mahābhārata*, 1.57.54–68.
20. A relatively common interpolation which occurs in the Devanāgarī version of Nīlakaṇṭha, as well as the Telugu version and several Grantha versions—thus in some manuscripts of the Central Group of the Northern recension and in some of the Southern recension. See the note on 1.57.38 in the critical edition. I have inserted the interpolation in the manner in which it is found in Nīlakaṇṭha's version.
21. Also known as Uparicara, founder of the *indradhvaja* festival and owner of a protective *unfading* garland given to him by Indra.
22. *Saraca indica* L. (= *Jonesia asoca* Roxb). According to Christophe Laudamiel, this has a "sweet, violet red fruit smell, with freesia peach undertones." E-mail to author, August 14, 2007.
23. *Magnolia champaca* (L.) Figlar (= *Michelia champaca* L).
24. *Symplocos racemosa* Roxb (?)
25. MW says this refers to a number of shrubs "surpassing pearls in whiteness." Apte says that it can refer to a creeper that embraces the mango tree. Here, is it classed "with other great trees," so perhaps it is, in fact, a tree? The commentary of Bhanūji Dīkṣita on Amara 4.26 gives a Hindi synonym as *tiniśa*, a tree, *Ougeinia oojeinensis* Hochr. (= *Dalbergia oojeinensis* W. Roxburgh).
26. *Calophyllum inophyllum* L.
27. *Pterospermum acerifolium* Willd.
28. *Mimusops elengi* L.
29. *Terminalia arjuna* Wight and Arn.
30. *Mahābhārata*, 1.57.38–40.
31. In the Sanskrit version of the *Mahābhārata* we are not told exactly how she smells. In the *Purāṇic Encyclopaedia*, Vettam Mani confidently asserts that Satyavatī's name changes from Matsyagandhī (fish-smelling) to Kastūrīgandhī (musk-smelling) because her new fragrant body smells of musk. There is no mention of this in the critical edition, and this may well refer to a vernacular version of this incident, perhaps in Malayalam, in which Vettam Mani first wrote the *Purāṇic Encyclopedia*. Also, Apte gives *yojanagandhā* as a synonym for musk, though it is unlikely that the term meant "musk" in the *Mahābhārata* which would appear to be otherwise devoid of references to musk. Perhaps when pungent musk appeared on the scene it was given Satyavatī's odorous epithet, and once this was established the incidences of her name in the *Mahābhārata* were interpreted to imply musk—a new supremely fragrant aromatic. This warrants future investigation (Mani 1979, 709).

32. *Mahābhārata* 1.94.41–45.
33. Johnston 2001, 203.

Chapter 5

Epigraph is from Gode 1961b, 53.

1. On the *kalās* see Ali 2004, 75–77; Chandra 1951–1952; Acharya 1929.
2. I base my account here on the texts collected by R. T. Vyas in his edition of the *Gandhasāra*, where he also presents most of the following sources (apart from the *Aṅgavijjā* and the *Haramekhalā*). For reasons of space, and because I wish to concentrate on fresh material and approaches, I will not dwell at length on many of these sources. I wish in this chapter to avoid reproducing the work of P. K. Gode and R. T. Vyas on this subject.
3. For example *Suśrutasaṃhitā, Cikitsāsthānam* 24 discusses the ideal daily routine, washing, massaging etc., though it does not discuss perfumes per se. The *Nāvanītakam* also contains similar material—not strictly perfumery. The mid-to-late eleventh century CE *Cikitsāsaṃgraha* contains materials on perfumery addressed later.
4. Such as the *Nāgarasarvasva* discussed later. For a thorough examination of materials on perfumery in erotic texts, see Sternbach 1962.
5. The *Bṛhatsaṃhitā* dicussed later. Also, the enormous Jain Prakrit text on signs and omens—the *Aṅgavijjā*—which contains material on almost every imaginable object/phenomenon that formed part of the lived-world of the period, contains a list of perfume preparations. Here the perfume preparations, just as in the *Bṛhatsaṃhitā*, are mentioned in the section on matters erotic. The introduction to this text, by Moti Chandra, provides a useful summary of the contents. The most up-to-date discussion of this important, fascinating, but very difficult text is by Dundas, who notes, "The whole world is approached from one sole perspective, namely, its capacity to signal meaning different from that which it ostensibly denotes . . .With the *Angavijjā* we can see Jainism attempting to align itself with the world of courtly power and luxury." For the summary of the perfumes, see *Aṅgavijjā*, intro., 51. For the date see *Aṅgavijjā*, intro., 36. Also see Dundas 2006, 405.
6. As in the thirteenth-century CE *Rasaratnākara*, in which the knowledge of the manufacture of gemstones and perfumes is praised as a means to wealth. Much of the material here seems to deal with the artifice of aromatic raw materials. See Gode's article for a summary of the material on perfumery here (1961d). Laufer 1896 translates and discusses a Tibetan translation of an Indian incense recipe attributed to Nāgārjuna, which, given that attribution, might also be taken from a work on alchemy. The text was translated by Rin Chen Bang Po with a Kashmiri collaborator. The text is called "gem necklace/garland of blending incense," *Dhūpayogaratnamālā*, in Sanskrit. The incense itself is very typical of a medieval Indian incense (musk, camphor, Kashmiri saffron, fragrant shell operculum, valerian/jatamansi (?), Indian frankincense, cinnamon, guggulu). I might note that the Tibetan term *nagi* which Laufer in unable to translate is no doubt *nakhī*, fragrant shell operculum. I am grateful to Arthur McKeown for his advice concerning this Tibetan source.
7. Too numerous to summarize here. See the accessible summary of a few of these materials in Ramachandra Rao 2005, 101–133.
8. See Gode 1961g; Gode 1961f.
9. Such as the *Mānasollāsa* and the *Śivatattvaratnākara* we discuss later.
10. The section on perfumes in this text has been discussed briefly in Krishnappa 1987. It appears from this synopsis that the perfumes described in this text (in the *Gandhayukti Krama*) are quite similar to those in such texts as the *Nāgarasarvasva*, and not unlike the preparations in the *Gandhasāra*, though I am unable to tell whether there is any literary embellishment of the formulae. An additional product Krishnappa mentions is the perfumed *tilaka*.
11. See Morita 1999. See also Aileen Gatten's excellent article on how taste in incense is used to portray character (1977). Also Bedini 1994, esp. ch. 2.

12. On this see Ali 2004, 99.
13. I note the dating of these different texts when I deal with them later.
14. *Gandhasāra* of Gaṅgādhara, intro., 9–14.
15. These chapter numbers refer to Bhat's well-known translation of this text. Please note that in Dvivedī's edition, with the commentary of Bhaṭṭotpala (1895–97), the chapter on perfumery is ch. 76.
16. For a clear discussion of Varāhamihira's contribution to combinatorics, see Wujastyk 2000. For a study of this chapter in particular see Hayashi 1987. Also see Kusuba 1993, 149–166.
17. Although Varāhamihira gives 174,720, this figure is incorrect. See the discussion in Kusuba 1993, 149–151.
18. See Wujastyk 2000, 486. More accurately, the bell ringing in question is a form of change ringing called "method ringing," in which bell ringers follow an algorithm to produce a potentially huge number of permutations of rings. On merchants and figures, see Baxandall 1988, 91.
19. *kacchapuṭa* is an interesting term, clearly referring to some sort of grid in which the aromatics are placed for the purposes of making this sort of mathematical perfume. Monier Williams in his dictionary, citing Varāhamihira, gives "a box with compartments." Hayashi notes that "this is not wrong, but it is not precise either" (1987, 161). Takanori Kusuba on the other hand was inclined to think it is not so much an instrument of some sort, but rather an abstract figure (1993, 162). It is possible that, as Kusuba suggests, Varāhamihira may have been simply referring to the notion of a figure, but in the later *Gandhasāra* the term also occurs several times and we are told:

    "Now, it is related here for the purpose of the preparation of all perfumes jointly in a *kacchapuṭa*: In a *kacchapuṭa* that is produced from nine lines by nine, that has enclosures equipped with iron depressions . . ."

    atha sakalagandhasiddhyai sāmānyaṃ procyate 'tra kacchapuṭe // 34cd
    navanavarekhājanite kacchapuṭe ayapadāṅkayutakoṣṭhe / 35ab
    Gandhasāra, 38, verse 34cd–35ab.

    This is the clearest description I have seen of a *kacchapuṭa* in the context of perfumery, and it provides a good idea of the object as it was understood in the medieval period. An ideal translation would seem to be "grid," implying both an abstract figure and a realized object: "grid" is ambiguous in the same way that *kacchapuṭa* may also have been. This resolves the tension between translating it as a "figure" or as an "instrument," and it also seems to confirm Hayashi's opinion. In the case from the *Gandhasāra*, it would seem to consist of a grid of nine lines by nine, forming eight squares by eight, though presumably these dimensions change according to the desired size of *kacchapuṭa*. This grid has enclosures (*koṣṭha*, also "chess squares" according to MW) equipped with iron depressions (*padāṅka*, literally "footprints"). It would be interesting to see whether such an object is still used in any context today in South Asia. The word has some phonetic similarities with the word *kakṣapuṭa*, meaning "armpit," though both Varāhamihira and this much later text clearly use the word *kacchapuṭa*.
20. Hayashi 1987, 162.
21. *Cinnamomum tamala*.
22. Bitumen, benzoin, or lichen.
23. Numerous possibilities, a particularly tricky word—perhaps *Agalia odorata*.
24. *Cyperus rotundus*. The bulb-like roots of this type of sedge are still used in Indian perfumery and incense making today.
25. Probably *guggulu: Commiphora mukul*.
26. Probably = *uśīra*. Vetiver: *Vetiveria zazanioides* = *Andropogon muricatus*.
27. I am not confident of a good identification here. Perhaps *Trigonella corniculata*.
28. *Valeriana jatamansi* = *V. wallichii* = *Nardostachys jatamansi*.
29. *unguis odoratus*/sweet hoof/*blattes de byzance*: the operculum of certain sea snails.
30. Amara gives as a synonym *sarala*: i.e., resin of *Pinus longifolia*.
31. Indian olibanum—*Boswellia serrata*.

32. *Bṛhatsaṃhitā* (Bhat) 77. 23–26, 714–715.
33. Meulenbeld provides an invaluable introduction to this text and also discusses the controversy surrounding the date, which is given in the text itself as the year 887 of an unspecified era. See HIML vol. 2a, 134–135. The text is also attested in eleventh-century Bengal, cited by Niścalakara in the *Ratnaprabhā* commentary on the mid-to-late eleventh century CE *Cikitsāsaṃgraha* of Cakrapāṇidatta, which I discuss later. See Bhattacharyya 1947, 123–155.
34. The author (or compiler) seems to have wanted to provide all the various possible applications of the many plant, animal, and mineral products (*materia medica* is not really an appropriate term in this context) of traditional India: the production of wonders such as ink that one can read in the dark; techniques to control lovers; as well as the preparation of medicines, perfumes, food, and so forth—as such it is a compendium of all useful formulae. I do not know a generic term for such a text in either Sanskrit or English (a "Book of Secrets"?), though clearly it would be of interest, and of use, to anyone who for one reason or another (e.g., practicing medicine or perfumery) had access to all these materials.
35. I base my summary closely on that in HIML vol.2a, 130–133.
36. "Māhuka . . . states he is a descendent of the great poet Māgha . . . The author was a Śaiva, as appears from the maṅgalācaraṇa, dedicated to Paśupati, and other references" (HIML vol. 2a, 134). As Whitney Cox pointed out to me, Māhuka might in fact be a Prakritized form of Māghaka (e-mail to the author, October 26, 2011).
37. According to Pingree, Bhaṭṭotpala, who lived in Kashmir, was active from 966–969 CE. It appears from the verses at the end that his commentary on the *Bṛhatsaṃhitā*, the *Saṃhitāvivṛti*, was composed in the year 967 CE (Pingree 1970, series A, vol. 4, 270).
38. I give the Sanskrit *chāyā*. *Haramekhalā*, verse 52, 17: *tailam idaṃ mṛgāṅkakiraṇāvaliśiśiram anaṅgadayitam.*
39. Bird formula—*Haramekhalā*, verses 97–98, 30–31. Elephant formula—ibid., verses 141, 42–43.
40. I am extremely grateful to Larry McCrea for his assistance in translating this verse and commentary—of course, all faults are my own.
41. *Haramekhalā*, 30–31.

    ghanaśīrṣatagaranayanacalagrīvaḥ kaṅkunirmitaśarīraḥ |
    kararuhaviracitapakṣo māṃsīmukho devīkṛtacaraṇaḥ ‖ 97
    eṣa vidagdhakāminīmānasasara[ḥ]saṅgavarditacchāyaḥ |
    madhumadhuraśabdasuraso dhūpaḥ kalahaṃsako nāma* ‖ 98

    I have emended a second *-śabdo* to *-suraso* based on the commentary and also the Prakrit *mahumahurasaddasuhao*. As Whitney Cox pointed out to me, this *suhao* might also be *subhaga*. I will however here remain faithful to the commentary as that text is in itself of interest. I also thank Dr. Cox for his emendation in the above verse (e-mail to author, October 26, 2011).
42. *Haramekhalā*, 31. *kalahaṃso hi mānasākhyasarasas sambandhe vardhitaśobho bhavati.*
43. Ibid. *laṭahavilāsinīnāṃ hṛdayajalāśayasamparkaviśeṣitaśobhaḥ.*
44. Ibid. *sundaradravyāṇāṃ kāvyavaicitryārthaṃ sāvayavarūpatā mātrā tu sarveṣāṃ samāṃśa iva.*
45. I base much of my account here on texts mentioned in the *New Catalogus Catalogorum*, vol. 4, 307–310.
46. *uktam īśvareṇa svasyāṃ gandhayuktau/*

    ollaṃmi ollao jo dijjai veha iti so bhaṇio/
    voho uṇa jo cuṇṇo cuṇṇaviṇi acchagandho so //
    editor's *chāyā:*
    ārdre ārdro yo dīyate vedha iti sa bhaṇitaḥ /
    bodhaḥ punar yaś cūrṇaś cūrṇite acchagandhaḥ saḥ //

    Bhaṭṭotpala's Commentary on *Bṛhatsaṃhitā* 76. 11. *Bṛhatsaṃhitā*, ed. Dvivedi, 948.
47. Professor Babulal Shukla Shastri, in his Hindi introduction to one recent edition, notes that the probable date of the text is around the final decades of the ninth century to the first half of the tenth century (*Nāgarasarvasva*, ed. Shastri, intro., 12–13.) This is also the date Zysk gives (2002, 8). Lienhard gives a latest possible date of the first half of the fourteenth century (1979, 98). I am inclined to agree with Daud Ali's more cautious assessment of our knowledge of the date of this text (2011, 42).

48. "Having collected the essential part of the perfume texts, which are difficult to understand by those who are not clever, [and] which are by Lokeśvara etc., I set [it] forth with very well known words" (*Nāgarasarvasva*, ed. Shastri, 4.1–2, 14).
49. Meulenbeld places Niścalakara in Bengal in the second half of the twelfth century CE, and Priya Vrat Sharma suggests a date later than 1250 CE. See HIML vol. 2a, 105. Also Sharma 1991, 107–112. In my account of perfumery texts quoted in this text, I relied on Meulenbeld's thorough analysis of this text. For the first description of this text, see also Bhattacharyya 1947.
50. Meulenbeld cites the opinion of G. Hāldār that this is the work of a certain Bhavadevabhaṭṭa. See HIML vol. 2b, 118, note 385.
51. Meulenbeld cites Hāldār's opinion that this is the work of a certain Pṛthvīsiṃha. See HIML vol. 2b, 118, note 387. I am inclined to think that this is a separate source.
52. Meulenbeld suggests another reading of *Gandhatattva* for both this and the following work, and believes this work is "distinct from the other treatises on *gandhayukti* quoted by Niścala." He notes that Hāldār's attribution of this text to a certain Bhavyadatta is an error. See HIML 2b, 118, note 388.
53. Meulenbeld usefully lists all these passages, HIML 2a, 95–105.
54. For a thorough discussion of Bhavadeva, see HDS, vol. 1.2, 639–653.
55. Ibid. 1.2, 642.
56. Ibid. 1.2, 647–648.
57. *Epigraphia Indica* 1900–1901, vol. 6, 203–207.
58. Ibid., verse 23, 207.
59. For the date see Sternbach 1974, 17.
60. As well as in the *Aṅgavijjā*.
61. Fragrant lichen, benzoin or bitumen.
62. *śaśinakhagirimadamāṃsījatubhāgo malayalohayor bhāgau /*
militair guḍaparimṛditair vastragṛhādīni dhūpayet caturaḥ // 3259
gandhadīpikāyāḥ/
Śārṅgadharapaddhati, 468.
63. Though it is not entirely clear if the two texts called *–pradīpa* are necessarily distinct. *Ṭoḍarānanda* part 3, respectively pages 376, 385, 386. See the appendix for a longer discussion of these lost texts. On the date and contents of the *Ṭoḍarānanda* see HIML 2a, 272–296. On the scholars responsible for the text as a whole see HIML 2a, 295–296; also HDS 1.2, 907–914.
64. It is not my intention here to track these correspondences in detail.
65. As Whitney Cox pointed out to me, some of the associations of verses to famous perfume texts and authors might in fact be pseudepigraphical attributions (e-mail to author, October 26 2011).
66. Carr 1962, 11.
67. Gode 1945a. Note there is a misprint in the reprint of this article in Indian Cultural History vol. 1: "A.D. 1530 and 1550." The original version has the dates given here.
68. *Gandhavāda*, sections 10 and 11. *Gandhasāra* of Gaṅgādhara, 57–58. As noted by Vyas in his introduction. *Gandhasāra* of Gaṅgādhara, intro., 73.
69. *Gandhavāda*, section 10. *Gandhasāra* of Gaṅgādhara, 58.
70. Gode 1945a, 191.
71. Meulenbeld usefully notes all these references to *ambara* and *lobān* as well as other unusual names of ingredients (HIML 2a, 510–511). Presumably *tavakṣīra* is *tabashīr* or bamboo manna, one of the varieties of "pearls" given in Sanskrit gemology texts, also commonly known by Sanskrit *vaṃśalocana*. In his discussion of the *Dhanvantarīyanighaṇṭu* Meulenbeld also notes references to a variety of *vaṃśarocanā* called *tvakkṣīrī* or *tugākṣīrī* that is no doubt the same term (*Dhanvantarīyanighaṇṭu* 2.57–59, see HIML 2a, 171). The history of the translation of this term into Indic languages would make an interesting short study.
72. Unpublished manuscript in the Anup Sanskrit Library Bikaner. 24 folios, complete. Old Anup catalog number 3974. New Anup catalog: general number 74, serial number 113.

73. The opening verses of the Anup *Gandhasāra* contain an interesting variant reading on one of the verses of the BORI *Gandhasāra* that I discuss in the next chapter. I am grateful to Larry McCrea for his advice on these verses:
    viriñcivaktrāṃbujarājahaṃsīdevī[ṃ] namaskṛtya ca gandhavādaṃ /
    gandhāgamajñadhvanitair vacobhir vakṣye sasāraṃ śubhagandhavādam //
    gandhavādam samudhṛtya gandhasāraś ca krī[i]yate /
    atra sarve 'pi yogāḥ saṃskṛtabhāṣayā ucyate //
    "Having paid homage to the goddess who is the royal goose to the lotus of Brahmā's mouth and to the lore of perfumery I will relate together with its essence the beautiful *Lore of Perfumery* with words suggested by experts in perfume-texts.
    Having thoroughly extracted the lore of perfumery (or *Lore of Perfumery*), the *Essence of Perfume* is produced. And in this [text] all the mixtures (or "methods") are related in Sanskrit."
74. In the Anup *Gandhasāra* the formulae for *covā* are compounded from several ingredients, whereas in the *Ā'īn-i Akbarī* the perfume called *chūva* is said to be simply distilled aloewood (Bochmann 1927, 86). In the *Ni 'matnāma, chūva* is also compounded. Indeed the formulae in the *Ni 'matnāma* for *chūva* appear to be quite similar to those in the Anup *Gandhasāra* (Titley 2005, 82). Did perhaps a precious oil of aloeswood lend its name to a compounded perfume or vice versa? (cf. the confusing perambulations of "frangipane" and "frangipani"). Were compounded artificial agarwoods perhaps very popular in their own right, just as compounded lavender perfumes were in nineteenth and twentieth century Europe?
75. *Śivatattvaratnākara* of Basavarāja of Keḷadi. See the introductions to volumes 2 and 3 for some general background to this text. The text contains about 35,000 verses.
76. A kingdom that is now part of Karnataka and Kerala.
77. *Śivatattvaratnākara* of Basavarāja of Keḷadi, *Kallola* 6, *Taranga* 15, vol. 2, 11–24.
78. As indicated by the editor in the notes for *lepas*.
79. Also indicated by the editor.
80. We will examine the phenomenon of the *parīkṣā* texts later.
81. Gaṅgādhara's name and the benedictory verse we see in the next chapter suggest he was a Śaiva, *Gandhasāra* of Gaṅgādhara, intro., 13. Gode 1945b, 52, does not venture to suggest a precise date in his paper on this text, noting it is post-1000 CE.
82. *Gandhasāra* of Gaṅgādhara, 36, verses 7–14. The *Haramekhalā* does not, however, use the term *javādi*, though it does seem to mention civet (*śāli, pūti*). References to civet as used in perfumery probably date the *Haramekhalā* sometime around the tenth century; a period when civet first appeared in Indic texts but when the term *javādi* had apparently yet to be used. For references and notes, see McHugh, forthcoming.
83. I should add that I only came to realize the import of this term for the dating of the *Gandhasāra* in the very final stages of copyediting this book, so it has not been possible to incorporate these materials fully.
84. Or so it appears on the surface. Later we will encounter the confusing possibility that this type of verse could have another "aromatic" reading. I have not attempted to produce such a reading for this verse.
85. *Gandhasāra* of Gaṅgādhara, 9 verse 1.
86. Ibid., 16, verses 1–3.
87. Ibid., 18, verse 1.
88. Ibid., 20, verse 1.
89. Ibid., 24, verse 1.
90. Ibid., 29, verses 66–69, and possibly until verse 71, though I am unclear on the bitextual readings of all these verses. The terms *kuca* (breast), *vadana* (face/mouth), and *netra* (eye) crop up in these other verses and possibly refer to parts of a burning incense stick.
91. In compound with the preceding.
92. *taralanayanavadanā gurujaghanā vipulakaṭhinakucayuktāḥ /*
    kāntā rāganibaddhā iva varttaya kaṃ [na] vaśayanti //
    Gandhasāra of Gaṅgādhara 29, verse 66.

93. *Gandhasāra* of Gaṅgādhara, 32, verse 1.
94. Kulkarni and Wright 1992. I adapt their translation here so as to be consistent later.
95. "Fracas" is a good translation into French of *kolāhala*, and given it is also the name of an important perfume by Robert Piguet it seemed an apt choice. Despite my best efforts, I have thus far been unable to identify the meter but as Kulkarni and Wright note this text might only scan in Prakrit.
Gandhavāda version:
sajjā kulavadhūlajjā paradhanaharaṇaṃ pāpasaṃjananam /
jinadharme adharmaḥ dhūpaḥ kolāhalo nāma // 1
ṭīkā
sajj(jjā) mhaṇatā la (vaṃ)ga / kulavadhūlajjā mhaṇatā nakha / paradhanaharaṇaṃ mhaṇije kacorā / pāpasaṃjananaṃ mhaṇatā kuṣṭḥ teṃ koṣṭḥ / jainadharme avarmu te jaṭāmāṃsī / he pāṃcai sama bhāgeṃ melavije / yā dhūpā nāv kolāhalo // 79
Gandhavāda in *Gandhasāra* of Gaṇgādhara, 83.
Gandhasāra version:
sarjjat kulavadhūlajjā paradhanaharaṇaṃ ca pāpasaṃbhūtam /
jinadharmasya vise(ro)dhī dhūpaḥ kolāhalo nāma //
Gandhasāra of Gaṅgādhara *Prakaraṇa* 2, verses 40–41, 27.
96. I take *sajjā* as a noun, thus meaning "dress" or "armor." I do not take it as an adjective meaning "ready," though my reading is far from certain.
97. It is R. T. Vyas who noticed this verse and mentions it in his introduction to the *Gandhasāra* of Gaṅgādhara, 6–7.
98. Kulkarni and Wright 1992. "The Marathi text is manifestly romancing on the basis of a preexisting, already corrupt Sanskrit text." Their "straightforward" reading of the verse makes sense in all respects except for the emphasis on a prohibition of incense in Jainism, yet it is a somewhat random collection of bad things, not the most pointed aphorism. In general Kulkarni and Wright are not pleased with the fascinatingly messy nature of the *Gandhavāda*. They do, however, usefully note that this particular verse might scan better in Prakrit—which might help make sense of the comment at the start of the Anup *Gandhasāra* to the effect that the formulae will be stated in Sanskrit in that text. Might a text called the *Gandhavāda* have existed in Prakrit in addition to the others discussed previously?
99. *Curcuma zedoaria*. An aromatic root not unlike ginger.
100. It appears that there is no consensus in texts on dharma on which particular bad deeds cause the disease *kuṣṭha*, through karmic retribution, though all the possibilities are very serious—the evil deeds range from incest to murdering a Brahmin, or killing a cow. See HDS, vol. 4, 174–178.
101. A Himalayan root important in perfumery and incense making to this day.
102. As Michael Witzel reminded me, the term *jina* can also refer to the Buddha, but here I believe the fact that the thing forbidden is meat suggests that a Jain *jina* is implied here. Buddhists, including monks, were not forbidden to eat meat in early South Asia.
103. See *Gandhasāra* of Gaṅgādhara, 47, verse 68.
104. The more unusual and suspect verses are *Gandhasāra* of Gaṅgādhara 24, verses 7–8, verse 1, 29, verse 70.
105. *gaurīkarajabhinnendukalāṃśarasamiśritam /*
gaṅgāsalilam īśasya snānakāri punātu vaḥ //
Gandhasāra of Gaṅgādhara, 18, verse 1.
106. Meulenbeld also notes this tendency in the *Gandhasāra* to refer to substances by terms uncommon in medical treatises, as well as by shortened forms of names, and synonyms of these shortened forms (HIML, vol. 2a, 175).
107. Just as in the reading of bitextual poetry specialized glossaries of monosyllabic words aided creative readings. See Bronner 2010, ch. 6.
108. Hasan-Rokem and Shulman 1996, intro., 3.
109. Both quotes are from Salomon 1996, 171.
110. Hasan-Rokem and Shulman 1996, intro., 4.

111. Ali 2004, 255.
112. As discussed in the only complete study of riddles in Sanskrit: Sternbach 1975.
113. Possibly a Buddhist who flourished at a period after Bāṇa (seventh century) and before the end of the eleventh century CE, Sternbach 1975, 94–95.
114. Hahn 2002, 3–81.
115. Ibid., 22.
116. Ibid., 22; 20.
117. My translation from the French, Balbir 2002, 181.
118. Ibid. 181.
119. See the table in which Balbir gives the contexts for the scenes of riddle exchanges she has analyzed. Ibid., 194–195.
120. *Nāgarasarvasvam* of Padmaśrī, ed. Shastri, ch. 5–11.
121. See the story of "Nūpurapaṇḍitā and the Jackal," from the *Sthavirāvalīcarita/Pariśiṣṭaparvan* of Hemacandra, in Fynes 1998, 69–82.
122. According to the *Hevajra Tantra*, as discussed in Davidson 2002, 263–264. Davidson also makes the intriguing suggestion that some of these code words might have sexual connotations in Dravidian South Asian languages. For example, he suggests the term *kakkola* (cubebs) might reflect the Dravidian *kakkulāte* meaning love or to make love (268–269). This might possibly add another level of erotic suspicion to the texts. However, I should qualify this by suggesting that for a medieval South Asian reader familiar with these very common terms for well-known aromatics, to understand these terms as having first and foremost perfumery-related meanings would undoubtedly have seemed natural. Also, in the two examples of musk (sometimes associated with deer genitalia) and white camphor, the rationale for the coded language seems relatively clear.
123. Bronner 2010, 168–169.
124. I am also grateful for the comments of Professor Nicholas Watson of Harvard University on this verse—that the association of the transgressive with the erotic is particularly noteworthy here.
125. Respectively: *Gandhasāra* of Gaṅgādhara, 12, verse 24; 17, verse 14; 30, verses 72, 73, 74; 31, verses 1–5. The *jāti* metres named in the verses do not appear to be exactly represented in the verses themselves, which are nevertheless in *jāti* metres. Probably the text here is somewhat corrupt (or translated?).

    Below is an example of the *śālinī* incense roll:
    vālā keśī ketakī corapuṣpī medhyā raktā g(r)anthiparṇī vihāṇī /
    chatrā kāntā koṣakāraiḥ kṛtā syāc cchubrāmodaiḥ śālinī dhūpavartiḥ //
    Gandhasāra of Gaṅgādhara, 30, verse 74.
126. E-mail to author, August 20, 2007. Professor Sarma notes that he once discussed this with a scholar in Mysore who cited other such instances from South India.
127. *Gaṇitasārasaṅgraha* of Mahāvīrācārya.
128. Ibid., ch. 2, 3, 4, 5.
129. Ibid., 69. My emphasis.
130. As Professor Sarma notes, given that the *Gandhasāra* was found in Maharashtra and the *Gandhavāda* has an old Marathi commentary, and also that this part of India is in many ways culturally part of South India, such a connection does not seem implausible (e-mail to author, August 20, 2007).
131. Pollock 2006, 179–180.
132. *bhojarājakṛta[ja]vādi . . .*

    . . . bhojanirmitā // 6
    Gandhavāda, in Gandhasāra of Gaṅgādhara, 70.
133. *Cārucaryā* of Bhoja. The text is a compilation and moreover, according to the editor, the attested manuscripts contain quite differing recensions—thus the text is not really a dateable entity. Nevertheless in B. Rama Rao's (collated) edition some materials on *javādi* suggest to me a date for those verses probably later than the thirteenth century CE. It is perhaps most important to note that the *idea* of a text by King Bhoja that contained materials on

perfumery appears to have been present in some circles in the later medieval period, even if the actual texts we possess are highly varied compilations.

134. Gode 1945b, 45.
135. *Gandhasāra* of Gaṅgādhara, 39.These numbers are not arranged in order, yet this is not a magic square. I have yet to understand if there is any rationale behind the order of the numbers in this square.
136. As Professor Lawrence McCrea noted when I showed this verse to him, it is clearly in a regular meter, except for the word *vallabhā*, which needs correcting to *vallabha* to make the meter consistent—this would also be consistent with the fact that the words in the third column seem to be the first part of compounds with words in the fourth; that this is semantically sound in the context can be seen from the compound in the top line: *parvata-putrī*:"daughter of the mountain." I have so far not been able decipher this table, nor have I identified the meter. It has eleven syllables per quarter, and the definition would be *ma ta ya ga ga*. (See table N.1)
137. See Pollock 2006, 5.
138. I believe it likely that there are other clever and deliberately puzzling features in this text that I have not noticed.
139. Note, for example, the scattered nature of the "metrical" recipes.
140. Some of the terms found in the formulae are clearly names, indicated by such terms as -*nāma* and –*saṃjñā* following the name. As Professor S. R. Sarma notes, these terms could be added *metri causa*, but, nevertheless, they suggest the terms are not merely adjectives describing the qualities of the aromatic preparations, and that they are actual names (e-mail to author, August 20, 2007). Some other names are of such an obviously poetic or metaphorical nature that they are also clearly names, not mere descriptions. For a more comprehensive list of these names, see McHugh 2008, appendix 2. Corbin also did some work on nineteenth-century French perfume names in their social and cultural context, see, for example Corbin 1986, 196, 199. Meulenbeld was also quite struck by the perfume names in this text, as he notes in his useful summary and discussion of it in HIML vol. 2a, 175.
141. *Gandhasāra* of Gaṅgādhara, 9, verse 9.
142. Ibid., 11, verse 13.
143. Ibid., 12, verse 8.
144. Ibid., 26, verse 28.
145. For example: *tripuraharavallabhākhya* at *Gandhasāra* of Gaṅgādhara, 12, verse 7.
146. See, for example *Gandhasāra* of Gaṅgādhara, 27, verse 10.
147. Ibid., 27, verse 34. Note that *darpa* can also mean musk.
148. Ibid., 22, verse 6.
149. Ibid., 25, verse 11.
150. Ibid., 21, verse 3.
151. Ibid., 21, verse 6.
152. Ibid., 25, verse 18.
153. As Professor Witzel and Professor S. R. Sarma immediately pointed out, this is a rare instance of a sentence compound (as in *kiṃkara* for servant). This may well have given our erudite audience even more to talk about. For such compounds see Wackernagel 1905, vol. 2i, section 123, 325–327.
154. *dhūpitasakalaśarīro janena gacchann ihocyate manujaḥ // 36cd*

Table N.1 **Table at the End of the *Gandhasāra***

varttiḥ	*padmā*	*parvata*	*putrī*	*devī*
gaurī	*yuktā*	*sajjana*	*raktā*	*viddhā*
candrā	*kāntā*	*bhīṣaṇa*	*keśī*	*caṇḍā*
viddhā	*proktā*	*vallabhā*	*saktā*	*śuddhā*

ko gacchatīti tasmāt kogacchati saṃjñako dhūpa / 37ab
Gandhasāra of Gaṅgādhara, *Prakaraṇa* 2, 27.

155. Ibid., 9, verse 8.
156. Ibid., 11, verse 14.
157. Ibid., 15, verse 21.
158. Ibid., 21, verse 2.
159. Ibid., 26, verse 23.
160. Ibid., 29, verses 58–64.
161. *diahe diahe je jaha kame(ṇa) vaccanti ṇiccamuvajoaṃ /*
cheāṇa te tahaccia bhaṇimo gandhaṃ samāseṇa //2
divase divase ye yathā krameṇa vraja(tyu? nti nityam u)payogam /
chekānāṃ tān tathaiva bha(ṇi? ṇā)mo gandhān samāsena //
Haramekhalā 5.2, 1.
162. In the text, the preparation of artificial versions of the aromatics are described.
163. I prefer the original reading *sahakārasthairyayuktiḥ* because in the text these are clearly methods to make *sahakāra* mangoes last longer.
164. *saṃgraho 'yam prayogāṇāṃ pañcamasya nibadhyate /*
tatrāmbuvāsanavidhir dantakāṣṭhavidhis tathā //
madhūcchiṣṭavidhir netraparikarmāñjanaṃ tathā /
mukhavāsādi tailāni tathodvartanasaṃvidhiḥ //
atha snānakriyā snānaṃ snānopakaraṇāni ca /
paṭavāsādi vartyā ca + sugandhādisaṃvidhiḥ //
kṛtiḥ kastūrikāyāś ca citragandhāsavakriyā /
karpūrakuṅkumanakhā aguroḥ sallakasya ca //
sahakārasya ca kṛtiḥ śaśitailakṛtis tathā /
lavaṅgatuṭikuṣṭhānāṃ kṛtayaś ca yathākramam //
sahakāra(rasairyu?sthairyay)uktiḥ sarvapuṣpadrutis tathā /
ketakīcampakādīnāṃ drutayaś ca tathā pṛthak //
Haramekhalā, commentary on final verse of part 5, 5.273, 77–78.
165. Hemacandra also mentions this preparation in his *Abhidhānacintāmaṇi*. Perhaps this was a popular formula in the centuries around the turn of the second millennium CE. It seems that the quantities used in making this paste came to be used as the name of the paste itself, much like the name "pound cake." As seen in the appendix, this was mentioned in a *Gandhaśāstra* quoted by Ballālasena in the *Adbhutasāgara*. There, a formula was given that was to be made in a *catuḥsama* manner (aloeswood, saffron, camphor, and sandalwood), and this was called *sarvagandha*. Unlike the recipes given by Padmaśrī and Hemacandra, the one quoted in the *Adbhutasāgara* lacks musk. In Hemacandra's version, the ingredients differ from those given in the *Nāgarsarvasva*, camphor being replaced by aloeswood. Thus it consists of sandalwood, aloeswood, musk, and saffron:
candanāgarukastūrīkuṅkumais tu catuḥsamam
Abhidhānakintāmani of Hemacandra, verse 639, 117.
The *Śabdakalpadruma* entry on this term discusses the "*sama*" in this name, concluding that it could imply either that the ingredients are added in *equal* quantity or that the ingredients are all used *together* in the preparation, *Śabdakalpadruma* of Rādhakāntadeva, vol. 2, 423.
166. Bühnemann 1988, 135–168. See also the brief instructions for a *pūjā* Bühnemann notes in the *Varāhapurāṇa*, *Adhyāya* 117. In that text, the rite of rubbing the body (*udvartanavidhi*) is described—starting with the teeth (verses 5–8); via *udvartana* rubbing substances (verses 25–28); all the way to incense (verses 36–39); and finishing with an offering of *tāmbūla* (verses 45–46).
167. *Kāmasūtra* 1.4.5.
168. Ibid., 1.4.10.
169. The editor in his introduction notes that this was "applied to the forehead on special occasions," and is still found in Maharashtra, where it is called *bukka*. The *bukka* I have seen is a black fragrant powder, *Gandhasāra* of Gaṅgādhara, intro. 3, n. 1.

170. This is only a brief and incomplete list of the twenty named *bhogas* in the text, but it gives a good idea of the progression.
171. *karpūrāgarudhūpaparimalavāsite*, *Vikramāṅkābhyudayam* of Someśvara, 27.

Chapter 6

1. Smith 1990, 52.
2. Identification uncertain in this context.
3. Ambiguous name.
4. *nāgakeśara*? (= *Mesua ferrea*).
5. Amarakośa gives *pūtiphalī* as a synonym of *vākūcī*: 2.4.96. Bhānujī Dīkṣita gives the vernacular for this as *vakucī*. *Useful Plants of India* notes this can refer to *Psoralea corylifolia*, which is used as a paste for skin conditions.
6. Or, as Lawrence McCrea suggested to me, "for twilight."
7. *Mānasollāsa* of Someśvara, vol. 2, 85.
8. As noted by Vogel, and this is especially so as the present form has been supplemented. Vogel also notes the opinion of P. V. Sharma that it dates from the tenth century (Vogel 1979, 374).
9. "Saffron, aloeswood, musk, camphor and sandalwood. Thus is related the great perfume by the name of *yakṣa* mud. This *yakṣa* mud is cool and removes skin diseases, is a perfume that beautifies as well as removing headache and poison."
   kuṅkumāgurukarpūrakastūricandanāni ca /
   mahāsugandha ity ukto nāmato yakṣakardamaḥ //
   yakṣakardama eṣa syāc chītas tvagdoṣahṛt tathā /
   sugandhiḥ kāntidaś caiva śirorttiviṣanāśanaḥ //
   Dhanvantarīnighaṇṭu, Miśrikādivarga 45–46.
   Dhanvantarīnighaṇṭuḥ, ed. P. V. Sharma, 267.
10. "Yakṣa mud is (made) with camphor, aloeswood, musk, and cubebs." *karpūrāgurukastūrīkakkolair yakṣakardamaḥ /*
   Amarakośa 2.6.133
11. "Yakṣa mud is (made) with mixed camphor, aloeswood, *kakkola*, musk, and sandalwood liquid."
   karpūrāgarukakkolakastūrīcandanadravaiḥ // 638 cd
   syād yakṣakardamo miśrair . . . 639 ab
   Abhidhānakintāmaṇi of Hemacandra, ed. and trans. Boehtlingk and Rieu, 143.
12. "Camphor and aloeswood, musk, as well as sandalwood and kakkola—yakṣa mud is (made) with these five."
   karpūram aguruś caiva kastūrī candanaṃ tathā /
   kakkolaṃ ca bhaved ebhiḥ pañcabhir yakṣakardamaḥ //
   Caturvargacintāmaṇi, Vratakhaṇḍa, Adhyāyaḥ 1.
   Chaturvarga Chintamani of Hemadri, vol. 72.2, 44.
13. *gandhadravyam yojayed yaḥ sa jñeyo gandhavittamaḥ /*
   prāṇināṃ prakṛtiṃ jñātvā vātapittakaphottarāṃ // 88
   udvartanāpi(di)kaṃ yuñjyāt tatra doṣapraśāntidam /
   āgneyaṃ vātale dravyaṃ pittale śītalaṃ hitam //89
   kaṭutiktakaṣāyaṃ tu yojayet sakaphe nare / 90 ab.
   Gandhasāra of Gaṅgādhara, *Prakaraṇa* 1, p. 8.
14. Zimmermann 1987a.
15. *Nāgarasarvasva*, ed. Shastri, 4.1–2, 14.
   nānāvidagdhavāsā mukhyā madanapradīpakāḥ khyātāḥ /
   varakāmukaḥ prayatnāc chikśyetādau sugandhaśāstrebhyaḥ //
   lokeśvarādikebhyo 'puṭamatidurbodhagandhaśāstrebhyaḥ /
   saṅgṛhya sārabhāgaṃ pravidhāsye suprasiddhapadaiḥ //
16. These two terms, *kumbha*, *ulūkhala* meaning "pot" and "mortar" respectively, can both also refer to the resin of *Commiphora mukul*—*guggulu*. See *Gandhasāra* of Gaṅgādhara, 48, verse 79ab.

17. *Azadirachta indica.*
18. *kumbholūkhalasarṣapabhujaṅganirmokanimbapatrakṛtaḥ /*
 dhūpo bhūtāveśaṃ nihanti doṣañ ca ḍākinyāḥ //
 Gandhasāra of Gaṅgādhara, 29 verse 59.
19. As noted earlier, this mountain-derived product could refer to lichen, bitumen, or benzoin resin. I tend to think it may be either benzoin or lichen, both still being used in the traditional Indian perfumery industry today.
20. Also called *sarala.*
21. *Shorea robusta* Steud.
22. *bhāgaiś caturbhiḥ sitaśailamustāḥ śrīsarjabhāgau nakhaguggulū ca /*
 karpūrabodho madhupiṇḍito 'yaṃ kopacchado nāma narendradhūpaḥ //
 Bṛhatsaṃhitā (Bhat), 77. 11.
23. For example at the beginning of the perfumery sections of the somewhat encyclopedic *Viṣṇudharmottarapurāṇa* and *Agnipurāṇa*. See *Gandhasāra* of Gaṅgādhara, intro., 44–46. Also *Gandhasāra* appendices 4 and 5.
24. In translating these two terms, I relied more on the commentary of Bhaṭṭotpala on *Bṛhatsaṃhitā*, ed. Dvivedi 76.11, where he gives a clearer definition of the two terms than given in the *Gandhasāra.*
25. I have not seen this process much used in traditional Indian perfumery today, but it is the principal method by which traditional Thai perfume, *Nam Op Thai*, is produced, though I have not yet been able to trace the origins of the method used there.
26. *bhāvanaṃ pācanaṃ bodho vedho dhūpanavāsane /*
 evaṃ ṣaḍ atra karmāṇi dravyeṣūktāni kovidaiḥ //
 Gandhasāra of Gaṅgādhara *Gandhasāra, Prakaraṇa* 1, p. 1, 6.
27. Lusthaus 1998.
28. On *enfleurage* see Groom 1997, 110–111.
29. *Gandhasāra* of Gaṅgādhara, p. 14, verse 1 to p. 15, verse 19.
30. For a nineteenth-century account of the production of perfumed sesame oil in India, see Buchanan 1936, 633–635.
31. *Bhikkhunīvibhaṅga, Pācittiya* 89. *Vinaya Piṭaka*, ed. Oldenberg, vol. 4, 341.
32. I am grateful to Christophe Laudamiel for providing this particular comment, as well as for many other additions and improvements to this discussion of *enfleurage* (e-mail to author January 26, 2010). Dan Lusthaus also kindly provided some very useful comments concerning *vāsanā.*
33. This all depends, of course, on accepting that *vāsana* and *vāsanā* are both derived from the same Sanskrit verbal root, namely what Monier Williams gives as √*vās* "to perfume." This is not, however, the only possible root from which to derive the (more commonly philosophical) term *vāsanā*. The latter can be derived as a feminine noun according to Pāṇini 3.3.107 from √*vās*, taking this to be either a Class Ten root, a denominative root, or as a causative based on a number of simple roots √*vas*. *Vāsanam* on the other hand would appear to be derived from Pāṇini 3.3.115. This is a more general rule, according to which one may derive a neuter action noun either from a simple root *vas* (giving *vasanam*), or from a derivative root *vās* (giving *vāsanam*), regardless of whether this *vās* is Class Ten, denominative, or causative in origin. But what is the origin of this root √*vās*, and also of the related noun *vāsaḥ* "perfuming, perfume"? Manfred Mayrhofer (1953–80, Lieferung 20, 197–98) suggests that the origin of the noun *vāsaḥ* has not been satisfactorily explained, though a special derivation from one of the many √*vas* roots seems possible. As we see in my analysis, *vāsana* in perfumery means to transfer a fragrance from one object to another. Thus I propose the hypothesis that the fragrance-related *vās*- terms are derived from the causative of root √*vas* with the sense "to dwell," thus implying "to cause [fragrance] to dwell," or "to infuse [with fragrance]" or simply "to perfume." Such an origin as a general sense of "making *x* dwell in *y*" would also help explain the different yet entirely consistent uses of this terminology, both to mean "infusion [with fragrance]" and "enduring traces [of certain dispositions]." I am extremely grateful to James Benson for his advice on Pāṇini in this case; all mistakes and misunderstandings are my own.

34. As explored by Shulman 1987. Also, see Doniger 2005 (quoting Martha McClintock), 112–117.
35. *śatrūdāsīnamitrāṇi śāstrato yuktitas tathā /*
ajñātvā gandhayuktiṃ yaḥ kurute na sugandhavit //
Gandhasāra 6, verse 62.
36. *trividhāni ca dravyāṇi mitrodāsīnaśatravaḥ /*
yojanīyāni kāleṣu yathāśāstramataṃ budhaiḥ //
mitradravyaṃ samaṃ deyam udāsīnaṃ tadardhakaṃ /
śatrudravyaṃ pādikaṃ tu gandhayuktiṣu śasyate //
Gandhasāra, 6, verses 69–70.
37. Ibid., 7, verses 71–76.
38. Zimmermann 1987a, 31.
39. *Gandhasāra* of Gaṅgādhara, 42–49.
40. *Nāgarasarvasvam*, ed. Shastri, 4.1–2, 14.
41. *dhammatthakāmajasojīviāṇa je sāhaṇakkataḷḷicchā /*
te bhaṇṇanti viaḍḍhā ṇa uṇā paravañcaṇasataggā // 275
dharmārthakāmayaśojīvitānāṃ ye sādhanaikatatparāḥ /
te bhaṇyante vidagdhā na punaḥ paravañcanasatṛṣṇāḥ //
Haramekhalā 5.275, 86.
42. *viuḷāi mahāmaïviraïāï daṭṭhūṇa gandhasatthāï /*
aha pañcamo ṇibandho viaḍḍhadaïö pariccheo // 1
vipulāni mahāmativiracitāni dṛṣṭvā gandhaśāstrāṇi /
atha (vā?) pañcamo nibandho vidagdhadayitaḥ paricchedaḥ //
Haramekhalā 5.1, 1.
43. *iha ettiamattadoccia je upaujjanti vatthupajjāā /*
haramehaḷāṇibandhe viaḍḍhajaṇavaḍḍhiāṇandā // 277
ihaitāvanmātra eva ye upayujyante vastuparyāyāḥ /
haramekhalānibandhe vidagdhajanavardhitānandāḥ //
ia esa parisamappaï suvaṇṇaraaṇujjaḷā susandhāṇā /
haramehaḷā viaḍḍhāṇurāakaïviaṇāmaṅkā // 278
iheti parisamāpyate suvarṇaracanojjvalā susaṃsthānā /
haramekhalā vidagdhānurāgakṛtidvitīyanāmāṅkā //
Haramekhalā 5.277–278, 86–87.
44. *Gandhasāra* of Gaṅgādhara, 1, verses 1–5. As suggested by the editor and Professor McCrea, I have amended verse two from *parisaṃprasarpan-* to *pariprasarpan-*.
45. As Vyas suggests. *Gandhasāra*, intro., 8.
46. Lévi 1915, 19–138.
47. For important reflections on ornament in South Asia, see Dehejia 2009; Ali 1998, 162–182; and Coomaraswamy 1939.
48. For *guru* the commentary gives *gula* = *guḍa* i.e., molasses/sugar. This whole mixture reminds me somewhat of that used to make *nam ob tai* in Thailand, in which filled water jars are fumigated with a mixture of heated brown sugar, benzoin resin, and kaffir lime peel (prior to the addition of floral perfumes, camphor and talc). Minus the essential oils nowadays used to impart floral fragrance (previously maceration was used) and the talc, I imagine this perfume was similar to some described in these early Sanskrit texts. As far as I am aware, the water-fumigation method is unique today in world perfumery and produces a very pleasant resinous-gourmand note.
49. *gurumahu(pura?)kāḷāgurusāḷubbhavasakkarāhi sarisāhi /*
bhaṇio bhāaṇadhūo javanehi suandhateḷḷāṇa // 58
gurumadhukālāgaruśālodbhavaśarkasābhiḥ sadṛśābhiḥ /
bhaṇi(tai? to) bhājanadhūpo yavanaiḥ sugandhitailānām //
Haramekhalā 5.58, 19.
50. *Yavanair gandhayuktividagdhair aviśeṣair*. Commentary on *Haramekhalā* 5.58.

51. I am interested in the notion that the *trivarga*, and even the four *puruṣārthas* including *mokṣa*, create a complex and potentially helpful framework for the refinement of the notion of what constitutes the "use-value" of material things in a South Asian context.
52. Though a large number of professional perfumers are male.
53. The *Bṛhatkathāślokasaṃgraha* of Budhasvāmin was edited and translated by Félix Lacôte and was also recently well translated into English by James Mallinson (2005) as part of the *Clay Sanskrit Series*. This episode was also translated by J. A. B. Van Buitenen (1959).
54. Lacôte 1908, 146.
55. Lacôte suggests a date around the eighth or ninth century CE (1908, 147). Winternitz dismisses this as conjecture (1920, vol. 3, 316, n. 1). Agrawala (1974, 229) suggests it was composed "sometime in the Gupta period." I am grateful to Professor S. R. Sarma for these references (e-mail to author, August, 20, 2007).
56. S. R. Sarma has written a detailed study of the term *phalakasaṃpuṭe* and its meaning in this passage. Though the term has caused difficulties to translators in the past, it is clear from Professor Sarma's article that it refers to a pair of boards (either for writing or painting) joined together. Given the context, it would appear that in this case the boards are painting boards with a white ground on which is painted a portrait of princess Nalinikā (Sarma 1985, 175–196).
57. *Bṛhatkathāślokasaṃgraha* of Budhasvāmin, ed. Lacôte 19.62–74, Books XVIII–XX, Texte Sanskrit, 290–291. (Translations of Sanskrit are mine.)
58. I am not entirely happy with this translation, though it accords with that of Lacôte (Traduction Francaise 184).
59. A type of being that has a human body and horse's head.
60. *Bṛhatkathāślokasaṃgraha* of Budhasvāmin, ed. Lacôte, 19.104–106, Books XVIII–XX, Texte Sanskrit, 290–291.
61. Ibid., 19.138–149, Books XVIII–XX, Texte Sanskrit, 297–298.
62. Ibid., 19.184–187, Books XVIII–XX, Texte Sanskrit, 302.
63. Named after the French 75mm field gun.
64. *Magnolia champaca* L. Figlar (= *Michelia champaca* L).
65. *Jasminum sambac* or Arabian jasmine.
66. Uncertain.
67. *Stereospermum suaveolens* DC.
68. *Mimusops elengi* L.
69. *Jasminum grandiflorum* L. synonym of *Jasminum officinale* f. *grandiflorum* L.
70. *Jasminum auriculatum* Vahl.
71. *Gomphrena globosa* L.
72. Only one manuscript has this reading, which nevertheless is quite close to the name of a flower *kuraba*—I am at a loss of how to go further without consulting more manuscripts.
73. *Mānasollāsa* of Someśvara, 3.7. 41–48ab, vol. 2, 90–91.
74. Kusuba 1993, 138–139.
75. *Varāha-Purāṇa* 116.35, 401.
76. For more reflections on this, see McHugh 2011.
77. "*paccakarpūra*."
78. I am extremely grateful to Dr A. V. Ramana Dikshitulu, Pradhana Archaka, and Agama Advisor, T. T. Devasthanams, Tirumala for explaining to me the composition and weekly preparation of the *namam* of Lord Venkateśvara in a personal interview, June 12, 2010.
79. Pollock 2006, 15.
80. *Mānasollāsa* of Someśvara, vol. 1, 2.
81. This ostensible structure, at least the first two parts, associating what are effectively the values of *dharma* and *artha* with the creation and maintenance of the kingdom respectively, somewhat echoes the logical order of the "characterological slots" of the formulaic genealogies given in *praśastis* as discussed by Pollock, where "the founder of the dynasty himself is typically credited with the achievement of great *vaidika* rites; one descendent masters the

world of political practice with its three powers; another evinces personal resolve and bravery" (Pollock 2006, 120).

82. *Vikramāṅkābhyudayam* of Someśvara.

Chapter 7

Epigraph is from Finot 1896, 33–34, my translation of the Sanskrit.

1. Finot (1896, intro., 10) suggested a tentative *terminus ad quem* of the eighth century CE and believes the work may date from quite some time before this. Meulenbeld states the various opinions on his date from the fifth century to the twelfth century CE. Likewise opinions vary as to whether he was a Buddhist, but at the very least, one attested form of this text shows Buddhistic features (HIML 2a, 780).
2. *nalikā* is a difficult term, possibly a variety of cassia cinnamon.
3. Finot 1896, intro., 14–19.
4. I adopt the well-known and useful analogy of Kopytoff 2003.
5. Often known for its yellow color in Europe and America, saffron, in fact, has a strong and attractive fragrance. The fruits of *Piper cubeba*, also called "tailed pepper," are very aromatic and somewhat like black peppercorns but with a quite different aroma. Resins include varieties of myrrh and frankincense from South Asia and the Arabian peninsula, as well as (probably at a later stage?) benzoin from Southeast Asia. Benzoin is a very prominent incense in South India today (*sambrani*), and a study of the history of this aromatic in India is a desideratum.
6. As seen in the *Dhanvantarinighaṇṭu* and the *Rājanighaṇṭu*. *Dhanvantari-Nighaṇṭuḥ*, ed. P. V. Sharma, 91–120. *Rājanighaṇṭusahito Dhanvantarīyanighaṇṭuḥ*, 93–133.
7. For a short discussion of medical classifications of "spices" see Zimmermann 1987b.
8. Vogel 1979, 309–310.
9. As of 2.4.122 starting with *elāvāluka* (as Meulenbeld states: "Much confusion exists concerning this substance," 1974, 530–532) there are listed a number of aromatics, for example, *sallakī* resin at 2.4.124 and the important *kuṣṭha* at 2.4.126.
10. The perfumery *nighaṇṭu* that Bhaṭṭotpala gives in his commentary on the *Bṛhatsaṃhitā* suggests that *kālīyaka* is a type of aloeswood: *kālīyakaṃ joṅgakaṃ lohaṃ khalaḥ kārpāsako 'guruḥ* (*Bṛhatsaṃhitā*, ed. Dvivedi, 941).
11. Perhaps another kind of pine resin/turpentine.
12. Vogel 1979, 335.
13. After naming the parts of the body, cosmetics, baths, and massage, Hemacandra takes up the raw materials of perfumes in a different order than the *Amarakośa*, giving synonyms for types of aloeswood (stanza 640–641); types of sandalwood (641–642); nutmeg, camphor, and musk (643–644); saffron (644–645); cloves, cubebs, *kālīyaka* (646); *sal* tree resin (647); and, finally, frankincense and deodar cedar resin (648). This list, though less clearly structured than the one in the previous lexicon, nevertheless names more or less the same aromatics: aloeswood, sandalwood, nutmeg, camphor, musk, saffron, cloves, cubebs, and a number of resins. As for other aromatics—the "herbs"—they seem to be listed amongst the plants in the *Vanaspatikāya* section, for example, *uśīra*/vetiver (1158).
14. *Vikramāṅkābhudaya* of Someśvara, 10–15.
15. Darnton 1984, 123.
16. Indra's divine garden.
17. The name of one of the divine trees in Indra's garden.
18. I am very grateful for the assistance of Professor S. R. Sarma and Professor L. J. McCrea for advice on this passage.

    ubhayato 'py ekaparipāṭiparighaṭitadvibhūmikasaudhapaṅktibhiḥ, prativaṇiggṛhalabhyamānatrai lokyadurlabhādurlabhapadārthasārthaiḥ, pratyakṣanidhipratinidhibhiḥ, jaladharadivasair iva bahughanasāraiḥ, nīcair iva śrīkhaṇḍollasitaiḥ, nāstikair iva sāguruvāsanaiḥ, gaṅgāpravāhair iva bahumārgaiḥ, nandanapradeśair iva saharicandanaiḥ, chandobhir iva gītaśāstrair iva smārtair iva vanair iva dṛṣṭabahujātiphalaiḥ . . . vipaṇisadanair alaṅkṛtāḥ . . . kalyāṇābhidhānā rājadhānī

    Vikramāṅkābhudaya of Someśvara, p. 11 line 24; p. 12 line 1; p. 12, line 11; p. 15, line 15.

19. The *Delight of the Mind, Mānasollāsa*, which, like this text, is attributed to Someśvara III contains a detailed formula for *puṃlliṅga* (masculine) perfume in the section in *vilepanas*, about which it is said "that perfume is called Masculine (?), which has a divine smell and is captivating." *puṃlliṅgaṃ nāma taṃ prāhur divyagandhaṃ manoharam. Mānasollāsa* of Someśvara, vol. 2, 87, verse 3.
20. Vikramāṅkābhudaya of Someśvara, 12, lines 16–17.
    (i)taratra sugandhāmalakasāndrapuliṅgamṛganābhirkardamacandanadravagandhatailapuṣpaniryāsa karpūrakākatuṇḍadevadāruśarkarāmadhusilhā(rasa)... varttimukhavāsapaṭavāsapānīyavā sādyavandhye[!]saugandhikavyavahāraiḥ...
21. Levey 1961, 397.
22. Gode 1961a.
23. Vogel 1979, 331–332.
24. *athāmbaram nāke 'tigandhadravye ca syād. Trikāṇḍaśeṣa* of Puruṣottamadeva, 86, verse 327–328.
25. Blochmann 1927, 78, 83.
26. Levey 1961, 403–04.
27. Freedman 2008, 8.
28. Kashmiri saffron is of course the exception. Saffron is also exceptional in that its high price derives from the enormous labor involved in producing it, and thus even when grown locally it is a relatively expensive product.
29. Just as we see the abundance of luxury materials in Buddhabhaṭṭa's description of the land of emeralds.
30. Polanyi 1975, 149–151.
31. Ibid., 133.
32. Ibid.
33. Ibid., 135.
34. This whole passage is discussed at length in Chandra 1945, 84–85.
35. Or "precious things."
36. *Mahābhārata* 2.46.35–2.47.2.
37. See the discussion of aloeswood in the nineteenth century in Watt 1889, vol. 1, 279–282. Nowadays, luxury and extinction often go hand in hand, adding another, relatively modern, ethical dimension to the consumption of many precious substances that is often correlated to their consumption by people. According to a recent CITES report, wild aloeswood is virtually exhausted in Arunachal Pradesh; wild *Aquilaria malaccensis* (one of the sources of aloeswood in India) is almost extinct in Assam; and wild aloeswood is very heavily depleted in all surrounding states (CITES, Fourteenth Meeting of the Plants Committee, 2004).
38. The editor of the critical edition notes the alternative reading of *kārūṣe ca* for *vāriṣeṇa*.
39. As noted, this is possibly another type of aloeswood.
40. *Mahābhārata* 2.48.8–11.
41. Note that the list of attributes could refer to separate groups of kings as I have taken it (given the *ca*-s), or all these terms may qualify the *Kirāṭas*.
42. I prefer here the reading of the 1892 edition, which I have not in general used: *ekam ajaryaṃ saṃgatam apahāya kāsty anyā* ... (*Harṣacarita* of Bāṇa, ed. Parab and Vaze, 245).
43. I am unable to make sense of this compound as given in the 1909 edition of A. A. Führer, but the 1892 edition of Parab and Vaze gives *-stabakitapadaṃ*, which I used here, though even this seems unsatisfactory.
44. I take the *mahārhapapadmarāga* to be a mistake in Führer's edition.
45. *Harṣacarita* of Bāṇa, ed. Führer, 291–293.
46. For a short discussion of this material, as well as some examples, see Losty 1982, 9, 139–141. I am also very grateful to Professor S. R. Sarma for providing me with the following additional information about the use of aloeswood bark as a writing material in

Assam: "Books made up of the *agaru* bark are known to the poet Bāṇa; in his *Harṣacarita* (ed. with Śaṅkara's comm., Varanasi 1958, 378) he enumerates *aguru-valkala-kalpita-sañcayāni subhāṣitabhāñji pustakāni* among the gifts brought from Assam. On the method of processing the bark for writing, see Sir Edward Gait, *A History of Assam*, second revised edition, Calcutta and Simla: Thacker, Spink & Co. 1926, p. 375: Appendix D: 'Description of Ahom Manuscript Records.' The processed sheets are called *sāncī pāt*. A notable manuscript copied and illustrated on *agaru* bark is the *Hastividyārṇava* which was published in a facsimile edition: *Hastividyārṇava*, ed. Pratāpachandra Chowdhuri, Gowhati 1976."

47. I am not at all certain what this substance is.
48. *La Kāvyamīmāṃsā* of Rājaśekhara, trans. Stchoupak and Renou, 2. Rājaśekhara refers to this text (*madbhuvanakośam*) *Bhuvanakośa* at the end of *Adhyāya* 17 of the *Kāvyamīmāṃsā* (*Kāvyamīmāṃsā* of Rājaśekhara, ed. Dalal, 98).
49. For an extensive discussion of Rājaśekhara, see Pollock 2006.
50. *Kāvyamīmāṃsā* of Rājaśekhara, ed. Dalal, 89.
51. Ibid., 94.
52. Or possibly *jātī* in the sense of *Jasminum grandiflorum* L., but since all the other plants mentioned here are traded commodities/spices it seems more likely that this means nutmeg. This would have been traded from the small Banda islands in the Malay archipelago, the only source until recent times.
53. *Kāvyamīmāṃsā* of Rājaśekhara, ed. Dalal, 92.
54. Ibid., 93.
55. As described, ibid., 93.
56. Monier Williams gives *Averrhoa acida* = *Cicca acida*.
57. Meulenbeld (1974, 552) gives several possibilities of which *Artemesia vulgaris*, mugwort, is indeed aromatic. He also notes that it is a synonym of *coraka*—*Angelica glauca*, another aromatic. The *nighaṇṭu* glossary of the *Gandhasāra* gives this name in the root section with some synonyms:

    granthiparṇaṃ śukaṃ śīlaṃ śuṣkapuṣpaṃ śūkacchadam // gāṃṭhivana (*m*), *Gandhasāra* of Gangādhara, 46, verse 62.

    Bhānuji Dīkṣita in commenting on this term in the *Amarakośa* gives the vernaculars *granthiparṇa* and *kukkuravadrā*, Amarasiṃha, with the Commentary of Bhānuji Dīkṣit, 2.4.132, 197–198.
58. *Kāvyamīmāṃsā* of Rājaśekhara ed. Dalal, 93.
59. Ibid.
60. Ibid., 94. Stchoupak and Renou (*La Kāvyamīmāṃsā*, 247) are unable to identify this town, though they note it is mentioned in the *Kathāsaritsāgara*. They also point out that one variety of sandalwood mentioned in the *Arthaśāstra* is called *daivasabheya, Arthaśāstra*, 2.11.47. See *Arthaśāstra*, ed. Kangle, part 1, 53.
61. *Capperis aphylla* Roth, a plant related to the caper with edible flower buds called *kurrel* or *karer* in Hindi. See UPI, 102.
62. *Salvadora persica*.
63. The resin of *Commiphora mukul* Engl., also called Indian bdellium, a dark brown resin from a tree related to the myrrh tree, which may be burnt in incense. I discuss this aromatic at length in ch.10. Ingalls, in his translation of the *Subhāṣitaratnakośa*, suggests that this may in fact be ambergris (1965, 546–547). I am inclined not to agree, especially as ambergris, once introduced as an aromatic, was *not* identified as the same substance, and moreover the passage Ingalls discusses (about Dvarkā) appears to use *guggulu* for precisely this sort of characterization of the Western region. Furthermore, this type of myrrh: *guggulu*, or *guggul*, is still quite commonly used today in India.
64. *Karabha* may mean either "young elephant" or a "camel." I am inclined to agree here with the translation of Stchoupak and Renou as "camel."
65. *Kāvyamīmāṃsā* of Rājaśekhara, ed. Dalal, 94.

66. Stchoupak and Renou suggest this is modern Pehoa/Pehowa (*La Kāvyamīmāṃsā*, 248).
67. *Pinus longifolia* Roxb. the resin of which, a form of rosin and source of turpentine, is used in some medieval perfumery formulae.
68. *Cedrus deodara* Loud. Also used in some perfumes.
69. Fly whisks were an indispensable part of royal regalia.
70. *Kāvyamīmāṃsā* of Rājaśekhara, ed. Dalal, 94.
71. I did not use the medical glossaries, since I am, above all, interested in these aromatics as located in a discourse associated with worldly pleasure.
72. For ease of presentation, I abridged the citation format in the following notes. The key here is as follows, including the method of citation:
    A. = *Amarakośa*, by section and verse;
    H. = Hemacandra's *Abhidhānacintāmaṇināmamālā*, by verse number;
    Gs. = *Gandhasāra*, by page number and verse;
    Bh. = the glossary (*nighaṇṭu*) in Bhaṭṭotpala's commentary on the perfumery chapter of the *Bṛhatsaṃhitā* of Varāhamihira (ed. Dvivedi), by page number.
73. A. 2.6.126.
74. A 2.6.126; H. 640.
75. Hemacandra's commentary on this term: *joṅgakagiribhavatvāt.*
76. H. 640.
77. H. 640.
78. *jāpakādribhavatvāj jāpakam.* H. 646 and commentary.
79. A. 2.6.131.
80. A. 2.6.131; H. 641.
81. Hemacandra's comentary on this term: *tailaparṇo girir ākāro 'sty asya.*
82. A. 2.6.131; H. 641.
83. Hemacandra's comentary on this term: *gośīrṣagiribhavatvād.*
84. H. 641 and commentary: *rohaṇācalasya drumo.*
85. Gs. p. 45, verse 48.
86. Bh. p. 941.
87. A .2.6.129.
88. A. 2.6.129.
89. Gs. p. 48, verse 83. Possibly implies civet too, the two products were frequently conflated.
90. Gs. p. 48, verse 83.
91. Bh. p. 941.
92. Bh. p. 941.
93. A. 2.6.124.
94. A. 2.6.124.
95. Bh. p. 941.
96. Side comment on *Gandhasāra* of Gaṅgādhara, 44, verse 29. It would be helpful to examine the manuscript before reading too much into this term.
97. As already noted, saffron from Kashmir is not exotic. It would be interesting to discover whether representations of saffron produced in Kashmir differ generally from those produced elsewhere. In one notable case, the poet Bilhaṇa claimed that people of taste, like actual saffron flowers, were only to be seen in Kashmir (Cox 2011). This conceit relies on the fact that saffron production and Sanskrit literary production/appreciation were known to overlap. One wonders if writers in Southeast Asia ever wrote in a similar manner in Sanskrit about camphor and other local products? If not, why not?
98. *Mahābhārata* 2.28.52–53ab.
99. Pods are also called "cods," implying the scrotum/testicles (as in "cod-piece"), which suggests there was the same confusion in England about the exact origin of the product as in India.
100. For a thematic survey of *subhāṣitas* concerning sandalwood, as well as other important plants as given in collections, see Majumdar 1938, 409–428.
101. *Hitopadeśa* of Nārāyaṇa, 59.

102. Of course, other aspects of sandalwood are exploited in other metaphors, but here we limit ourselves to its dangerous origins.
103. As Professor S. R. Sarma also notes "*Dhātuvāda* is both metallurgy and alchemy" (e-mail to the author, December 23, 2007). For some discussion of *dhātuvāda* see also Sarma 1995, 149–162.
104. The color of certain sapphires is compared to the wings of the bee. According to Amara 2.5.29 *bhramara* = *bhṛṅga*. In the section of the *Mānasollāsa* devoted to the inspection of gemstones, a certain type of sapphire is described as *bhṛṅgapakṣasamaprabhā*, *Mānasollāsa*, 2.4.503, vol. 1, 74.
105. A bright yellow pigment derived from cow bile. Still available in India, it is prepared from cow gallstones, and in my experience it is sold somewhat "under the counter."
106. Professor Sarma also notes: "Perhaps "surabhi," the source of *gorocana*, should be understood as the common cow and not necessarily as the divine wishing cow" (e-mail to the author, December 23, 2007).
107. Professor Sarma again adds: "*Camaraṃ gopucchāo* is interesting. Sanskrit literature generally imagines that the *cāmara* comes from the Himalayan *camarī-mṛga*, i.e. a kind of deer! Here Pherū correctly states that it is an ox and not a deer," ibid.
108. See Gaeffke 1954.
109. Note the use of the peacock tail whisk, almost as an item of regalia, by some Jain ascetics.
110. This could also possibly be *yavādi*, so "barley and so on."
111. Professor S. R. Sarma, who has studied the works of Ṭhakkura Pherū for many years, kindly provided this translation, as well as the many invaluable comments relating to this passage I have noted. I have slightly modified the translation of the final two lines (*Dhātūtpatti* of Ṭhakkura Pherū, 39).

    ruppaṃ ca maṭṭiyāo naï—pavvayareṇuyāu kaṇao ya /
    dhāuvvāo ya puṇo havanti dunnivi mahādhāū // 1
    paṭṭaṃ ca kīḍayāo miyanāhīo havei katthūrī /
    goromayāu duvvā kamalaṃ paṅkāu jāṇeha // 2
    maūraṃ ca gomayāo gorocaṇa honti surahipittāo /
    camaraṃ gopucchāo ahimatthāo maṇī jāṇa // 3
    unnā ya bukkaḍāo danta gaïṃdāu piccha romā (morā?)o /
    cammaṃ pasuvaggāo huyāsaṇaṃ dārukhaṇḍāo // 4
    selāu silāiccaṃ malappavesāu hui javāi varaṃ /
    iya saguṇehi pavittā upattī jaïya nīyāo // 5

112. Zimmermann 1987a.
113. I think it quite likely that many contemporary North Americans would not be prepared to touch a real musk-pod with their bare hands.
114. Pollock 2006, 216.
115. It would be especially interesting to consider references to aromatics in texts from Assam, Java, and Cambodia.

Chapter 8

1. See the excellent discussion of knowledge and commodities in Appadurai 2003, 41–56.
2. Groom 1997, 302–303.
3. Gamble 1922, 259–261.
4. Asouti and Fuller 2008, 116–117, 135. I am also very grateful to Dr. Fuller for answering my questions regarding these theories (e-mail to the author, November 6, 2009).
5. Gamble 1922, 586.
6. Watt 1889–93, vol. 6, part 2 (Sabadilla to Silica), 464.
7. Gamble 1922, 586–587.
8. Fischer 1938, 461; Yule and Burnell 2000 (1903), 789–790.
9. Metcalfe 1935.
10. I often relied on Gode's paper in my selection of pertinent passages (Gode 1961c). Fischer (1938) also provides some analysis of these complexities.

11. Southworth 2005, 76, 239, 274. See also Mayrhofer 1953, part 1, 373.
12. *Nirukta* of Yāska 11.5.
13. Kahrs 1998, 14.
14. *Mahābhāṣya* on Pāṇini 2.2.8.
15. Gode 1961c, 326.
16. *Mahābhārata* 7.58.7–12ab.
17. *Mahābhārata* 9.10.45 ab.
18. *Mahābhārata* 5.166.38.
19. *Mahābhārata* 1.118.19a; 1.118.22a; 1. 213.032c.
20. *Mahābhārata* 7.111.24ab; *Rāmāyaṇa* 2.30.9.
21. *Rāmāyaṇa* 2.70.16.
22. Possibly *Prunus puddum* = *Prunus cerasoides*.
23. For example, *Mahābhārata* 2.10.8.
24. *Arthaśāstra* 2.11.43–56. *Arthaśāstra* of Kauṭalya, part 1, 53, part 2, 115–116.
25. *Arthaśāstra*, 2.11.56, *Arthaśāstra* of Kauṭalya, part 1, 53.
26. HIML vol. 2a, 169.
27. Ibid., 172–173.
28. *Dhanvantarīnighaṇṭuḥ*, ed. P. V. Sharma, 3.1, 91.
29. The identification of *kucandana* as sappan wood is somewhat supported by the fact that one of the Sanskrit synonyms *pataṅga* and cognates are also used in many Indian vernacular languages for this wood. See UPI, 94.
30. *Dhanvantarīyanighaṇṭu*. ed. P. V. Sharma, 3.1–3.3, 91.
31. Ibid. 3.10, 92.
    sarvāṇy etāni tulyāni rasato vīryatas tathā /
    gandhena tu viśeṣaḥ syāt pūrvaṃ śreṣṭhatamaṃ guṇaiḥ // 3.10
32. Perhaps also the white *candana* that Gode hoped to identify in his paper (1961c).
33. *Gandhasāra* of Gaṅgādhara, 49–51, verses 91–118.
34. *Mānasollāsa* of Someśvara, part 2, 85–86. *Viṃśati* 3. Sandalwood = 984 cd–946 ab; Musk = 992 cd–995 ab.
35. Called the *Kastūrīparikṣā* and consisting of one folio. No. 3842 in the *Catalogue of the Anup Sanskrit Library*. NCC vol. 3, 294. I am grateful to Ryan Overbey for bringing this reference to my attention.
36. I rely here very closely on the detailed account of his life and works by S. R. Sarma, given in the introduction to his translation of Thakkura Pherū's work on gemology, the *Rayaṇaparikkhā*, 1–20.
37. See Jackson 1999, 156–157.
38. I closely follow S. R. Sarma's account of this incident. *Rayaṇaparikkhā* of Ṭhakkura Pherū, 4–5. Sarma takes as his source the *Kharataragacchālaṃkāra-yugapradhānācārya-gurvāvalī*, a chronicle of the pontiffs of the Kharataragaccha from the eleventh century until 1336 by Jinapāla. From what little I have read of this text, I agree with Professor Sarma when he writes, "It is an immensely valuable document and deserves close study," ibid., 5. The text itself is pages 1–88 in the *Kharataragaccha-bṛhadgurvāvali* of Jinapāla.
39. On this usage see, Thapar 2004, 361–364. Also Chattopadhyaya 2004.
40. An early use of this term in a Jain context that might be of interest to some readers.
41. *śrīpūjyānām agra eva rājadvāre lakṣasaṃkhyamlecchahindukapratyakṣam yaṣṭimuṣṭilakuṭādipra hāraiḥ kuṭṭayitvā vigopayitvā ca bandī kṛtaḥ.*
    Karataragacchālaṃkāra-yugapradhānācārya-gurvāvalī (p. 67 in *Kharataragaccha-bṛhadgurvāvali* of Jinapāla). Note that page numbers are not consistent in the text as a whole.
42. *Ratnaparīkṣādi Sapt-Granth Saṃgrah* of Ṭhakkura Pherū, 104–106.
43. Ibid., 1–16. Also *Rayaṇaparikkhā* of Ṭhakkura Pherū, trans. S. R. Sarma.
44. *Ratnaparīkṣādi Sapt-Granth Saṃgrah* of Ṭhakkura Pherū, 1–40. Note the page numbers start from "1" again here.
45. Ibid., 75–103.
46. Ibid., 17–38.
47. This text has been published with translation and mathematical commentary by S. R. Sarma, Takanori Kusuba, Takao Hayashi, and Michio Yano, or SaKHYa.

48. *Ratnaparīkṣādi Sapt-Granth Saṃgrah* of Ṭhakkura Pherū, 39–44.
49. As pointed out in the introduction to *Rayaṇaparikkhā*, ed. S. R. Sarma, 11. For the verse in question see *Ratnaparīkṣādi Sapta-Grantha Saṃgraha* of Ṭhakkura Pherū, 38, verse 149.
50. It is interesting to remark that Sir Isaac Newton was for over twenty-seven years the master of the mint.
51. Baxandall 1988, 11.
52. Ibid., 86.
53. As with the literati and puns. Baxandall makes a very similar point, ibid., 91.
54. Ramachandra Rao notes *daśāṅgha* incense is commonly used in worship (2005, 125).
55. As part of an alternative twofold classification of sandalwood as *beṭṭa* and *sukvaḍi*. Evidently, this latter name for a type of sandalwood was more widely used in the later medieval and early modern periods. *Beṭṭa* means "mountain" in Kannada and Kodagu according to the *Dravidian Etymological Dictionary* (Burrow and Emeneau 1961), but I have not been able to interpret *sukvaḍi*. The *Rājanighaṇṭu* passage begins as follows:

    "Sandalwood is said to be of two types, called *beṭṭa* and *sukvaḍi*. *Beṭṭa* is moist when cut, and *sukvaḍi* is dry on its own accord. The mountains located in the vicinity of Malaya mountain are called *beṭṭa*. And the sandalwood produced there is to be called *beṭṭa* in some opinions."

    candanaṃ dvividhaṃ proktaṃ beṭṭasukvaḍisaṃjñakam. beṭṭaṃ tu sārdravicchedaṃ svayaṃ śuṣkaṃ tu sukvaḍi. malayādrisamīpasthāḥ parvatā beṭṭasaṃjñakāḥ. tajjātaṃ candanaṃ yat tu beṭṭavācyam kvacinmate (*Rājanighaṇṭusahito Dhanvantarīyanighaṇṭu*, 93).
56. HIML vol. 2a, 269–270.
57. *Arthaśāstra* of Kauṭalya, 2.11.56, 53.
58. Perhaps the Nilgiri mountains where sandalwood does grow.
59. Uncertain.
60. This quite possibly refers to the East African town of Malindi, on the coast of present day Kenya, making this a rare, very specific reference to an African town in an Indic language text of this period. Indian sandalwood from *Santalum album* is, of course, not found in Africa, but a variety known as East African sandalwood from *Osyris tenuifolia* Engl. is indeed found there. It appears that sandalwood (presumably this variety) was indeed an item of export from East African ports in the thirteenth century. See Ricks 1970, 355. Though some of his citations are unreliable, Ricks mentions the account of the products of this coast by a Chinese writer of the thirteenth century CE, Zhao Rugua, who notes that Zanzibar (Ts'ŏng-pa) was a source of yellow sandalwood (for the passage Ricks refers to, see Hirth and Rockhill 1911, 126–127). I am very grateful to Professor Ali Asani and Ryan Overbey for their comments on this matter.
61. Professor Sarma suggests this may be Sanskrit *gomukhī*.
62. Possibly the same as the *barbarika* variety of *candana* mentioned in the *Dhanvantarinighaṇṭu*.
63. Again, Professor S. R. Sarma has kindly provided me with a translation of this text, as well as many useful comments. The translation of the final verse is in part my own.

    Ratnaparīkṣādi Sapt-Granth Saṃgrah of Ṭhakkur-Pherū, 43–44:
    malayagiri pavvayaṃmi siricaṃdaṇataruvaraṃ ca ahinilayaṃ /
    aïsīyalaṃ suyaṃdhaṃ taggaṇdhe sayalavaṇagaṇdhaṃ // 47
    siricaṃdaṇu taha caṃdaṇu nīlavaī sūkaḍissa jāi tiyaṃ /
    taha ya malindī kauhī vavvaru iṃya caṃdaṇaṃ cchavihaṃ // 48
    vīsaṃ vāraṭṭha igaṃ tihāu pā visuva caṃdaṇaṃ seraṃ /
    paṇa tiya du pāu ṭaṃkā jaïthala caü tinni kami mullaṃ // 49
    siricandanassa ciṇhaṃ vanne pīyaṃ ca ghasiya rattābhaṃ /
    sāe kaḍuyaṃ sagaṃṭhi saṃtāva nāsayaraṃ // 50
64. It would appear that during the reign of Quṭb al-Dīn Mubārak Shāh, one *taṅka* was worth 48 *jītals* (Wright 1936, 107–109). Professor S. R. Sarma generously provided me with a useful analysis and tabular presentation of this data:

    "Pherū grades the quality of sandalwood in a scale of 20 (*visuva*). See verse 52 where the musk from Nepal and Kashmir is said to have the grade 20, and that from elsewhere is

Table N.2

S.No.	*Name of the variety*	*Quality in a scale of 20 (visuva)*	*Price of 1 ser*
1	*Śrīcandana*	20	5 taṅka
2	*Nīlavaī*	12	3 taṅka
3	*Sūkaḍḍissa*	8	2 taṅka
4	*Malindī*	1	1/4 taṅka
5	*Kaūhī*	1/3	1/12 taṅka (4 jītals)
6	*Vavvaru*	¼	1/16 taṅka (3 jītals)

Source: S. R. Sarma

graded at 10 or 8. The first half of verse 49 mentions the grades of the six varieties, where the *śrīcandana* is stated to have the grade of 20. The second half of the verse mentions the prices of 1 ser of each of these six varieties. This can be tabulated as follows:" [table N.2]

65. We know of the weights and measures, and some prices of the time of 'Ala' al-Dīn, as well as of the weights and measures of the time of Fīrūz Shāh Tughluq (reigned 1351–1388). The information on weights for the periods gives slightly differing modern weights for the sandalwood (Lal 1967, 197–225):

    1. In the time of 'Ala' al-Dīn, according to the writer Ferishta:
    1 *man* = 40 *sers*
    1 *ser* = 24 *tolas*

    S. R. Sarma, in discussing the weights given in the *Rayaṇparikkhā* (73–74) notes:
    1 *tola* = 11 grams, applied to Ferishta system given above, 1 *ser* = 264 grams

    2. In time of Firoz Tughlaq:
    1 *man* = 40 *sers*
    1 *ser* = 70 *misqāls*
    1 *misqāl* = approx 72 grains

    So, in this latter system:

    1 *ser* = 5040 grains avoirdupois
    1 pound av. = 7000 grains av.
    1 pound av. = 453.59237 grams
    so 1 *ser* = 326.59 grams

    So a *ser* may be either 264 g or 326 g—very approximately 2/3 to 3/4 of a pound av.
66. Professor S. R. Sarma also adds: "The prices of superior gems like diamonds are given in gold tanka; inferior gems and aromatics in silver tanka, which is the standard currency" (e-mail to the author, December 23, 2007).
67. Pollock 1985, 500.
68. Latour 2004, 210.
69. From *Boswellia serrata*.
70. *Haramekhalā*, commentary on final verse of part 5, 5.273.
71. *Gandhasāra* of Gaṅgādhara, 35–36, verses 1–6.
72. See McHugh, forthcoming.
73. *Gandhasāra* of Gaṅgādhara, 36, verses 10–11.
74. Ibid., 36, verses 14cd–17.
75. Ibid., 37, verses 24cd–29.

76. Ibid., 38, verses 30–32ab.
77. Ibid., 38, verses 32 cd–33ab.
78. Ibid., 38, verses 33 cd–34 ab.
79. I rely on the relevant text given as an appendix to Vyas' edition of the *Gandhasāra* of Gaṅgādhara as I have been unable to see a copy of the original edition containing this section. I have also consulted the excellent article by P. K. Gode in which he brings attention to the material on perfumery in this text (1961d).
80. HIML vol. 2a, 664–665. See also Wujastyk 1984.
81. Note that both this chapter, and also Pherū's text on aromatics, in addition to material on fakery and evaluation respectively, also give a small number of formulae for blending the aromatics.
82. I follow Meulenbeld's detailed summary (HIML vol. 2a, 657).
83. *Rasaratnākara, Vādikhaṇḍa, Adhyāya* 9, 89–91 (*candana*), 92–96 (*karpūra*), 104–114 (*kastūri*), 115–118 (*kuṅkuma*) respectively.
84. This somewhat difficult passage is a lot easier to read if we take *-vāda* as neuter. My translation is somewhat tentative, and I am grateful to Larry McCrea for his advice on this:
    saṃsāre sārabhūtaṃ sakalasukhakaraṃ suprabhūtaṃ dhanaṃ vai
    tat sādhyaṃ sādhakendrair gurumukhavidhinā vakṣyate tasya siddhyai /
    ratnādīnāṃ viśeṣāt karaṇam iha śubhaṃ gandhavādaṃ samagraṃ
    jñātvā tat tat susiddhaṃ hy anubhavapathagaṃ pāvanaṃ paṇḍitānām // 1
    Gandhasāra of Gaṅgādgara, appendix 12, 170.
85. It is interesting to remark how, in this period, the status of *guggulu* has fallen since the time of the references to it in the *Atharvaveda* and those in the *Mahābhārata* that we see in ch. 10. Where it was once the most prestigious resin, it is used to fake other aromatics in this passage. This is not to say that *guggulu* ceased to be used as an aromatic, just that its relative prestige appears to have changed over time.
86. *Gandhasāra* of Gaṅgādhara, appendix 12, 170. Neem tree: *Azadirachta indica* A. Juss = *Melia azadirachta*.
87. Latour 1999, 151.
88. Zimmermann 1987a, 206.

Chapter 9

1. I offer the briefest account of *avadāna* literature and its context, since the purpose of this section is to examine the mercantile imaginary reflected here. Also Rotman has produced thorough studies of both this genre and its mercantile context (2003, 2008, 2009).
2. *The Divyāvadāna*. For the *Pūrṇāvadāna* see 24–55.
3. Rotman 2008, 19.
4. For a recent detailed discussion of this, see Rotman 2003, 38–64.
5. Fortunately Tatelman 2001 has produced a translation and thorough study of this text, and thus I provide a basic introduction to move as soon as possible to our examination of the commercial aspects of aromatics in the text. I use here Tatelman's translation as a basis for my summary. There is also an excellent translation of this text by Rotman 2008, 71–117.
6. Now the village of Sopāra, 37 miles north of Mumbai. See Tatelman 2001, 1–2 and notes.
7. Or sealing, or perhaps both.
8. *Divyāvadāna*, 26. I provide my own translation for all the passages of this text that we shall examine in order to emphasis certain similarities with other texts I explored in this book.
9. Sastri discusses the ideal education of other groups as represented in the *avadāna* literature (Sastri 1945, 9–10). See also Rotman 2008, 402, note 216.
10. *Divyāvadāna*, 100.
11. As Cowell and Neill observe in the note to this passage, these replacements are found on pages 3, 26 and 58 of their edition. Ibid., 100.

12. As Tatelman states (2001, 83, notes 15, 16), wood examination is mentioned in the Tibetan version as presented by Shackelton Bailey (1959, 174).
13. I retain the narrative present in translation because I find it works quite well in English and conveys the rather fast-moving narrative tone of the original. As Rotman notes, it appears that Pūrṇa takes the sandalwood on credit (2008, 404, note 246). *Divyāvadāna*, 30–31.
14. See Burnouf 1876, 557–559; see also the numerous references to this type of sandalwood in Rotman 2009.
15. Or explicitly learned, according to the Tibetan version.
16. *Divyāvadāna*, 31.
17. Ibid.
18. *rājñaś cakravartino 'rthāya dhāryate*, *Divyāvadāna*, 42. There is, in fact, a technical term in Sanskrit to refer to a royal monopoly, *prakhyāta*, though it is not used here. In the *Mānavadharmaśāstra* certain items are referred to as *rājñaḥ prakhyātabhāṇḍāni*, *Mānavadharmaśāstra*, 8.399 in *Mānavadharmaśāstra*, ed. Olivelle, 188 and note, 740. Wezler has provided a good discussion of this term as found in both the *Mānavadharmaśāstra* and the *Arthaśāstra* (Wezler 2000, 496–501).
19. Kopytoff 2003, 73.
20. What exactly is implied by this term is not clear, though for our purposes what matters is that this building is substantially made of ox-head sandalwood. For a discussion of this, see Tatelman 2001, 144 and notes. Also Rotman 2008, 408, note 307.
21. *Divyāvadāna*, 42–43.
22. Ibid., 43.
23. I am grateful to Phyllis Granoff for highlighting the importance of rock crystal in this narrative (personal communication).
24. Strong 1977, 396. See also Tatelman 2001, 143–144.
25. Rotman 2008, 151–153.
26. Evidently, this is a Buddhist attempt to incorporate the Indra festival; here Indra is a Brahmin who converts to Buddhism, the pole is the measure of the Buddha, and it is the Buddha who gives Indra permission to establish this festival. See also Rotman 2009, 123. For a study of the Indra festival see Baltutis 2008.
27. *Divyāvadāna*, 262–289. I am also very grateful to Andy Rotman for providing me with a draft of his translation of this text.
28. *Cullavagga* 5 .8. *The Vinaya Piṭaka*, ed. Oldberg, vol. 2. For a translation see *Vinayapiṭaka*, trans. Horner, vol. 5(*Cullavagga*), 149–152. A similar story occurs in other sources as Rotman notes (2009, 233, n. 28). In the version that Rotman notes is contained in the *Divyāvadāna*, the *Jyotiṣka-avadāna*, the bowl is made of ox-head sandalwood, as we would expect from that text (*Divyāvadāna*, 274, line 19). In this version, however, the bowl is not broken, and sandalwood is not mentioned in the subsequent list of permissible bowls (but neither is it mentioned as a material for bowls to be rejected).
29. On this object, see Strong 2004, 63–64.
30. For an English translation see Mitra 1882, 101. For a Sanskrit edition see *Lalitavistara, Raritavisutara no kenkyū*, ed. Kōichi Hokazono, 402.
31. Mitra suggests "wood that has the essence of serpents in it" (1882, 115). The same variety also appears in other Buddhist texts (e.g., *Saddharmapuṇḍarīkasūtra* 237, line 24; *Sukhāvatīvyūha* 237, line 29), and a comparison of Buddhist and other texts in terms of varieties of sandalwood might show some interesting patterns. Might, for example, *uragasāra* sandalwood be more associated with the luxury material hyperbole seen in texts considered more Mahāyāna in flavor, and the *gośīrṣa* variety be more common in narrative contexts that portray a world of mercantile abundance? Are such differences related to historical period, to region, to educational practices and lexicons, to an undiscovered coded meaning of these sandalwood varieties, or even to an actual division in usage of real sandalwood in practice?
32. *Lalitavistara, Raritavisutara no kenkyū*, ed. Kōichi Hokazono, 404.
33. Mitra, 1882, 182. *Raritavisutara no kenkyū*, 526.

34. For a detailed recent discussion of this image, together with thorough notes and bibliography, see Swearer 2004, 14–24. See also the detailed discussion in Soper 1959, 259–265.
35. *Bṛhatsaṃhitā*, trans. M. R. Bhat, 59.5, vol. 2, 565; 79.2, vol. 2, 729.
36. Cort 2010, 194. For a definitive recent discussion of this sandalwood Jina, see Cort, ch. 4.
37. I am painfully aware that it is hard to be certain of statements such as this, especially given the vast extent of Sanskrit texts, as well as the uncertain date of many texts. I would hope that future scholarship will complicate this picture by paying attention to the uses of sandalwood as described in texts.
38. I will not concern myself here with the issue of whether these objects actually ever existed—however, we can be certain that people told stories about them and imagined them.
39. See Tatelman 2001 appendices 1 and 2 for translations of the *Puṇṇovādasuttavaṇṇanā* from the *Papañcasūdanī*, and the *Puṇṇatheragāthāvaṇṇanā* from the *Paramatthadīpanī* respectively. On the *Papañcasūdanī*, see von Hinüber 1997, 112–123. On the *Paramatthadīpanī*, see von Hinüber 1997, 136–142.
40. Tatelman 2001, 182. For the Pali, see *Papañcasūdanī* of Buddhaghosa, part 5, suttas 131–152, 88.
41. Tatelman 2001, 190. For the Pali, see *Theragāthā-Aṭṭhakathā Paramatthadīpanī*, vol. 1, 230.
42. On the date and location of Buddhaghosa, see von Hinüber 1997, 102–103. On Dhammapāla, see von Hinüber 1997, 136–137; and also Pieris 1978.
43. "He didn't distinguish between being cut by a blade and being anointed with sandalwood paste" (Rotman 2008, 94, 407 note 294). Reconstructed from *Divyāvadāna*, 282, line 2: *vāsīcandanakalpo*. Monius notes that in the *Periyapurāṇam*, a twelfth-century Tamil hagiographical text, Mūrtti, "denied access to sandalwood by an evil Jain king begins to grind his own arm against a stone." Again, sandalwood is also rather vividly contrasted with tactile pain (Monius 2004, 114).
44. *Aṅgavijjā*, intro., 41.
45. Ibid., 48. The text in question is *sāravaṃtesu heraṇṇikasuvaṇṇikacaṃdaṇadussikasaṃjukārakā devadā veti viṇṇeyā* (*Aṅgavijjā*, 160, line 27).
46. Cutler 1983, 433.
47. Penny 1993, 30.
48. Malgouyres 2003, 11. I translate the French.
49. See under *candana* in Böhtlingk and Roth.
50. Malgouyres 2003, 187–189.
51. See Cutler 1983, 455.
52. Coomaraswamy, 1939, 377. See also the observations of Daud Ali on the importance of ornament in early medieval India (2004, 162–182); as well as Dehejia's recent discussion of adornment in South Asian Art (2009).
53. Mrozik 2007.
54. Hopkins 2007.
55. *Divyāvadāna*, 45.
56. Of course, the sandalwood Jina Cort discusses is also a sandalwood icon of a liberated person. Yet, as noted, since that story seems derived from the story of the sandalwood Buddha, I do not wish to make too much use of the sandalwood Jina narrative to support my theory. Nevertheless, the narrative of the sandalwood Jina by no means contradicts what I propose. In his comprehensive study of narratives of Jain image worship, Cort also mentions that in Digambara image-consecration rites pieces of sandalwood are burnt in order to reenact the cremation of the deceased body of the Jina (2010, 23–24). This would very much seem to support my theory, as here sandalwood is used as a material substitute for an enlightened being. But, again, I do not wish to make too much of this, since as we have seen, sandalwood has long been a prestigious component of funeral pyres, and it is not clear to what extent wood used in this manner counts as an artifact.
57. See Cort 2010, 13–16.
58. I translate Bandmann 1969, 90.

59. As Tatelman (2001, 140) similarly notes: "Pūrṇa's rescue of the merchants transforms the fruit of mercantile ambition into an edifice that unites in itself the material substance of wealth and the spiritual 'substance' of devotion."
60. Although, for many years, sandalwood oil was particularly valued as a treatment for gonorrhea, including in the colonial context. See "Santalum" in Watt 1889.
61. Although scholars of these texts are generally quite aware of the conventional cooling powers and economic value of sandalwood—I do not wish to criticize a straw man.

Chapter 10

1. The interesting question of the worship of fully liberated beings in Jainism who by definition do not possess aesthetic sensibilities (or sensibilities of any variety) has been well addressed. See Babb 1996; Humphrey and Laidlaw 1994; Cort 2010.
2. See Fitzgerald 2003, 810–811. Cf. Hiltebeitel 2005, 241–261.
3. Fitzgerald 2006, 258.
4. *Mahābhārata*, critical edition, vol. 17.1, intro., 47.
5. For example, giving perfumes is said to make one fragrant: "With respect to a gift of perfume, a man becomes fragrant" *Mahābhārata* 13.57.35 (*gandhapradāne surabhir naraḥ syāt*). This is a very clear example of what Strong called the "rūpalogical fruit" of a deed. This is a term he created when discussing offerings in a Buddhist context to describe certain correspondences between the physical object of a gift and its karmic, physical/*rūpa*-related consequences (1979).
6. Oberlies notes this exceptional plural (*oṣadhyo*) of *oṣadhi* f. (2003, 82–83).
7. According to the critical edition, several manuscripts, including the "vulgate" of Nīlakaṇṭha have in place of those rather confusing lines:

   "With him gods are indeed satisfied, and satisfied, they impart prosperity."
   tasya tuṣyanti vai devās tuṣṭāḥ puṣṭiṃ dadaty api.
8. *mālya*: suited to garlands.
9. Possibly this implies secret rites.
10. It is tempting to read accusative *martyān* in place of *martyānām*. I am very grateful to Stephanie Jamison for her comments on this line and on the meaning of the root √*bhū* in this context (e-mail to author, February 26, 2009). I am also grateful to Guy Leavitt for his comments on this line.
11. In light of what we have learned in this book about the term *sāra* "(fragrant) heartwood," I have used here another reading that the critical edition notes is found in many manuscripts. The critical edition itself gives *saralaś* meaning pine resin, from *Pinus roxburghii*, yet as we shall see, this does not correspond to the breakdown of types of incense given in the subsequent discussion, where the gods and *asuras* enjoy resins, other beings such as *yakṣas* prefer heartwoods such as aloeswood, and humans enjoy what would appear to be compounded incenses. This context suggests that *sāriṇaś* (heartwood-possessing things) is a better reading.
12. Indian "frankincense" from *Boswellia serrata*.
13. Or the resin of *Vateria indica*, Sharma 1996, 386.
14. *Mahābhārata* 13.101.1–43.
15. In *adhyāyas* 58 and 60 of the critical edition.
16. *Mahābhārata* 13.58.19.
17. See *Mahābhārata*, 17.1 intro. 43–45. Dandekar also notes in connection with the manuscripts that "it is not without significance that the MS. of Ca on *Dānadharma* has become available as a separate MS. with separate numbering of folios" (ibid., 44).
18. See HDS, vol. 2, part 2, 837–842 for a brief summary of Vedic materials relating to *dāna*.
19. The implications of *etasminn antare* in this context are not entirely clear, though perhaps the period in question is after the origin of *dharma*, for dharma is said to originate "immediately after" the origin of *tapas*: *tasmād anantaram*.

20. *tulyajātaya*—this implies the same nature as either nectar or poison, or alternatively of an "indifferent" nature i.e., neither simply nectar or poison.
21. We might recall the prominence of the odors of plant parts in the earlier Buddhist classifications of odor.
22. Wujastyk 2003–2004; also see Zimmermann 1987a, 131, 145, 198, 220.
23. Wujastyk 2003–2004, 347; ibid., 366.
24. *Niryāsa*: a term used to classify one type of incense in the passage.
25. *Mahābhārata*, 1.16.25–26.
26. Zimmermann 1987a, 102.
27. One of the basic concepts of Indian pharmacology—though the meaning may not be so specific in this case. Perhaps this term is here synonymous with *śakti*, as *vīrya* sometimes is in medical literature. See Meulenbeld 1987, 11–14.
28. The sense qualities here are not in any recognizable order as discussed in ch. 2.
29. This twofold classification of odor is not the same as the more complex classification we examined from the *Mahābhārata* in ch. 2. There I suggested that the twofold classification was possibly a later development in the brahmanic schools of thought. If that is the case, then a later date for this passage is possible.
30. Though we should note Coomaraswamy's association of *yakṣas* with the "Water Cosmology." We will return to Coomaraswamy's important work on *yakṣas* at the end of the chapter. (Coomaraswamy 1993).
31. Note that at this time roses do not appear to be known in India, avoiding the problem of how to classify them in this system.
32. *Īśānaśivagurudevapaddhati* of Iśānaśivagurudevamisra, part 3, 52, verses 74–75.
33. Note that in *Cooking the World*, Charles Malamoud explains, "The very odour of the cooked food, the *pakvagandha*, is a constituent part of the sacrificed animal. In the *aśvamedha*, the dismembered victim sates the hunger of every creature: while the serpents feed on the odour of its blood, the birds receive the odour of the cooked flesh as their portion" (1996, 38).
34. I am grateful to Professor Michael Witzel for his comments on this matter, as well as to Professor Stephanie Jamison (e-mail to the author, February 23, 2007). This particular verse is highlighted by Keith 1925, 286–287, fn. 1.
35. RV 7.11.5, my emphasis. *Rig-Veda-Sanhita* ed. Müller, vol. 3, 942–943.
36. Kane gives a good account of this complicated rite characterized by the prominence of the number seventeen: it lasts for seventeen days, seventeen animals are sacrificed, and so on. It was performed in the autumn, and also involves a ritualized chariot race (HDS, vol. 2, part 2, 1206–1212).
37. *Mahābhārata* 5.119.9–12.
38. For a recent short bibliography of the literature on the date of this text see Willis 2009, 331, note 261.
39. *Mahābhārata* 12.323.12ab.
40. Malamoud 1996, 36.
41. *Madhuca indica* (= *Bassia latifolia*).
42. We should note that *niryāsa* was used in the passage to refer to the resins that flowed into the churning milk ocean, and which appear to be partly responsible for the production of nectar (*amṛta*).
43. Zysk 1993, 14.
44. For the numerous references in the *Śrauta Sūtras*, see "bdellium" in the index to volume 2 of Dandekar 1962.
45. *Taittirīya Saṃhitā* 6.2.8.6
46. *Śatapatha Brāhmaṇa* 3.5.2.16.
47. *Aitareya Brāhmaṇa* 1.28.
48. *Rigveda Brahmanas: The Aitareya and Kauṣītaki Brāhmaṇas of the Rigveda*, trans. Keith, 129. See also *Das Aitareya Brāhmaṇa*, ed. Aufrecht, 23.
49. Keith's translation. *Taittiriya Sanhita*, ed. Keith, part 2, 6.2.8.6. Harvard Oriental Series, vol. 19, 510. See also *Die Taittirīya-Saṃhitā*, ed. Weber, part 2 kāṇḍa 5–7, p. 167.

50. *Śatapatha Brāhmaṇa* 3.5.2.16. *Śatapatha-Brāhmaṇa*, trans. Eggeling, part 2, books 3 and 4, 125. See also *Śatapatha Brāhmaṇa*, ed. Weber, 272.
51. Dated by MacDonell to no later than 400 BCE. Tokunaga dates the two recensions between the first and fifth centuries CE and between the seventh and eleventh centuries CE. This uncertainty as to the date need not concern us terribly here—what is most important about the reference to Agni's flesh becoming *guggulu* in this text is that is was evidently a relatively widespread notion in early orthodox Vedic circles. For a full discussion of the controversy over the date of this text see Patton 1996, 11–12, and 465–474. A comment by Vyas in his introduction to the *Gandhasāra* first made me aware of this passage, and this led to my discovering the other Vedic passages (*Gandhasāra* of Gaṅgādhara, intro. 22).
52. *Bṛhaddevatā* 7.78. Translated by MacDonell in *The Bṛhad-Devatā attributed to Śaunaka*, ed. and trans. MacDonell, part 2, translation and notes, 271. See also ibid., part 1, text, 85.
53. Michael Witzel, e-mail to author, August 16, 2011.
54. *Pañcaviṃśa Brāhmaṇa* 24.13. 2–5. Caland's translation, and I added the Sanskrit terms. *Pañcaviṃśa-Brāhmaṇa*, trans. Caland, 615–616. Sanskrit: *Tāṇḍya Mahābrāhmaṇa*, ed. A. Vedāntavāgīśa, vol. 2, 757–759.
55. Hiltebeitel 2001, 131. Quoted in Fitzgerald 2003, 807.
56. Both quotes from Granoff 2008, 60.
57. Frequently mentioned in the *Mahābhārata*, but as we have seen this is generally in the form of a paste.
58. Coomaraswamy 1993, 80.
59. Ibid., 73–74.
60. Hopkins 1915, 68–69.
61. This is doubly unfortunate, since this association of *yakṣas* with water plants might have further strengthened Coomaraswamy's "Water Cosmology" thesis.
62. See Willis 2009, 112; and Thieme 1957–58. For a discussion of early medieval court protocol that reveals similarities with the later terminology of worship see Ali 2004, ch. 3. The tribute gift to King Harṣa we examined also shows many similarities with later *pūjā* rites, including the more sophisticated nature of the offerings and the reciprocal gift of favor. The offering of aromatics such as incense to a king as a tribute gift is, of course, quite different to the king's daily consumption of his own aromatics prepared by servants. Noting such distinctions and the terminologies associated with them might be useful in understanding later forms of temple worship in future research.
63. Bühnemann 1999, 305.
64. Or possibly "mixed with."
65. *Īśānaśivagurudevapaddhati* of Iśānaśivagurudevamiśra, part 3, 54.

    dhūpadravyeṣu sarveṣu śreṣṭhaḥ kṛṣṇāgarur bhavet // 86
    karpūram adhikaśreṣṭham agarūpahitaṃ tathā /
    guggulur mahiṣākṣākhyaḥ śreṣṭha eva śivapriyaḥ // 87
    candanośīrake caiva madhyame tu prakīrtite /
    śrīvāsasarjāv adhamau tato lākṣā ghṛtaṃ madhu // 88
    sarvair etaiḥ sitopetair dhūpa ukto daśāṅgakaḥ /

66. I expand the observations of Willis to include the impact of donations on long-distance trade (Willis 2009, 163–164).
67. *Gandhasāra* of Gaṅgādhara, 26, verses 19–25.
68. *Gandhasāra* of Gaṅgādhara, 26, verse 20:

    kāntākesarajaladharabhujaṅgagurukarajacapalajatusarjaiḥ /
    madhupavimṛdu(di)to dhūpas tripuraharānandako bhavati //

69. Or *nāgakesara*.
70. Dehejia 2009, 17.
71. In the discourses and practices of religious asceticism engagement with materiality and the pleasures of the senses is, of course, quite the inverse of the worldly life. See Ali 1998, 159–184.

Epilogue

1. *yuktaṃ pāpakṛtāṃ gandhair*, *Mahābhārata*, 18.2.17.
2. *kuṇapadurgandham aśivaṃ*, *Mahābhārata*, 18.2.22.
3. *Mahābhārata*, 5.34.32. As discussed in Sternbach 1963, 46.
4. And a book such as Süskind's *Perfume* is acclaimed as a striking anomaly.
5. For a rare and amusing exception see the Jain story of "The Prince who Loved Sweetmeats" translated by Granoff 2006, 173–176. This story also contains a verse that notes that the musk from the musk deer can turn into a stench. Given the importance of corporeal wind and breaths, a study of the history of the fart in India is a desideratum.

Appendix

1. The NCC also mentions a medical text called the *Parimalapārijāta* that I have not had the opportunity to examine (NCC vol. 11, 229). It is possible that this text might deal with perfumery.
2. For a list of references see P. V. Sharma's introduction to the *Cakradatta-Ratnaprabhā*, 16.
3. *Ṭoḍarānanda*, 386. To illustrate the textual sharing, the section on civet (*khaṭṭāśo 'nūpajaḥ*) attributed to the *Gandhatantra* by Niścalakara (*Cakradatta-Ratnaprabhā*, 395), is contained in the longer section on civet in the *Ṭoḍarānanda* 390, verse 882.
4. *Ṭoḍarānanda*, 384.
5. For references see P. V. Sharma's introduction to the *Cakradatta-Ratnaprabhā*, 21.
6. Ibid., 16.
7. Ibid., text, 390, 391. In the discussion of *nakha* the part attributed to Bhavadeva lists just the varieties of *nakha*, and that from the "Bengali treatise" discusses the uses of the varieties. The two passages are stylistically and metrically quite different so this might well be another text.
8. *Adbhūtasāgara* of Ballālasena, Benares, ed. M. Jha, 273. On the date Pingree notes: "Ballalasena began the *Adbhutasāgara* in Śaka 1090 = A.D. 1168; it was completed by his son and successor, Lakṣmaṇasena, who ruled Bengal from *ca.* 1178 till *ca.* 1200" (series A vol. 4, 237).
9. *Ṭoḍarānanda*, 376.
10. For references see P. V. Sharma's introduction to the *Cakradatta-Ratnaprabhā*, 21.
11. For example, *Ṭoḍarānanda*, 406, verse 961 on *nakhī* is very similar to the quote from Pṛthvīsiṃha at *Ratnaprabhā*, 390. *Ṭoḍarānanda* on purification, 385, verse 863ab = Pṛthvīsiṃha at *Ratnaprabhā*, 391.

BIBLIOGRAPHY

Abbreviations

HDS Kane, P. V. 1930–1962. *History of Dharmaśāstra (Ancient and Mediaeval Religious and Civil Law in India)*. Poona: Bhandarkar Oriental Research Institute.

HIML Meulenbeld, G. J. 1999–2002. *A History of Indian Medical Literature*. Groningen: E. Forsten.

MW Monier-Williams, M. 2000 (1899). *A Sanskrit-English Dictionary*. New ed. Oxford: Oxford University Press.

NCC Raghavan, V., ed. 1949–. *New Catalogus Catalogorum: An Alphabetical Register of Sanskrit and Allied Works and Authors*. Madras: University of Madras.

PTS Rhys Davids, T. W., and Wilhelm Stede, eds. 1959. *Pali-English Dictionary*. London: Pali Text Society.

T Taishō shinshū daizōkyō, ed. Takakusu Junjirō and Watanabe Kagyoku. Tōkyō: Taishō Issaikyō Kankōkai,Taishō 13-shōwa 7 [1924–1932].

UPI Ambasta, S. P., ed. 2000. *The Useful Plants of India*. New Delhi: National Institute of Science Communication, Council of Scientific & Industrial Research.

Primary Sources

Abhidhānakintāmaṇi of Hemacandra. Ed. O. Boehtlingk and C Rieu. St. Petersburg: Kaiserliche Akademie der Wissenschaften, 1847.

Abhidhānacintāmaṇināmamālā of Hemacandra. Ed. Śrī Hemacandravijayo Gaṇiḥ. Ahmedabad: Jain Sahitya Vardhak Sabha, 1975–1976.

Abhidharmakośa of Vasubandhu. Ed. and trans. B. C. Hall, "Vasubandhu on 'Aggregates, Spheres, and Components': Being Chapter one of the Abhidharmakośa." PhD diss., Harvard University, 1983.

Abhidharmakośa and Bhāṣya of Ācārya Vasubandhu with the Sphūtārthā Commentary of Ācārya Yaśomitra. Ed. Swāmī Dwārikādās Śāstrī. Varanasi: Bauddha Bharati, 1998.

Ācārañga-sūtra. Ed. W. Schubring. In *Abhandlungen für die Kunde des Morgenlandes*, Band XII.4. Leipzig: Deutsche Morgenlänische Gesellschaft, 1910.

Adbhutasāgara of Ballālasena. Ed. M. Jha. Benares: Prābhākarī Yantrālaya, [1905?].

Das Aitareya Brāhmaṇa. Ed. T. Aufrecht. Bonn: Adolph Marcus, 1879.

Amarasiṃha. *The Nāmalingānuśāsana of Amarasinha with the Commentary (Vyākhyāsudhā or Rāmāśramī) of Bhānuji Dīkṣit (Son of the Grammarian Bhattoji Dīkṣit)*. Ed. Paṇḍit Śivadatta. Bombay: Tukārām Jāvajī, 1905.

Amarasiṃha. *The Nāmalingānuśāsana (Amarakosha) of Amarasimha with the Commentary (Amarakoshodghāṭana) of Kṣīrasvāmin*. Ed. K. G Oka. Poona: Law Printing Press, 1913.

Amarasiṃha. *Amarakosa with the Commentary of Maheśvara*. Ed. V. Jhalakikar and R. G. Bhandarkar. Delhi: Eastern Book Linkers, 2002.

Añgavijjā. Ed. Muni Shri Punyavijayaji. Banaras: Prakrit Text Society, 1957.

Aristotle. *On the Soul, Parva Naturalia, On Breath*. Trans. W. S. Hett. Loeb Classical Library. Cambridge, MA: Harvard University Press, 1936.

Arthaśāstra of Kauṭalya. *The Kauṭilīya Arthaśāstra*. Ed. R. P. Kangle. Bombay: University of Bombay, 1963.

Atthasālinī of Buddhaghosa. London: Pali Text Society, 1897.

Bhagavatīsūtram Jainācāryajainadharmadivākarapūjyaśrīghānasīlālajīmahārājaviracitayā prameyacandrikākhyayā vyākhyayā samalaṅkṛtam. Rājakoṭa: A. Bhā. Śve. Sthā Jainaśāstroddhā rasamitipramukhaḥ Śreshṭhi-Maṅgaladāsabhāī-Mahodayah, 1961.

Bṛhatkathāślokasaṃgraha of Budhasvāmin. *Bṛhat-kathā Çlokasaṃgraha*. Ed. and trans. Félix Lacôte. 4 vols. Paris: Imprimerie Nationale, 1908–1929.

Bhāṣāpariccheda of Viśvanātha Nyāyapañcānana Bhaṭṭācārya. Ed. E. Roer. Bibliotheca Indica. Vol. 8. Osnabruck: Biblio Verlag, 1980.

Bṛhaddevatā of *Śaunaka*. *The Bṛhad-Devatā Attributed to Śaunaka*. Ed. and trans. A. A. MacDonell. Part 2, Translation and Notes. Harvard Oriental Series 6. Cambridge, MA: Harvard University, 1904.

Bṛhatsaṃhitā of Varāhamihira, with the commentary of Bhaṭṭotpala. Ed. Sudhakara Dvivedi. E. J. Lazarus, Benares 1895–97.

Bṛhatsaṃhitā of Varāhamihira. Trans. and notes by M. Ramakrishna Bhat. Delhi: Motilal Banarsidass, 2003.

Cakradatta-Ratnaprabhā: The Cakradatta (Cikitsā-San'graha) of Cakrapāṇidatta with the Commentary Ratnaprabhā by Mahāmahopadhyāya Śrī Niścala Kara. Ed. Priya Vrat Sharma. Jaipur: Swami Jayaramdas Ramprakash Trust, Anaj Mandi, Jauhari Bazar, 1993.

Caraka-saṃhitā. Ed. and trans. Priyavat Sharma. Varanasi: Chaukhambha Orientalia, 1981.

Cārucaryā of Bhoja. *Cārucaryā: A Medieval Work on Personal Hygiene*. Ed. B. Rama Rao. Hyderabad: Indian Institute of History of Medicine, 1974.

Caturvargacintāmaṇi of Hemādri. *Chaturvarga Chintamani by Hemadri*. Osnabrück: Biblio Verlag, 1989.

Daśakumāracarita of Daṇḍin. Ed. M. R. Kale. 4th ed. Delhi: Motilal Banarsidass, 1966.

Dhammapada. Ed. O. von Hinüber and K. R. Norman. Oxford: Pali Text Society, 1994.

Dhammasaṅgani. Ed. Edward Müller. London: Pali Text Society, 1985.

Dhanvantarīnighaṇṭuḥ. Ed. P. V. Sharma. Jaikrishnadas Ayurveda Series 40. Varanasi: Chaukambha Orientalia, 1998.

Dharmasaṅgraha of Nāgārjuna, *Buddhist Technical Terms: An Ancient Buddhist Text Ascribed to Nāgārjuna*. Annotated Kenjiu Kasawara. Ed. F. Max Muller and H. Wenzel. Reprint. Delhi: Orient, 1984.

Dharmasūtras. Ed. and trans. Patrick Olivelle. Oxford: Oxford University Press, 1999.

Dhātūtpatti of Ṭhakkura Pherū. *Ratnaparīkṣādi Sapt-Granth Saṃgrah*. Jodhpur: Rajasthan Oriental Research Institute, 1996.

Dīgha Nikāya. Ed. T. W. Rhys Davids and J. Estlin Carpenter. London: Pali Text Society, 1890.

Divyāvadāna: A Collection of Early Buddhist Legends. Ed. E. B. Cowell and R. A. Neill. Cambridge: Cambridge University Press, 1886.

Gandhasāra of Gaṅgādhara and *Gandhavāda*. *Gaṅgādhara's Gandhasāra and an Uunknown Author's Gandhavāda, with Marathi Commentary*. Ed. Ramkrishna Tuljaram Vyas. Gaekwad's Oriental Series, 173. Vadodara, India: Oriental Institute, 1989.

Ganeśapurāṇa. Part I: Upāsanākhaṇḍa. Introduction, notes, and index by Grey Bailey. Purāṇa Research Publications Tübingen. Vol. 4, part. 1.Weisbaden: Harrassowitz Verlag, 1995.

Gaṇitasārakaumudī of *Ṭhakkura Pherū*. Ed. S. R. Sarma, Takanori Kusuba, Takao Hayashi, and Michio Yano [SaKHYa]. *Gaṇitasārakaumudī: The Moonlight of the Essence of Mathematics by Ṭhakkura Pherū*. New Delhi: Manohar, 2009.

Gaṇita-sāra-Sangraha of Mahāvīrācārya with English Translation and Notes. Trans. M. Raṅgācarya. Madras: Government Press, 1912.

Haramekhalā of Māhuka with commentary. Part 2. Ed. K Sāmbaśiva Śāstrī. Trivadrum Sanskrit Series 136. *Śrī Citrodayamañjarī* 25. Trivandrum: Government Press, 1938.

Harṣacarita of Bāṇa. *The Harshacharita of Bāṇabhatta with the Commentary (Saṅketa) of Sankara*. Ed. Kāśīnāth Pāṇdurang Parab and Śāstrī Dhondo Paraśūrām Vaze. Bombay: Tukaram Javaji, 1892.

Harṣacarita of Bāṇa. *Bāṇabhaṭṭa's Biography of King Harshavardhana of Sthāṇvīśvara with Śaṅkara's Commentary, Saṅketa*. Ed. A.A. Führer. Bombay Sanskrit and Prakrit Series, no. 66. Bombay: Government Central Press, 1909.

Hitopadeśa of Nārāyaṇa. Ed. M. R. Kale. Delhi: Motilal Banarsidass, 1998.

Īśānaśivagurudevapaddhati of Iśānaśivagurudevamiśra. Ed. T. Ganapati Śāstrī. Trivandrum Sanskrit Series 77. Trivandrum: Government Press, 1922.

Jayamaṅgalā. Ed. H Sarma. Calcutta Oriental Series, no. 19. Calcutta: N. N. Law, 1926.

Kālikāpurāṇaṃ. Ed.B. Śāstrī. *Jaikrishnadas-Krishnadas Prachavidya Granthamala* 5. Varanasi: Chowkamba Sanskrit Series Office, 1972.

Kalyāṇasaugandhikavyāyoga of Nīlakaṇṭhakavi. *Bhīma in Search of Celestial Flower: Kalyāṇasaugandhikavyāyoga*, Ed. Dr. K. G. Paulose. Delhi: New Bharatiya Book Corporation, 2000.

Kāmasūtra of Vātsyāyana. *The Kama Sutra of Vatsyayana*. Trans. R. Burton and F. F. Arbuthnot. London: George Allen and Unwin, 1963.

Kāmasūtra of Vātsyāyana. Trans. and ed. W. Doniger and S Kakar. Oxford: Oxford University Press, 2002.

Kāmasūtra of Vātsyāyana. Ed. Devadatta Śāstrī. Varanasi: Chakhambha Sanskrit Sansthan, 2003.

Karpūramañjarī of Rājaśekhara. *Rāja-Çehkara's Karpūra-Mañjarī: A Drama by the Indian Poet Rājaćekhara*. Ed. Sten Konow, trans. Charles Rockwell Lanman. Harvard Oriental Series 4. Cambridge, MA: Harvard University, 1901.

Kāśyapa-saṃhitā or Vṛddhajīvakīya Tantra. Ed. and trans. P. V. Tewari, Haridas Ayurveda Series 2. Varanasi: Chaukhambha Visvabharati, 1996.

Kathāvatthu. Ed. A. C. Taylor. London: Pali Text Society, 1897.

Kāvyamīmāṃsā of Rājaśekhara. Ed. C. D. Dalal. Gaekwad's Oriental Series 1. Baroda: Central Library, 1916.

La Kāvyamīmāṃsā. Trans. Nadine Stchoupak and Louis Renou. Paris: Imprimerie Nationale, 1946.

Kharataragaccha-bṛhadgurvāvali of Jinapāla. *Jinapālopādhyāyādi-saṅkalita Kharataragaccha-bṛhadgurvāvali*, prathama saṃskaraṇa sampādaka, Muni Jinavijaya; saṃśodhaka evaṃ punarsampādaka, Vinayasāgara. Jayapura: Prākṛta Bhāratī Akādamī; Sāñcora: Śrī Jaina Śve. Kharataragaccha Saṅgha, 2000.

Kiraṇāvalī of Udayanācāryya. Ed. Mahāmahopādhyāya Siva Chandra Sārvvabhouma. Calcutta: Asiatic Society, 1989.

Lalitavistara: Raritavisutara no kenkyū. Ed. Kōichi Hokazono. Tokyo: Daitō Shuppansha, Hensi, 1994.

The Mahābhārata for the First Time Critically Edited by Vishnu S. Sukthankar [et al.] *Illustrated from Ancient Models by Shrimant Balasaheb Pant Pratinidhi*. Poona: Bhandarkar Oriental Research Institute, 1933–.

Mahābhāratam with the Bharata Bhawadeepa Commentary of Nīlkaṇṭha. Ed. Pandit Ramchandrashastri Kinjawadekar. New Delhi: Oriental Books Reprint, 1979.

Mahāvyutpatti. Csoma de Körös, Alexander. "Sanskrit-Tibetan-English Vocabulary, Being an Edition and Translation of the Mahāvyutpatti." Ed. E. D. Ross and M.S.C. Vidyābhūsana. *Memoirs of the Asiatic Society of Bengal*. Vol 3, no. 1, 1–127.

Mānasollāsa of Someśvara. Ed. G. K. Shrigondekar. Gaekwad's Oriental Series 28, 84, 138. Baroda: Oriental Institute, 1925–1961.

Mānavadharmaśāstra. The Commentary of Govindarája on Mánava-Dharma Śástra (Being a Supplement to Mánavadharmaśástra with the Commentaries of Medhátithi, Sarvajñanáráyana, Kulluka, Rághavánanda, Nandana, and Rámachandra). Edited with notes by V. N. Mandlik. 2 vols. Bombay: Ganpat Krishnaji's Press, 1886.

Mānavadharmaśāstra. Manu's Code of Law: A Critical Edition and Translation of the Mānava-Dharmaśāstra. Ed. Patrick Olivelle. Oxford: Oxford University Press, 2005.

Mānavadharmaśāstra with the *Manubhāṣya* of Medhātithi. Trans. Mahāmahopādhyāya Gangānātha Jhā. Allahabad: University of Calcutta, 1926.

Mānavadharmaśāstra with the *Manubhāṣya* of Medhātithi. *Manusmṛti Medhātithibhāṣyasamalaṅkṛtā*. Kalakattā: Udayācal Press, 1967–71.

Mātaṅgalīlā of Nīlakaṇṭha. Ed. T. Gaṇapati Śāstrī. Trivandrum Sanskrit Series 10. Trivandrum:

Travancore Govt. Press, 1910.
Meghadūta of Kālidāsa. Text with translation by M. R. Kale. Delhi: Motilal Banarsidass, 2002.
Mṛcchakaṭika of Śūdraka. Ed. and trans. M. R. Kale. Bombay: Booksellers, 1962.
Mūlasarvāstivāda Vinaya. Bhaiṣajyavastu. Gilgit Manuscripts. Ed. H. Dutt and S. S. Sastri. Vol. 3, pt. 1. Bibliotheca Indo-Buddhica 16. Delhi: Sri Satguru, 1984.
Nāgarasarvasva of Padmaśrī. Ed. Paṇḍit Bhagīrathasvāmī. Śrīveṅkaṭeśvar Pustak Agency, Kalkattā 1929.
Nāgarasarvasva of Padmaśrī. Ed. Babulal Shukla Shastri. Delhi: Eastern Book Linkers, 1994.
Nirukta of Yāska. Ed. V. K. Rajavade. 2nd ed. Government Oriental Series Class A, no. 7. Poona: Bhandarkar Oriental Research Institute, 1993.
Nyāyamañjarī of Jayantabhaṭṭa. Ed. K. S. Varadacharya. 2 vols. Oriental Research Institute Series 116 and 139. Mysore: Oriental Research Institute, 1969 and 1983.
Nyāyasūtra of Gautama. *Nyāyasūtra: gautamīyanyāyadarśana with Bhāṣya of Vātsyāyana.* Ed. A Thakur. New Delhi: Bhāratīyadārśanikānusandhānapariṣatprakāśitam: Distributed by Munshiram Manoharlal, 1997.
Pañcaviṃśa-Brāhmaṇa The Brāhmaṇa of Twenty Five Chapters. Trans W. Caland. Calcutta: Asiatic Society of Bengal, 1931.
Papañcasūdanī of Buddhaghosa. *Papañcasūdanī Majjhimanikāyaṭṭhakathā of Buddhaghosācariya.* Part 5, suttas 131–152. Ed. I. B. Horner. London: Published for the Pali Text Society by Oxford University Press, 1938.
Periplus Maris Erythaei. Trans. Lionel Casson. Princeton, NJ: Princeton University Press, 1989.
Pliny. *Natural History.* Trans. H. Rackham. Cambridge, MA: Harvard University Press, 1945.
Praśastapādabhāṣyam of Praśasta Devāchārya. Chowkhambā Sanskrit Series 61. Benares: Chowkhamba Sanskrit Series Office, 1930.
Pravacanasāra of Kundakunda. Trans. and ed. A. N. Upadhye. 2nd ed. Bombay: Shetha Manilal Revashankar Jhaveri, 1935.
Pūjāprakāśa of Mitramiśra in the *Vīramitrodaya.* Chowkhamba Sanskrit Series. Vol. 4. Benares: Chowkhambā Sanskrit Book-Depot, 1913.
Raghuvaṃśa of Kālidāsa with the Commentary Sañjīvanī of Mallinātha. Cantos I–V. Ed. and trans. M. R. Kale. Delhi: Motilal Banarsidass, 1997.
Rājanighaṇṭusahito Dhanvantarīyanighaṇṭuḥ, Ānandāśramasaṃskṛtagranthāvaliḥ 33. 2nd ed. Pune: Anandasrama Press, 1927.
Rāmāyaṇa of Vālmīki. General editors G. H. Bhatt and U. P. Shah. Baroda: Oriental Institute, 1960–75.
Rasaratnākara of Nityanātha. *Rasāyanakhanda: Fourth Part of Rasaratnākara.* Ed. Vaidya Jāvadjī Tricumjī Āchārya. Haridas Sanskrit Series. Vol. 95. Varanasi: Caukhambā Samskṛta Pustakālay, 1939.
Ratnāvalī of Harṣa. Ed. and trans. M. R. Kale. Delhi: Motilal Banarsidass, 2002.
Ratnaparīkṣādi Sapt-Granth Saṃgrah of Ṭhakkura Pherū. Jodhpur: Rajasthan Oriental Research Institute, 1996.
Rayaṇaparikkhā of Ṭhakkura Pherū. Trans. S. R. Sarma. Aligargh: Viveka, 1984.
Rigveda Brahmanas: The Aitareya and Kauṣītaki Brāhmaṇas of the Rigveda. Trans. A. B. Keith. Harvard Oriental Series 25. Cambridge, MA: Harvard University Press, 1920.
Rig-Veda-Sanhita the Sacred Hymns of the Brahmans; Together with the Commentary of Sayanacharya. Ed. Max Müller. Vol 3. London: William H. Allen, 1856.
Ṛtusaṃhāra of Kālidāsa. Introduction, notes, and trans. M. R. Kale. Delhi: Motilal Banarsidass, 2002.
Śabdakalpadruma of Rādhakāntadeva. Calcutta: Baptist Mission Press, 1886.
Saddharmapuṇḍarīkasūtra. Buddhist Sanskrit Texts no. 6. Ed. P. L. Vaidya. Darbhanga: Mithila Institute, 1960.
Saṃyutta-Nikāya, part 4 Saḷāyatana-vagga. Ed. M. Leon Feer. London: Pali Text Society, 1960.
Sarvārthasiddhi of Pūjyapāda. *Sarvartha Siddhi of Pujyapad, the Commentary on Acharya Griddhapiccha's Tattwartha Sutra.* Ed. Pt. Phoolcandra Siddhant Shastry. Kashi: Bharatiya Jnanapitha, 1955.
Śārṅgadharapaddhati. The Paddhati of Sarngadhara—A Sanskrit Anthology. Ed. Peter Peterson. Bombay: Government Central Book Depot, 1888.

Śatapatha-Brāhmaṇa. Çatapatha-Brāhmaṇa in the Mādhyandina-Çākhā with extracts from the commentaries of Sāyaṇa, Harisvāmin and Dvivedananga. Ed. A. Weber. Berlin: 1855.

Śatapatha-Brāhmaṇa According to the Text of the Mādhyandina School. Trans J. Eggeling, part 2, books 3 and 4. Sacred Books of the East, vol. 26. Oxford: Clarendon Press, 1885.

Saugandhikāharaṇa of Viśvanāthakavi. Ed. Paṇḍit Śivadatta and Kāśīnāth Pāṇḍurang Parab. Kāvyamālā. Vol. 74. Bombay: Tukārām Jāvajī, 1902.

Śivatattvaratnākara of Basavarāja of Keḷadi. Ed. S, Narayanaswamy Sastry, R. Rama Shastry, H. P. Malledevaru. 3 vols. Mysore: Oriental Research Institute, 1964–1983.

Śṛṅgāraprakāśa of Bhoja. part 1. Ed. V. Raghavan. Harvard Oriental Series 53. Cambridge MA: Harvard University Press, 1998.

Sthavirāvalīcaritra of Hemacandra. *Sthavirāvalīcaritra or Pariśishṭaparvan Being an Appendix of the Tr ishashṭiśalākapurushacarita*. Ed. Herman Jacobi. Bibliotheca Indica, no. 513. Calcutta: Asiatic Society of Bengal, 1884.

Sukhāvatīvyūha (vistaramātṛkā). In *Mahāyāṇa-sūtra-saṃgraha*, part 1. Buddhist Sanskrit Texts, no. 17. Ed. P. L. Vaidya. Darbhanga: Mithila Institute, 1961.

Suśruta Saṃhitā. Ed. Vaidya Jādavjī Trivikamjī Ācārya and Nārāyaṇ Rām Ācārya Kāvyatīrtha. Krishnadas Ayurveda Series 51. Varanasi: Krishnadas Academy, 1998.

Suśrutasaṃhitā: with English Translation of Text and ḍalhaṇa's Commentary along with Critical Notes. Ed. Priya Vrat Sharma. Varanasi: Chaukhambha Visvabharati, 1999–2001.

Die Taittirīya-Saṃhitā. Ed. Albrecht Weber. Part 2, kāṇḍa 5–7. Indische Studien: Beiträge für die Kunde des indischen Alterthums, Band 12. Liepzig: F. A. Brockhaus, 1872.

Taittirīya-Saṃhitā. The Veda of the Black Yajus School entitled Taittiriya Sanhita. Ed. A. B. Keith. Part 2, VI.2.8.6. Harvard Oriental Series 19. Cambridge, MA: Harvard University Press, 1914.

Tāṇḍya Mahābrāhmaṇa with the commentary of Sāyaṇa Āchārya. Ed. A. Vedāntavāgīśa. 2 vols. Calcutta: Asiatic Society of Bengal, 1870–1874.

Theophrastus. *Enquiry into Plants*. Trans. Sir Arthur Hort. London: William Heinemann, 1916.

Theragāthā-Aṭṭhakathā Paramatthadīpanī. Ed. A. Chaudhary. Vol. 1. Nālanda: Nava Nālandā Mahāvihāra, 1976.

Timaeus of Plato. *Plato's Cosmology: The Timaeus of Plato Translated with a Running Commentary*. Trans. Francis MacDonald Cornford. New York: Humanities Press, 1952.

Ṭoḍarānanda: Diagnosis and Treatment of Diseases in Āyurveda, Based on Āyurveda Saukhyaṃ of Ṭoḍarānanda. Part 3. Trans. B. Dash and L Kashyap. Ṭoḍarānanda Āyurveda Saukhyaṃ Series, no. 5. New Delhi: Concept, 1984.

Trikāṇḍaśeṣa of Puruṣottamadeva. Ed. R. S. Bhattacharya. Ratnabharati Granthamālā 13. Varanasi: Ratna, 1995.

Vaiśeṣikasūtra of Kaṇāda. *Vaiśeṣikadarśanam*. Ed. Pt. Kṛpā Rām Śarma. Banāras: Kvapārām Bookseller, 1889.

Vaiśeṣikasūtra of Kaṇāda with the Commentary of Candrānanda. Ed. Muni Srī Jambuvijayi. Baroda: Oriental Institute, 1961.

The Varāha-Purāṇa with English translation. Trans. A. Bhattacharya, ed. A. S. Gupta. Varanasi: All-India Kashiraj Trust, 1981.

The Vibhanga, Being the Second Book of the Abhidhamma Pitaka. Ed. Mrs. Rhys Davids. London: Pali Text Society, 1904.

Vikramāṅkābhyudayam of Someśvara. Ed. M. L. Nagar. Gaekwad's Oriental Series 150. Baroda, India: Oriental Institute, 1966.

Vinayapiṭaka. The Book of the Discipline (Vinaya-Piṭaka) volume 5 (Cullavagga). Trans. I. B. Horner London: Luzac, 1963.

The Vinaya Piṭaka. Ed. Hermann Oldenberg. Oxford: Pali Text Society, 1993.

Secondary Sources

Abu-Lughod, Janet L. 1989. *Before European Hegemony: The World System A.D. 1250–1350*. New York: Oxford University Press.

Acharya, P. K. 1929. "Fine Arts." *Indian Historical Quarterly* 5.2: 188–218.

Agrawala, V. S. 1953. *India as Known to Pāṇini*. Lucknow: University of Lucknow.
———. 1974. *Bṛhatkakathāślokasaṃgraha: A Study*. Varanasi: Prithivi Prakashan.
Alter, R. 1981. *The Art of Biblical Narrative*. New York: Basic Books.
Apte, V. S. 2003. *The Practical Sanskrit-English Dictionary*. Revised and enlarged edition. Delhi: Motilal Banarsidass.
Ali, Daud. 1998. "Technologies of the Self: Courtly Artifice and Monastic Discipline in Early India." *Journal of the Economic and Social History of the Orient* 41.2: 159–184.
———. 2004. *Courtly Culture and Political Life in Early Medieval India*. Cambridge: Cambridge University Press.
———. 2011. "Padmaśrī's *Nāgarasarvasva* and the World of Medieval Kāmaśāstra." *Journal of Indian Philosophy* 39:41–62.
Ambasta, S. P., ed. 2000. *The Useful Plants of India*. New Delhi: National Institute of Science Communication, Council of Scientific & Industrial Research.
Appadurai, Arjun, ed. 2003 (1986). *The Social Life of Things: Commodities in Cultural Perspective*. Cambridge: Cambridge University Press.
Asouti, Eleni, and Dorian Fuller. 2008. *Trees and Woodlands of South India: Archaeological Perspectives*. Publications of the Institute for Archaeology, University College. Walnut Creek, CA: Left Coast Press.
Atre, Shubangana. 1987. "Many Seeded Apple: The Fruit of Fertility." *Bulletin of the Deccan College Research Institute* 46:1–6.
Auboyer, J. 1961. *La Vie Quotidienne dans L'Inde Ancienne*. Paris: Hachette.
Babb, Lawrence. 1996. *Absent Lord: Ascetics and Kings in a Jain Ritual Culture*. Berkeley: University of California Press.
Bailey, D. R. Shackleton. 1950. "Notes on the Divyāvadāna, Part 1." *Journal of the Royal Asiatic Society*, n.s., 3/4:166–184.
Balbir, Nalini. 2002. "Théorie et pratique de la devinette en milieu jaina: I. Les *Cent soixante et une devinettes* de Jinavallabha; II. Devinettes en contexte." *Bulletin d'Études Indiennes* 20.2: 83–243.
Baltutis, Michael. 2008. "The Festival of Indra: The Construction of a South Asian Urban Celebration." Ph.D. diss. The University of Iowa.
Bandhu, Vishva. 1960. "An Appreciation of Professor P. K. Gode." *Professor P. K. Gode Commemoration Volume*. Ed. H. L. Hariyappa and M. M. Patkar. Poona Oriental Series 93. Poona: Oriental Book Agency.
Bandmann, Günter. 1969. "Bemerkungen zu einer Ikonologie des Materials." *Städel-Jahrbuch* 2:75–100.
Banerjee, M., and Miller, D. 2003. *The Sari*. Oxford: Berg.
Baxandall, M. 1988. *Painting and Experience in Fifteenth Century Italy*. 2nd ed. Oxford: Oxford University Press.
Bechert, H., and G. von Simson, eds. 1979. *Einführung in die Indologie*. Darmstadt: Wissenschaftliche Buchgesellschaft.
Bedini, Silvio A. 1994. *The Trail of Time: Time Measurement with Incense in East Asia*. Cambridge: Cambridge University Press.
Benavides, G., and E. Thomassen. 2007. "Religion through the Senses." *Numen* 54:371–373.
Bhattacharyya, D. C. 1947. "New Light on Vaidyaka Literature." *Indian Historical Quarterly* 23.2: 123–155.
Bhattacharya, R. S. 1983. "A Purāṇic Objective Division of Smell (Gandha) Not Found in the Works on Philosophy." *Purāṇa* 25.2: 246–253.
Blackburn, Anne. 1999. "Looking for the Vinaya: Monastic Discipline in the Practical Canons of the Theravada." *Journal of the International Association of Buddhist Studies* 22.2: 281–309.
Bloch, Marc. 1974. *Apologie pour l'histoire ou métier d'historien*. Paris: A. Colin.
Blochmann, H. 1927. *Āʾīn-I Akbarī* of Abū 'l-faẓl 'allāmī. Calcutta: Asiatic Society of Bengal.
Böhtlingk, Otto von, and Roth, Rudolph. 1855–75. *Sanskrit-wörterbuch heraugegeben von der Kaiserlichen akademie der wissenschaften, bearbeitet von Otto Böhtlingk und Rudolph Roth*. St. Petersburg: Buchdr. der K. Akademie der wissenschaften.
Borges, Jorge Luis. 1964. "The Nightingale of Keats." In *Other Inquisitions, 1937–1952*, 121–124. Austin: University of Texas Press.

Bronkhorst, J. 2000. "Abhidharma and Jainism." In *Abhidharma and Indian Thought: Essays in Honor of Professor Doctor Junsho Kato on His Sixtieth Birthday*, ed. The Committee for the Felicitation of Professor Doctor Junsho Kato's Sixtieth Birthday, 598–581. Tokyo: Shunju-sha.

Bronner, Yigal. 2010. *Extreme Poetry: The South Asian Movement of Simultaneous Narration*. New York: Columbia University Press.

Brown, Robert L. 2006. "The Nature and Use of Bodily Relics of the Buddha in Gandhāra." In *Gandhāran Buddhism: Archaeology, Art, Texts*, ed. Pia Brancaccio and Kurt Behrendt, 183–209. Toronto: UBC Press.

Bryant, Edwin F. 2003. *Krishna: The Beautiful Legend of God (Śrīmad Bhāgavata Purāṇa*. Book X). London: Penguin Books.

Buchanan, Francis. 1936. *An Account of the Districts of Bihar and Patna in 1811–1812*. Patna: Bihar and Orissa Research Society.

Bühnemann, G. 1988. *Pūjā: A Study in Smārta Ritual*. Ed. Gerhard Oberhammer. Publications of the De Nobili Research Library, vol. 15. Vienna: Institut für Indologie der Universität Wien, Sammlung De Nobili.

———. 1999. "Buddhist Deities and Mantras in the Hindu Tantras: I The Tantrasārasaṃgraha and the Īśānaśivagurudevapaddhati." *Indo-Iranian Journal* 42:303–334.

Buitenen, J. A. B. van. 1959. *Tales of Ancient India*. Chicago: University of Chicago Press.

———. Trans. 1973. *The Mahābhārata*, 1. *The Book of the Beginning*. Chicago: University of Chicago Press.

Burke, Peter. 2004. *What is Cultural History?* Cambridge, UK: Polity Press.

Burnouf, E. 1876. *Introduction a l'histoire du buddhisme indien*. 2nd ed. Paris: Maisonneuve et cie.

Burrow, T., and M. B. Emeneau. 1961. *A Dravidian Etymological Dictionary*. Oxford: Clarendon Press.

Buswell, Robert E. Jr. 1996. "The 'Aids to Penetration' (*Nirvedabhāgīya*) According to the Vaibhāṣika School." *Journal of Indian Philosophy* 25:589–611.

Campany, Robert F. 1992. "Xunzi and Durkheim as Theorists of Ritual Practice." In *Discourse and Practice*, ed. Frank Reynolds and David Tracy, 197–231. Albany: SUNY Press.

Carr, E. H. 1962. *What is History?* New York: Alfred A. Knopf.

Caseau, B. 1994. "Euodia: The Use and Meaning of Fragrances in the Ancient World and Their Christianization (100–900 AD)." PhD diss. Princeton University.

Catalogue of the Anup Sanskrit Library. 1946. Prepared by C. K. Raja, and C. M. Krishna. Bikaner.

Chandra, Moti. 1940. "Cosmetics and Coiffure in Ancient India." *Journal of the Indian Society of Oriental Art* 8: 62–145. Reprinted in Moti Chandra. 1973. *Costumes Textiles Cosmetics and Coiffure in Ancient and Medieval India*. Delhi: Oriental.

———. 1945. *Geographical and Economic Studies in the Mahābhārata: Upāyana parva*. Lucknow: U.P. Historical Society.

———. 1951–1952. "Technical Arts in Ancient India." *Journal of the Uttar Pradesh Historical Society* 23–25: 161–185.

Chattopadhyaya, B. 2004. "Representing the Other? Sanskrit Sources and the Muslims (Eighth to Fourteenth Century)." In *Subordinate and Marginal Groups in Early India*, ed. A. P. Sen, 374–404. New Delhi: Oxford University Press.

CITIES. *Fourteenth Meeting of the Plants Committee*. 2004. Windhoek (Namibia). (Feb.): 16–20. Review of Significant Trade *Aquilaria malaccensis*. PC14 Doc. 9.2.2, Annex 2, 5.

Classen, C., D. Howes, and A. Synnott, eds. 1994. *Aroma: The Cultural History of Smell*. London: Routledge.

Clayton, John. 2006. *Religions, Reasons and Gods: Essays in the Cross-Cultural Philosophy of Religion*. Prepared by Anne M. Blackburn and Thomas D. Carroll. Cambridge: Cambridge University Press.

Coomaraswamy, Ananda K. 1939. "Ornament." *Art Bulletin* 21.4: 375–382.

———. 1993. (1928–1931.) *Yakṣas: Essays in the Water Cosmology*. Ed. Paul Schroeder. New ed. Delhi: Oxford University Press.

Corbin, Alain. 1982. *Le miasme et la jonquille: l'odorat et l'imaginaire social XVIIIe–XIXe siècles*. Paris: Aubier Montaigne.

———. 1986. *The Foul and the Fragrant: Odor and the French Social Imagination*. Cambridge, MA: Harvard University Press.

———. 2005. "Charting the Cultural History of the Senses." In *The Empire of the Senses: The Sensual Culture Reader*, ed. David Howes, 128–139. New York: Berg.
Cort, John. 2010. *Framing the Jina: Narratives of Icons and Idols in Jain History*. Oxford: Oxford University Press.
Cox, Whitney. 2011. "Saffron in the Rasam." In *South Asian Texts in History: Critical Engagements with Sheldon Pollock*, ed. Yigal Bronner, Whitney Cox, and Lawrence McCrea, 177–202. Ann Arbor, MI: Association for Asian Studies.
Craddock, Harry. 1999. *The Savoy Cocktail Book*. London: Pavilion Books.
Cutler, Anthony. 1983. "Prolegomena to the Craft of Ivory Carving in Late Antiquity and the Early Middle Ages." In *Artistes, artisans et production artistique au Moyen Age: colloque international, Centre national de la recherché scientifique, Université de Rennes II, Haute-Bretagne, 2–6 mai 1983*, vol. 2, 431–475. Paris: Picard.
Dandekar, R. N. 1962. *Śrautakośa*. English Section. Poona: Vaidika Saṃśodhana Maṇḍala.
Darnton, Robert. 1984. *The Great Cat Massacre and Other Episodes in French Cultural History*. New York: Basic Books.
Dasgupta, S. 1963. *A History of Indian Philosophy*. Vol. 1. Cambridge: Cambridge University Press.
Davidson, Ronald M. 2002. *Indian Esoteric Buddhism: A Social History of the Tantric Movement*. New York: Columbia University Press.
Dehejia, Vidya. 2009. *The Body Adorned: Dissolving Boundaries Between Sacred and Profane in India's Art*. New York: Columbia University Press.
Deleu, Jozef. 1970. *Viyāhapannati (Bhagavaī): The Fifth Anga of the Jaina Canon*. Bruges: De Tempel.
Detienne, Marcel. 1972. *Les jardins d'Adonis*. Paris: Gallimard.
Dezsö, Csaba. 2004. "'Much Ado About Religion.' A Critical Edition and Annotated Translation of the Āgamaḍambara, a Satirical Play by the Ninth Century Kashmirian Philosopher Bhaṭṭa Jayanta." D.Phil. diss. University of Oxford, UK.
Doniger, Wendy. 2005. *The Woman Who Pretended to Be Who She Was: Myths of Self-Imitation*. New York: Oxford University Press.
Douglas, Mary. 1966. *Purity and Danger*. London: Routledge and K. Paul.
Drobnick J., ed. 2006. *The Smell Culture Reader*. New York: Berg.
Dundas, Paul. 2002. *The Jains*. 2nd ed. London: Routledge.
———. 2006. "A Non-Imperial Religion? Jainism in Its 'Dark Age.'" In *Between the Empires: Society in India 300 BCE to 400 CE*, ed. P. Olivelle, 383–414. Oxford: Oxford University Press.
Duroiselle, Charles. 1905. "Notes sur la géographie apocryphe de la Birmanie; à propos de la légende de Pūrṇa." *Bulletin de l'Ecole française d'Extrême-Orient* 5:146–67.
Eastaugh, Nicholas. 2004. *The Pigment Compendium: A Dictionary of Historical Pigments*. Oxford: Elsevier Butterworth-Heinemann.
Eck, Diana. 1981. *Darśan: Seeing the Divine Image in India*. Chambersburg, PA: Anima Books.
———. 1999. *Banaras: City of Light*. New York: Columbia University Press.
Eichinger Ferro-Luzzi, Gabriella. 1996. *The Smell of the Earth: Rajanarayanan's Literary Description of Tamil Village Life*. Napoli: Istituto Universitario Orientale.
Epigraphia Indica. 1900–1901. Vol. 6. Ed. Hultzsch. Calcutta: Office of the Superintendent of Government Printing.
Filliozat, J. 1934. "Liste des manuscrits etc. de la collection Palmyr Cordier conservés à la bibliothèque nationale." *Journal Asiatique* 224:155–73.
Filliozat, Pierre-Sylvain. 1990. "*Yukti*, le quatrième *pramāṇa* des medecins (*Carakasaṃhitā, Sūtrasthāna* XI, 25)." *Journal of the European Āyurvedic Society* 1:33–46.
Finot, Louis. 1896. *Les Lapidaires Indiens. Bibliothèque De L'école Des Hautes Études. Sciences Philologiques Et Historiques, 111. Fasc.* Paris: É. Bouillon.
Fischer, C. E. C. 1938. "Where Did the Sandalwood Tree (Santalum album Linn.) Evolve?" *Journal of the Bombay Natural History Society* 40:458–66.
Fitzgerald, James L. 2003. "The Many Voices of the Mahābhārata." Review of *Rethinking the Mahabharata: A Reader's Guide to the Education of the Dharma King*, by Alf Hiltebeitel. *Journal of the American Oriental Society* 123.4 (Oct.–Dec.): 803–818.
———. 2006. "Negotiating the Shape of 'Scripture': New Perspectives on the Developments and

Growth of the Mahābhārata between the Empires." In *Between the Empires: Society in India 300 BCE to 400 CE*, ed. P. Olivelle, 257–286. New York: Oxford University Press.

Flood, Finbarr. 2009. *Objects of Translation: Material Culture and Medieval "Hindu-Muslim" Encounter*. Princeton, NJ: Princeton University Press.

Frauwallner, E. 1973. *History of Indian Philosophy*. Trans. V. M. Bedekar. Delhi: Motilal Banarsidass.

———. 1995. *Studies in Abhidharma Literature and the Origins of Buddhist Philosophical System*. Trans. S. F. Kidd. Albany: SUNY Press.

Freedman, Paul. 2008. *Out of the East: Spices and the Medieval Imagination*. New Haven, CT: Yale University Press.

Fynes, R. C. C. 1998. *The Lives of the Jain Elders*. Oxford: Oxford University Press.

Gaeffke, Peter. 1954. "The Snake-Jewel in Ancient Indian Literature." *Indian Linguistics*, 14:581–94.

Gait, Edward. 1926. *A History of Assam*. 2nd ed. Calcutta: Thacker, Spink.

Gamble, J. S. 1922. *A Manual of Indian Timbers*. London: Sampson Low, Marston.

Gatten, Aileen. 1977. "A Wisp of Smoke: Scent and Character in the Tale of Genji." *Monumenta Nipponica* 32.1: 35–48. Reprinted in Drobnick, Jim. 2006. *The Smell Culture Reader*, 331–341. New York: Berg.

Gell, Alfred. 1998. *Art and Agency: An Anthropological Theory*. Oxford: Clarendon Press.

Getty, Alice. 1962. *The Gods of Northern Buddhism*. Rutland, VT: Charles E. Tuttle.

Gode, P. K. 1940. "Date of the Rājavinoda of Udayarāja, a Hindu Court-poet of Mahamūd Begḍā—Between A.D. 1458 and 1469." *Journal of the University of Bombay* 9.2: 116–125.

———. 1945a. "Studies in the History of Indian Cosmetics and Perfumery: A Critical Analysis of a Rare Manuscript of Gandhavāda and its Marathi Commentary." *New Indian Antiquary*, 7:185–193.

———. 1945b. "Studies in the History of Indian Cosmetics and Perfumery—The Gandhasāra of Gaṅgādhara, an Unknown Treatise on Gandhaśāstra and its Critical Analysis." *Journal of the Bombay University* 14.2: 44–52.

———. 1947. *Thirty Years of Historical Research or Bibliography of the Published Writings of P. K. Gode*. 3rd ed. Poona: Samarth Bharat Press.

———. 1952. "Presidential Address to the Section of Technical Sciences and Fine Arts." *All India Oriental Conference, Fourteenth Session, Darbhanga 15–18 October 1948*. Part 1. 127–139. Poona: All India Oriental Conference.

———. 1958. "Notes on the History of the Camel in India—Between 500 B.C. and A.D. 800." *Janus* 3:133–138.

———. 1961a. "History of Ambergris in India Between about A.D. 700 and 1900." In *Studies in Indian Cultural History*, vol. 1, 9–14. Hoshiarpur: Vishvarananand Vedic Research Institute.

———. 1961b. "Perfumes and Cosmetics in the Royal Bath." In *Studies in Indian Cultural History*, vol. 1, 53–56. Hoshiarpur: Vishveshvaranand Vedic Research Institute.

———. 1961c. "Some Notes on the History of Candana (Sandal) in General and of Sveta-Candana (White Sandal) in Particular—Between B.C. 500 and 900 A.D." In *Studies in Indian Cultural History*, vol. 1, 314–46. Hoshiarpur: Vishveshvaranand Vedic Research Institute.

———. 1961d. "Some Recipes about Perfumes and Cosmetics in the Gandhavāda Section of the Rasaratnākara of Nityanātha Siddha (13th Century A.D.)." In *Studies in Indian Cultural History*, vol. 1, 88–93. Hoshiarpur: Vishveshvaranand Vedic Research Institute.

———. 1961e. *Studies in Indian Cultural History*. Vol. 1. Hoshiarpur: Veishveshvaranand Vedic Research Institute.

———. 1961f. "The Gandhayukti Section of the Viṣṇudharmottara and its Relation to Other Texts on the Gandhaśāstra." In *Studies in Indian Cultural History*, vol. 1, 74–87. Hoshiarpur: Veishveshvaranand Vedic Research Institute.

———. 1961g. "Verses Pertaining to Gandhayukti in the Agnipurāṇa and Their Relation to the Topics Dealt with in Gaṅgādhara's Gandhasāra." In *Studies in Indian Cultural History*, vol. 1, 68–73. Hoshiarpur: Veishveshvaranand Vedic Research Institute.

———. 1961h. "Indian Science of Cosmetics and Perfumery." In *Studies in Indian Cultural History*, vol. 1, 3–8. Hoshiarpur: Vishveshvaranand Vedic Research Institute.

———. 1969. *Studies in Indian Cultural History*. Vol. 3. P. K. Gode Studies 6. Poona: Prof. P. K. Gode

Collected Works Publication Committee, Bhandarkar: Oriental Research Institute.

Granoff, Phyllis. 1998. "Maitreya's Jewelled World: Some Remarks on Gems and Visions in Buddhist Texts." *Journal of Indian Philosophy*, 26: 347–371.

———. 2004. "Luxury Goods and Intellectual History: The Case of Printed and Woven Multicolored Textiles in Medieval India." *Ars Orientalis*, vol. 34, *Communities and Commodities: Western India and the Indian Ocean, Eleventh-Fifteenth Centuries*: 151–171.

———. 2006. *The Forest of Thieves and the Magic Garden: An Anthology of Medieval Jain Stories*. London: Penguin Books.

———. 2008. "Relics, Rubies and Ritual: Some Comments on the Distinctiveness of the Buddhist Relic Cult." *Rivista degli Studi Orientali* 81.1–4: 59–72.

Greenwood, David R., Dan Comeskey, Martin B. Hunt, and L. Elizabeth L. Rasmussen. 2005. "Chemical Communication: Chirality in Elephant Pheromones." *Nature* 438 (December 21): 1097–1098.

Groom, Nigel. 1981. *Frankincense and Myrrh: A Study of the Arabian Incense Trade*. London: Longman.

———. 1997. *The New Perfume Handbook*. 2nd ed. London: Blackie Academic and Professional.

Gupta, Shakti M. 1996. *Plants in Indian Temple Art*. Delhi: B.R.

Hacker, Paul. 1959. "Two Accounts of Cosmogony." In *Jñānamuktāvali: Commemoration Volume in Honor of John Nobel*, ed. C. Vogel. Sarasvati Vihara Series 38, 77–91. Delhi: International Academy of Indian Culture.

———. 1961. "The Sāṅkhyization of the Emanation Doctrine Shown in a Critical Analysis of Texts." *Wiener Zeitschrift für die Kunde Süd- und Osasiens*. Band V: 75–112.

Hahn, Michael. 2002. "Ratnākaraśānti's *Vidagdhavismāpana:* An Old and Unpublished Work on Sanskrit Riddles." *Bulletin d'Études Indiennes* 20.2: 3–81.

Hara, Minoru. 2010. "A Note on Sanskrit Gandha." Studia Orientalia 108. *Anantaṃ Śāstram: Indological and Linguistic Studies in Honour of Bertil Tikkanen*, ed. Klaus Karttunen, 65–86. Helsinki: Finnish Oriental Society.

Hariyappa, H. L., and M. M. Patkar, eds. 1960. *Professor P. K. Gode Commemoration Volume*. Poona Oriental Series 93. Poona: Oriental Book Agency.

Harper, R., E. C. Bate Smith, and D. G. Land. 1968. *Odour Description and Odour Classification: A Multidisciplinary Examination*. New York: Elsevier.

Harvey, Susan Ashbrook. 2006. *Scenting Salvation: Ancient Christianity and the Olfactory Imagination*. Berkeley: University of California Press.

Hasan-Rokem, Galit, and David Shulman, eds. 1996. *Untying the Knot: On Riddles and Other Enigmatic Modes*. New York: Oxford University Press.

Hayashi, Takao. 1987. "Varāhamihira's Pandiagonal Magic Square of the Order Four." *Historia Mathematica* 14. 2: 159–166.

Heim, Maria. 2004. *Theories of the Gift in South Asia: Hindu, Buddhist, and Jain Reflections on Dāna*. New York: Routledge.

Heppell, David. 2001. "The Chank Shell Industry in Modern India." *Princely States Report* 2.2, (Apr.). Accessed 1 June 2006. http://www.princelystates.com/ArchivedFeatures/fa-03-03a.shtml.

Hiltebeitel, Alf. 2001. *Rethinking the Mahabharata: A Reader's Guide to the Education of the Dharma King*. Chicago: University of Chicago Press.

———. 2005. "On Reading Fitzgerald's Vyāsa." Review of *The Mahābhārata, vol. 7:11. The Book of the Women; 12. The Book of Peace, Part One*, trans. and ed. James L. Fitzgerald. *Journal of the American Oriental Society* 125.2 (Apr.–Jun.): 241–261.

Hinüber, O. von. 1997. *A Handbook of Pali Literature*. New Delhi: Munishiram Manoharlal.

Hirth, Friedrich, and Rockhill, W. W., ed. and trans. 1911. *Chau Ju-kua: His Work on the Chinese and Arab Trade in the Twelfth and Thirteenth Centuries, Entitled Chu-fan-chï*. 2nd ed. St. Petersburg: Printing Office of the Imperial Academy of Sciences.

Hopkins, E. Washburn. 1907. "The Sniff Kiss in Ancient India." *Journal of the American Oriental Society* 28: 120–134.

———. 1915. *Epic Mythology*. Strassburg: K. J. Trübner.

Hopkins, Steven P. 2007. *An Ornament for Jewels: Love Poems for the Lord of Gods by Vedāntadeśika*. Oxford: Oxford University Press.

Howes, David, ed. 2005. *The Empire of the Senses: The Sensual Culture Reader*. New York: Berg.

Humphrey, Caroline, and Laidlaw, James. 1994. *The Archetypal Actions of Ritual: A Theory of Ritual Illustrated by the Jain Rite of Worship*. Oxford: Clarendon Press.

Hurlbut, Cornelius S. Jr., and W. Edwin Sharp. 1998. *Dana's Minerals and How to Study Them*. New York: Wiley.

Husain, Ali Akbar. 2000. *Scent in the Islamic Garden: A Study of Deccani Urdu Literary Sources*. Oxford: Oxford University Press.

Huysmans, J.–K. 1991. *À rebours*. Paris: Gallimard.

———. 2003. *Against Nature (À rebours)*. Ed. Patrick McGuiness. Trans. Robert Baldick. London: Penguin Books.

Inden, Ronald. 2000. "Imperial Purāṇas: Kashmir as Vaiṣṇava Center of the World." In *Querying the Medieval: Texts and the History of Practices in South Asia*, ed. Ronald Inden, Jonathon Walters, and Daud Ali, 29–98. Oxford: Oxford University Press.

Ingalls, Daniel, H. H. (1965). *An Anthology of Sanskrit Court Poetry, Vidyākara's "Subhāṣitaratnakoṣa"*. Harvard Oriental Series 44. Cambridge, MA: Harvard University Press.

Isaac, Erich. 1959. "The Citron in the Mediterranean: A Study in Religious Influences." *Economic Geography* 35.1: 71–78.

Jackson, Peter. 1999. *The Delhi Sultanate: A Political and Military History*. Cambridge: Cambridge University Press.

Jacobi, Hermann. 1968. "Jaina Sutrās." *Sacred Books of the East*. Ed. M. Muller. vols. 22, 45. Delhi: Motilal Banarsidass.

Johnston, Mark. 2001. "The Authority of Affect." *Philosophy and Phenomenological Research* 63.1: 181–214.

Jung, Dinah, ed. 2010. *An Ethnography of Fragrance: The Perfumery Arts of 'Adan/Laḥj. Islamic History and Civilization*. Vol. 84. Leiden: Brill.

Jütte, Robert. 2005. *A History of the Senses: From Antiquity to Cyberspace*. Trans. J. Lynn. Cambridge, UK: Polity Press.

Kahrs, Eivind. 1998. *Indian Semantic Analysis: The Nirvacana Tradition*. Cambridge: Cambridge University Press.

Kane, P. V. 1930–1962. *History of Dharmaśāstra (Ancient and Mediaeval Religious and Civil Law in India)*. Poona: Bhandarkar Oriental Research Institute.

Keith, A. B. 1925. *The Religion and Philosophy of the Veda and Upanishads*. Harvard Oriental Series 31. Cambridge, MA: Harvard University Press.

King, Anya. 2007. "The Musk Trade and the Near East in the Early Medieval Period." PhD diss. Indiana University.

———. 2008. "The Importance of Aromatics in Arabic Culture: Illustrations from Pre-Islamic and Early Islamic Poetry." *Journal of Near Eastern Studies* 67.3: 175–89.

———. 2011. "Tibetan Musk and Medieval Arab Perfumery." In *Islam and Tibet: Interactions Along the Musk Routes*, ed. A. Akasoy, C. Burnett, and R. Yoeli-Tlalim, 145–161. Burlington, VT: Ashgate.

King, Richard. 1999. *Orientalism and Religion: Postcolonial Theory, India and "The Mystic East."* London: Routledge.

Kinsley, David R. 1986. *Hindu Goddesses*. Berkeley: University of California Press.

Kittel, F. 1983. *A Kannada English Dictionary*. New Delhi: Asian Educational Services.

Kopytoff, Igor. 2003. (1986.) "The Cultural Biography of Things: Commoditization as Process." In *The Social Life of Things: Commodities in Cultural Perspective*, ed. Arjun Appadurai, 64–91. Cambridge: Cambridge University Press.

Krishnamachariar, M. 1970. *History of Sanskrit Literature*. Delhi: Motilal Banarsidass.

Krishnappa, M. V. 1987. "Perfumery Industry as Described in Lokopakara." *Journal of the Mysore University*, n.s., Section A-Arts, 49: 17–20.

Kulkarni, V., and Wright, J. C. 1992. Review of *Gaṅgādhara's Gandhasāra and an Unknown Author's Gandhavāda with Marathi Commentary*, ed. R. T. Vyas. *Journal of the Royal Asiatic Society of Great Britain & Ireland*, 3rd series, 2.1: 90–91.

Kusuba, T. 1993. "Combinatorics and Magic Squares in India: A Study of Nārāyaṇa Paṇḍita's

'Gaṇitakaumudī', Chapters 13–14." PhD diss. Brown University.
Lacôte, Félix. 1908. *Essai sur Guṇāḍhya et la Bṛhatkathā suive du texte inédit des chapitres XXVII a XXX du Nepāla-Māhātmya*. Paris: Ernert Leroux.
Lafleur, William R. 1998. "Body." In *Critical Terms for Religious Studies*, ed. Mark C. Taylor, 36–54. Chicago: University of Chicago Press.
Lal, Kishori Saran. 1967. *History of the Khaljis A.D. 1290–1320*. Bombay: India Pub. House.
Langdale, A. 1999. "Aspects of the Critical Reception and Intellectual History of Baxandall's Concept of the Period Eye." In *About Michael Baxandall*, ed. Adrian Rifkin, 17–35. Oxford: Blackwell.
Larson, Gerald J. 1979. *Classical Sāṃkhya: An Interpretation of its History and Meaning*. Delhi: Motilal Banarsidass.
———. 1987. *Encyclopedia of Indian Philosophies*. Vol. 4, *Sāṃkhya A Dualist Tradition in Indian Philosophy*. Delhi: Motilal Banarsidass.
Latour, Bruno. 1994. *We Have Never Been Modern*. Trans. Catherine Porter. Cambridge, MA: Harvard University Press.
———. 1999. *Pandora's Hope: Essays on the Reality of Science Studies*. Cambridge, MA: Harvard University Press.
———. 2004. "How to Talk About the Body? The Normative Dimension of Science Studies." *Body and Society*, 10.2–3: 205–229.
Laufer, Berthold. 1896. "Indisches Recept zur Herstellung von Räucherwerk." *Verhandlungen der Berliner Gesellschaft für Anthropologie, Ethnologie und Urgeschichte*, 18: 394–398.
Le Goff, Jacques. 1988. *The Medieval Imagination*. Trans. A. Goldhammer. Chicago: University of Chicago Press.
Lévi, Sylvain. 1915. "Le Catalogue géographique des *yakṣa* dans la Mahāmāyūrī." *Journal Asiatique* 11.5: 19–138.
Levey, Martin. 1961. "Ibn Māsawaih and His Treatise on Simple Aromatic Substances: Studies in the History of Aromatic Pharmacology I." *Journal of the History of Medicine and Allied Sciences* 16.4: 394–410.
Lienhard, Siegfried. 1979. "Observations Concerning a Buddhist Text on Erotics: The Nāgarasarvasva of Padmaśrī." *Central Asiatic Journal* 23.1–2: 96–103.
Losty, Jeremiah P. 1982. *The Art of the Book in India*. London: British Library Reference Division.
Lusthaus. Dan. 1998. "Buddhism, Yogācāra School of." *Routledge Encyclopedia of Philosophy*. Ed. E. Craig. London: Routledge.
Majumdar, G. P. 1935, "Toilet [Man's Indebtedness to Plants]." *Indian Culture* 1.4: 651–666.
———. 1938. *Some Aspects of Indian Civilization (In Plant Perspective)*. Calcutta: The Author, at Calcutta Oriental Press.
Malamoud, Charles. 1996. (1989.) *Cooking the World: Ritual and Thought in Ancient India*. Trans. David White. Delhi: Oxford University Press.
Malgouyres, Philippe. 2003. *Porphyre: La Pierre pourpre des Ptolémées aux Bonaparte*. Paris: Editions de la Réunion des musées nationaux.
Mallinson, James. 2005. *The Emperor of the Sorcerers*. Clay Sanskrit Series, 2 vols. Ed. and trans. Sir James Mallinson. New York: JJC Foundation and New York University Press.
Malvania, D. D. 1981. "Beginnings of Jaina Philosophy in the Acaranga." In *Studien zum Jainismus und Buddhismus*, ed. Klaus Bruhn and Albrecht Wezler, 152–153. Wiesbaden: Franz Steiner Verlag Gmbh.
———. 2000. "Beginnings of Jaina Philosophy." In *Abhidharma and Indian Thought: Essays in Honor of Professor Doctor Junsho Kato on His Sixtieth Birthday*, ed. The Committee for the Felicitation of Professor Doctor Junsho Kato's Sixtieth Birthday. Tokyo: Shunju-sha.
Mani, Vettam. 1979. *Purāṇic Encyclopaedia*. Delhi: Motilal Banarsidass.
Mayrhofer, Manfred. 1953–80. *Kurzgefasstes etymologisches Wörterbuch des Altindischen. A Concise Etymological Sanskrit Dictionary*. Heidelberg: C. Winter.
McHugh, James. 2007. "The Classification of Smells and the Order of the Senses in Indian Religious Traditions." *Numen: International Review for the History of Religions* 54.4: 374–419.
———. 2008. "Sandalwood and Carrion: Smell in South Asian Culture and Religion." PhD diss. Harvard University.

———. 2011 "Seeing Scents: Methodological Reflections on the Intersensory Perception of Aromatics in South Asian Religions." *History of Religions* 51:2: 156–177.

———. Forthcoming. "The Disputed Civets and the Complexion of the God: Secretions and History in India." *Journal of the American Oriental Society*.

Metcalfe, C. R. 1935. "The Structure of Some Sandalwoods and Their Substitutes and of Some Other Little Known Scented Woods." *Bulletin of Miscellaneous Information (Royal Gardens, Kew)* 4:165–195.

Meulenbeld, G. J. 1974. "Appendix Four: Sanskrit Names of Plants and their Botanical Equivalents." In *The Mādhavanidāna and its Chief Commentary Chapters 1–10*, trans. G. J. Meulenbeld, 520–611. Leiden: E. J. Brill.

———. 1987. "Reflections on the Basic Concepts of Indian Pharmacology." In *Studies in Indian Medical History*, ed. G. Jan Meulenbeld and Dominik Wujastyk, 1–17. Groningen Oriental Studies 2. Groningen: Egbert Forsten.

———. 1988. "Additions to Sanskrit Names of Plants and their Botanical Equivalents." In *Das Wissen von der Lebensspanne der Bäume: Surapālas Vṛkṣāyurveda*, ed. and trans. Rahul Peter Das, 425–465. Alt- und Neu-Indische Studien 34. Stuttgart: Franz Steiner Verlag Wiesbaden Gmbh.

———. 1997. "Aspects of Indian Psychiatry." In *History of Psychiatric Diagnoses, Proceedings of the 16th International Symposium on the Comparative History of Medicine—East and West*, 183–237. Toyko: Ishiyaku EuroAmerica.

———. 1999–2002. *A History of Indian Medical Literature*. Groningen: E. Forsten.

Miller, Daniel, ed. 2005. *Materiality*. Durham, NC: Duke University Press.

———. 2010. *Stuff*. Cambridge, UK: Polity Press.

Mitra, Rajendralala, trans. 1882. *The Lalita-Vistara or Memoirs of the Early Life of Sakya Sinha*. Fasc. 2. Calcutta: Asiatic Society.

Monier-Williams, M. 2000. *A Sanskrit-English Dictionary*. New ed. Oxford: Oxford University Press.

Monius, Anne E. 2004. "Love, Violence, and the Aesthetics of Disgust: Śaivas and Jains in Medieval South Asia." *Journal of Indian Philosophy* 32: 113–172.

———. 2009. "Purāṇa/Purāṇam: Modes of Narrative Temporality in Sanskrit and Tamil." In *Passages: Relationships between Tamil and Sanskrit*, ed. Francois Gros and M. Kannan, 217–236. Berkeley: University of California Press.

Morita, Kiyoko. 1999. *The Book of Incense: Enjoying the Traditional Art of Japanese Scents*. New York: Kodansha International.

Mrozik, Susanne. 2007. *Virtuous Bodies: The Physical Dimensions of Morality in Buddhist Ethics*. Oxford: Oxford University Press.

Mukhopadhyaya, G. 1923–29. *History of Indian Medicine: Containing Notices, Biographical and Bibliographical, of the Ayurvedic Physicians and Their Works on Medicine, from the Earliest Ages to the Present Time*. 3 vols. Calcutta: University of Calcutta.

Nambiar, D. 1979. *Nārada Purāṇa: A Critical Study*. Varanasi: All Kashiraj Trust.

Needham, Joseph and Gwei-Djen, Lu. 1971. *Science and Civilization in China*. Vol. 5, *Chemistry and Chemical Technology*. Part II, *Spagyrical Discovery and Invention: Magisteries of Gold and Immortality*. Cambridge: Cambridge University Press.

Oberlies, Thomas. 2003. *A Grammar of Epic Sanskrit, Indian Philology and South Asian Studies*. Vol. 5. New York: Walter de Gruyter.

Olivelle, Patrick, ed. 2006. *Between the Empires: Society in India 300 BCE to 400 CE*. Oxford: Oxford University Press.

Panofsky, E. 1976. *Gothic Architecture and Scholasticism: An Enquiry into the Analogy of the Arts, Philosophy, and Religion in the Middle Ages*. New York: New American Library.

Patton, Laurie. 1996. *Myth as Argument: The Bṛhaddevatā as Canonical Commentary*. New York: Walter de Gruyter.

Penny, Nicholas. 1993. *The Materials of Sculpture*. New Haven, CT: Yale University Press.

Pieris, A. 1978. "The Colophons to the Paramatthamañjūsā and the Discussion on the Date of Ācariya Dhammapāla." In *Buddhism in Ceylon and Studies on Religious Syncretism in Buddhist Countries*, ed. Heinz Bechert, 61–77. Abhandlungen der Akademie der Wissenschaften in Göttingen, no. 108. Göttingen: Vandenhoeck & Ruprecht.

Piesse, Charles H., ed. 1891. *Piesse's Art of Perfumery*. 5th ed. London: Piesse and Lubin.

Pingree, David. 1970–. *Census of the Exact Sciences in Sanskrit*. Series A. Philadelphia: American Philosophical Society.

Pischel, R. 1973. *Grammatik der Prakrit-Sprachen*. Hildesheim: Georg Olms Verlag.

Platts, John T. 2000. *A Dictionary of Urdū Classical Hindī and English*. New Delhi: Munshiram Manoharlal.

Polanyi, Karl. 1975. "Traders and Trade." In *Ancient Civilization and Trade*, eds. J. A. Sabloff and C. C. Lamberg-Karlovsky, 133–154. Albuquerque: University of Mexico Press.

Pollock, Sheldon. 1985. "The Theory of Practice and the Practice of Theory in Indian Intellectual History." *Journal of the American Oriental Society* 105.3: 499–519.

———. 2006. *The Language of the Gods in the World of Men: Sanskrit, Culture, and Power in Premodern India*. Berkeley: University of California Press.

Potter, Karl., ed. 1977. *Encyclopedia of Indian Philosophies*. Vol. 2, *Indian Metaphysics and Epistemology, the Tradition of Nyāya-Vaiśeṣika Up to Gangeśa*. Delhi: Motilal Banarsidass.

———, ed. 1996. *Encyclopedia of Indian Philosophies*. Vol. 7, *Abhidharma Buddhism to 150 A.D.* Delhi: Motilal Banarsidass.

Preisendanz, Karin. 1989. "On *ātmendriyamanorthasannikarṣa and the* Nyāya-Vaiśeṣika Theory of Vision." *Berliner Indologische Studien* 4/5: 141–213.

Raghavan, V., ed. 1949–. *New Catalogus Catalogorum: An Alphabetical Register of Sanskrit and Allied Works and Authors*. Madras: University of Madras.

Raja, C. K., and Sarma K. M. K. 1993. *Catalogue of the Anup Sanskrit Library*. Bikaner: Maharaja Ganga Singh Ji Trust.

Ramachandra Rao, S. K. 2005. *The Āgama Encyclopaedia*. Vol. 7, *Preparations for Pūjā*. 2nd ed. Delhi: Sri Satguru.

Rasmussen, L. E. L., H. S. Riddle, and V. Krishnamurthy. 2002. "Chemical Communication: Mellifluous Matures to Malodorous in Musth." *Nature* 415 (Feb. 28): 975–976.

Ray, P. C. 1902–1909. *History of Hindu Chemistry from the Earliest Times to the Middle of the Sixteenth Century, A.D.* Calcutta: Bengal Chemical and Pharmaceutical Works.

Review of Significant Trade: Aquilaria malaccensis. 2003. PC14 Doc. 9.2.2, Annex 2 (Nov.). Accessed July 31, 2007, http://www.cites.org/eng/com/PC/14/E-PC14-09-02-02-A2.pdf.

Ricks, Thomas M. 1970. "Persian Gulf Seafaring and East Africa: Ninth-Twelfth Centuries." *African Historical Studies* 3.2: 339–357.

Robinson, Jancis. 2003. *Jancis Robinson's Wine Course*. 3rd ed. New York: Abbeville Press.

Rotman, Andy. 2003. "Monks, Merchants, and a Moral Economy: Visual Culture and the Practice of Faith in the *Divyāvadāna*." PhD diss. University of Chicago.

———. 2008. *Divine Stories. Divyāvadāna Part 1*. Boston: Wisdom.

———. 2009. *Thus Have I Seen: Visualizing Faith in Early Indian Buddhism*. New York: Oxford University Press.

Rumpf, Georg Eberhard. 1999. *The Ambonese Curiosity Cabinet*. Trans. and Ed. E. M. Beekman. New Haven, Connecticut: Yale University Press.

Salomon, Richard. 1996. "When Is a Riddle Not a Riddle? Some Comments on Riddling and Related Poetic Devices in Classical Sanskrit." In *Untying the Knot: On Riddles and Other Enigmatic Modes*, ed. Galit Hasan-Rokem and David Shulman, 168–178. New York: Oxford University Press.

Sanderson, Alexis. 1988. "Śaivism and the Tantric Traditions." In *The World's Religions: The Religions of Asia*, 128–172. London: Routledge.

Sarma, S. R. 1985. "Writing Material in Ancient India." *Aligarh Journal of Oriental Studies* 2.1–2: 175–196.

———. 1995. "Gushing Mercury, Fleeing Maiden: A Raśaśāstra Motif in Mughal Painting." *Journal of the European Āyurvedic Society* 4:149–162.

———. 2003. "The Mango Motif in Sanskrit Poetry." *Journal of Sukṛtīndra Oriental Research Institute* 5.1: 72–88.

Sastri, K. A. 1945. Nilakantha. *Gleanings on Social Life from the Avadānas*. Calcutta: Indian Research Institute.

Schafer, Edward H. 1963. *The Golden Peaches of Samarkand: A Study of Tang Exotics*. Berkeley: University of California Press.

Scharfe, Hartmut. 1993. *Investigations in Kauṭalya's Manual of Political Science*. Wiesbaden: Harrassowitz Verlag.

———. 2002. "The Language of the Physician." In *Indian Linguistic Studies, Festschrift in Honor of George Cardona*, eds. M. Deshpande and P. Hook, 344–346. Delhi: Motilal Banarsidass.

Schopen, Gregory. 1997a. "Burial Ad Sanctos and the Physical Presence of the Buddha." In *Bones, Stones, and Buddhist Monks*, 114–147. Honolulu: University of Hawai'i Press.

———. 1997b. "The Buddha as an Owner of Property and Permanent Resident in Medieval Indian Monasteries." In *Bones, Stones, and Buddhist Monks*, 258–289. Honolulu: University of Hawai'i Press.

Schubring, Walther. 2000. *The Doctrine of the Jainas Described after the Old Sources*. Trans. Wolfgang Beurlen. 2nd ed. Delhi: Motilal Banarsidass.

Shapin. Steven. 2009. "Changing Tastes: How Foods Tasted in the Early Modern Period and How They Came to Taste Differently Later On." Talk delivered at Tasty Philosophers, Smelly Scientists: Taste and Smell in the Early Modern Period and Beyond. Radcliffe Institute for Advanced Study, Harvard University, May 18.

Sharma, P, V. 1991. "Some New Information about Niścala's Commentary on the Cakradatta." In *Medical Literature from India, Sri Lanka and Tibet*, ed. G. Jan Meulenbeld, 107–112. Vol. 3, *Panels of the VIIth World Sanskrit Conference*. Gen. ed. J. Bronkhorst. Leiden: Brill.

———, ed. 1992. *History of Medicine in India*. New Delhi: Indian National Science Academy.

———. 1996. *Classical Uses of Medicinal Plants*. Varanasi: Chaukhambha Visvabharati.

Shaw, Ian, J. Bunbury, and R. Jameson. 1999. "Emerald Mining in Roman and Byzantine Egypt." *Journal of Roman Archaeology* 12:203–215.

Shulman, David. 1987. "The Scent of Memory in Hindu South India." *Res* 13 (Spring): 123–33. Reprinted abridged in *The Smell Culture Reader*, ed. Jim Drobnick, 411–426. New York: Berg, 2006.

Slotow, Rob, Gus van Dyk, Joyce Poole, Bruce Page, and Andre Klocke. 2010. "Older Bull Elephants Control Young Males." *Nature* 408 (Nov. 23): 425–426.

Smith, Frederick M. 2006. *The Self Possessed: Deity and Spirit Possession in South Asian Literature and Civilization*. New York: Columbia University Press.

Smith, J. Z. 1990. *Drudgery Divine: On the Comparison of Early Christianities and the Religions of Late Antiquity*. London: School of Oriental and African Studies.

Smith, Mark H. 2007. *Sensing the Past: Seeing, Hearing, Smelling, Tasting, and Touching in History*. Berkeley: University of California Press.

Soper, A. C. 1959. *Literary Evidence for Early Buddhist Art in China*. Artibus Asiae Supplementum 19. Ascona, Switzerland: Artibus Asiae

Southworth, Franklin C. 2005. *Linguistic Archaeology of South Asia*. New York: Routledge.

Stamelman, R. 2006. *Perfume: Joy, Obsession, Scandal, Sin: A Cultural History of Fragrance from 1750 to the Present*. New York: Rizzoli.

Sternbach, Ludwik. 1962. "Review of *Studies in Indian Cultural History*, vol. 1, by P. K. Gode." *Journal of the American Oriental Society* 82.2: 222–229.

———. 1963. "Mahābhārata Verses in Cāṇakya's Compendia." *Journal of the American Oriental Society* 83.1: 30–67.

———. 1974. *Subhāṣita, Gnomic and Didactic Literature*. Ed. Jan Gonda. *History of Indian Literature*. Vol. 4.1. Wiesbaden: Otto Harrassowitz.

———. 1975. *Indian Riddles: A Forgotten Chapter in the History of Sanskrit Literature*. Hoshiarpur: Vishveshvaranand Vedic Research Institute.

Strong, John S. 1977. "*Gandhakuṭī*: The Perfumed Chamber of the Buddha." *History of Religions* 16.4: 390–406.

———. 1979. "The Transforming Gift: An Analysis of Devotional Acts of Offering in Buddhist Avadāna Literature." *History of Religions* 18.3: 221–237.

———. 2004. *Relics of the Buddha*. Princeton, NJ: Princeton University Press.

Swearer, Donald K. 2004. *Becoming the Buddha: The Ritual of Image Consecration in Thailand*. Princeton, NJ: Princeton University Press.

Tachikawa, M. 1981. *The Structure of the World in Udayana's Realism*. Dordrecht: D. Reidel.

Takakusu, Junjirō. 1904. "La Sāṃkhyakārikā étudiée à la lumière de sa version chinoise (II)." *Bulletin de l'École Française d'Extrême-Orient*, 4:978–1064.

Taruskin, R. 1989. "Resisting the Ninth." *19th-Century Music* 12.3 (Spring): 241–256.

Tatelman, Joel. 2001. *The Glorious Deeds of Pūrṇa: A Translation and Study of the Pūrṇāvadāna*. Delhi: Motilal Banarsidass.

Tatia, Nathmal, trans. 1994. Umāsvāti's *That Which Is*. San Francisco: Harper Collins.

Taylor, Mark C., ed. 1998. *Critical Terms for Religious Studies*. Chicago: University of Chicago Press.

Ter Haar, Barend J. 1999. "Teaching with Incense." *Studies in Central and East Asian Religions*, 11:1–14.

Thapar, R. 2004. "The Tyranny of Labels." In *Subordinate and Marginal Groups in Early India*, ed. A. Parasher-Sen, 349–373. New Delhi: Oxford University Press.

Thieme, Paul. 1957–58. "Pūjā." *Journal of Oriental Research*, 27: 1–16.

Thomas, E. J. 1931. "Gandhayukti in the Lalitavistara." *Bulletin of the School of Oriental Studies, University of London*, vol. 6, no. 2. *A Volume of Indian Studies Presented by His Friends and Pupils to Edward James Rapson, Professor of Sanskrit in the University of Cambridge, on His Seventieth Birthday, 12th May, 1931*: 515–517.

———. 1933. *The History of Buddhist Thought*. New York: A. A. Knopf.

Thuillier, Guy. 1977. *Pour une histoire du quotidien au XIXe siècle*. Paris: Mouton.

Tikekar, S. R. 1964. *On Historiography: A Study of the Methods of Historical Research and Narration of J. N. Sarkar, G. S. Sardesai and P. K. Gode*. Bombay: Popular Prakashan.

Titley, Norah M. 2005. *The Ni'matnāma Manuscript of the Sultans of Mandu: The Sultan's Book of Delights*. London: Routledge Curzon.

Vallée Poussin, Louis de la. 1971. *L'Abhidharmakośa de Vasubandhu, Traduction et Annotatations, Nouvelle édition anastatique présentée par Étienne Lamotte*. Bruxelles: Institut Belge des Hautes Études Chinoises.

Vogel, C. 1979. *Indian Lexicography. History of Indian Literature*. Vol. 5 fasc. 4. Wiesbaden: Harrassowitz.

Wackernagel, Jakob. 1905. *Altindische Grammatik*. Göttingen: Vandenhoek and Ruprecht.

Watt, George. 1885–1893. *A Dictionary of the Economic Products of India*. Calcutta: Superintendent of Government Printing.

Waugh, Evelyn. 1973. *Brideshead Revisited*. Boston: Little, Brown.

Wezler, Albrecht. 2000. "Some Remarks on the 135th Adhikaraṇa of the 'Kauṭilīya' *Artha-śāstra* Entitled 'Policy towards Saṃghas.'" *Studia Indologiczne 7: On the Understanding of Other Cultures*, 489–503. Warszawa: Instytut Orientalistyczny Uniwersytet Warszawski.

Wijeratne, R. P., and Gethin, Rupert, trans. 2002. *Abhidhammatthavibhāvinī* of Sumangala. *Summary of the Topics of Abhidhamma (Abhidhammatthasaṅgaha) by Anuruddha, Exposition of the Topics of Abhidhamma (Abhidhammatthavibhāvinī) by Sumangala*. Oxford: Pali Text Society.

Willis, Michael. 2009. *The Archaeology of Hindu Ritual: Temples and the Establishment of the Gods*. Cambridge: Cambridge University Press.

Winternitz, M. 1920. *Geschichte der Indischen Litteratur*. Vol. 3. Leipzig: C. F. Amelangs Verlag.

Witzel, Michael. 2006. "From the Mauryas to the Guptas: Reactions to Foreign Influences, Social and Religious Change." In *Between the Empires: Society in India 300 BCE to 400 CE*, ed. P. Olivelle, 457–499. Oxford: Oxford University Press.

Wright, H. Nelson. 1936. *The Coinage and Metrology of the Sultans of Delhi, Incorporating a Catalogue of the Coins in the Author's Cabinet Now in the British Museum*. Delhi: Manager of Publications.

Wujastyk, D. 1984. "An Alchemical Ghost: The Rasaratnākara of Nagarjuna." *Ambix* 31.2: 70–83.

———. 1999. "Miscarriages of Justice: Demonic Vengeance in Classical Indian Medicine." In *Religion, Health and Suffering*, eds. John R. Hinnells and Roy Porter, 256–275. New York: Kegan Paul.

———. 2000. "The Combinatorics of Tastes and Humours in Classical Indian Medicine and Mathematics." *Journal of Indian Philosophy* 28:479–495.

———. 2003. *The Roots of Ayurveda*. Rev. ed. London: Penguin Books.

———. 2003–2004. "Agni and Soma: A Universal Classification." *Studia Asiatica* 4–5: 347–369.

Yule, Henry, and A. C. Burnell. 2000 (1903). *Hobson Jobson*. Ed. William Crooke. New ed. Delhi: Munshiram Manoharlal.

Zimmermann, Francis. 1987a. (1982.) *The Jungle and the Aroma of Meats: An Ecological Theme in Hindu Medicine*. Trans. Janet Lloyd. Berkeley: University of California Press.

———. 1987b. "Les épices dans la literature savante indienne." In *Parfums de Plantes*, 42–44. Paris: Muséum National d'Histoire Naturelle.

Zysk, Kenneth G. 1991. *Asceticism and Healing in Ancient India: Medicine in the Buddhist Monastery*. New York: Oxford University Press.

———. 1993. *Religious Medicine: The History and Evolution of Indian Medicine*. New Brunswick, NJ: Transaction.

———. 2002. *Conjugal Love in India*. Leiden: Brill.

INDEX

Page numbers in italic refer to tables.

artificial sandalwood produced with, 197–198
used to fake other aromatics, 288n85

Hara, Minoru, on the Sanskrit word *gandha* (odor, perfume), 14
Haramekhalā (*Girdle of Hara*) of Māhuka: about, 111–113
Bṛhatkathāślokasaṃgraha compared with, 148
daily routine and the organization of aromatic preparations in, 131–133
and the lifestyle of the "cultivated man," 144
perfumery by *yavanas* described in, 147
preparations for artificial substances in, 196
Harṣacarita by Bāṇa: about, 169–170
tribute brought to King Harṣa in, 170–171, 293n62
Harvey, Susan Ashbrook, 9, 17
hierarchy: class-based smell prejudices, 87, 96
of elephants in the *Play of Elephants*, 83–85
Greek hierarchy of the senses, 22
high-status of the cow in South Asian culture, 67
of the senses in cosmogonic accounts, 50–51
of the senses in South Asia, 21–22
social hierarchy and classifications of odor and odorants, xiii, 163–165
and the territory associated with various beings, 87
historical periodization: and aromatic material culture/olfactory aesthetic sensibilities, xi
Baxandall's notion of the "period eye," 17–18
and olfactory aesthetic sensibilities, xi, 19
historiography, and the senses, 22

Ibn Māsawaih *Treatise on Simple Aromatic Substances*, 165
imaginary worlds: forest of Ox-head Sandalwood guarded by *yakṣas*, 205
and the origins of exotic materials, xiii, 159–160
snakes associated with the origin of sandalwood, 211
immateriality, 5
incense: bedchamber use of, 133
and benzoin (*sambranī*), 280n5
for driving away various beings, 77–78, 139
and the ingredients suitable to recipients, 232–237
origin myth of, 78
and other valued aromatics, xiii
intestinal gas, 245, 294n5
Islam in South Asia: and the *Ain-i Akbari*, 165, 271n74
olfactory sensibility of Islamic culture, 165, 243
and the study of smell and perfumery, x, 14

Jainism: classification of beings according to the number of senses they have, 30, 46, 230
mathematical "mental habits" of, 191, 192
order of the senses, 30, 46–47
ox-head sandalwood image of the Jina Mahāvīra, 211, 290n56
perfumery as one of seventy-two arts (*kalās*), 107
vegetarian lifestyle of, 30, *See also* Pherū, Ṭhakkura (Jain scholar and arithmetician)

kacchapuṭa ("grid"), 268n19
kalās, the 64 or 72 "arts", 105, 106, 107, 125, 267n1
Kālidāsa, *Raghuvaṃśa* by, 69, 70–71
Kalyāṇa (royal capital city), depicted by Someśvara, III, 163–164
kāma (pleasure): and artha (power and profit), 146, 162, 197
perfumes associated with, 107, 146–147, *See also* *trivarga* (three aims of life)
kāmaśāstra, perfumery in, 107, 267n4
Kāmasūtra's description of the room of the man-about-town, 17, 68, 132
kāvya. *See* poetry
King Someśvara III. *See* Someśvara III
kissing: and erotic names associated with mouth perfumes, 131
sniffing-as-kissing, 13
kṣatriyas, and the smell of sandalwood, 97
kuṣṭha. *See* costus root

language: and the description of Sanskrit odors, 61, 64–65
synonyms for aromatics, 174–176
used to describe smells, 65
the word "flower" in Sanskrit invoked to explain offering of, 227, 242, *See also* terminology
lapis lazuli, 191–192, 213
Latour, Bruno: on substances as institutions, 199
on words and perceptions as one "articulation," 195
Laudamiel, Christophe (perfumer), 89, 141
Law Code of Manu (*Mānava Dharmaśāstra*): Sāṃkhya features of, 50–51
and smelling as a sin, 26–27
and use of flowers in rituals, 224, *See also* *śāstric* technical literature
Lōkōpakāra, Kannada encyclopedic text, 107, 267n10
long-distance trade, and aromatic materials, 8, 178
lotus-smell (*padmagandha*), 70–71
lotus breath, 70–71
luxury materials, and regional production, 147

Mahābhārata (Indian epic): arousing nature of fragrances in, 95–96, 129
candana not used for construction of material objects in, 210
candana used as a paste in, 186
and the churning of the milk ocean, 227
and the cultural history of smells in South Asia, xiii, 219
five senses attributed to plants in, 29–30

20033838R00206

Printed in Great Britain
by Amazon